MARK DORRIAN holds the Forbes Chair in Architecture at the University of Edinburgh.

FRÉDÉRIC POUSIN is Professor at École Nationale Supérieure de Paysage de Versailles.

'Flying became possible because it was imagined. This is what a history of seeing from above discloses: we visualised angelic mobility before we could design it. In this fascinating collection the open eye of Google Earth retains at its vanishing point a turbulent history of self-elevation: new suburbs far below look like ancient cities – or are they bomb sites? Birds, mountains and clouds serve as armatures for cameras. An extraordinarily timely survey of earth from the sky, full of virtuosic new insights, ethical as well as aesthetic implications, and not without its share of vertigo.'

Paul Carter, author and artist

'This uplifting collection of essays accounts comprehensively and for the first time for one of the most important reorientations in the history of perception and the senses, the capacity to see the world from above. The volume gives historical reach to the idea of the aerial, tracking it back before the era of flight to earlier arguments and speculations. Encompassing ballooning, architecture, photography, painting, cartography, urban planning, military history and internet imaging, *Seeing from Above* assembles a dizzyingly delicious panorama of ideas and arguments. In its mapping of what has become our defining world picture, this is truly explication in excelsis.'

Steven Connor, Grace 2 Professor of English, University of Cambridge

'In order to move deeper into the history of our modernity, one has to move upward. But our gaze was not all that went with us into the altitudes; it was joined by cameras, leaflets, bombs and computers, not to mention our poetic, philosophical and existential contemplations. This book brings out aeriality's multiple dimensions with such force that by the end one feels that – despite our imprisonment to gravity – we really live not *on* the earth, but at the bottom-most layer of a vast exospherical mirror filled with everything that makes us human, from our highest ideals to our basest thoughts and ambitions.'

Mark Jarzombek, Professor of the History and Theory of Architecture, School of Architecture and Planning, MIT

'In the last decades of the twentieth century, aerial and satellite photography pervaded our ways of seeing, but also our means of representing and managing the terrestrial surface. Paradoxically, until now there has been little research investigating the drives and consequences of such a change. *Seeing from Above* brings an innovative perspective to the history of art, architecture and landscape and sheds new light on the construction of images and their uses. This remarkable collection of richly illustrated essays – which encompasses the analysis of etchings, of early cinematography, of views from balloons and of Google Earth – will become a landmark for any scholar interested in the field of visual culture.'

Vincent Piveteau, Director, École Nationale Supérieure de Paysage, Versailles

SEEING FROM ABOVE

THE AERIAL VIEW IN VISUAL CULTURE

EDITED BY MARK DORRIAN AND FRÉDÉRIC POUSIN

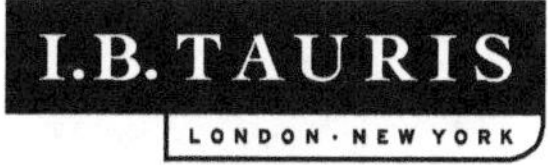

Published in 2013 by I.B.Tauris & Co. Ltd
6 Salem Road, London W2 4BU
175 Fifth Avenue, New York NY 10010
www.ibtauris.com

ISBN: 978 1 78076 460 3 (HB)
ISBN: 978 1 78076 461 0 (PB)
eISBN: 978 0 85773 432 7
ePDF: 978 0 85772 289 8

A full CIP record for this book is available from the British Library
A full CIP record is available from the Library of Congress

Library of Congress Catalog Card Number: available

Contents

Figures

CHAPTER 1
Intimate Communiqués

CHAPTER 2
The Meaning of Roman Maps

CHAPTER 3
Thomas Baldwin's *Airopaidia*, or the Aerial View in Colour

CHAPTER 4
European Cities from a Bird's-eye View

CHAPTER 7
Aerial Views and Cinematism, 1898–1939

CHAPTER 8
'The Domain of Rrose Sélavy'

CHAPTER 9
The Aviator and the Photographer

CHAPTER 10
From the Sky to the Ground

CHAPTER 11
The Figure from Above

CHAPTER 12
The City Seen from the Aeroplane

CHAPTER 13
Vectors of Looking

CHAPTER 14
The Aerial View and the *Grands Ensembles*

CHAPTER 15
Robert Smithson and *Aerial Art*

CHAPTER 16
On Google Earth

Acknowledgements

This book is the result of a programme of seminars and conferences held in Edinburgh and Paris between February 2007 and October 2008 under the title *The Aerial View: Spatial Knowledges and Spatial Practices*. We are extremely grateful to the British Academy and the Centre national de la recherche scientifique (CNRS) for their award of a 'Joint Partnership' grant, which funded the series. Our thanks extend to all those who contributed to the seminars, which – in addition to the chapter authors – includes Olivier Archambeau, Catherine Bruant, Wilson Poon and Iain Woodhouse. The meetings in Edinburgh were held at the University of Edinburgh and the Fruitmarket Gallery, and those in Paris at the Institut de géographie and the University of Chicago Center in Paris. We are indebted to these institutions and to those who chaired the sessions that took place at them – Marie-Noëlle Bourguet, Ella Chmielewska, Viviane Claude, Martin Hammer, Panos Mantziaras, Olivier Schefer and Tamara Trodd – and to Laura Marcus, who led the discussion at the final event. We are especially grateful to Stacy Boldrick for her important review of the first meeting, published in *Architectural Research Quarterly*, and for her key role in facilitating and organising the closing conference.

Translation of the French papers has been funded through a production grant awarded by the Graham Foundation for Advanced Studies in the Fine Arts. Chapters 3, 4, 10 and 12 were translated by Manuela Antoniu, Chapters 7 and 9 by Jane Yeoman, Chapter 14 by Alice Holt and Jane Yeoman, and Chapter 15 by Michael Crawley and Jane Yeoman. Additional translation is by Mark Dorrian.

Contributors

Stephen Bann is Emeritus Professor and Senior Research Fellow at the University of Bristol. He is a Fellow of the British Academy and the Society of Antiquaries, and was awarded CBE in 2004. His work has ranged widely, from studies of historical representation and print culture to modernist and contemporary art. He is the subject of a collection of essays, *About Stephen Bann* (ed. Cherry, 2006). His most recent books are *Ways Around Modernism* (2007) and *Distinguished Images: Prints in the Visual Economy of Nineteenth-Century France* (2013). In 2010 he acted as Guest Curator for an exhibition of the work of Paul Delaroche, which took place at the National Gallery London.

Jean-Marc Besse is a philosopher and holds a doctorate in History from the University of Paris 1 Panthéon–Sorbonne. He is a director of research at CNRS, where he leads the team EHGO (UMR Géographie-cités, CNRS/Paris I/Paris VII), and is a co-editor of the journal *Les Carnets du paysage.* His research takes the form of a wide-ranging anthropological inquiry on the form and content of modern representations and experiences of space. His studies are distributed across three themes: the historical epistemology of modern geography; the history of representations and theories of landscape; and the epistemology of contemporary geography. His books include: *Le goût du monde. Exercices de paysage* (2009); *Face au monde. Atlas, jardins, géoramas* (2003); *Les grandeurs de la terre. Aspects du savoir géographique à la Renaissance* (2003); and *Voir la terre. Six essais sur le paysage et la géographie* (2000).

Michael Bury was educated at the University of Cambridge and at the Courtauld Institute in London. He became a lecturer in the History of Art at the University of Edinburgh in 1972 and worked there until his retirement in 2008. His research interests have centred on Italian art and architecture of the fifteenth and sixteenth centuries. He has published in many journals, including the *Burlington Magazine*, the *Mitteilungen des kunsthistorischen Institutes in Florenz*, the *Annali di Architettura* and *Print Quarterly*. His exhibition, *The Print in Italy 1550–1620*, was organised for the British Museum in 2001. The catalogue won the Eric Mitchell Prize as the best English-language exhibition catalogue of the years 2000–01. He was Balsdon Fellow at the British School at Rome for 2008–09.

Teresa Castro is Associate Professor of Film Studies at the University of Paris 3 – Sorbonne Nouvelle. A former grantee of the Fundação de Ciência e Tecnologia (Portugal), her research focuses on visual culture (in particular aerial views in cinema and photography and photographic and cinematographic atlases) and the relations between cinema and contemporary art. Her book *La Pensée cartographique des images. Cinéma et culture visuelle* was published by Aléas, Lyon, in 2011. She acted as an Associate Curator (Film) for the exhibition *Views from Above*, held at the Centre Pompidou Metz from May to October 2013.

Ella Chmielewska is Senior Lecturer and Director of the Cultural Studies Programme at the University of Edinburgh. Her research has focused on urban visual culture, the materiality of writing, and practices of commemoration and display. Among her publications are 'Framing Temporality: Montréal Graffiti in Photography' in Annie Gérin and James S. McLean, eds, *Public Art in Canada: Critical Perspectives* (University of Toronto Press, 2009); 'Semiosis Takes Place, or the Radical Uses of Quaint Theories' in A. Jaworski and C. Thurlow, eds, *Semiotic Landscapes: Language, Image, Space* (Continuum, 2010); 'Material errata: Warsaw neons and Socialist modernity', *The Journal of Architecture*, 15(1) (2010); and 'Writing with the Photograph: Espacement, Description and an Architectural Text in Action' in Anna Dahlgren, Nina Lager Vestberg and Dag Patersson, eds, *Representational Machines: Photography and the Production of Space* (Aarhus University Press, 2013).

Mark Dorrian holds the Forbes Chair in Architecture at the University of Edinburgh, and is co-director of the art, architecture and urbanism atelier *Metis*. His books include (with Adrian Hawker) *Metis: Urban Cartographies* (Black Dog Publishing, 2002), (with Gillian Rose) *Deterritorialisations: Revisioning Landscapes and Politics* (Black Dog Publishing, 2003), (with Jane Rendell, Jonathan Hill and Murray Fraser) *Critical Architecture* (Routledge, 2007) and *Warszawa: Projects for the Post-socialist City* (University of Edinburgh, 2009). His volume of collected essays, *Writing on the Image: Architecture, the City and the Politics of Representation*, will be published by I.B.Tauris in 2014.

David Hopkins is Professor of Art History at the University of Glasgow, where he teaches and researches in Dada and Surrealism and post-war art. His latest book, *Dada's Boys: Masculinity After Duchamp* – which follows in the wake of the exhibition *Dada's Boys* at the Fruitmarket Gallery, Edinburgh (2006) – was recently published by Yale University Press. His numerous other publications include *Marcel Duchamp and Max Ernst: the Bride Shared* (Clarendon Press, 1998), *After Modern Art* (Oxford University Press, 2000) *Neo-Avant-Garde* (Rodopi, 2006) and (with Dawn Ades and Neil Cox) *Marcel Duchamp* (Thames and Hudson, 1999).

Christina Lodder is a Professor of the History and Philosophy of Art at the University of Kent and a Fellow of the Royal Society of Edinburgh. She specialises in the history and theory of twentieth-century Russian art and design and related European developments. Her publications include numerous articles and several books: *Russian Constructivism* (Yale University Press, 1983) and *Constructive Strands in Russian Art* (Pindar Press, 2005), as well as (with Martin Hammer) *Constructing Modernity: The Art and Career of Naum Gabo* (Yale University Press, 2000), *Gabo on Gabo: Texts and Interviews* (Artists Bookworks, 2000) and (with Charlotte Douglas) *Rethinking Malevich* (Pindar Press, 2007). She has also been involved as an advisor for several exhibitions and was a member of the curatorial team for the exhibition *Modernism* at the Victoria and Albert Museum, London (2006).

Olivier Lugon is an art historian and professor at Lausanne University (Film History Department and Centre for the History of Culture). His research has focused on German and American photography of the inter-war years, documentary photography and exhibition design. Among his publications are *La Photographie en Allemagne. Anthologie de Textes, 1919–1939* (Chambon, 1997), *August Sander. Landschaften* (Schirmer/Mosel, 1999), *Le Style Documentaire. D'August Sander à Walker Evans, 1920–1945* (Macula, 2002), (co-edited with Laurent Guido) *Between Still and Moving Images* (John Libbey Publishing, 2012), *Exposition et médias. Photographie, cinéma, télévision* (L'Age d'Homme, 2012) and (with François Bon and Philippe Simay) *Le Pont transbordeur de Marseille – Moholy-Nagy* (INHA/Ophrys, 2013). He is currently director of the research project 'The modern exhibition of photography, 1920–1970' and is preparing a book on the topic.

John Macarthur is Professor of Architecture at the University of Queensland, Australia, where he directs the research centre ATCH (Architecture, Theory, Criticism, History). He writes on the cultural history and aesthetics of architecture. His work has appeared in *Assemblage, Architectural Research Quarterly, The Journal of Architecture, Architectural Theory Review* and *OASE*. His book *The Picturesque:*

Architecture, Disgust and other Irregularities was published by Routledge in 2007. He is currently working on projects on the twentieth-century reception of Baroque architecture, on criticism and aesthetics, and on the architecture of Queensland, Australia.

Frédéric Pousin is an architect and a director of research at CNRS. He currently teaches as a professor at the École Nationale Supérieure du Paysage de Versailles (ENSP). His research focuses on urban landscape and the epistemological value of visuality in architecture and urbanism and has appeared in *Annales de la recherche urbaine, Cahiers de la recherche architecturale et urbaine, Rassegna, Werk* and *Bauen+Wohnen*. He is a member of the editorial board of *Les Carnets du paysage*. His books include *Figures de la ville et construction des savoirs: architecture, urbanisme, géographie* (CNRS Éditions, 2005), (with S. Robic) *Signes, Histoire, Fictions. Autour de Louis Marin* (Arguments, 2003) and (with H. Jannière) *Paysage urbain: genèse, représentations, enjeux contemporains* (Strates, 2007). His essay 'Urban Cuttings: Sections and Crossings' is published in Christophe Girot and Fred Truninger, eds, *Landscape, Vision, Motion*, Landscript 1 (Jovis Verlag, 2012).

Marie-Claire Robic is a director of research at CNRS, specialising in the history and epistemology of geography. Her work focuses on the classic texts of French geography, concepts of human geography in the different national traditions that have developed since the late nineteenth century, and the iconographic systems by which geographers have produced different modern geographical paradigms. Within these interests, she has published – alone or in collaboration – on fieldwork, on the use of photography in the development of cartography and on the historic form of the 'atlas', as well as on graphic schematisation.

Nathalie Roseau is an architect and engineer who graduated from the École Polytechnique. She holds a PhD in Urbanism from Université Paris-Est. After having been in charge of urban studies for the Paris Region (French Ministry of Planning), she joined the architecture office led by Paul Andreu in the Paris Airports Corporation. Since 2003, she has been a research member of the Laboratoire Techniques, Territoires et Sociétés (Université Paris-Est) and an associate professor at the École nationale des ponts et chaussées, where she directs the urban planning masters programme. She is a guest professor in the Facultà di Architettura of the Politecnico di Milano. Her research focuses on the contemporary dynamics of the metropolis, the imaginary of the city and the relations between infrastructure and architecture. Recent publications include 'Airports as Urban Narratives', *Transfers* 2(1) (2012) and the book *Aerocity: Quand l'avion fait la ville* (Éditions Parenthèses, 2012).

Marie Thébaud-Sorger is a scholar whose work focuses on the cultural history of eighteenth-century technologies. Following a position as Marie Curie Research Fellow at the Department of History at the University of Warwick, she is currently working at CNRS as a research fellow on a project studying the history of industrial risks (École des hautes études en sciences sociales – Centre de recherches historiques). Her doctoral thesis was on the first balloon flights, and has recently been published as *L'aérostation au temps des lumières. Sciences et techniques à la rencontre du public, 1783–1785* (Presses Universitaires de Rennes, 2009). Other recent publications include 'L'aérien et ses publics. Une histoire longue de la mise en scène de la technique' in Mathieu Flonneau and Vincent Guigueno, eds, *De l'histoire des transports à l'histoire de la mobilité?* (Presses Universitaires de Rennes, 2009); 'La mesure de l'envol à la fin du XVIIIe siècle. Les premiers ballons: affaires d'opinions ou d'exactitude?', *Histoire et Mesure*, 21(1+2) (2006); and 'La conquête de l'air, les dimensions d'une découverte', *Dix-huitième siècle*, 31 (1999). In 2008, together with Nathalie Roseau and Patrice Bret, she organised the international colloquium *La Culture Aérienne. Objets, imaginaire, pratiques de l'aéronautique XVIII–XXe siècle* (13–15 November, CNAM, Cité des sciences de La Villette et Musée de l'air).

Gilles A. Tiberghien is a philosopher and is an assistant professor at the University of Paris 1 Panthéon–Sorbonne where he teaches aesthetics. He has written on land art, sculpture in landscape, photography and cinema. His books include *Land Art* (éditions Carré, 1993; and Princeton Architectural Press, 1995 [new expanded edition 2012]); *Nature, art, paysage* (Actes-Sud/ENSP, 2001); *Notes sur la Nature, la cabane et quelques autres choses* (éd du Félin, 2005); *FINIS TERRAE: Imaginations et imaginaire cartographique* (Bayard, 2007); (with Gilles Clément) *Dans La Vallée. Dialogues. Biodiversité, art et paysage* (Bayard, 2009); and *Pour une république des rêves* (Les presses du réel, 2011). He is a member of the editorial board of *Les Cahiers du Musée national d'art moderne* (Centre Georges Pompidou) and is co-editor of *Les Carnets du paysage* (Actes-Sud/ENSP).

Marina Warner is a writer of history, cultural studies and fiction. Her mother was Italian and her father English, and she was brought up in Egypt, Belgium and Cambridge, England. She has been a writer since she was young, specialising in mythology and fairy-tales, with an emphasis on the part women play in them. Her award-winning books include *From the Beast to the Blonde* (1994) and *Phantasmagoria: Spirit Visions, Metaphors, and Media* (2006), a study of phantasms and modern technologies. She has curated exhibitions, including *The Inner Eye* (1996), *Metamorphing* (2002–3) and *Only Make-Believe: Ways of Playing* (2005). Her recent book, *Stranger Magic: Charmed States & the Arabian*

Nights, was given the Sheikh Zayed award, 2013. She is Professor of Literature, Film and Theatre Studies at the University of Essex and a fellow of All Souls College, Oxford.

Introduction

Mark Dorrian and Frédéric Pousin

From the late eighteenth century onward, the phenomenon of human flight generated profound transformations in the cultural imagination. It changed the way that the environments in which we live were seen, and formed one of the main vectors of the modern expansion of mobility that has led to the construction of a visually comprehensive global space throughout which – thanks to contemporary digital technologies – it is now possible to browse. The aerial, with all the upheavals it engendered and conquests it permitted, is central to the modern imagination and, indeed, might even be claimed to be its emblematic visual form: as László Moholy-Nagy declared in his seminal publication *The New Vision*, 'the most essential for us is the airplane view, the complete space experience'.[1]

To understand the transformation in seeing brought about by flight, the study of images is essential. On one hand, these reflect the experience of flight, but on the other they give rise to practices through which the environment in which we live is interpreted and shaped. At the same time, however, the question of the aerial – despite its intimate relation with modernity – cannot be directly linked and naively restricted to the physical possibility of ascension, as the existence of overhanging perspectives, city portraits and bird's-eye views produced from the Renaissance, and even earlier, shows.

Recognising the complex cultural history of aerial imagery and the shifting contexts of its production and reception, this book considers its subject in terms of a *longue durée*. Its primary aim is to develop a cross-disciplinary consideration of the aerial view in relation to spatial practices, knowledge construction and affect. Given the extensiveness and intricacy of the topic, the book can make no claims to be exhaustive. Instead, it is structured through a series of 'episodes' or representative case studies that have a strategic value and eloquence in relation to the long cultural history of aerial images. This approach permits the various phenomena it considers, which have hitherto been isolated from one another, to be thought relationally in a new way. Moreover, the essayistic format allows the individual case studies to be developed in the detail that is demanded by the complexity of the subject matter, while at the same time locating them within a wider historical context of shifting ideas, technologies, cultures and meanings. The chapter sequence – which is broadly chronological – facilitates the historicisation of each of the episodes and helps to make legible the connections, transformations and developments between them.

Throughout the volume, an interrogative and critical approach to the topic is maintained, which involves directing questions toward the concepts with which the book deals, as well as toward the material that it examines. While focused on its own material, each chapter is developed in relation to a common series of questions that motivate the collection as a whole and ensure its coherence. Thus we ask – what is the aerial view; that is to say, how do we define it in relation to other visual modes, positions and so on, and what are its constitutive limits? Within what discourses have practices of the aerial view emerged, and how have they been variously staged or conceptualised within them? What, in specific historical and cultural contexts, have been the discursive or ideological effects and agencies of the aerial view? In what representational forms has the aerial view been historically anticipated or mediated (drawing, models, photography, cinema, etc.), and how do we analyse the specific effects and utilities that these forms present? How are these representational documents then deployed? And how do they interact with other images and what kinds of knowledge and practice do they make possible or, alternatively, foreclose?

The collection opens with a chapter by Marina Warner, which reflects on the work of the Danish artist, Melchior Lorck, who travelled to Turkey in 1555 as part of the embassy of the Emperor-elect, Ferdinand I, to the court of Sultan Suleiman the Magnificent. Pointing out the narrative powers and possibilities that are endowed by the aerial view, she identifies it with the unboundedness and mobility that third-person narrative bestows upon the imagination, transporting readers across space and time and into secret and otherwise hidden locales. This is a relationship that underpins a drawing by Lorck of a view from his window that was made, she argues, during the period in which the ambassadors were confined after their arrival. This interplay of intimate and even forbidden knowledge with overview, which Lorck's drawing makes visible, would find a more literally expanded articulation in his extraordinary *Prospect of Constantinople,* in the foreground of which the artist's aerial eye registers himself at work. Warner finds the aspirations of the earth-bound artist for mobility – whether aerial or within the aqueous medium of the fishes of which he so admiringly wrote – pictured in his remarkable drawing of a large tortoise passing blimp-like above a walled town and wryly inscribed with the note 'Made in Venice from Life'.

Michael Bury's paper transports us to Rome, two decades on from Lorck's *Prospect,* and to two bird's-eye views of the city, those of Etienne Dupérac (1577) and Antonio Tempesta (1593). Analysing these with reference to the specific choices of viewpoint and representational technique employed, Bury examines the interpretations of the city that the images promoted. Structured through a visual rhetoric on the relation between the modern city and its ancient predecessor, these images carry meanings that are enabled by the particular agency of the bird's-eye view. Dupérac's image, in which an orthographic plan is combined with the rendering of buildings from an oblique viewpoint, pictorially emphasises the ruins of the ancient city and relegates the contemporary city to background. In Tempesta's *Prospectus,* however, the graphic suppression of the countryside beyond the city walls supports the vision of a modern city that has flourished to succeed the ancient, whose environs it is now pictured as filling.

The following chapter moves us into the era of flight, and to a unique early account of the effects upon the senses of altitude and the so-called aerostatics of the balloon. This is *Airopaidia,* the treatise published by the Englishman Thomas Baldwin following his ascent in 1785 in the balloon of the Italian aeronaut Lunardi, who was then visiting Chester. Baldwin had carried with him various instruments with which to take readings, and when his publication appeared it was accompanied with a set of engravings of an unprecedented kind. Here, in her study of *Airopaidia,* which she calls a 'treatise on the sensations experienced in a balloon in motion', Marie Thébaud-Sorger describes Baldwin's efforts to articulate the conditions of a new kind of vision, one whose objects had undergone radical transformation by virtue of the way in which they were now viewed. Considering the remarkable circular illustration in Baldwin's publication titled *A View from the Balloon at its Greatest Elevation,* she notes his novel and close attention to atmosphere, weather and light – a concern so alien to the cartographic tradition – and his characterisation of a chromatically complex and shifting world in which the contour of objects gives way to colour.

Jean-Marc Besse's study of the work of Alfred Guesdon maintains the atmospheric theme, although now the clouds to which we are directed are those that issue from the chimneys of the industrial plants of mid-nineteenth-century European cities. Guesdon, whose work is historically poised on the cusp of a new era of photographic reproduction, from 1845 travelled for about 15 years in France, Italy, Spain and Switzerland, producing over 100 bird's-eye views of cities. Besse's analysis of Guesdon's drawings situates them in a complex and longstanding discourse on perspectival technique and construction, within which the elevated viewpoint played a very specific role. Moreover, he notes how, for certain Fourier and Saint-Simon-inspired architectural theorists of the nineteenth century, the aerial view carried a diagnostic force, which made it a privileged vehicle for the comprehension of the city. Guesdon's views of the modernising urban landscape of Napoleon III's France, and other countries, shows cities that are in movement, infused with the energy of work and machinic force and whose emblems of industrialisation – such as the billowing smoke from factories – attain a newly assertive presence.

The closing years of Guesdon's activities overlapped with the start of the aerial exploits of the photographer Nadar, which would lead to his successful photographic recording of a view from a balloon in 1858. Following this aerial achievement Nadar quickly embarked on a new project to photograph the Paris catacombs under artificial light and, in his chapter, Stephen Bann explores this suggestive interplay between the aerial and the subterranean. If, as he argues, the mid-eighteenth century saw a new conjunction between the two, and an awareness of their relation, as antiquarians calibrated patterns evident on land seen from above with new understandings of what lay below derived from excavation, then by the mid-nineteenth century the earth's surface had come to be seen as less a limit than an interface between two different kinds of knowledge. Examining Nadar's writing, Bann detects a shift from an understanding of the aerial view that was deeply shaped by intellectual tradition and literary precedent, to one committed to the progressive potential of this new and powerful way of seeing for which the photographic apparatus played the role of necessary complement and stabilising device.

Suprematism, established around 1913 by Kazimir Malevich, was a movement that was deeply saturated with the powers and potentialities of the aerial view. Christina Lodder's chapter examines this relationship and – in particular – the role that aerial photography played in the development of the Suprematist imaginary. Certainly, this is a relation that Malevich explicitly articulated in the 1920s in his book *Die Gegenstandlose Welt* (translated as *The Non-Objective World*), but Lodder goes further back to examine the concepts and meanings associated with the aerial view present in the milieu in which Malevich developed Suprematism during the previous decade. Showing how the transfigured sight of the aviator could be analogised with the metaphysical vision of the icon painter (famously Malevich compared his *Black Square* with a traditional icon), she also explores the links between the aerial view and the *ostranenie* (estrangement) of the Russian formalists, and the concept of the fourth dimension as it was elaborated in the philosophy of Peter Ouspensky. Her essay closes with a reflection upon Malevich's drawing for the libretto of the Futurist opera *Victory Over the Sun*, a celebration of the transcendence of technology over cosmic forces, for which flight held paradigmatic status. Here, at the inception of Suprematism, the black square is anticipated as, in Malevich's word, a 'louse' that absorbs and cancels the radiance of the sun.

In her chapter, Teresa Castro considers in detail the connection between aerial mobility and the cinematographic imagination, a relationship that the opening remarks of Marina Warner's essay have already alerted us to. Examining the coupling of the technology of the moving image with that of the aircraft, Castro's analysis stresses the importance of the sensation of flight and mobility in three dimensions that film made possible and that indeed was fundamental to the very concept of cinematic vision as – for example – articulated by the Soviet film-maker Dziga Vertov. World War I gave powerful impetus to the development of aerial imaging techniques, and Castro discusses the case of Lucien Le Saint who had experimented with fixing his camera to a gun-mount and who was involved in the production of a remarkable aerial film made in the aftermath of the conflict. Produced to document the post-war devastation, this was part of a larger effort to amass information to aid planning for reconstruction in France. However, Castro finds that, in excess of its documentary function, the mobile camera becomes a source of emotion, in which the pleasure of free aerial movement and the new perspectives of the earth it allows are mixed with the scrutiny of a devastated terrain that now takes on the new aspect of a wounded body. Her discussion of cinematography from above concludes with a suggestive consideration – by way of Siegfried Kracauer's theorisation of the mass ornament – of Busby Berkeley's Hollywood musicals of the 1930s.

With David Hopkins' new reading of Man Ray's photograph *Dust Breeding* (*Elevage de poussière*) we remain above the battlefields of World War I. Taken in Marcel Duchamp's studio in New York in 1920, this close-up photograph of the artist's *Large Glass* was subsequently published in the Dadaist magazine *Littérature* with the caption 'Vue prise en aéroplane'. Connecting the image, with its strange collapse of proximity and distance, to World War I aerial reconnaissance photography, Hopkins' argument explores the significance of the dust that has settled upon the artwork in relation to the remains of the war dead and to Duchamp's female alter-ego Rrose Sélavy, whose domain the photograph was declared to depict. Here the (war) game-like scenario of *Elevage de poussière* represents, Hopkins suggests, a process of mourning, but one in which the horror of the conflict and the ensuing loss has been displaced by the ludic. Meanwhile, Rrose herself is figured as a medium through which the spirits of the dead – and of Duchamp himself, on the 'other side', in New York – are transmitted.

Walter Mittelholzer – the Swiss pilot, photographer and entrepreneur – is the subject of Olivier Lugon's essay, which analyses both the construction of his identity as national aviator-hero and the specific relations between his practice and the mountain landscape of Switzerland, with its tradition of high-level views associated with alpine tourism and ascensional (and morally freighted) sporting activities. Trained as an aerial photographer during World War I, Mittelholzer subsequently co-founded an aerial photographic and transportation company that would in time become the national airline carrier Swissair. Lugon shows how Mittelholzer's practice emerged at the intersection of the discourses of science and adventure. In Mittelholzer's books the roles of pilot and photographer merged into one, while the presentation and narrative framing of his photographs, which emphasised the physical effort involved in their capture, ensured that Mittelholzer himself was the constant reference and in a sense the perpetual subject of his practice. This in turn was reflected in what Lugon describes as a unique form of aeronautic-ethnographic view that Mittelholzer developed during his trans-Africa crossing from Zurich to Cape Town: a low-level photograph, taken from the cabin of the landed aircraft, whose aim appears to have been less to see its subjects 'in themselves' than to register their surprise and admiration in the presence of their observer.

Marie-Claire Robic locates her account of the aerial view in French geographical discourse during the 1920s in relation to an underlying tension between the rational or reflective contact with terrain at a distance as mediated and made possible through documents such as the map and the direct personal experience of a place that had, by the beginning of the twentieth century, been newly valorised. Holding these together within what Robic describes as a 'mixed epistemology', the modern French geographers developed a concept of the *vue raisonnée* of the earth, and it is the particular ability of aerial photography to embody this, by negotiating its internal tension, combining 'the verticality of the gaze with the feel of the terrain', upon which Robic specifically concentrates. She goes on to discuss a series of case studies, which include Jean Brunhes' jubilant response to aerial photography as that which – through its very constitutive distance – was capable of registering the extent of the humanisation of the earth. Also considered here is the uptake of techniques and approaches that were pioneered in World War I, such as those developed in Morocco by the French military, whose photographs then formed the basis for a series of articles by the young geographer-pilot Jules Blache between 1919 and 1921. In her analysis Robic emphasises the importance of the experience of the aerial view for the new centrality and programmatic status that the term 'landscape' (*paysage*) gained in French geographical circles in the first decades of the twentieth century.

The distinction between vertical and oblique, discussed by Robic, plays a recurring and crucial role in conceptualisations of the aerial view. It is to the fore again in John Macarthur's chapter, which reads a 1919 article on aerial photography by Gordon Holt, published in the British journal *The Architectural Review*, in light of Louis Marin's celebrated analysis of the maps of Paris by Mathieu Mérian (1615) and Jacques Gomboust (1652). In his article Holt describes the techniques of orthographic vertical photography but also sets out the virtues of oblique views, especially those with a steep incidence which are thereby capable of conveying both the three-dimensional formation of the urban fabric and an understanding of its arrangement in plan, in a way that is otherwise impossible when the view is more laterally directed. If Holt's promotion of this kind of view is based on its ability to mediate between 'figuration' (or 'urban character') and abstraction (the diagrammatic overview of the plan), then it resembles the seventeenth-century maps of Paris whose semiotics were analysed by Marin as holding an array of structural oppositions together within a totalising utopic view. And here Macarthur sees a correspondence between the disappearance of the horizon in Holt's steeply angled shots and the utopic indeterminacy of the viewpoint of the maps that Marin discusses. While the image that is constituted as the totality of the city finds its addressee in the eye of the sovereign, Macarthur suggests that we might find a corresponding image for the liberal polity in the fragmented collage urbanism promoted by the English architectural critic, historian and urbanist Colin Rowe, whose compositional position – abstract because 'in the air', as the essay puts it – implicitly secures the distance from tradition required before historic urban form can become material for the procedures of collage.

Nathalie Roseau's study considers the impact of aerial mobility and representation on the way the modern city was imagined and examines its connection with the new infrastructural conditions of the airport in relation to which it developed. Her account moves us – by way of Hugh Ferris, Le Corbusier, Paul-Henry Chombart de Lauwe and the aerial urbanism of the architect-engineer Eugène Hénard – from the large-scale public demonstrations of the new technologies of aerial locomotion at the beginning of the twentieth century to the spectacle of the airport itself. Airports have frequently been characterised as being like cities in their own right, and Roseau interprets their evolution in terms of the history of representations – and here the aerial view was of fundamental importance – within which the image of the city of the future as a spectacle was constructed. Here she finds a crucial moment in the New York World's Fair of 1939–40, in which diverse media and technological installations were deployed in order to provide simulated experiences of flight: such, for example, was the 'Futurama', designed by Norman Bel Geddes, in which the spectacle of the future city was disclosed through the mechanism of a simulated aircraft journey.

The next chapter takes us to 1944 and to a view from above that is also to do with a certain vision of the urban future, but this time of a radically different kind. For these 'bird's-eye views' of Warsaw were taken by an *Owl,* or more precisely a Focke-Wulf 189A *Eule,* the reconnaissance aircraft whose twin-boom arrangement resulted in it being nicknamed 'The Frame'. In her essay Ella Chmielewska reflects on a sequence of photographs drawn from the Luftwaffe's aerial survey of the city that year, a project that recorded and memorialised the city as a prelude to its intended total destruction. Her text, which meditates on the experience of looking at these photographs, reflects on images of ruins, on ruined images and on the complex moment and movement of photographic capture. Her discussion of the photographs re-establishes the importance of image sequence as it relates to the flight-path of the aircraft, whose frame-like shadow we find imprinted on Warsaw's surface, while her close reading of them draws out the quotidian life of the fractured city below. She shows how figures on the ground – and in the past – at certain moments turn toward the aircraft overhead and, beyond it, to the observer of the image and her present. Thus, a kind of destabilisation in the survey document is effected, in which the directionality of the gaze from above that is monumentalised in the photograph is unsettled by the witness of those below.

Taking as his case study Firminy vert – the important new town constructed near St Étienne after 1953 – Frédéric Pousin examines the role of aerial photography in the discourse on urbanism in France during the period of its post-World War II reconstruction. Noting the intimate relation between the elevated eye and the very concept of planning, he observes the importance that images taken from helicopters and other aircraft had assumed in technocratic thinking by the late 1950s. In the pursuit of its mission, the Ministère de la Reconstruction et de l'Urbanisme (MRU) amassed a vast array of documentary photography that recorded and promoted its modernising activities and that retrospectively bore witness to the emergence of a landscape that was, as Pousin puts it, fundamentally new but extraordinarily banal. The town of Firminy vert was to be different, however. Conceived by its mayor in opposition to the limitations of the 'grands ensembles', the imaging of Firminy by the Basque photographer Ito Josué from 1960 also responded to new conditions: the task was no longer to produce a bureaucratic documentation of the construction process but rather was to visually forge the identity of the new town, and this entailed a different kind of photographic practice. By studying not only Josué's images, but also their dissemination through publications and interlinkage with other images, texts and diagrams, Pousin's analysis demonstrates the symbolic role and effects of the aerial view with regard to this emblematically modern project.

Gilles A. Tiberghien's study takes up the conception of 'aerial art' developed by the American artist Robert Smithson, locating its beginnings in the project for Dallas regional airport for which Smithson acted as a consultant to the architectural practice Tippetts-Abbett-McCarthy-Stratton. It was here, as Smithson later reflected, that his thinking on earthworks developed, this leading to his famous *Spiral Jetty* of 1970. Deeply interested in the experience of descent and ascent in an aircraft and the scaling effects that it produced, Smithson's proposals included a series of earthworks to be built at the margins of the airport. Tiberghien's essay shows the link between this work and the artist's *Alogon* series – produced around the same time as the work on the airport – whose title refers to the Greek term for irrational numbers. His analysis connects the shifting scales disclosed by flight, and a Pascalian understanding of the incommensurability of differing 'orders', to what Smithson would describe as the 'world that cannot be expressed by number or rationality' of *Spiral Jetty*.

The final chapter, by Mark Dorrian, considers the rise of Google Earth, analysing it in the context of the company's holistic ideology and its stated mission to 'organize the world's information and make it universally accessible and useful'. Dorrian reflects on the agency of image capture devices and of the programme's interface in the construction of a world picture that, while underpinned by a recognisable cultural image, at the same time presents us with something radically new. It is a picture that seems to offer us a new kind of political map, one that is no longer primarily structured by boundary lines and coloured territories, but instead through a politics of image resolution, this in turn being linked to – among other factors – national legislation governing data release that pertains in the specific countries in which satellite imaging companies are registered and out of which they operate. Dorrian suggests that the unprecedented mass availability of satellite imagery has led to a newly intensive mediation of the terrestrial surface by aerial images according to the logic of commercial branding. Today hybrid 'mashups' of text, diagram and photographic imagery – phenomena previously entirely virtual – are realised as physical constructions on the ground which has itself become a media surface, this testifying to the mass migration of the eyes of consumers into space. Under these conditions the elevated eye can no longer be thought of in terms of coolness, objectivity and detachment, but has to be reconceptualised as something that, by its very presence, produces concrete material effects.

Our goal – to sum up – is for this book to offer a way of thinking about its topic, and a range of material, that will be of importance and interest to image-based research across the humanities and social sciences and that will stimulate new theoretical approaches and directions for research. Moreover, it tries to do this at a time when the aerial view has become virtually ubiquitous. In recent years we have seen an ever-increasing cultural appetite for aerial views, as well as an extraordinary efflorescence of technologies to produce them. Today the aerial view pervades popular and consumer culture, while at the same time its uses and the key epistemic role it plays across a range of discourses – scientific, aesthetic, political, military – have continued to expand. Through this episodic historical study of the pleasures, powers and anxieties of the aerial view, we hope that new kinds of understandings of the development of our contemporary visual culture can come into focus and that new critical possibilities for thinking about it will be opened.

NOTES

1 László Moholy-Nagy, *The New Vision: From Material to Architecture* (New York: Brewer, Warren and Putnam, Inc, 1932), p.178.

1

Intimate Communiqués

Melchior Lorck's Flying Tortoise

Marina Warner

The bird's-eye view gives a vantage point of great power; from this height and synoptic angle, hitherto unknown experiences and information can be unified and displayed. Paradoxically, however, this heroic and often vast vision can also give access to small, personal glimpses of private scenes, and so become a vehicle for gaining entry to secrets – and for transmitting intimate communiqués to the viewer. Furthermore, an aerial viewpoint defies the laws of time and space, and gives the narrator a chance to fly free of these constraints. It is significant that the *Tales of a Thousand and One Nights,* which were first translated in Europe by the French scholar Antoine Galland at the beginning of the eighteenth century, associate such views from above with the power and knowledge of flight, brought about on behalf of humans by magic – either by djinn or by enchanters' devices. The vantage point magic makes possible grants the flyer superior powers – to see farther, to know and control more. The magic carpet, which figures in some of the tales, acts as a vehicle for the characters' transport – in both senses, as travel and as rapture; and it has since been established as the pre-eminent figure – the richest and most versatile metonym – for the workings of the imagination itself. On the part of the narrator in the story (and beyond him or her stands Scheherazade, who is telling all), the carpet bodies forth a literal, dream pun on flight of fancy on the one hand, and the rush of enhanced knowledge – enlightenment – on the other. More generally it also comes to stand for the book, play or film, in relation to its readers or audience, for they themselves become transported on a fantastic journey alongside the heroes of the adventure – a journey which is sometimes airborne at a distance.

Such aerial mobility, providing a common ideal vantage point to pursue a narrative and communicate its free play with time and place, functions analogously to the omniscient third-person point of view, above the action and detached from it. But at the same time, with startling flexibility, it can also imply a single observer, a first-person perceiver who is uniquely, almost prophetically, equipped to see all. It operates in the manner of the generalised eye of fate, oracular and god-like, but can also slip into the persona of an individual questor, even a peeping Tom, who is able to uncover things normally hidden from view.

The exhibition of the Indian epic, the *Ramayana,* held in the British Library in London between May and September 2008, showed this tradition at work in the story scrolls that unfold the complex and multifarious episodes of the sacred epic.[1] The most remarkable sequence of all, in what was a dazzling exhibition about visual narrative, was painted by Sahib Din and his studio in the reign of Jagat Singh in the mid-seventeenth century. At numerous points in the adventures, the painter-storyteller rises above the scene to create the picture, and to do so he combines two vantage points: one oblique to the action, the other airborne, as in one scene when the travellers stop for the night, and lay their rugs on the ground. From above, the viewer can see the divine Rama and Sita side by side on the right, but the horses beneath them are painted in profile, as is the cart and their departure the next day on the left. Many other scenes similarly offer a double viewpoint, one sharing the plane of the characters, the other floating disconnected from the earth above the *mêlée*. The compositions cannot be attributed to lack of skill – though they can be to an absence of Renaissance perspective – but they convey a keenly experienced desire to follow, by means of visual devices, the fluid motion of stories. The language of cinema would later describe these narrative manoeuvres as crane shots, panning shots and long distance sweeps (interestingly, the Indian epic artists include no close-ups).

This magnificent *Ramayana* cycle makes an illuminating comparison with contemporary European narrative arts and their use of viewpoint; it reveals how, alongside the geometry of perspective and observer, as established in Western art, artists elsewhere were multiplying positions and entry points into a drama, giving them freewheeling mobility in handling a story.

The Danish-born artist Melchior Lorck (1526–7–after 1588) travelled to Turkey in 1555–9 to gather information for his patron, Ferdinand I, heir to the Holy Roman Emperor; his stay in the Ottoman empire makes him an invaluable early witness, so it is surprising that he has been so little explored – the catalogue raisonné of his work was published only recently.[2] The art of this sixteenth-century traveller does not focus on flying as such, but has frequent recourse to an elevated position – the better to report on the mysterious realm of Islamic power. One of the first Western European observers to travel in the region and record what he was observing in visual, artistic form, Lorck was producing intelligence about the power and culture of the threatening rival Ottoman empire; his numerous drawings and prints give an unprecedented and often proto-Surrealist record of Turkish customs, architecture, costumes and devices. Lorck's prime intention being to draw up an inventory of data and communicate it clearly, he adopted the omniscient narrator's view from above for several key works. One of his greatest creations is the vast, synoptic 'Prospect of Constantinople', a panoramic watercolour drawing of the city of Istanbul, but two other pieces reveal the intimate communiqués which the aerial view can also achieve: in a superb drawing surveying the roofs of Istanbul from the artist's lodgings, he discovers a pair of lovers on a balcony; and in one of his many prints, he flies over Mecca to disclose the arrangement of the shrines inside the sacred precinct.

Lorck drew the first scene from life, but imagined the second. In literature composed before the invention of flight, the use of the aerial view frequently serves narrators who want to reveal intimate information to the reader. Born a year or two before Dürer died, Lorck was an attentive and admiring apprentice, and drew a powerfully severe portrait of his great predecessor. Besides emulating the scrutinising accuracy of Dürer, Lorck also had a quirky, even comic imagination, and a taste for odd juxtapositions and discrepancies of scale: a superb sketch, now in the British Museum, reveals his scientifically objective zoological interests, but he has transformed a tortoise into an object of wonder by positioning the animal in the sky above a Venetian coastal scene (Figure 1.1). Lorck has also added the sly inscription 'Made in Venice from Life'. To all intents and purposes like a tortoise, the creature has been identified by the cataloguers as a certain species of turtle from the Venetian lagoon, though its paws do not resemble flippers but rather the claws of the terrestrial species.[3] In any case, with such a legend, the artist dares the viewer to see the creature flying overhead like some kind of colossal, fabulous, reptilian version of the giant Rukh, the huge raptor from the Arabian nights who lifts Sinbad and can also carry off an elephant. Lorck does not give an aerial view here, though he invites his viewers to imagine the tortoise's view of the city below. But other works of his reveal that for him an elevated vantage point served both the purposes of intimate disclosure and of synoptic sweep or overview.

Melchior Lorck was born in Flensburg in Schleswig-Holstein, which was under the Danish king at the time of his birth. Called by the well-to-do Lorcks after one of the Magi (his brothers were Caspar and Balthasar), Melchior was slender

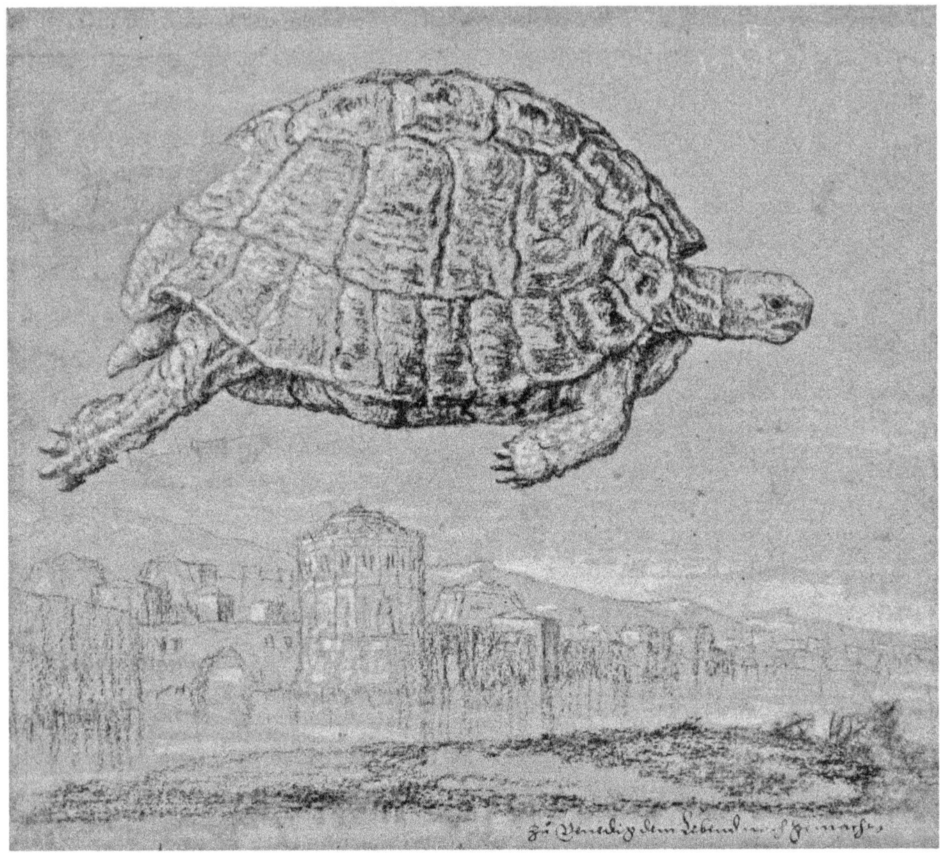

[1.1] Melchior Lorck, Tortoise, with a view of a walled coastal town in the Veneto.

and charming-looking (angelic, even, if his self-portrait serves), well educated, peripatetic and versatile. Trained as a goldsmith in Lübeck, and polished in Italy on a Grand Tour subsidised by the Danish king Frederick II, he liked to turn his hand to any kind of art – portraits, maps, prospects, engineering charts, medals, triumphal arches, emblems, calligraphy, heraldry, bestiaries, religious caricature and propaganda. In demand in his lifetime all over Europe, patronised by kings and emperors, he remained a footloose cosmopolitan and anxious to advance: he enjoyed adding exquisitely penned curlicues to his family coat of arms, granted by the Emperor for services rendered.

Lorck first emerges clearly in 1555 when he was attached to the embassy of Augier Ghiselin Busbecq (1522–92), who was being sent by the Emperor-elect, Arch-Duke Ferdinand I, to negotiate with the Sultan Suleiman the Magnificent (also known as Suleiman the Lawgiver) in an attempt to prevent the sultan's continuing assaults across the border to his Western European neighbours in Hungary and Austria. The Hapsburgs in Vienna ruled the vast possessions of the ancient Holy Roman Empire; contiguous to them, the Ottomans – under Suleiman the Magnificent and later under Suleiman II – held power over an immense territory that ranged from Armenia in the east to North Africa in the south. Suleiman had laid siege to Vienna in 1529 and been beaten back, but the vulnerability of the empire was a continued pressing matter, and the mission of 1555 aimed to negotiate greater stability. (Incidentally, this was the journey that first brought back the tulip – and the lilac. It named the first flower after the Turkish word for turban, possibly because the Turks wore the flower in their headgear, and when a traveller pointed to the flower to ask what it was, the dragoman, or interpreter, thought he must be inquiring after the turban and so the word was switched, and stuck.)[4] But unlike the diplomats, who returned home, Lorck stayed on another four years until 1559, enduring hardships and troubles, which he reported in bitter complaints and lamentations to his patrons.

Melchior Lorck's time in the Ottoman empire was the longest visit made by any artist from Western Europe during a period when the two great powers in Europe co-existed in a permanent state of live tension and perpetual conflict, and he produced a fabulously rich and rare catalogue of the customs, technology, costumes and – above all – the military arrangements of the Turks. His project presents an astonishing album of reconnaissance material: Lorck successfully compiled the detailed and acute report of an enterprising spy, a proto-photo journalist's open-eyed output and at the same time created a marvellous work of bizarre imagination. His drawings show him to be highly responsive to aesthetic ornament, and display a penchant for bizarre poses and elaborate gestures. In these last, the influence of the Mannerist Italians, among whom the Northern European Melchior Lorck went to study, can be seen.

Lorck's oeuvre is surprising for many reasons: first, that it is so little known, indeed almost unknown; second, that his Ottoman hosts gave him such a freedom of access and movement in their military encampments, places of worship and, it seems, even their harems; and third, that the spirit of his observations of Turkish culture and Islam departs so categorically from the approach we now know as 'Orientalism'. For all his flamboyant fantasy, Lorck is not an Orientalist in that sense: he observes, but does not slaver or condemn. He was gathering information about the Ottomans in order to understand them and pass it on to his Hapsburg patrons, in order to help them resist Ottoman power.

When the embassy reached Constantinople, the party was put up in the Austrian emperor's embassy near the forum of Constantine, but under reportedly uncomfortable conditions – Lorck referred to their imprisonment.[5] Indeed, on arrival, the diplomatic party was held for a year and a half under house arrest in

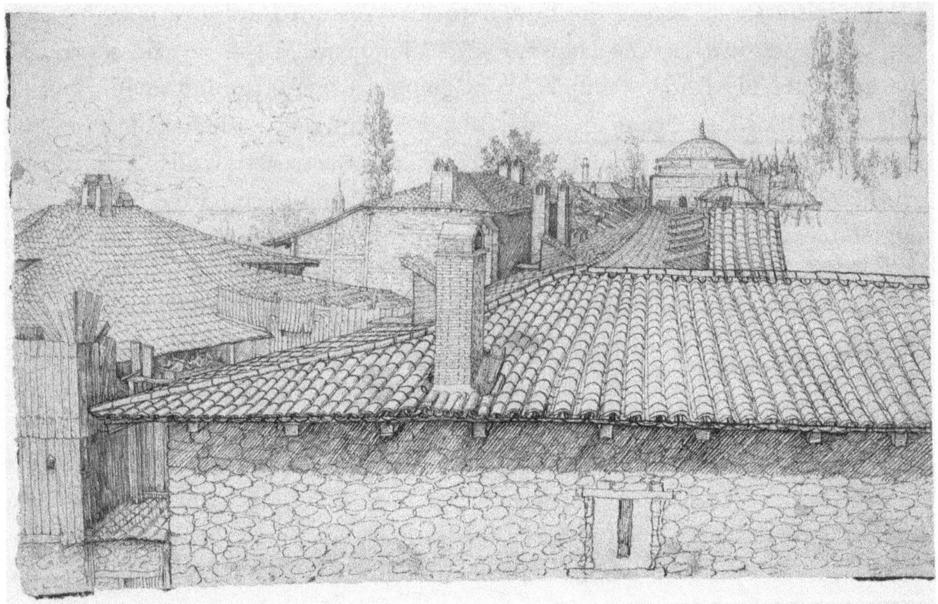

[1.2] Melchior Lorck, View over roofs toward the Column of Arcadios in Constantinople.

the caravanserai of Elçi Hani in Constantinople near the Atik Ali Pasha Mosque; Busbecq showed great talent in enduring this and eventually extricating a treaty (the English did not risk a mission until 1583).

During their confinement, the artist drew the view from his room in the eaves: a detailed pen-and-ink drawing shows some of the landmarks of the great city – the Column of Arcadios in the distance (a monument from the Byzantine era, now lost), as well as the Sea of Marmara on the horizon, where Busbecq reported he could 'see the dolphins leaping and sporting in the water'[6] (Figure 1.2). This work is one of the very few original drawings to survive from Lorck's stay in Turkey, and it is a very fine, unshowy, exemplary act of meditative attention by a new arrival in another country.

The artist's eyes scan the scene laid out before him apparently as it lay beneath his gaze; he does not compose it to conform with a pastoral landscape or a structured cityscape, but commits it dispassionately to paper, recording the mortared stonework on the wall facing him, a blank expanse except for one small window and a brick chimney stack almost in the middle of the view. His admiration for Dürer again shows in the penmanship and detail of his attention – to the masonry, the woodwork, the rendering, to the curve and irregular tiling of rooftops and shallow domes of the adjoining mosque's madrasa, and to the shuttered mansard windows which were built to face the prevailing wind from the sea and freshen upper floors in hot weather. He records the various palings and fences and screens erected between the buildings, some even bristling fanwise from the top of one fence, which has been raised on top of another. The whole drawing gives a virtuoso inventory of different building fabrics and textures, of what amounts to a series of screens or veils. It is a view of a view that is turning away from the viewer: a portrait of a scene that has brought its hands instinctively to cover its face or wants to present its back.

Busbecq reported wearily that the embassy building was

> open to all the breezes and is therefore regarded as a healthy place of residence; the Turks, however, grudging such amenities to foreigners, not content with having blocked the view with iron bars on the windows, have added parapets, which impede both the view and the free enjoyment of fresh air. This appears to have been done in deference to the complaints of the neighbours, who declared they had no privacy from the gaze of the Christians.[7]

Lorck was probably trying deliberately to overcome these constraints when he looked out of the window, or perhaps his curiosity had been aroused by them; then, as his cartographer's eye sweeps over the view below his window, his hand follows and he captures in a tiny vignette a couple making love on a terrace screened by rushes (Figure 1.3).

The striking quality of the drawing comes from the inconsequentiality of Lorck's treatment: the temperature of his penmanship does not rise; without emphasis of any kind, without drawing attention to the lovers' presence in his roofscape, or reference to erotic couplings from the repertory of the Renaissance (for example Giulio Romano's *I modi*, published 1524), conveying neither titillating expressiveness, bawdiness, nor disapproval, Lorck simply sets down what he saw. In this drawing, his way of looking does not reach for the excitement of the grotesque juxtaposition, but remains equable, almost affectless; his sepia ink accords one tile as much interest as the next, in the manner of a surveyor measuring and recording in a manner very radical for its time – it would be hard to date the work accurately without further context. The day is hot, the atmosphere inside is stuffy, the balcony is screened. Apart from Rembrandt's tender intimacies – and occasional frank scatology – it is difficult to think of another artist making so little fuss about looking at sex.

Nor is it possible to read into this scene a vision of the Orient as a place of *luxe, calme, et volupté*. Later, when the mission was given permission to travel and observe the country and Melchior Lorck began to draw the inhabitants and their customs, he shows a similar inexpressive absorption in the details of décor,

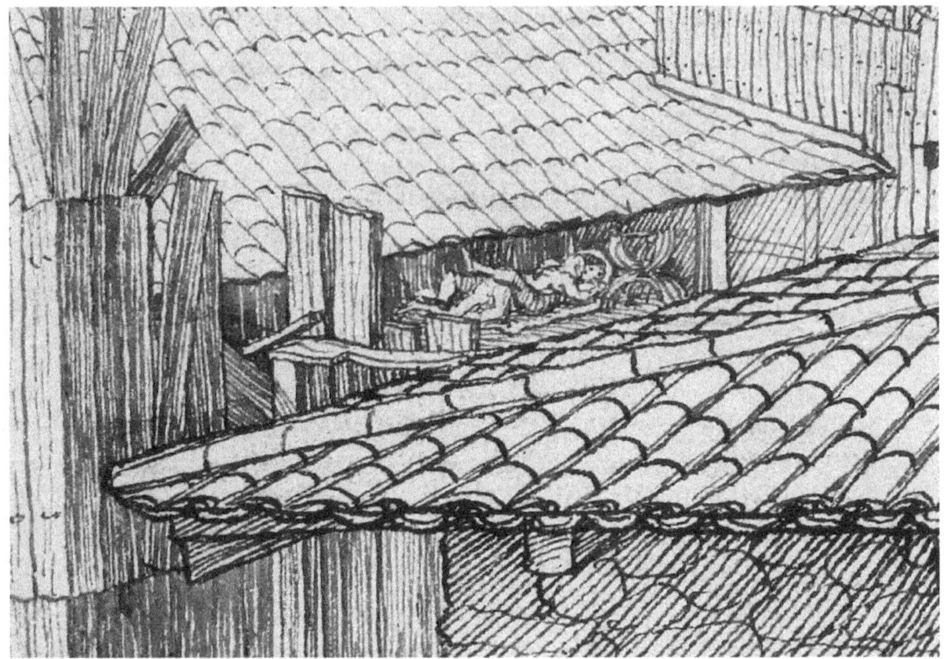

[1.3] Melchior Lorck, Detail, View over roofs toward the Column of Arcadios in Constantinople.

ornament and cladding, with little concern for subjective interactions with his subjects, though he could be a trenchant and impressive portraitist, as in the two images he made from life of the Sultan himself (Figure 1.4). However fanciful, Lorck's drawings, from this image onwards, build into an awed tribute to Ottoman wealth and efficiency: not a trace announces those Orientalist preconceptions about languor and effeminacy and debauch, as emphasised in commentaries excoriated by Edward Said – that tendency comes later, a good 200 years after Lorck travelled in Turkey.

Nevertheless, the foreigner kept confined for diplomatic reasons looks out of his window and at some point during the making of his drawing, sees the lovers without intending to: seeing from above gives him access to something private not intended for the eyes of others. The aerial view, as we now know from surveillance systems, also offers a keyhole view.[8]

Lorck was set on this kind of looking: his Turkish drawings include a set of studies showing women in domestic interiors – one group at prayer, the other sitting down to a meal. In both cases they are gathered in their own quarters – so how did he gain access, if at all? Are these convincing looking sketches inventions? Or the result of something more clandestine? Disguise? Bribery?

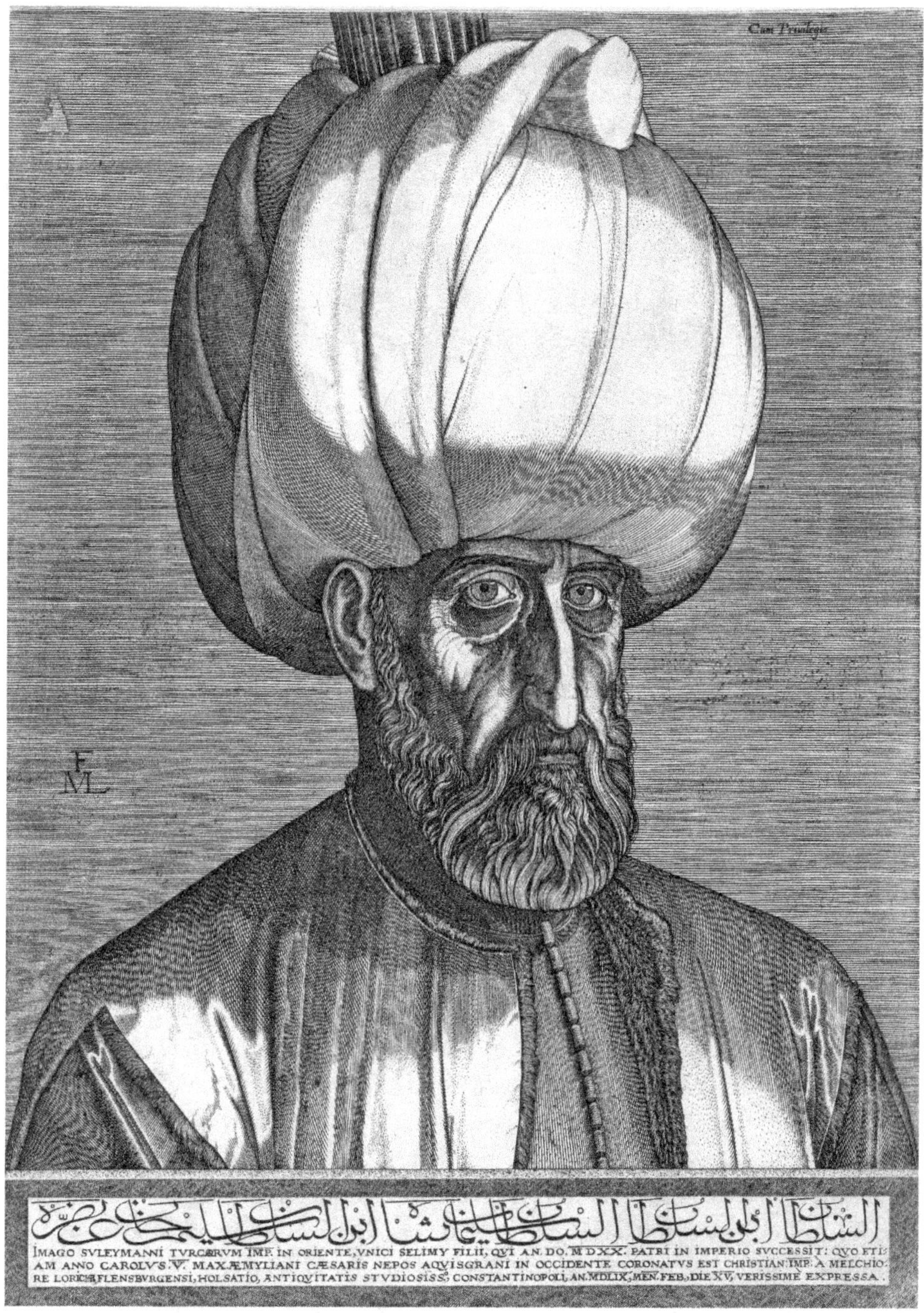

[1.4] Melchior Lorck, Portrait of Suleiman.

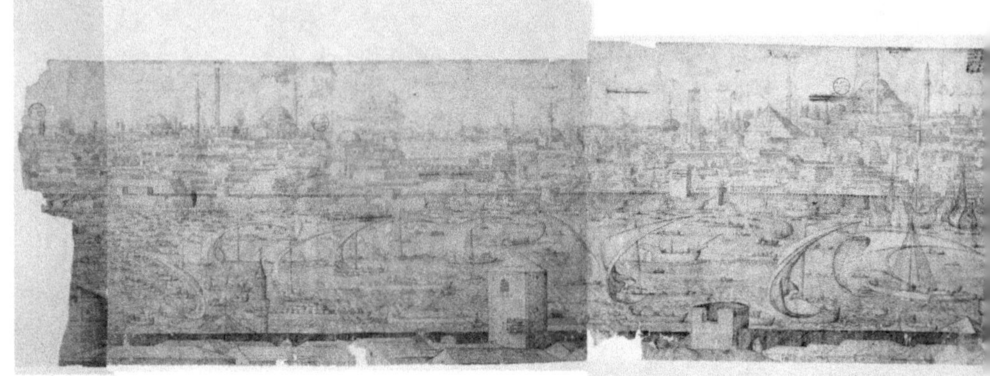

[1.5] Melchior Lorck, Prospect of Constantinople (section).

Whatever the circumstances of his obtaining the information, the artist communicates it without prurience, without exclamation. The unfamiliar scenes he appears to be capturing do not arouse defensiveness or superiority on his part – or on ours, viewing his work later. Lorck is a traveller in the Orient before Orientalism, and in his images, he views the Turks without the condescension, the exclamatory distance, or the hostility that come to be characteristic of later eighteenth-century reports.

Lorck uses the elevated view in two other ways, but in both the connection to forbidden knowledge persists. First, empirically, when he unfurls the magnificent panorama of the city of Constantinople, and second, fantastically, when he takes his audience into the sanctuary of Mecca.[9]

The panorama is a great work by any standard and makes Lorck's neglect all the more surprising. The 'Prospect of Constantinople', signed and dated 1559, is the artist's most ambitious achievement and the first eyewitness view of the city made in situ from a unified geographical vantage point, as if anticipating widescreen cinemascope[10] (Figure 1.5). It was originally made up of 21 sheets of paper glued together, which have now been separated for conservation purposes, but the whole astonishing work is reproduced in facsimile, leporello-style, in vol. 4 of the catalogue raisonné, with a commentary that transcribes the inscriptions Lorck entered in his spiky and lovely handwriting; he identified the palaces and mosques, classical antiquities, churches, aqueducts and schools, and, in the roads of the Golden Horn, the teeming shipping. The Prospect was given to the library in Leiden almost as soon as it was completed, and used to hang in the reading room, but it was then rolled up and left in an attic and only salvaged in the nineteenth

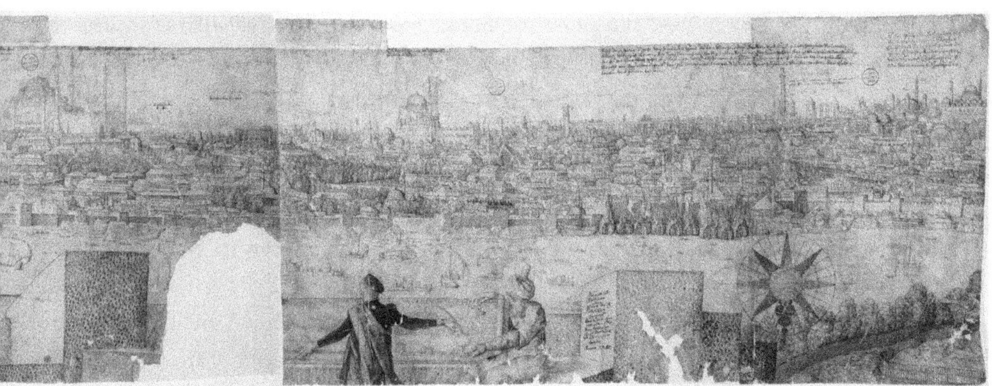

century; the extensive damage it had suffered looks like the work of rats, not only damp. What remains is still a wonder, though.

A magnificent 11.32 metres long, the scroll unfolds a vast, synoptic overview of the city of Istanbul, rendered from the heights of the fortifications in the Galata district on the European side of the Bosphorus, across the Golden Horn thronged by the graceful cross-rigged dhows of the Turkish merchants, fishing boats, naval vessels, ferries and skiffs, plying the waters under sail, and sweeping across 'from the Seraglio Point to the mountains beyond the walls that protect the city peninsular from the hinterland'.[11] This Olympian vista is in itself fantastic – the artist has united eight different vantage points into a single illusory, aerial synopsis, which gives his penmanship a chance to play wonderfully with the bellying shapes of the sails against the stacked forms of the city's massive splendour.[12] As the art historian Erik Fischer comments, 'It is sensational, for it was the first large and detailed picture the West saw of this mysterious, glorious city so rich in memories.'[13]

In the foreground, the artist has included himself at work with a flourishing gesture of his quill; the scroll and a chalice for his ink and paint (there are washes of green and pink on the drawing) are being held for him by a seated Ottoman grandee, who is wearing the huge rolled turban that marked out the status of a Mufti or an Emir, both pre-eminent definers and upholders of the law.

The composition communicates to us that the sweeping view of the great Ottoman capital has been granted to a gifted humanist artist and gentleman traveller; his self-portrait shows Lorck, then in his early thirties, as a Renaissance courtier, a graceful youthful figure with elongated fingers as in a painting by his contemporary Parmigianino, and a suitable recipient of a king's bursary who has studied in Italy and garnered the benefits. He is executing his art with élan under the benevolent supervision of a high-placed protector, or so it would appear, and the relationship discloses the tensions in the commission: the Ottoman official is being helpful, even admiring, but he remains present and no doubt vigilant. The visiting artist from Europe is able to record the city, its layout, its dwellings, its fortifications, its trade and shipping, but only by permission, and that permission is granted because the Turkish empire has nothing to fear from its magnificence and business being revealed to foreigners, so confident are its citizens – the seated figure holding the scroll proclaims – in what they have achieved and what they are. So the Prospect is triple-faced: an act of intelligence-gathering by a visitor from a hostile power, a reverent homage to a munificent and enthralling host country, and a message to the neighbouring European empire about what it has to reckon with.

The Italians began making comparable *vedute* of the Turkish capital after Gentile Bellini's return from his visit to the Ottoman court in 1479–81, and the genre took root in Venice.[14] A magnificent mapping of Cairo was made by Matteo Pagano, for example, in 1549(?),[15] and a very fine Venetian woodcut of 1520 bears the same title as Lorck's – *Byzantium sive Constantineopolis* – which pointedly overlooks the Turks' own name for their city, Istanbul. In this print by Giovanni Vavassore, Christian interests dominate and the Muslim presence – especially the conversion of churches into mosques – has been smudged, even effaced (only two religious buildings of non-Christian origin are included). Although Lorck quotes the Venetian, he does not follow his tendency to propaganda. He also seems to have been shown a highly detailed pictorial and coloured Turkish map of Istanbul, made in 1537–8;[16] as in that image, the religious monuments of all denominations are included in Lorck's panorama, with Hagia Sophia, Justinian's great basilica from the Byzantine past, and its brand new offspring, the architect Sinan's Suleimaniye Mosque, dominating the skyline.

His depiction of what he saw rather than what European interests wanted to see is worth exploring further, as it bears on religious struggles in the artist's time and gives context to the position of his birthplace in Reformation Europe; but it also has relevance to current approaches to religion and politics. However, while this Prospect counts as an oblique aerial view, as it fulfils some of the criteria (an elevated vantage point, a uniform attention to data laid out for inspection and a flattening of distance and proximity into pattern and repetition), Melchior Lorck also took wing to satisfy the curiosity of his patrons by producing from imagination a fantastic bird's-eye view of Mecca, with all the tombs and shrines surrounding the Kaba itself, as represented in Islamic tradition, but he has mischievously added other sacred buildings from east and west, including a fanciful cathedral, arranged in a kind of capriccio around its walls (Figure 1.6).[17]

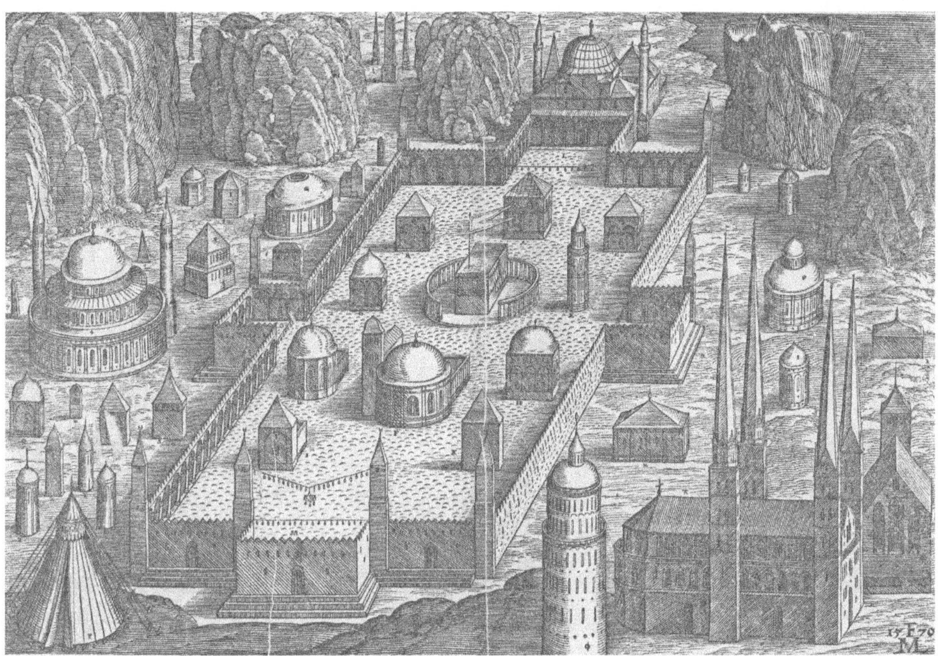

[1.6] Melchior Lorck, View of Mecca.

Lorck had this image engraved for the album of his Turkish travels which he planned to publish after his return; he seems to have tilted his material to meet the taste of his Christian patrons. But this project was never carried out, which accounts for the artist's comparative neglect. Towards the end of his life, he was employed by Rudolph II in Prague, and that patron's fanciful tastes are indeed foreshadowed by Lorck's own way of seeing. The art historian Peter Ward-Jackson noticed Lorck's luminous oddness in an article in 1955 (one of the very few about him), and comments on 'the almost hallucinatory quality that is often present in Lorck's work'.[18]

Eventually, Lorck disappears from view. The last known drawings by him depict two African figures, 'A Woman of Nigeria' and 'A Woman of the Gambia', so he probably continued his explorations of countries far beyond his native Denmark. After his death, his drawings were again edited and engraved, and began to appear in different collections – a volume of 1574 (known in a single copy, destroyed in the bombing of Hamburg) and, finally, in 'The Turkish Publication' of 1626.[19]

With regard to early uses of the aerial view, Melchior Lorck's threefold approach throws light on the mobility of narrative viewpoint according to very ancient and hence almost invisible conventions, and a certain humorous yearning for such days of cosmic ubiquity fills the drawing of the airborne tortoise. Interestingly, Lorck invokes his desire for such counter-intuitive mobility in a letter he wrote on his return from Constantinople to the new King of Denmark, Frederick II. Pleading for his royal patronage in the steps of his father, Lorck presented his work, offering, in particular, his portraits of Suleiman the Magnificent:

> I do not bring home gold, pearls, and treasures, for they were not the cause of my travels [...] therefore I present what I have [...] For (to speak what is already on my tongue) if it were possible for me to move freely about in the sea, then I would rather imitate the fish – especially the large ones – than begin groping for pearls and precious stones.[20]

Then, after this expression of unusual sympathy with large fish, he tries to persuade his prospective protector of his good faith as an artist; he then switches to another metaphor and another point of identification: 'Indeed,' he continues, 'could I bodily step in and out of heaven, neither effort nor danger would restrain me.'[21] In Lorck's chain of metaphors, the surprising affinity he expresses with large fish swimming comfortably in the sea segues into another kind of mobility, an aerial mobility between earth and sky; these two points of identification are both embodied in his fantastic tortoise above Venice. The airborne creature, so little a natural candidate for flight, conveys through the joking, punning conjugations of the unconscious, an ideal alter ego for a struggling artist-traveller, a lumbering grounded animal who can yet soar in order to spy out the lie of the land, the laying of lovers and the secret precincts of worshippers of another faith.

NOTES

1 J. P. Losty, *The Ramayana: Love and Valour in India's Great Epic – The Mewar Ramayana Manuscripts*, 16 May–14 Sept 2008 (London: British Library, 2008). See plates 25, 26.

2 Erik Fischer, Ernst Jonas Bencard, Mikael Bøgh Rasmussen, *Melchior Lorck* (Copenhagen: The Royal Library and Vandkunsten Publishers, 2009) (hereafter abbreviated ML-Fischer). A review of this catalogue was published as 'A View of a View' in *The London Review of Books*, 32(10), 27 May (2010): 15–17.

3 ML-Fischer, Number 1553-3, vol. 1, p.19.

4 Anna Pavord, *The Tulip* (London: Bloomsbury, 1999), pp.56–62.

5 On sheet VIII of Prospect of Constantinople. Erik Fischer, *Melchior Lorck in Turkey: Texts by Erik Fischer and Melchior Lorck* (Copenhagen: Royal Museum of Fine Arts, 1990), p.4.

6 ML-Fischer, vol. 1, p.96; the drawing is in the collection of the Statens Museum for Kunst, Copenhagen, where it is dated *c*.1559, but the content of the work suggests an earlier period during Lorck's visit to Turkey.

7 ML-Fischer, vol. 1, pp.96–7.

8 These two angles of view were also assimilated in early cinema, see for example *The Magic Glass* (1914), in Marina Warner, 'The Uses of Enchantment' in Duncan Petrie, ed., *Cinema and the Realms of Enchantment* (London: British Film Institute, 1993), pp.13–35; p.35.

9 See Venetia Porter et al., eds, *Hajj: Journey to the Heart of Islam* (London: British Museum, 2011).

10 The full reference in the Leiden Library catalogue is: *Byzantium sive Constantineopolis.* [Door] Melchior Lorichs. Bladen [6]–[12], pentekening in sepia, 600 x 355 mm. [Constantinopel/Wenen, 1559 [1561(?)] – (BPL 1758); reproduced in facsimile in ML-Fischer, vol. 4.

11 Erik Fischer, *Melchior Lorck in Turkey,* op. cit., p.9.

12 Marco Iuliano, 'Melchior Lorck's Constantinople in the European Context', in Fischer, op. cit., vol. 4, pp.25–60; pp.51–60.

13 Fischer, *Melchior Lorck in Turkey,* op. cit., p.9.

14 Iuliano, op. cit., pp.30–41.

15 See Nicholas Warner, *The True Description of Cairo: A Sixteenth-Century Venetian View,* 3 vols (Oxford: the Arcadian Library with Oxford University Press, 2006), esp. 'Contexts', vol. 1, pp.115–35.

16 Iuliano, op. cit., p.41.

17 See various pilgrimage certificates in *Hajj Journey to the Heart of Islam,* ed. Venetia Porter et al., op. cit. (London: British Museum, 2012), Figs 8, 14, 79, these examples all being made later, however, than Lorck's.

18 Peter Ward-Jackson, 'Some rare drawings by Melchior Lorichs in the collection of Mr John Evelyn of Wotton, and now at Stonor Park, Oxfordshire', *Connoisseur,* 135(544), March (1955): 83–93; 87; Ward-Jackson also draws attention to 'the morbid trend of his imagination' and 'his predilection for the weird and the sinister', 90.

19 ML-Fischer vol. 3 reproduces 'The Turkish Publication' in full.

20 Melchior Lorck: 'An Autobiographical Letter, written on Jan 1 1563', from Erik Fischer, *Melchior Lorck in Turkey,* op. cit., p.13; a paraphrase is included in ML-Fischer, vol. 1, p.176.

21 Ibid., p.13; cf. ML-Fischer, vol. 1, p.176.

2

The Meaning of Roman Maps

Etienne Dupérac and Antonio Tempesta

Michael Bury

The subjects of this chapter are two representations of Rome which have always been considered among the very finest of the sixteenth century: Etienne Dupérac's of 1577, etched and engraved on 4 plates with the title *Nova Urbis Romae Descriptio,* and Antonio Tempesta's of 1593, etched on 12 plates, with the title *Recens prout hodie iacet almae urbis Romae cum omnibus viis aedificiisque prospectus accuratissime delineatus*[1] (Figures 2.1 and 2.2). Although they would almost certainly have been printed in relatively large numbers at the time they were made, surviving examples are extremely rare. This reflects a general fact that multi-plate prints, mounted to form very large single units for purposes of display, were immensely vulnerable to physical deterioration and eventual destruction. Only one impression of the Dupérac survives (in the map collection of the British Library) and only a few of the Tempesta (at Stockholm, Leiden and the Vatican).[2]

What I argue is that each can be seen as a carefully constructed visual system for organising information and conveying meaning. Both of them are of the type known as bird's-eye views, but each shows immense ingenuity in the command of visual invention. By comparing them, I will try to demonstrate what very different kinds of meaning were communicated using essentially the same conventions. In terms of the factual information they convey, there are major differences, the consequence of the different positions from which the city is pictured in each, and the exact projections chosen to present it. But what I want to bring out particularly is that behind each is an

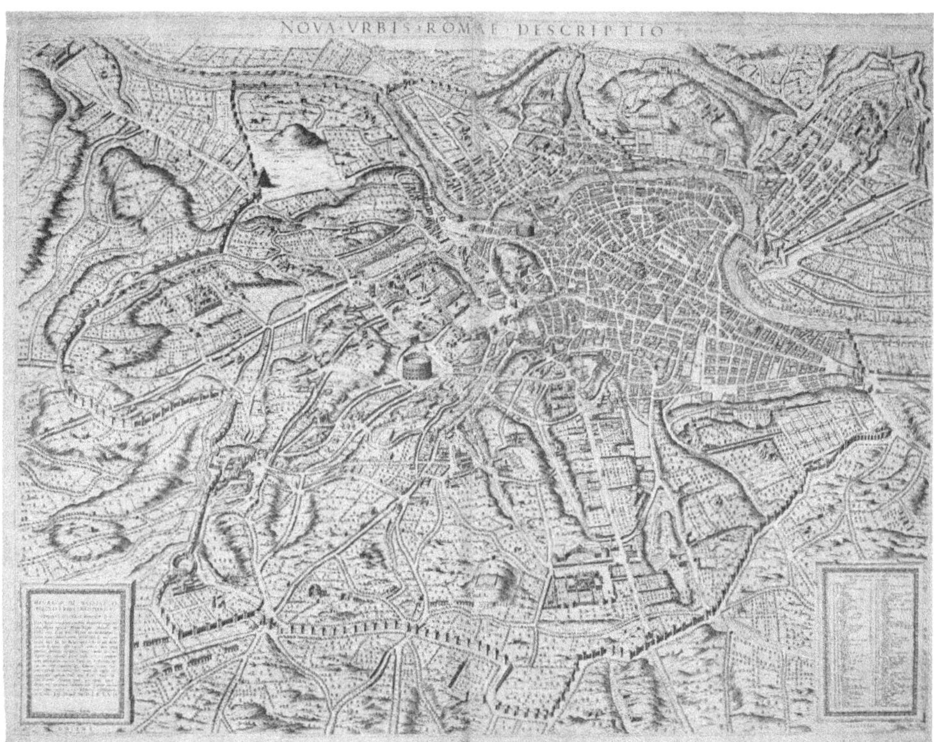

[2.1] Etienne Dupérac, *Nova Urbis Romae Descriptio*, 1577.

explicit rhetorical purpose: both of them were intended to convey meanings that required, but went beyond, their factual contents.[3] My argument will be that both Dupérac and Tempesta signalled their different purposes very clearly and created representations that achieved those purposes in a very consistent manner.

Dupérac defined the extent and shape of the city in a vertical projection. For this purpose he made use of an earlier print: the remarkable orthogonal plan of Rome, printed from 24 wood blocks, designed by the geometer and military engineer, Leonardo Bufalini, and first published in 1551[4] (Figure 2.3). This was not at all a common form for city maps in the sixteenth century. Although there is no direct evidence for Bufalini's motives in adopting this method, which was based on a measured survey of the city, the relationship between his and an earlier plan allows one to infer something of his thinking. The plan of ancient Rome that Bartolomeo Marliani introduced into the 1544 edition of his book on the city's antiquities is a similar orthogonal representation, in which a system of shading like Bufalini's is employed to bring out the relief

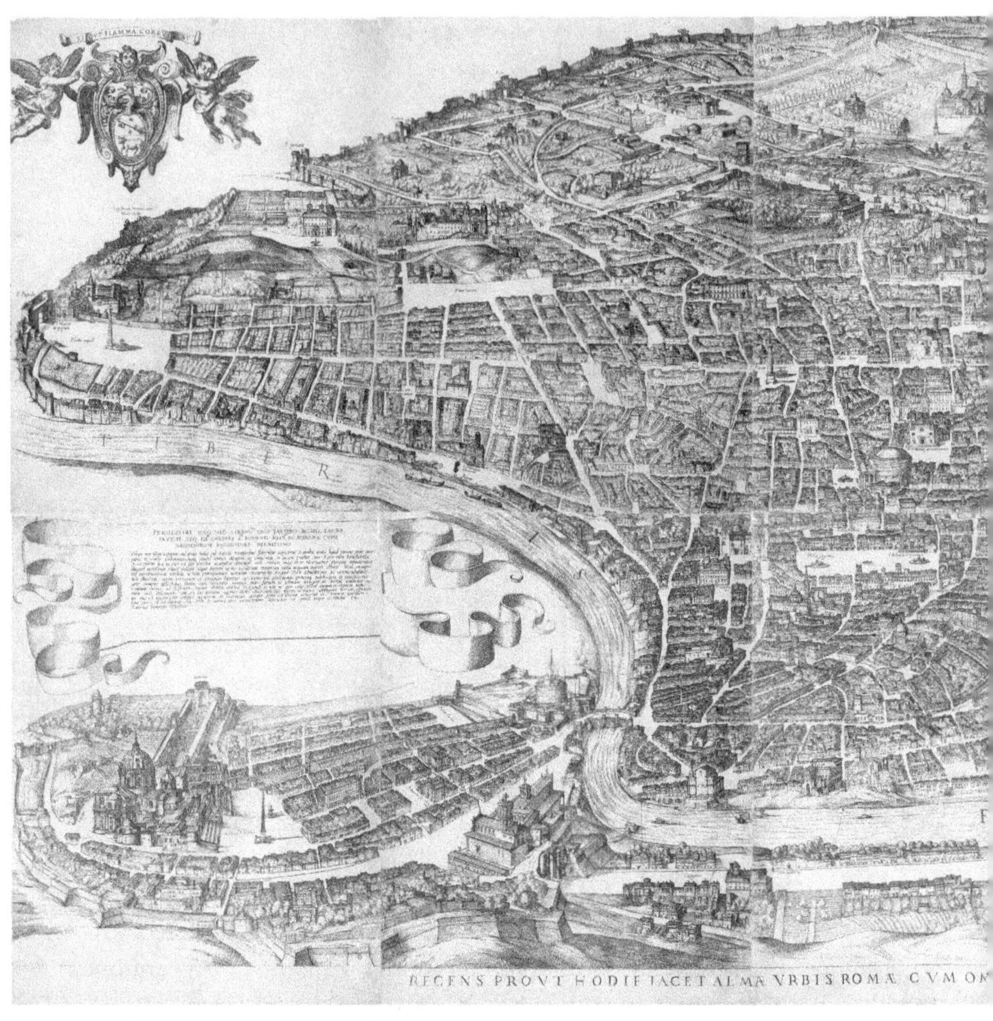

[2.2] Antonio Tempesta, *Recens prout hodie iacet almae Urbis Romae … Prospectus*, 1593.

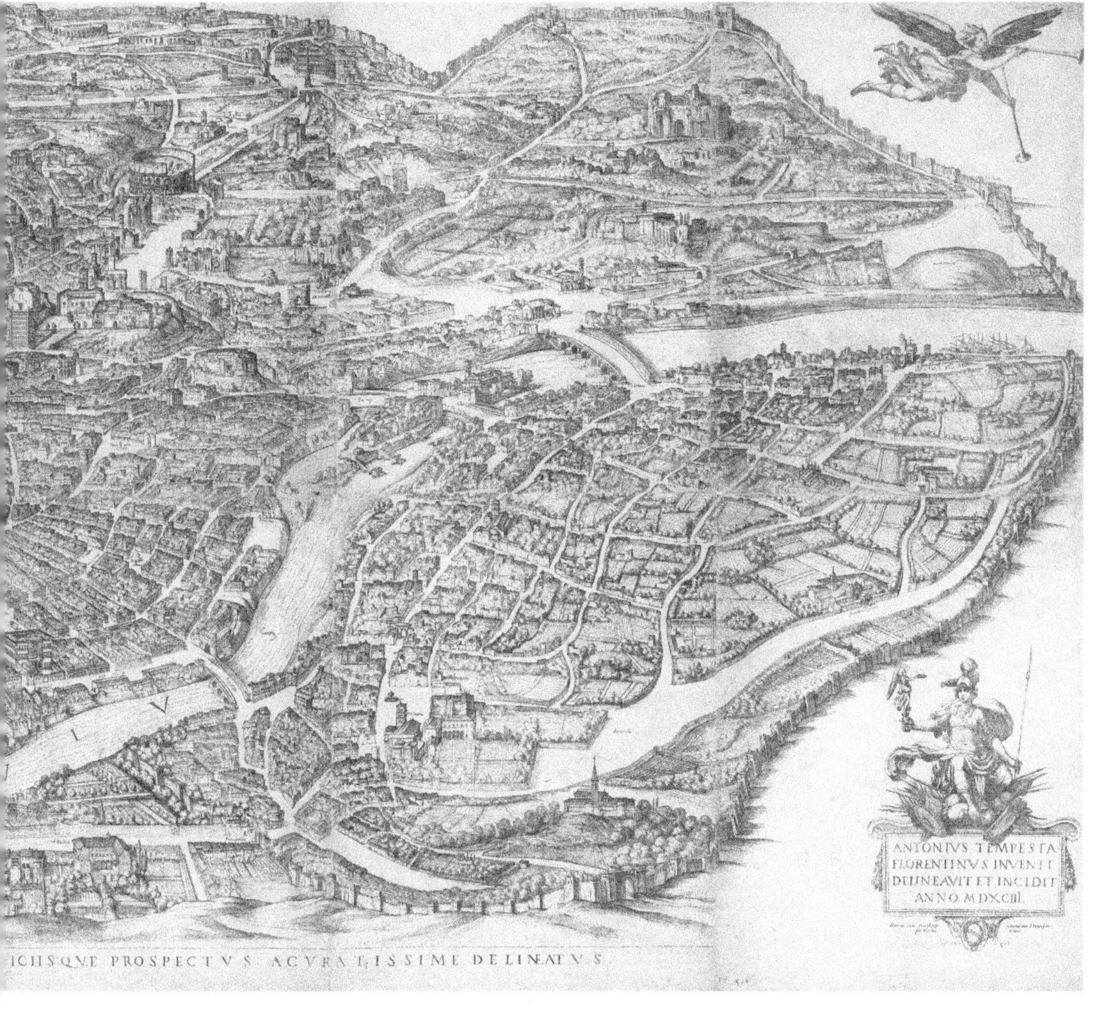
ANTONIVS TEMPESTA
FLORENTINVS INVENIT
DELINEAVIT ET INCIDIT
ANNO MDXCIII.
ICHSQVE PROSPECTVS ACVRATISSIME DELINEATVS.

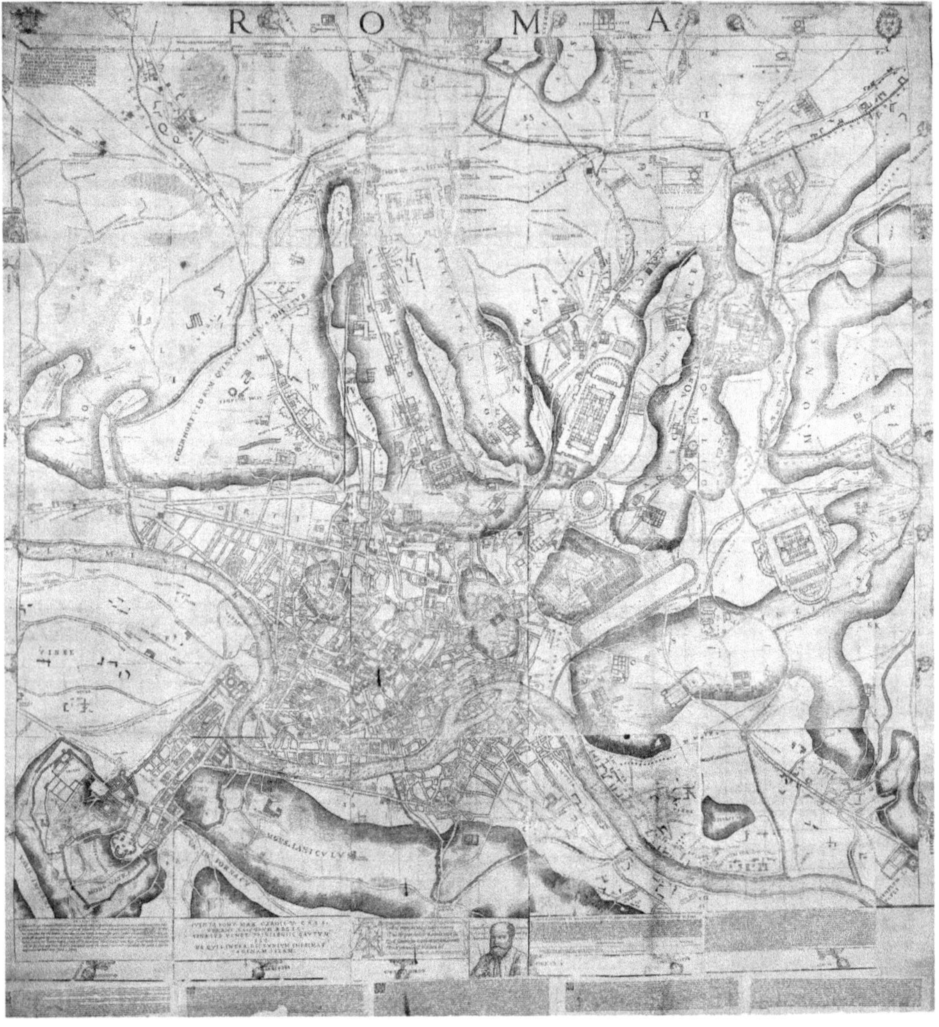

[2.3] Leonardo Bufalini, *Roma*, 1551 (1560 reprint).

of the ground (Figure 2.4). Whether Bufalini was influenced by Marliani, or whether Marliani obtained from Bufalini a preliminary draft of his plan, they cannot have been conceived independently of one another.[5] Marliani provided the following instructive justification for his approach:

> [I]f we had wished to present in relief this figure and the following ones, according to natural perspective, it would have happened that, with all the sides of the hills (except one) hidden, it would have been impossible to place the buildings on their sites. Therefore since we thought it better, for the benefit

> of all, for it to be consultable, rather than to amuse certain people with a useless picture, we presented the figures flat. We took care however to shade the sides of the hills according to their height, so that the valleys would thereby be easily distinguished.[6]

Marliani acknowledges that there would be a demand for a pictorial perspective view, while making clear his disapproval. In the early seventeenth century, Floriano dal Buono, was to justify his use of a low viewpoint for his pictorial representation of Bologna in the following terms:

> To represent [the city of Bologna] in plan would have been to indulge myself with a fiction and with satisfying the imagination rather than the sense of sight. Portraits of cities do not consist in their plans, valuable for anyone who might intend to attack them with mines or to build others similar, but in their representation exactly as the eye sees them from a determinate point of view.[7]

Dupérac combined Bufalini's orthogonal plan with the elevations of the ancient and modern buildings of the city as seen in a bird's-eye perspective, approximately from the north-east. Thus he was able to incorporate the accurate relational information of the orthogonal plan not only with an indication of the relief of the ground but also with something of the actual appearance of the buildings. By this means he succeeded to some degree in avoiding the drawbacks of a perspectival representation as conceived by Marliani. Dupérac had not invented this method. Francesco Paciotto's plan of 1557, engraved by Béatrizet and published by Antonio Lafreri, had earlier taken advantage of the existence of Bufalini's surveyed plan in a comparable manner.[8] Dupérac himself had earlier adopted the same system for his great reconstruction of the ancient city at its apogee.[9] In the dedication of his representation of the modern city to the King of France, Henry III, he referred to that previous work. Instead of a celebration of the glory of Rome as it had once been, he now proposed to show the city as it was in the present, with the injurious effects of time on the ancient monuments: a stimulus to a meditation on the vicissitudes of human achievement.[10]

The effect of Dupérac's choices was to emphasise the disparity between the ancient city and the modern. Not only was the full extent of the uninhabited areas within the Aurelian wall clearly revealed, but the choice of the north-east as the point from which the buildings were viewed gave special prominence to those areas, occupied as they were only by the massive ruins of the ancient city. The perspective viewpoint for the buildings implied a foreground and background, so that the populated parts of the modern city appeared as if in

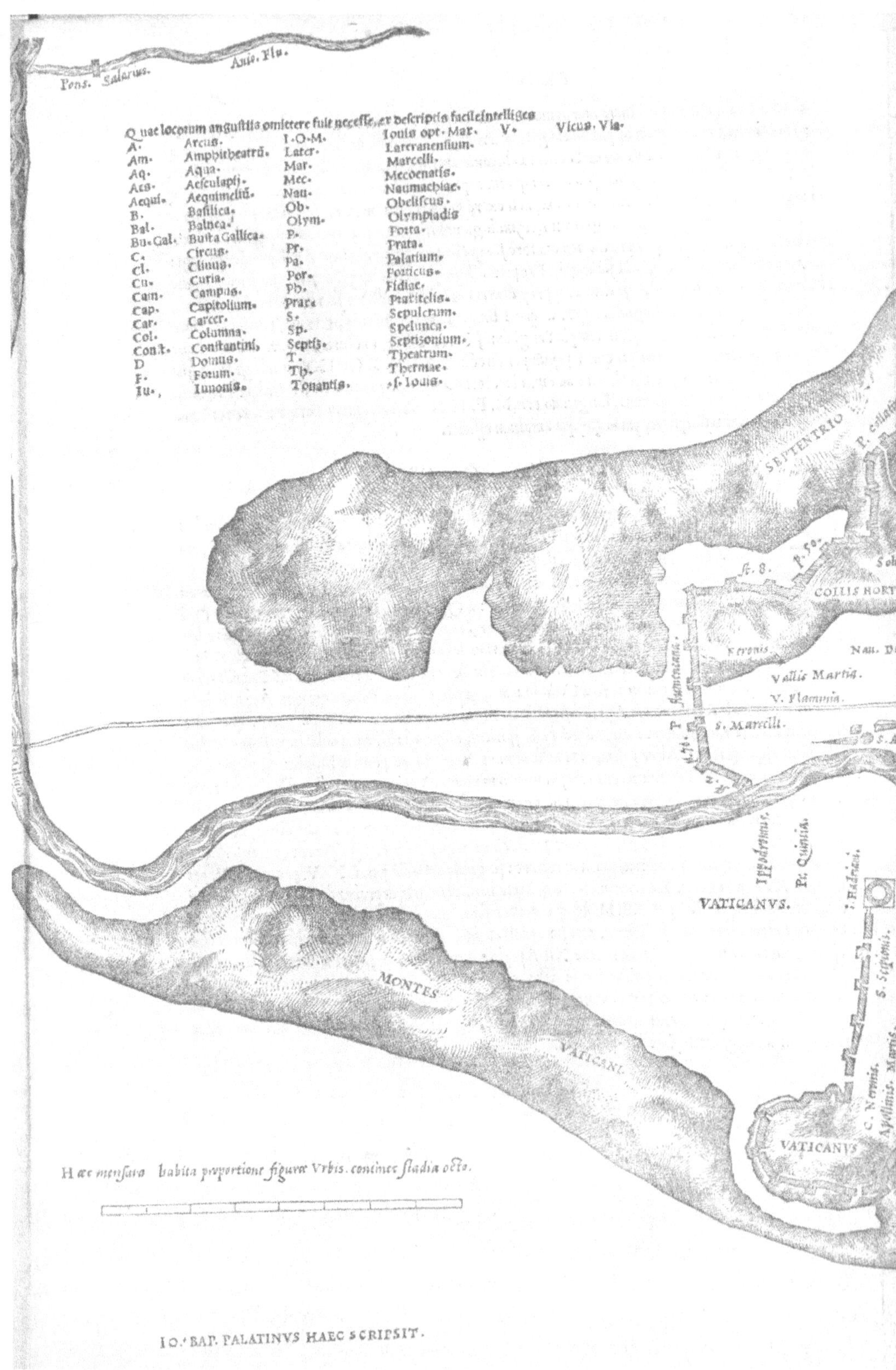

[2.4] Bartolomeo Marliani, Plan of Ancient Rome, 1544.

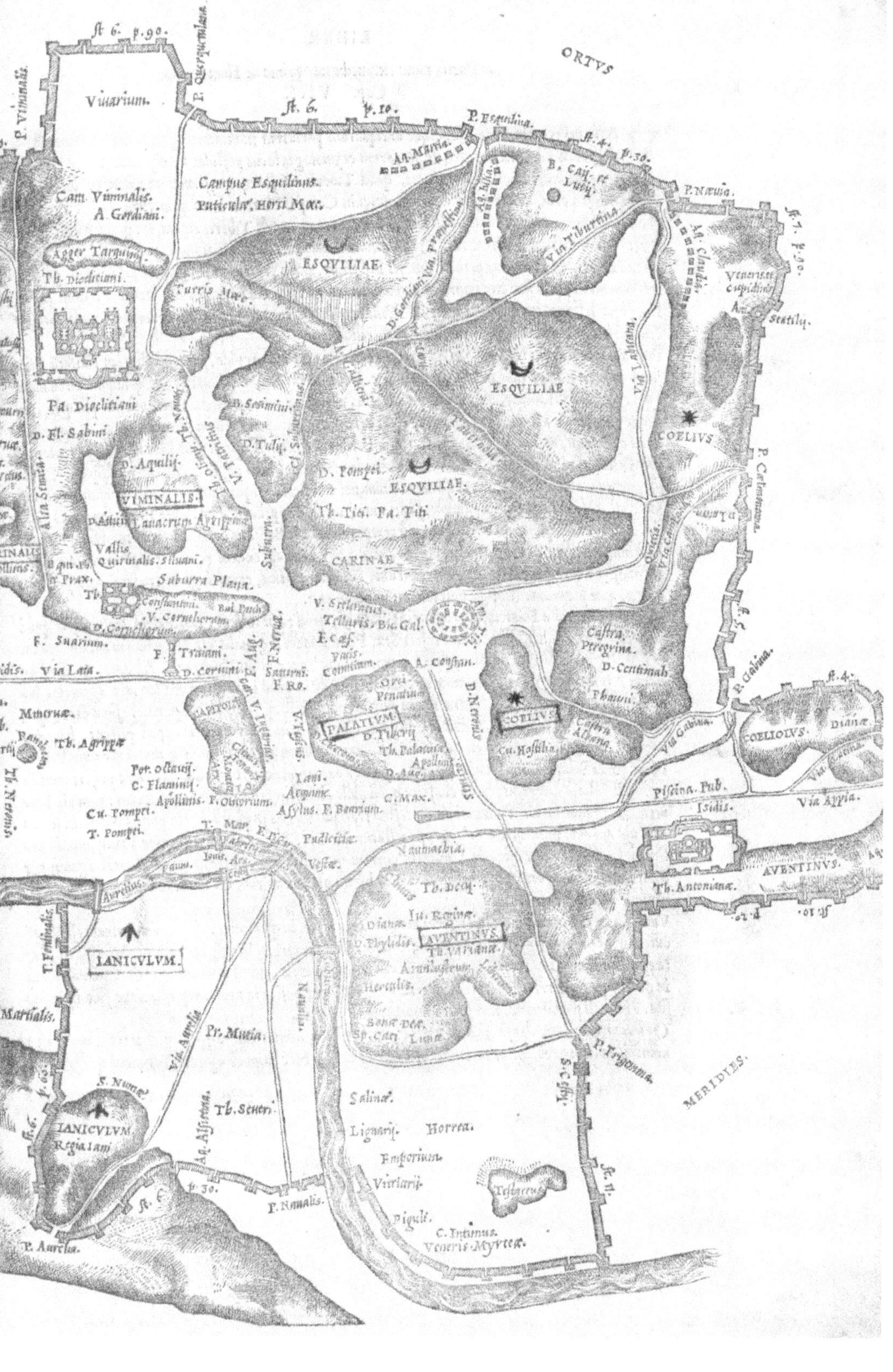
ORTVS
Viuarium.
P. Viminalis.
P. Esquilina.
P. Næuia.
Ag. Martia.
Campus Esquilinus.
Puticulæ, Horti Mæc.
Cam Viminalis.
A. Gordiani.
Agger Tarquinij.
Th. Diocletiani
Turris Mæc.
ESQVILIAE
Via Tiburtina
Ag. Claudia.
Veneris et Cupidinis.
A. Statilij.
Pa. Diocletiani
D. Fl. Sabini.
D. Aquilij.
VIMINALIS
ESQVILIAE
D. Pompei.
Th. Titi. Pa. Titi
CARINAE
COELIVS
Via Labicana.
P. Celimontana.
Vallis Quirinalis.
Suburra Plana.
Th. Constantini.
V. Corneliorum.
D. Corneliorum.
F. Suarium.
F. Traiani.
Via Lata
V. Sceleratus.
Telluris.
Castra Peregrina.
D. Centimali
Faunni.
CAPITOLIVM
Th. Agrippæ
C. Flaminij
Apollinis.
Cu. Pompei.
T. Pompei.
PALATIVM
D. Tiberij
Th. Palatinæ
Apollinis
D. Aug.
COELIVS
Castra Albana.
Cu. Hostilia.
P. Gabiusa.
COELIOLVS.
Dianæ.
Via Latina
Piscina Pub.
Isidis.
Via Appia.
Lani.
Asylus. F. Boarium.
C. Max.
Pudicitiæ.
Naumachia.
Th. Antonianæ.
AVENTINVS
Aurelius.
IANICVLVM
Th. Decij
Iu. Reginæ.
Dianæ.
AVENTINVS
Herculis.
Bonæ Deæ.
P. Trigemina.
MERIDIES.
Via Aurelia
Pr. Mutia.
Th. Seueri
Ag. Alsietina.
S. Numæ
IANICVLVM
Regia Iani
Salinæ.
Lignarij.
Horrea.
Emporium.
Vitriarij.
Testaceus.
P. Naualis.
P. Aurelia.
Figuli.
C. Intimus.
Veneris Myrteæ.

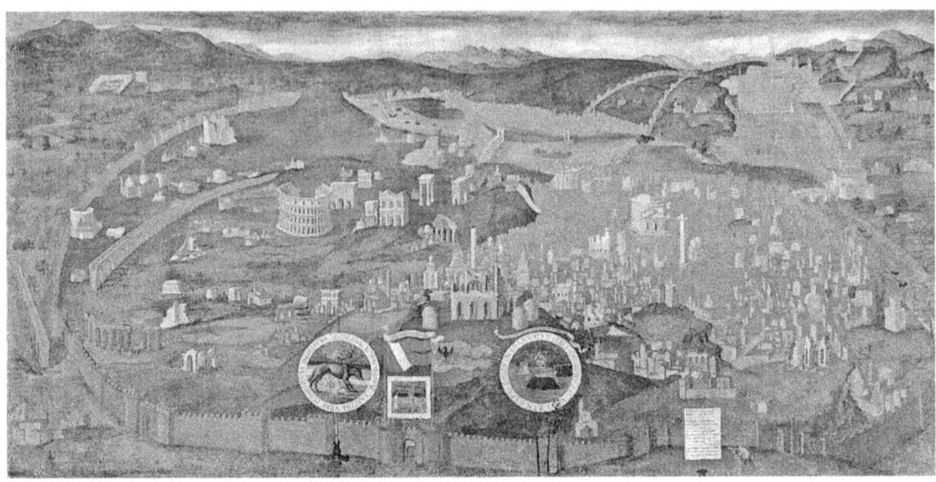

[2.5] Anonymous, View of Rome, copied from the original of Francesco Rosselli.

the background, huddled into a small area beside the Tiber. By such means the representation stressed decline and decay.

There were other sixteenth-century representations that showed the city from the north-east. This was the case, for example, with one of those engraved by Béatrizet in 1557, but this had the very specific purpose of showing the fortifications that had been put in place for the Naples war.[11] More relevant for what Dupérac did was the lost Rosselli view, designed before 1490 (Figure 2.5). It was a pictorial perspective showing the city in a high oblique but not quite bird's-eye view, with the ruins of the ancient city given an exaggerated size.[12] It was still known and used in the sixteenth century. The painted version of it in the ducal palace at Mantua, dating from after 1538, has a series of inscriptions proclaiming Rome as mistress of peoples and prince of provinces and, echoing Dante, as founded to rule the world and receive the papal mantle. In the present she fulfilled her destined role as the holy city of the popes, but the ruins of the ancient city were the monumental signs of a now-transcended phase of that millennial purpose.[13] And they are emphasised not only by their scale: a *titulus* carries the inscription 'Only the ruins show how great I once was'. The point is further developed in the 14 lines of a poem, written on what purports to be a banner displayed to the lower right, with the figure of Father Time with a scythe beside it.[14]

The intended meaning of Dupérac's *Descriptio* was less complex than Rosselli's view, but the emotional charge is nevertheless a powerful one. Looking at details such as the delineation of the Pantheon or of the Theatre of Marcellus

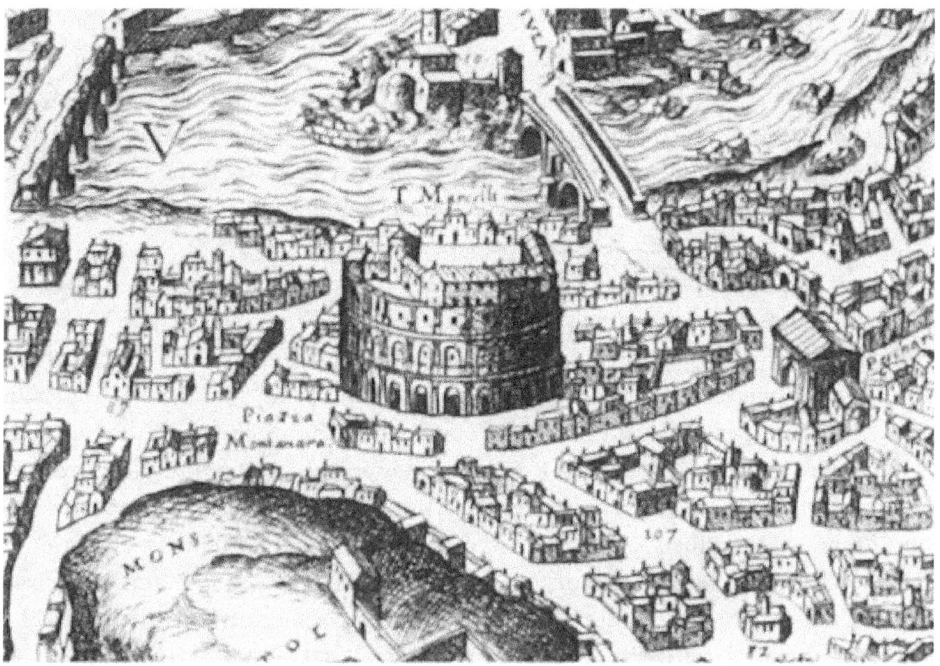

[2.6] Detail of Dupérac, 1577: Theatre of Marcellus with modern buildings within it.

between the Capitoline hill and the river, with houses within and around it, one recalls how the modern buildings attached to the ancient remains had reminded Montaigne of the nests built by martins and crows in ruined churches[15] (Figure 2.6). In general it is noticeable how small in size the modern buildings are, especially the anonymous generic forms of those not individually studied. Dupérac's representation was structured by an explicit rhetorical purpose.

Tempesta's representation too is explicitly an attempt to present the city as it is, but with a quite different twist: he is concerned 'not to show the old but the city that we see today flourishing under the popes'.[16] Tempesta chose a bird's-eye view for both the ground and the buildings. Onto the receding ground plane he raised the elevations of the buildings, presented as if seen from high above the Janiculum in the west. He wanted to emphasise the inhabited areas; the modern city is unchallenged by the remains of the ancient. It is interesting that in the 1580s, Sixtus V had laid out an extensive road network intended to open up the largely uninhabited areas of the Roman hills. But this was far from central to Tempesta's concern, and the idea, which has sometimes been proposed, that he conceived his work as a homage to Sixtus V seems perverse.[17] To judge the effect of his work it should be compared to a representation which, although known today only in late states, was probably first published at much the same time as, or just before Tempesta's.[18] This lays out the elevations of the buildings from a bird's-eye viewpoint above the Janiculum, but, unlike Tempesta, the unforeshortened, orthogonal ground plane allows a full appreciation of the new road systems.[19] Tempesta's perspective, by contrast, projected the built-up parts of the modern city into the foreground, while reducing the unpopulated spaces traversed by the new roads to a diminished distance.

A viewpoint from the west had become the one most commonly adopted by Roman mapmakers; prominent examples are Pirro Ligorio's work of 1552, Ugo Pinard's of 1555 – which Jacob Bos engraved – and Cartaro's of 1576.[20] It was the *Urbis Romae descriptio* of Pinard which was perhaps the most important model for Tempesta, because there too both the ground plane and the buildings are shown in perspective as if from high above the Janiculum[21] (Figure 2.7). Pinard's view, which had been published by Antonio Lafreri, was much copied and immensely influential, its status confirmed when its scheme was chosen as the basis for the representation of Rome included by Georg Braun and Franz Hogenberg in their *Civitates Orbis Terrarum*, published at Cologne in 1572.[22] When compared with Pinard's it can be seen that Tempesta intensified the effects of perspective recession. From his chosen viewpoint in the west, he described in extensive detail the city as far east as the papal palace on the Quirinal and the church of S. Trinità dei Monti, but beyond, the space suddenly diminishes. Great monumental complexes within that contracted eastern area, such as the Lateran and S. Maria Maggiore, are given a quite disproportionately large scale. Tempesta thereby stresses, even more than Pinard had done, the buildings of the modern city.

Comparing Tempesta with Dupérac it is easy to see how differently they deployed the bird's-eye view. Dupérac's arrangement of the buildings implied a viewer occupying a particular position, even if it was not a position that anyone could have actually taken up: Dupérac had constructed it in his mind, never seen it. On the other hand, any straightforward pictorial illusion is contradicted by the vertical projection of the ground plane, which is independent of any viewer. He called the result a *Descriptio*, a term that could be used equally well to refer to a verbal, as to a visual representation. The overall purpose was, as we have seen, to communicate his message of the vicissitudes of fortune as clearly and elegantly as possible.

Tempesta's representation of the city is apparently more homogeneous in the sense that both the ground plane and the elevations are treated in perspective. The point of view is conceived as being high above the Janiculum – a favourite place with visitors from which to view Rome. Thus Montaigne's diary reports on 26 January 1581: 'M. de Montaigne went to see the Janiculum Hill beyond the Tiber [...] and the view of the whole of Rome which can be surveyed more clearly from that spot than from any other.'[23] Tempesta indeed calls what he did a *Prospectus*.[24] But his is far from being a straightforward view of the city, either. First of all there are important adjustments.[25] Tempesta introduced a very significant distortion of reality in his treatment of the course of the Aurelian wall in the south-western zone of the city (Figure 2.8). In reality the wall on the Trastevere side of the river ended with a tower that looked across the water towards the Aventine hill, at the foot of which, running along the river bank, was a longish section of wall that at a certain point turned east, away from the river, towards the Pyramid of Cestius and the Porta S. Paolo. Tempesta, by means of a radical displacement of the port of Rome, the Ripa, relative to the opposite bank of the river, created the quite false impression that the sections of wall running west to east on either side of the river directly corresponded to one another.

Any sense that the use of perspective for both ground plane and elevations was being used by Tempesta to present his work as if it were truly a view, is finally subverted by the way he artificially isolates the city from its surrounding territory, making it almost like one of those models carried by a town's patron saint to be seen in many Renaissance paintings. It has been argued that the relationship between a city and its countryside was usually falsified in sixteenth-century representations, perhaps in order to emphasise the visual cohesion of the city.[26] A very good example of this is provided by Dupérac's treatment of the relationship between Rome and the country around it in his 1577 *Descriptio*. To focus on just one detail (Figure 2.9): Dupérac's representation of the Porta Latina, near the Lateran, may be compared with a carefully observed drawing by Michiel Gast to reveal how Dupérac eliminated the buildings clustering around the outside of the gate, thereby heightening the distinction between the inside and the outside of the city.[27]

However, Tempesta's device of entirely eliminating the surrounding country had no precedents among the earlier printed representations of the city, although it was to influence some of his seventeenth-century successors.[28] It communicates the idea that the representation is of some completely self-contained entity, conceptual rather than phenomenal in kind. It may have been a desire to reinforce this appearance that motivated his manipulation of the true course of the Aurelian wall, for the effect of the displacements described above is to enhance the sense of the city as a compact unit. This, in turn, provided the space and opportunity for allegory: in the blank corners we find not only the image of *Roma Victrix* to the lower right, but also, upper right, an angel blowing the trumpets of Fame.[29]

It has sometimes been supposed that Tempesta's *Prospectus* was intended for a papal patron.[30] But the dedication to Giacomo Bosio (1544–1627) and the prominent display of his arms detaches this work from the papal orbit.

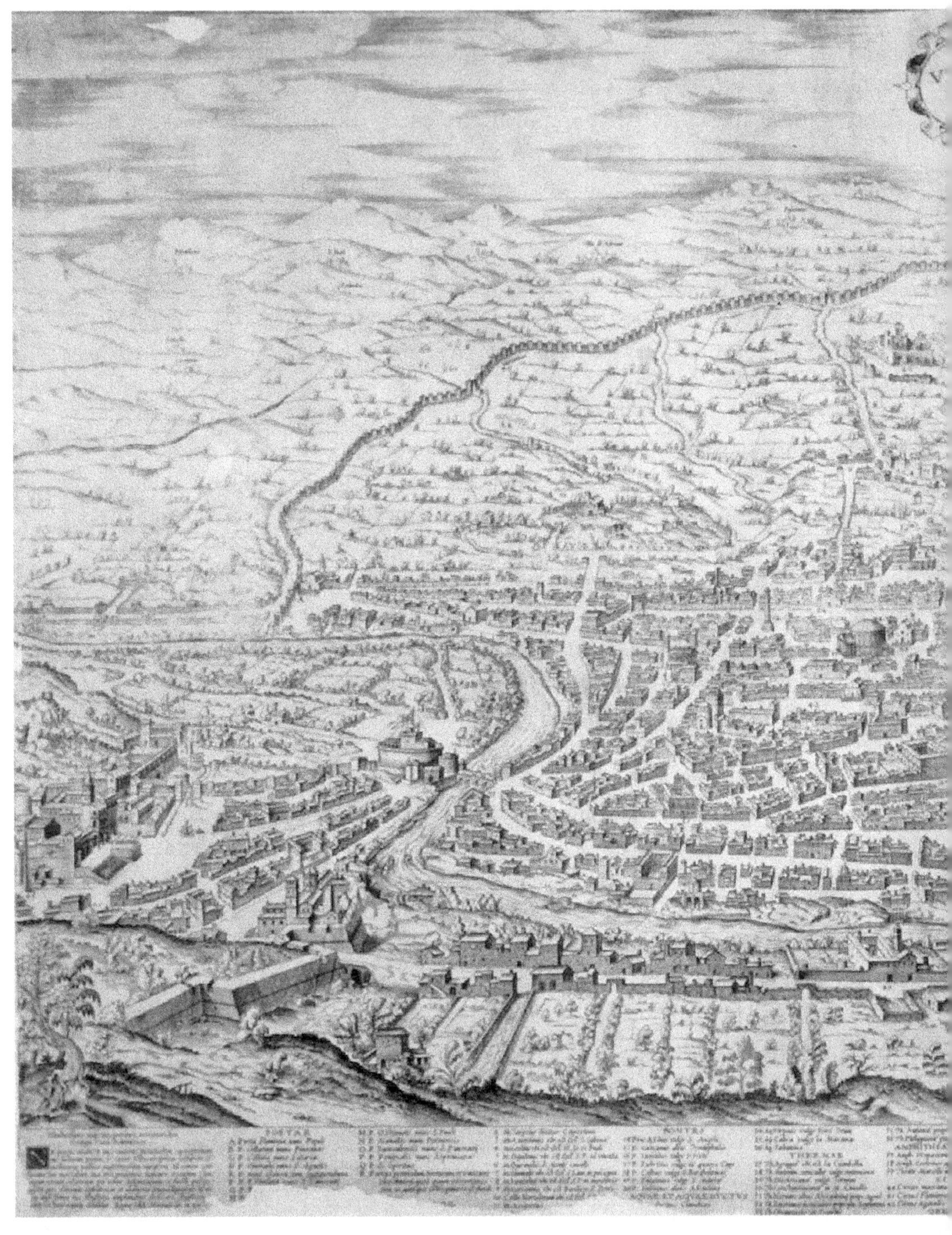

[2.7] Ugo Pinard, *Urbis Romae Descriptio* (engraved by Jacob Bos), 1555.

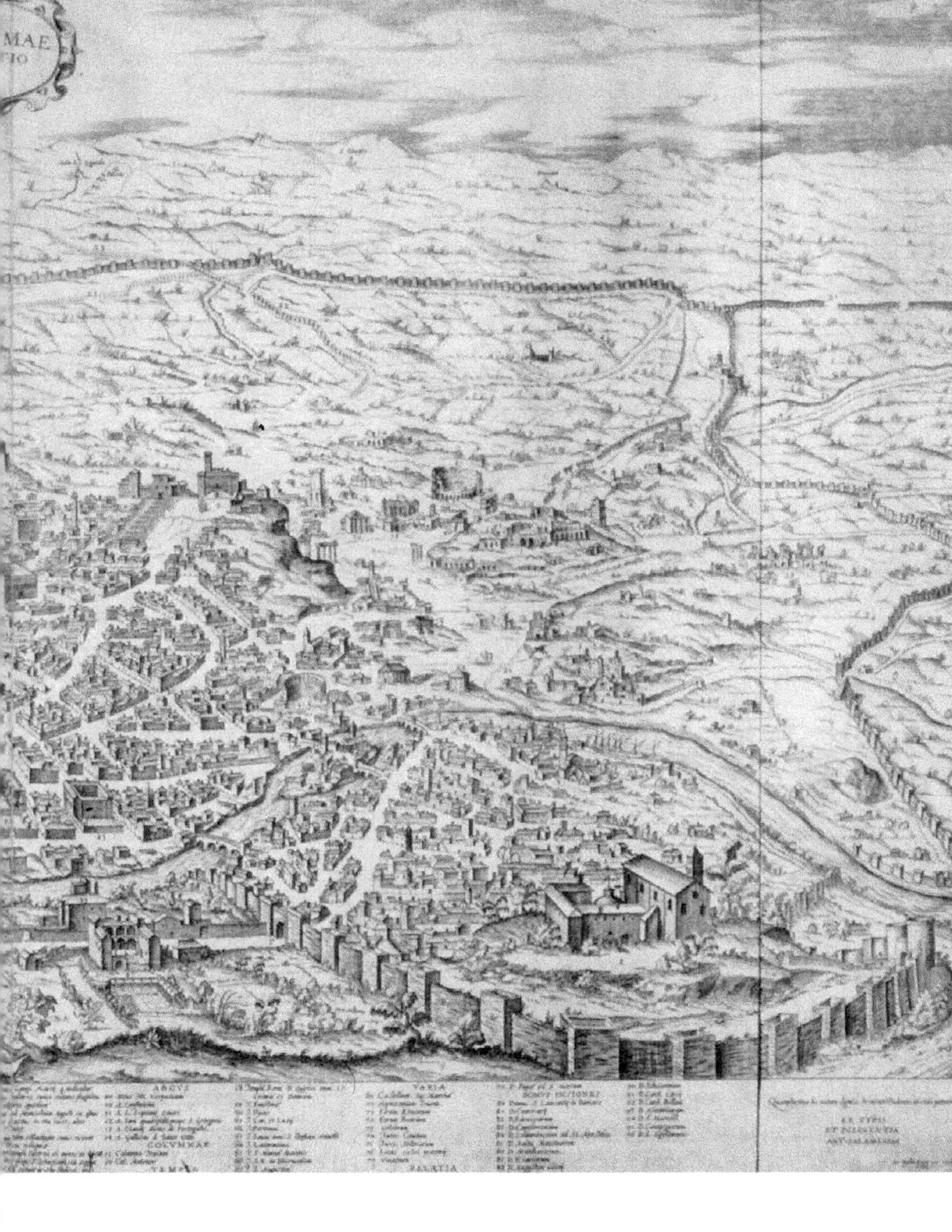

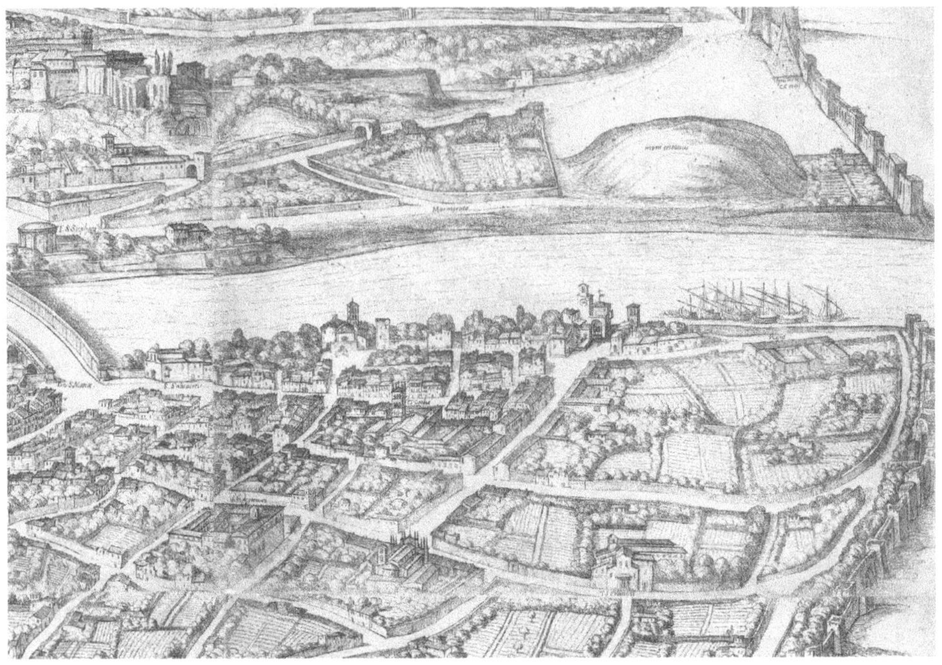

[2.8] Detail of Tempesta, 1593: south-west zone of the city.

Bosio was a collector, an antiquarian and a historian of the military Order of St John of Jerusalem. He was himself a knight of that Order and, from 1574, its official representative at Rome.[31] It is interesting that if thought about from a simple ecclesiastical point of view, the representation could hardly be considered adequate, not least because of the way it excluded some of the major churches that formed an essential part of any definition of Rome as a great spiritual centre. S. Paolo fuori le Mura, for example, one of the four basilicas which in Jubilee years every pilgrim had to visit in order to gain full advantage of the indulgences, was included by Dupérac, and by the author of the so-called 'plan of 1590', but, being located outside the walls, it is necessarily omitted by Tempesta's choice of borders for his representation.[32] He intended to convey a message quite the opposite of Dupérac's: a message not of decline but of the rise of the modern city to fill the space of the ancient and thus become its worthy successor. The measure is the immense circuit of the Aurelian wall, now apparently filled with a thriving population, making it possible to celebrate it with the triumphal symbolism of a personified Fame trumpeting conquering Rome. It is in that sense that Tempesta does praise the popes. It is under their rule that the city has flourished; a point that is stated clearly in the dedication – '*sub Sanctis Pontificibus florentem*'.[33]

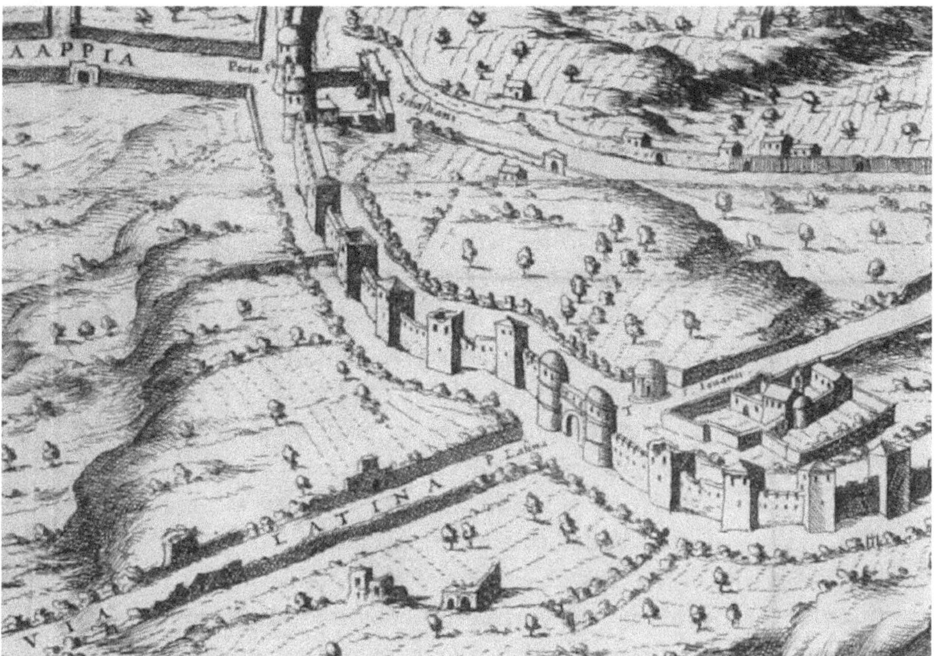

[2.9] Detail of Dupérac, 1577: Porta Latina.

Anton Francesco Doni, around 1550, described how a citizen might introduce a stranger to his city, first taking him to visit the public and well-known sites, then to the less well-known:

> finally he takes him onto the top of some building that commands the city, or onto some hilltop, and there shows him the length and the breadth of the site, familiarising him with the public buildings, the streets and everything, so that from this elevated position he comes to fix in his mind an image of the place (*'egli viene a stabilirsi nell'Idea la imaginatione della terra'*).[34]

The large size of both Dupérac's and Tempesta's multiple-plate prints allows them to depict in great detail many of the principal monuments of the city, and their efforts to present what often amount to portraits of individual buildings give immense value to their work. Thus they produced synthetic images packed with factual information, and their works can be and are used for the purpose of extracting detailed information about the individual buildings, streets and squares of the city as they were in the sixteenth century. The two prints were constructed independently of one another and adopt different viewpoints, but with respect to the individual elements these differences are potentially complementary. They can often be used together to gain a remarkably full understanding of the reality, because they describe the same things in different ways.[35]

The adoption of a bird's-eye view also provides the viewer with the relational information to form an image of the whole as well as of the parts. However, in terms of the 'meaning of the place' that each of the prints communicates, their differences are incommensurable. Each of the maps had an explicit rhetorical purpose toward which matters such as the choice of viewpoint and manner of projection were directed. That larger purpose – which worked on both emotive and visual-didactic levels – had, of course, an impact on the details. This can be seen in the adjustments that were made to particular areas in order to make them conform to the desired image – as we have seen in the Tempesta with the circuit of the Aurelian wall in the south-western sector of the city; it can be seen in the construction of ideal relationships as, for example, between the ancient and the modern, and between the city and its surrounding countryside; and it can be seen in the way the elements were standardised by each mapmaker so that the parts could be put together to constitute what would convey, with consistency, the desired picture of the city. The representation of ordinary houses is an important case in point, where almost certainly no individual studies underlie what we are shown. While Dupérac presents us with houses that are overwhelmingly one- and two-storey structures, Tempesta presents two- or three-storey ones. Jean Delumeau tried to use this in order to track the distribution of a supposed large increase in the population between the reigns of Gregory XIII (1572–85) and Clement VIII (1592–1605), but that seems a dangerous procedure.[36] These representations of Rome communicate knowledge of what was there, but it is – as I have argued – knowledge that is directed toward certain and specific ends. The outcome of both close observation and pictorial invention, these persuasive documents are immensely sophisticated negotiations between reality and imagination.

NOTES

1 For the Dupérac (815 x 1042 mm), see Franz Ehrle, *Roma prima di Sisto V: la pianta Du Pérac-Lafréry del 1577* (Rome: Biblioteca Vaticana, 1908), passim; Christian Huelsen, *Saggio di bibliografia ragionata delle piante icnografiche e prospettiche di Roma dal 1551 al 1748* (Rome: Bardi, 1969), p.66, XIV (73) (originally published by the Archivio della Società Romana di Storia Patria, Rome, 1915); Amato Pietro Frutaz, *Le piante di Roma*, 3 vols (Rome: Istituto Studi Romani, 1962) I, p.186, no. CXXVII; and Michael Bury, *The Print in Italy 1550–1620* (London: The British Museum, 2001), p.136, no. 83. For the Tempesta (1090 x 2450 mm), see

Huelsen, op. cit., p.74, XVIIIa (84); Franz Ehrle, *Roma al tempo di Clemente VIII: la pianta di Roma di Antonio Tempesta* (Rome: Biblioteca Vaticana, 1932), passim; Frutaz, op. cit., I, p.192, no. CXXXIV; and Eckhard Leuschner, *Antonio Tempesta, ein Bahnbrecher der römischen Barock und seine europäischen Wirkung* (Petersberg: Imhof, 2005), pp.365–9.

2 The Vatican example comes from the collection of Thomas Ashby; it is mentioned in Mario Gori Sassoli, ed., *Roma Veduta. Disegni e stampe panoramiche della città dal XV al XIX secolo* (Rome: Artemide, 2000), p.156.

3 My project was inspired by Juergen Schulz's work on Jacopo de'Barbari's view of Venice. See Juergen Schulz, 'Jacopo de'Barbari's view of Venice. Map Making, City Views and Moralized Cartography before the year 1500', *Art Bulletin*, LX (1978): 425–74. A revised version was published in Italian in a collection of Schulz's essays on mapmaking, entitled *La cartografia tra scienza e arte. Carte e cartografi nel Rinascimento italiano* (Modena: Panini, 1990), pp.13–63.

4 1980 x 2040 mm. See Franz Ehrle, *Roma al tempo di Giulio III: la pianta di Roma di L. Bufalini* (Rome: Biblioteca Vaticana, 1911), passim; Huelsen, op. cit., pp.18 and 38, I (1); and Frutaz, op. cit., I, p.168, no. CIX.

5 Bartolomeo Marliani, *Urbis Romae topographia* (Rome: Valerius and Aloysius Doricus, 1544); the great plan of the ancient city is printed over pp.12–13. See Huelsen, op. cit., p.30, Frutaz, op. cit., I, p.56, no. XII and Margaret Daly Davis, *Archäologie der Antike 1500–1700* (Wolffenbüttel: Herzog August Bibliothek, 1994), p.44, no. 2.7. See also Jessica Maier, 'Mapping Past and Present; Leonardo Bufalini's Plan of Rome 1551', *Imago Mundi*, 59, pt.1 (2007): 1–23; 6.

6 Cited in Rebecca Zorach, 'The public utility of prints', in *The Virtual Tourist in Renaissance Rome. Printing and Collecting the Speculum Romanae Magnificentiae* (Chicago: Joseph Regenstein Library, 2008), p.66; I have altered the translation to some extent. '*Si hanc figuram, et sequentes, secundum naturalem prospectum attollere voluissemus: contigisset ut omnibus partibus montium, una excepta, occultatis, aedificia in suo situ locari non potuissent. Qua propter cum melius putaremus utilitati omnium esse consulendum, quam inani pictura quosdam oblectare: figuras ipsas planas posuimus: curavimus tamen latera montium secundum illorum altitudinem ita inumbrare, ut convalles ab ipsis facile distinguantur*' (Marliani, op. cit., p.2).

7 '*Il farla in Pianta saria stato un dilettarmi nell'impossibile et in sodisfare all'imaginatione piu che alla vista. Non consistono i ritratti delle citta nelle Piante loro a proposito per chi le volesse minare o altre simili fabricare, ma nel rapresentarle tali quali l'occhio da una determinata vista le puo vedere.*' For these points about the representation of boundaries between the city and the countryside, see Hilary Ballon and David Friedman, 'Portraying the City in Early Modern Europe: Measurement, Representation and Planning', in D. Woodward, ed., *Cartography in the European Renaissance*, part 1 (Chicago and London: University of Chicago Press, 2007), pp.680–704; p.692.

8 Huelsen, op. cit., p.51, VI (29) and Frutaz, op. cit., I, p.175, no. CXVI. Mario Cartaro's modern Rome of 1576 used this method too; see Huelsen, op. cit., p.65, XIII (72) and Frutaz, op. cit., I, p.185, no. CXXVI.

9 It is dated 1574; see Huelsen, op. cit., p.60, XI (56) and Frutaz, op. cit., I, p.67, no. XXII.

10 The text of the dedication reads in part: '*Veteris Romae immaginem a veteribus monumentis, magno meo labore diligenter expressum, Henrice Regum Maxime, superioribus annis dicavi Karolo IX fratri tuo* [...] *Nunc tibi eius Romae quae hodie est non minus accurate descriptam offero, expressis etiam iis quae tempor. iniuriam effugerunt antiquitatis reliquiis. Munus non indignum, quo aliquando pascas oculos, et in quo humanarum rerum vicissitudinem agnoscas.*'

11 Béatrizet illustrated the fortifications erected by Paul IV to meet the dangers of an attack on Rome during the war with Naples. See Huelsen, op. cit., p.49, V (25) and Frutaz, op. cit., I, p.172, no. CXIII.

12 The distinction between a high oblique and a bird's-eye view does not pretend to any scientific status. The considerable diminution in the size of the elements further away, seen for example in the drawing of the city walls, and the way of presenting the dense urban fabric without, for the most part, showing streets and squares, gives the Rosselli view more the character of a cityscape drawn from an elevated viewpoint than the more abstracted, map-like qualities of a bird's-eye representation.

13 The source was perhaps the Francesco Rosselli view of Rome, shown as it was just before 1490 (Schulz, 1990, op. cit., p.15; also Frutaz op. cit., I, p.151, no. XCVII who dates it after *c.*1484 – the key to this dating is that S. Agostino is shown incomplete). The Mantua version can confidently be dated after 1538, for the Marcus Aurelius outside the Lateran has an inscription saying that it had been moved to the Capitoline, an event that occurred in 1538. M. Fagiolo, '*Quanta ego iam fuerim sola ruina docet*', in Gori Sassoli, op. cit., pp.69–77, pointed out (p.71) the inscription above the banner flying on the Porta S. Agnese with its reference to Dante's *Inferno* II, 20-27. Whether these inscriptions were present in the original, or were added later cannot be decided.

14 The *titulus* reads: '*Quanta ego iam fuerim sola ruina docet*', Schulz, 1990, op. cit., p.39. The poem begins: 'Ubi son Roma gli honor de' tempi prisci ...'.

15 Michel de Montaigne, 'Journal de voyage en Italie', in *Oeuvres complètes*, ed. Maurice Rat (Paris: Gallimard, 1962), pp.1099–1342; p.1213: '*que les bastimans de ceste Rome bastarde qu'on aloit à cette heure atachant à ces masures, quoi qu'ils eussent de quoi ravir en admiration nos siecles presans, lui faisoint resouvenir propremant des nids que le moineaux et les corneilles vont suspendant en France aus voutes et parois des eglises que les Huguenots viennent d'y démolir.*'

16 '*Urbem non illam veterem, sed quam hodie sub sanctis Pontificibus florentem aspicimus*'.

17 Borsi argued that it was prepared with Sixtus V in mind: Stefano Borsi, *Roma di Sisto V: la pianta di Antonio Tempesta, 1593* (Rome: Officina edizioni, 1986), p.9.

18 Huelsen discussed what he called '*la pianta del 1590*', op. cit., pp.21–4 and 72–3, XVIIa (82). The state with the address of Francesco de Paoli, the earliest to survive, post-dates 1623, Frutaz, op. cit., I, p.207, no. CXLVI. Imperfect erasures show that the plates had originally been published by the heirs of Claudio Ducchetti. It is printed on 12 sheets. There is also a copy, published by De Veen at Leiden in 1593, on 12 sheets, see Huelsen op. cit., p.73, XVIIb (83). The presence of the address of the heirs of Ducchetti provides a *terminus postquem* of 1584, while a *terminus antequem* of 1593 is established by De Veen's copy.

19 Frutaz noted updatings, incorporating the urban changes of the first two decades of the seventeenth century: op. cit., I, p.207, no. CXLVI.

20 Gori Sassoli, op. cit., p.81. Exceptionally, the north had been chosen by Dosio for his view of 1561, see Huelsen, op. cit., p.51, VII (30) and Frutaz, op. cit., I, p.176, no. CXVII.

21 Huelsen, op. cit., pp.19–20 and 45, IV (17), and Frutaz, op. cit., I, p.171, no. CXII.

22 Georg Braun and Franz Hogenberg, *Civitates Orbis Terrarum, Cities of the World*, ed. Stephen Füssel (Hong Kong, Cologne, London, etc.: Taschen, 2008) pp.112 and 114–15. Braun and Hogenberg's view of Rome did not depend directly on Pinard's, but on an intermediary: a print published at Venice by G. F. Camocio in 1569. See Huelsen, op. cit., p.48, IV (21) and Frutaz, op. cit., I, p.181, no. CXXII.

23 Montaigne, op. cit., p.1212: '*M. de Montaigne étant allé voir le mont Janculum, delà le Tibre* [...] *et contempler le sit de toutes les parties de Rome, qui ne se voit de nul autre lieu si cleremant.*'

24 This was noted by Frangenberg: Thomas Frangenberg, 'Chorographies of Florence. The Use of City Views and City Plans in the Sixteenth Century', *Imago Mundi*, 46 (1994): 41–64; 59, note 16.

25 Leuschner, op. cit., p.368 pointed out that the orientation of St Peter's had been altered, because its facade would not have been visible from the supposed point of view.

26 Ballon and Friedman, op. cit., pp.680–704; p.692.

27 For Gast, who was in Rome from 1538 until (?)1558, see Nicole Dacos, *Roma Quanta Fuit ou l'invention du paysage de ruines* (Brussels: Somogy, 2004), pp.94–5.

28 Greuter's representation of 1618 (Huelsen, op. cit., p.81, XXI (102), and Frutaz, op. cit., I, p.205, no. CXLV) and Falda's of 1676 (Huelsen, op. cit., p.95, XXVII (130) and Frutaz, op. cit., I, p.221, no. CLVIII) give only the most minimal indications of the country outside the walls.

29 One of the derivatives of Pinard's view of Rome, Camocio's version of 1569 (see above note 21), is actually titled 'ROMAE VICTRICIS NOVA DESCRIPTIO'.

30 Borsi suggested Sixtus V, see above note 16.

31 G. De Caro in *Dizionario Biografico degli Italiani*, 13 (1971): 261–4.

32 For the Jubilee, see Thurston, 1925, pp.68ff. Of the other important basilicas outside the walls that were part of the prominent devotion to the seven churches, S. Lorenzo fuori le Mura does not appear on the Dupérac, although it does on the 'plan of 1590'; San Sebastiano appears on neither.

33 The population of Rome in 1592 was 97,000; it is difficult to know what change there had been since 1577. The only accurate figures before 1592 are from the census of 1526–7 which recorded the population, just before the city was sacked in 1527, as being about 55,000, see Jean Delumeau, *La Vie économique et sociale de Rome dans le seconde moitié du XVIe siècle*, I (Paris: De Boccard, 1957), pp.280–1.

34 Frangenberg, op. cit., p.48, citing Anton Francesco Doni, *I Mondi* (Venice, 1552), f.3r-v. See M. Marziano Guglielminetti and Patrizia Pellizzari, eds, *Anton Francesco Doni, I Mondi e gli Inferni* (Turin: Einaudi, 1994), p.7: '*Bisogna dunque fare a noi* [...] *come fa quel cittadino nato, allevato e pratico nella sua patria, il quale guida una persona nuovamente venuta nella terra per vedere ogni cosa che v'è di bello. Prima costui lo mena ne' luoghi generali e conosciuti e poi ne' particolari riposti, ultimamente lo conduce sopra qualche edificio che signoreggi la citta o sopra qualche monticello, e quivi gli fa vedere il sito, la larghezza, lunghezza e gli fa conoscere i publici edifici, le strade e tutte le cose onde: da questo luogo superiore, egli viene a stabilirsi nell' idea la imaginazione della terra.*'

35 A good example is Milton Lewine's article 'Vignola's Church of Sant'Anna de' Palafrenieri in Rome', *Art Bulletin*, 47 (1965): 199–229.

36 Delumeau, op. cit., I, pp.280ff. and especially p.286.

3

Thomas Baldwin's *Airopaidia*, or the Aerial View in Colour

Marie Thébaud-Sorger

The invention of balloons did not immediately give rise to pictorial representations of the vistas that they enabled. In the interval between 1783 – when the Montgolfier brothers' invention launched the hot-air balloon – and Nadar's aerial photography, the emergence of this technology did not prove decisive in determining the aerial view.[1] Indeed, technical advancements remained something of a paradox at a time when mapping and the panorama could render views in elevation and at 360º.[2] It would seem that balloon flights had, above all, a theoretical appeal and undertaking them opened up a field of conceptual possibilities. Audiences had been captivated by feats of aerial adventure, but it was not until 1867 – when large-scale captive balloons appeared on the scene at successive Universal Exhibitions – that a wider public was able to gain immediate experience of the view from the air, which until then had been the preserve of a select few. And yet it was precisely the accounts written by the latter, the flight experiences of these privileged travellers, that began to nourish a gaze that sought to partake in the various modalities of seeing from above,[3] and that was expressed in the enthusiasm for mountain climbing, the taste for panoramic vistas, and suchlike, all of which contributed to the emergence of an elevational view that gradually took shape in the stories and images of the second half of the nineteenth century.[4]

I have written elsewhere on the asynchrony between, on the one hand, the conditions that enabled instant access to a zenithal aerial view and, on the other hand, the means of representing this view; certainly the balloonists saw the world from above, but they could not transcribe it.[5] This problem, which stemmed in part from their difficulty of adjusting their way of looking and of comprehending what they saw from on high, allows us to appreciate the complexity of the process through which categories of vision are constructed.[6] This is especially so as the balloonists' main interest at the time lay primarily in the understanding of aerial navigation. Focused as they were on the behaviour of their flying machines, the panoramic view – although described using superlatives – did not constitute the purpose of their flights. As a result, detailed accounts are rare and pictorial representations of directly experienced views from the balloon's basket are non-existent. Or rather, almost non-existent, for there is a single exception, that of the airborne journey of the Englishman Thomas Baldwin, whose balloon flight around Chester in 1785 yielded several engravings and thus, we might say, gave birth to the aerial view as a record of the direct experience of flight. These representations are something of an enigma, as no other traveller from the era had produced anything similar. What is more, it seems unlikely that they stirred much interest in the readership of the time; instead, they remained known only to collectors and connoisseurs, generating neither subsequent reprints nor imitations. We shall therefore reopen the file on the aerial view from the balloon at the end of the eighteenth century by looking at this unique treatise, *AIROPAIDIA: CONTAINING THE NARRATIVE OF A BALLOON EXCURSION from CHESTER, the eighth of September, 1785* (Figure 3.1). Written in the third person singular, the treatise attempts not only to articulate the emotions experienced by the aeronaut, but also to understand this new way of perceiving the world and even, in the process, to establish some rules relating to the aerial view.

BALDWIN'S JOURNEY: FROM FEELING TO NARRATIVE

Having failed to construct his own flying machine by subscription in Chester,[7] Thomas Baldwin subsequently carried out a successful flight in a balloon belonging to the 'Daredevil Aeronaut' Lunardi. The flight was undertaken as a full-blown expedition, whose account he subsequently published in 1786 in the form of an unusual treatise, combining as it did a flight narrative with a genuine experimental programme that involved instruments, sensations and descriptive analyses. The work is conceived in three parts: the first is an overview of the flight itself; the second presents a series of observations on specific aspects of the journey; and the third part is made up of technical appendices. While maintaining a learned tenor throughout, the work is nevertheless permeated by

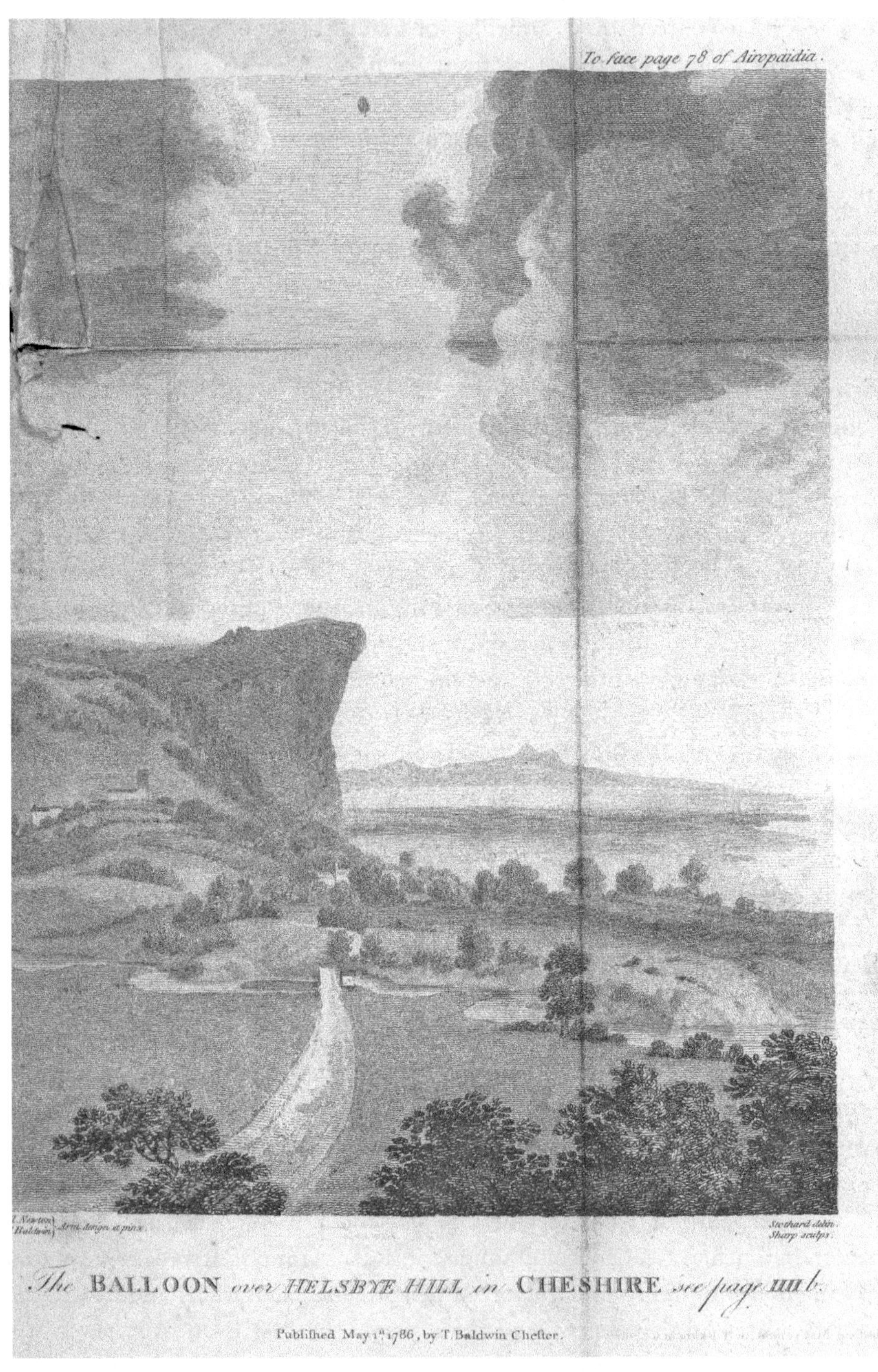

[3.1] *The* BALLOON *over* HELSBYE HILL *in* CHESHIRE, from Thomas Baldwin, *Airopaidia* (1786).

a curiosity that is particularly manifest in the first of the three parts, entitled *Airopaidia* or *aerial recreation*:[8]

> Balloon-Voyagers have likewise been particularly defective in their Descriptions of aërial Scenes and Prospects: those Scenes of majestic Grandeur which the unnumbered Volumes of encircling Clouds, in most fantastic Forms and various Hues, beyond Conception glowing and transparent, portray to a Spectator placed as in a Center of the Blue Serene above them: contemplating at the same Instant, and *apparently* at some Miles Distance immediately below, a most exquisite and ever-varying Miniature of the *little Works of Man*, heightened by the supreme Pencil of Nature, inimitably elegant, and in her highest Colouring.[9]

On the face of it, Baldwin's account of the flight does little to make it stand out from those of his contemporaries; in fact, it emphasises their numerous similarities.[10] Indeed, at first, like other balloonists such as Charles or Pilâtre de Rozier, Baldwin is quite taken with the novel sensations provided by the flight. Initially, he finds narration impossible and so the story starts by unfolding at the expense of description, for that which he experiences far surpasses his imagination. He therefore lacks both the concepts and – even more so – the words that would fit the occasion. The verbalisation of his feelings builds up the story. This presents him with the task of having to reconcile the articulation of his sense-impressions with what he sees. In the wake of Condillac's philosophy, which holds that the senses give us an intuitive knowledge of objects, the descriptions of the French balloonists seem to have been decidedly influenced by a radical sensationist approach; the senses became therefore the primary means whereby the reality of the flight could be recalled in its particulars. Baldwin's own approach is steeped just as much in Locke's empiricism. His account, which is effectively a treatise on the sensations experienced in a balloon in motion, revolves around a key tenet: that our sphere of knowledge expands in direct proportion to the sphere of sensations. By bringing to the fore sensations hitherto unknown, Baldwin's flight truly expands the realm of the imaginable and opens it up to another dimension, especially as the mind seems to be buoyed by the purity of the ambient air.[11] The historicity of sensations has been analysed by Alain Corbin, who studied the evolution of the human perception of natural phenomena. With the advent of the Age of Enlightenment, interest in these phenomena gave rise to a new sensibility in respect of natural landscapes such as shores, horizons, alpine and maritime panoramas. Confronted with the grandeur of the scenery, and out of sheer emotion at attempting to describe the magnificence of what he saw, beauty moved Baldwin to shed 'A Tear of pure Delight' which 'flashed in his Eye'.[12] He found no terms of comparison or equivalence for that beauty, and his 'Imagination itself was more than gratified; *it was overwhelmed*'.[13] This description calls to mind that conceptual pairing that emerged in the twilight of the Enlightenment, which Baldwin explicitly invokes: that of the beautiful and the sublime. Indeed, the shifting perception of the aeronaut due to the motion of the balloon in its atmospheric milieu becomes reflected in a conceptual oscillation between – and sometimes unification of – the categories. The aerial experience engages Baldwin's whole body and he resorts primarily to superlatives in order to describe the nature of his feelings. The ascent sparked in him exaltation and enthusiastic rapture. His recourse to the category of the sublime seems a viable reaction to the immensity of the spectacle spread out before him.[14] In common with other balloonists before him, Baldwin records the disappearance of ordinary markers alongside those that would signal human existence: 'no Houses [...] No *public Roads* [...] No Voices'.[15] The reigning silence ceases to belong to the human realm, as the ear itself discovers new depths 'unknown to Mortals *upon Earth*'.[16] And while this might result in the 'Chearful Serenity' that Baldwin felt when he discovered 'the BEAUTIFUL and SUBLIME [...] united, in a manner perfectly novel and engaging',[17] equally the disorienting perceptions to which this dehumanised space gave rise threaten to bring the traveller close to non-being, to the brink of dread; for, when objects become drained of their beauty, the precarious boundary beyond which the sublime stretches out serves to demonstrate how close ecstatic submersion and annihilation can be.

And yet, even though it touches upon the sublime, Baldwin's project does so from within an eminently empiricist tradition, as it conjures up emotions and various sensations accurately; that is to say, without departing from the descriptive yet all the while retaining the picturesque. By means of this absolutely unique personal experience, it is nevertheless a practical work that is addressed to, in equal measure, the public at large as well as future investigators and those of a scientific bent, whom it equips with comparative material for consideration. While Baldwin's first-hand account structures the work so as to establish points of reference, his self-analysis informs the complete experience soliciting the totality of his senses.[18] To this end, he carries with him in the balloon's basket an array of carefully chosen instruments. Quite naturally, sight was the first of the senses to be investigated. His visual responses are detailed extensively (almost anatomically), while being embedded in all the changes that the body perceives through the other senses. The traveller listens to his body and uses it in order to comment on temperature or humidity, but also on the sense of taste. For that purpose, he brings along ginger, salt and pepper and compares their respective tastes with previous experiments that had been attempted high in the mountains.[19]

It is then a matter of noting how taste differs when the body is aloft from when it is on the ground, or even when it is on the ground as opposed to high up in the mountains. The differences actually turn out to be particularly pronounced. Far from being a frightful experience, the airborne journey is here imbued with a sense of tranquillity; in fact, it is uninterrupted wonder. Baldwin records the effects that upward and downward movements have on the body, movements that – not unlike those experienced in a swing – produce physical sensations of pleasure. As he leaves his native land for the very first time, Baldwin encounters unusual sensations. Recording these effects anchors his experience firmly in the concrete, marking its distance from a fiction or philosophical tale. Nevertheless, aiming to delight the reader, the author indulges in a comparison with Jonathan Swift's very popular story of Gulliver's 'Voyage to Lilliput', a diminutive land to which he compares the county of Chester when seen from the air. For although air travel has a long tradition in fiction,[20] by making this journey part of a scientific project, which is dotted with colourful remarks, it is given a sense of the real that attests to both its uniqueness and its authenticity. If at times sentences seem to outdo one another in the use of superlatives (enlisted to evoke the splendour to which they are witness), what distinguishes Baldwin from his British and French contemporaries is that – far from doing away with it – description becomes in fact the main goal. It is therefore a matter of forsaking the sublime for the beautiful, which will mean describing. Consequently, this is what he cheerfully and eagerly sets out to do, utilising the physical tools and conceptual framework at his disposal while pursuing a specific aim: that of communicating his perceptions of an ever-changing landscape that 'touches the senses and the imagination',[21] even when this landscape's appearance does not live up to his initial amazement:

> Unity and Sameness were there contrasted with *perpetual Variety*: Beauty of Colouring: Minuteness, and consummate Arrangement; – with *Magnificence* and *Splendor*: *actual* Immensity; – with *apparent* Limitation: – all which were *distinctly* conveyed to the Mind, at the *same* Instant, throu' the Intervention of the Organs of Sight: and, to complete the Scene, was added the Charm of NOVELTY'.[22]

Seeing the infinite variety of objects displayed at the same level, his perceptions and understanding are suspended in wonder and he is 'charmed' as if bewitched. Yet, in order to extricate himself from its magic spell, the traveller must tackle the aerial view in a methodical fashion and resist wallowing in the fascination exerted on the senses by the flight. This is a considerable challenge, because the fantastic transformation wrought upon things by this new perspective diverges so radically from the common understanding of them. At one point Baldwin compares what he sees to an oriental carpet, which 'is made to exhibit NO EXACT *Resemblance* to the Works either of Art or Nature',[23] while the bends on the River Mersey appeared 'so various and *fantastic* as to exceed the Limits of Credibility'.[24] In keeping with the accounts of French balloonists such as Pilâtre de Rozier or the abbé Carnus, he resorts to the metaphor of being in an amphitheatre to illustrate his description. The titles, subtitles, sections, numerals, tables and suchlike that are incorporated into the work help to organise it and mark its distance from what might otherwise appear as a mere story of amazement, situated somewhere between the platitudinous and the naive. Structured in chapters that are then subdivided into numbered sections, the book boasts a very thorough index and, in keeping with many English treatises, is annotated in the margins with paragraph summaries, which allow the main themes of each section to stand out from the profusion of details. Going beyond an evocation of wonders, the work lays down detailed descriptions of how things were perceived from the airship.

AVOIDING THE PITFALLS OF THE AERIAL GAZE AND LEARNING A NEW WAY OF SEEING

The task of understanding aerial vision is complex and is predicated upon a work of differentiation that equally calls for an adjustment of the senses and for proven abilities. Mobility disorientates all balloon pilots as it greatly increases the effects of rapid changes in scale, whilst the altered perception of sounds and objects requires constant readjustment. Coming to terms with this new way of seeing involves not only the enjoyment of its beauty, but also the ability to recognise the metamorphic effects that the ascent has on objects, therefore being able to outfox many a *trompe l'œil* and misleading impression. Throughout the treatise, Baldwin endeavours to pave the way for a new vision, especially in the second part, entitled 'OBSERVATIONS, HINTS, AND CONJECTURES, ON THE SUBJECT OF THE BALLOON AND EXCURSION FROM CHESTER'. Like other aerial travellers, he brings along various instruments: a barometer for measuring atmospheric pressure, a thermometer for temperature readings, together with other items such as thin ribbon, bottles, three flags, a speaking trumpet, a basket, 'Pepper Salt and Ginger'.[25] And if he must do without a telescope, because of its weight, he completes his equipment with a spyglass,[26] while in his pockets he takes along writing cards, knife, scissors, sharpened pencils and a map of Chester. Baldwin is a clever and able man. Nevertheless, as he mentions several times, his capacities as a draughtsman and natural philosopher require the leavening of his personal experience. It is precisely by virtue of his previous experiences that he can draw up comparisons – first, a local knowledge of the area surveyed from the air (the county of Chester) and, second, a knowledge of other countries that enables him to compare the local terrain to distant lands. He seems to have seen the mountains of Europe and also to have passed through a number of continental landscapes, for instance those of the big cities; he has personal knowledge of large-scale structures outside England and can tell a provincial village from a densely populated city, or else discern the view from a summit, despite being rather vague about the precise locations of his travels. In short, a bevy of recollections from far beyond the confines of Chester, although knowledge of the local landscape is essential for getting his bearings. However, as he finds, elevation progressively dissolves the scale of the immediate surroundings.

This levelling is coupled with the fact that, as the horizon line starts to bend, the edges change their appearance. Past a certain height, planimetry is replaced by a complex curvilinear phenomenon that is particularly difficult to fathom. Baldwin seeks to provide the reader with similes by means of which the sense-impressions of the pilot, who is invariably placed at the centre of the circle of vision, can be understood. For the sake of description, he resorts to a commonplace metaphor, that of comparing the air traveller flying over a landscape to an observer viewing a vast carpet. Baldwin imagines the visual effect that would entail if the observer, who was previously standing on the carpet, was to be gradually elevated. As he floated upward 'the distant Parts of the Carpet would *seem* to rise with him', producing a bowl-like effect.[27] Therefore, despite the earth being convex, the balloonist perceives himself within a concave space, as if he were inside a bowl and as if the lie of the land were like a miniature painted inside the bowl's rim, while the edges smooth out all around into a linear flatland. Consequently, for a traveller who finds himself above the clouds, at a distance of more than a mile from the earth's surface, the disappearance of markers becomes problematic. The shadows that help define objects are no longer seen as shadows at this distance, but as gradations of shade; everything is in colour and no living creatures can be seen – the pilot has now reached, and inhabits, the scale of the map. The miniature becomes smaller as the distance increases.[28] But the cartographic comparison remains ambiguous. At times it serves as an analytical filter through which terrestrial objects can be seen: while flying over the city of Chester, Baldwin remarks that the landscape resembles a colourful map, rather than a scale model, as this better indicates the complete loss of relief. On other occasions, though, the limitations of the cartographic comparison become obvious. Here the aerial view is of a different kind: on the one hand, because it is curved and achieved in motion; on the other hand, because the objects perceived are uncoupled from their usual contour-based graphic representation. Here objects present themselves to the eye of the pilot in an entirely different way – they are full, coloured and substantial – which totally changes the perception of them. Make-believe therefore always lies in wait for the aerial gaze, particularly as the flying machine travels along two vectors: one vertical, which effects changes of scale, and one horizontal, which transports the pilot unawares. This is where the unfurling of flags from the balloon's basket proves essential, as it helps ascertain the direction and force of the wind, if not also air resistance and flight direction. Although Baldwin brings along a map of the region, he only consults it after he has been airborne for some time, and then only to notice its shortcomings. How should one understand the landscape? Blended together are sounds, colours, vapours. Seen from above, the sea is still and its sandy shores are prominent in their whiteness; and when it disappears from view being obscured by fog, its relative proximity can be gauged by the lapping sound of the waves.[29] As the balloon ascends, perimeters draw nearer to each other and the pilot witnesses the disappearance of the field enclosures just as, once past a certain altitude, he no longer distinguishes the type of crops, let alone the ears of corn. And yet, it is precisely by being able to make out the presence or absence of livestock and crops that altitude can be ascertained, and the point established at which the identity of terrestrial objects ceases to be elusive, rendering them again recognisable. However, distortions are legion and he lists them meticulously. For instance, flying over woods, Baldwin remarks several times that the dark green of tree tops gives the false impression of an upward slope.[30] The eye is therefore constantly challenged.

The complexity lies in the classification of objects by size, for if the balloonist can indeed group them according to category (woods, bodies of water, dwellings), this may lead him to mix up elements belonging to the same genus. Urban entities are identifiable, but can appear almost interchangeable; their structural sameness blurs any distinguishing features, as the 'highest Buildings had no apparent Height: their Summits were reduced to the common Level of the Ground. Nor was the Cathedral distinguished; nor any Tower or Spire discerned'.[31] Thus, having previously seen a small-scale model of Paris, Baldwin has the impression that, from the air, Chester is not dissimilar to the European capital.[32] This is a veritable trap that blurs relative magnitudes and into which, were he not aware of the differences, he could fall by believing that, when viewed from above, the small town is equal to one of the most populous capitals on the Continent. By disrupting systems of reference through a shift in scale, the aerial view completely changes the perception of large objects, which become miniaturised. It is therefore a matter of discriminating between objects that on the ground are of different scale, yet to the aerial observer look similar. It becomes necessary to establish a classification of the objects seen from above in order to be able, at a given height, to spot their differences and assign to each its relative importance. For instance, the river is not the small stream it may appear to be and, conversely, the small town is not the capital to which it resembles.

This levelling is a first visual trap, for the observer can no longer gauge his altitude instantly, by means of accurately judging the height of objects with respect to the ground. And yet, if properly mastered, these markers can become highly relevant empirical tools for measuring altitude. In order to precisely determine his altitude, the balloon traveller needs to rely, in the first instance, on his ability to recognise from the basket the objects beneath (trees, buildings, livestock), their kind and their size. He can then process the way in which altitude has transformed their appearance. For, at a similar distance, the same object can appear smaller when seen from above than when viewed from the ground. Baldwin seeks therefore to understand why the rise produces this altered perception of distance. He puts forward hypotheses in conjunction with visual tests that he designs, which relate to his prior, non-aerial occasions of views from summits with which he is familiar and which also draw upon a store of memories from a variety of his experiences. His intention is to understand the relationship between the perception of the object, the eye and the ability to judge distance. To this end, he uses combinations of three parameters, one of which remains always unknown: the size of the object as it is perceived (the 'miniature'), the distance between the object and the balloon, and the dimension of the 'tangible Object'.[33] Then he tries to understand how the mind and the eye can adapt to each other such that they can agree on what they perceive. By understanding these relationships, the visual illusions of the aerial view can also be understood and therefore fully factored into it: if the distance from and dimensions of a tangible object are known, then the object can be surmised and the rules 'for its corresponding *Miniature* on the eye' can be established; second, when the miniature is seen and the distance from the object is known, then 'the Mind forms a *Judgment* of [the object's] tangible *Magnitude*'; and third, if 'the *Miniature* be seen, and [the] *Magnitude* of a tangible Object is known by Mensuration', the mind endeavours to estimate the object's distance from the eye'.[34] However, according to him, these non-rigorous empirical means allow the mind to acquire 'a tolerable Degree of Proficiency, in estimating *Distances* of familiar Objects, *known* from the Appearance of their respective Miniatures on the Fund or Bottom of the Eye'.[35] The input from other instruments, such as the barometer, which by measuring atmospheric pressure, indicates altitude, proves to be a valuable back-up. These new modalities that Baldwin attempts to systematise all aid in the understanding of the transformation of vision that results from a gain in altitude. However, they are only valid if undertaken in the same environment.

He compares this problem to the perception of celestial bodies on the horizon, for when the sun and moon rise or set, they appear much larger:

> as the Sun and Moon, at Setting or Rising, appear *large and oval*; but at their greatest Elevation, are *small* and *round*: because being seen, when passed out of a Medium impregnated with Vapours, which in some Measure intercept the Rays of Light.[36]

Thus he continues this line of reasoning with the analysis of the effects of air and vapours on the perception of objects according to their respective properties of being bright, reflecting light or absorbing it, which plays a key role in accurately determining their size. He then poses the question of the effects of refraction on the perception of objects. An object can be seen at the same distance but, depending on how bright it is each time, 'will *contract the Pupil* in Proportion to its Brightness'.[37] Light plays on the retina and hence determines the impression of size formed in the mind. If we were to apply the same reasoning to the balloon's ascent, then objects may not be as elevated as we might think, since their size is reduced, but this depends on the vapour saturation through which they are seen.[38] Consequently, Baldwin's estimation is that objects at the same height appear approximately five times smaller when seen from the balloon than if seen from the ground, at the same distance.[39] He also emphasises the presence of colours caught in the play of light.

A WORLD IN COLOUR, PERMEATED BY AIR, SUN AND WIND

Air and atmospheric density, the play of wind and fog, all conspire to blur perception and distort attempts at object identification. However, the elements on the ground, though neither drawn nor painted, are perceived in their full density. Theories of vision and chromaticism were an important topic at the time, having gained notoriety, in the wake of Newton's spectral theory, with, for example, the thesis of Louis Bertrand Castel and Goethe's *Theory of Colours*.[40] Baldwin puts into play a whole spectrum of knowledge and in his turn refers to Newton, all in an effort to understand the colour changes undergone by elements on the ground when seen from above. This refined understanding is rendered all the more complex when the colourless and expandable gases that make up the atmosphere are taken into account. On the one hand, he builds hypotheses by means of instruments used to measure air pressure and temperature. With these new tools he can establish from the balloon's platform a better understanding of both altitude and the air through which he travels. On the other hand, he incorporates the issue of air and atmospheric phenomena into the analysis of object perception as well as into the representation of aerial views crystallised at the level of the clouds[41] (Figure 3.2). Baldwin suggests all manner of ingenious lenses through which to adjust viewing from above: small glasses, a circular opening in the platform, and so on. By virtue of this enframing process and thanks to the perimeters supplied by the clouds' edges, he manages to sketch both an aerial description and its representation. In this process, the production of images plays a key role. Baldwin takes advantage of those moments during which the balloon is stable to trace – with the aid of carefully prepared implements (such as sharpened pencils) – its path on his map. This route, which shows a series of circumvolutions that the balloon had executed, is then transferred by Baldwin onto a final perspective that he designs. At first glance, this aerial perspective resembles a map.

In the first of the published engravings depicting the view from an altitude of two miles, one can only discern the largest objects. This limit coincides with that of the ocular field of view, resulting in a round image at the centre of a circle of clouds. Atmospheric phenomena are therefore inscribed in the overall view and offer readings on two different registers: first, the clouds become incorporated into the system of aerial representation, giving it a substantial reality – we can say that the aerial view has its genesis among the clouds; and second, the nebular crucially informs the overall perception, as light influences colour definition. Moreover, the clouds acquire an aesthetic function while arraying themselves as a frame for the eye, completely inverting the Baroque low-angle tiered view towards the heavens. The real perspective no longer stages godly figures in the clouds; here, it is the ground and its ordinary objects that constitute the focal point. The clouds are also the subject of extensive descriptions. Here we have a human being ascending among the clouds, if not above them, in an environment that is not even high in the mountains, but above plain English countryside. They help estimate altitude and the scale of things, as well as aid in the construction of a perspective that is relevant to the viewer. In addition, their materiality makes possible the perception of a world that is surrounded by atmospheric strata. The hydrogen balloon achieves stability by virtue of the relationship between the lightness of the gas that it uses and the air surrounding it, which becomes progressively colder and rarefied as the balloon ascends.[42] Furthermore, the issue of barometric measurement of the atmosphere at altitude, just as the issue of winds and currents, was a much-debated topic in the physics and applied mathematics of the time.[43] Baldwin undertakes an innovative investigation by promoting a new object of study: he analyses especially the colour of the clouds, from the pure white of a 'sea of cotton'[44] to the 'vast Assemblage of *Thunder-Clouds*'.[45]

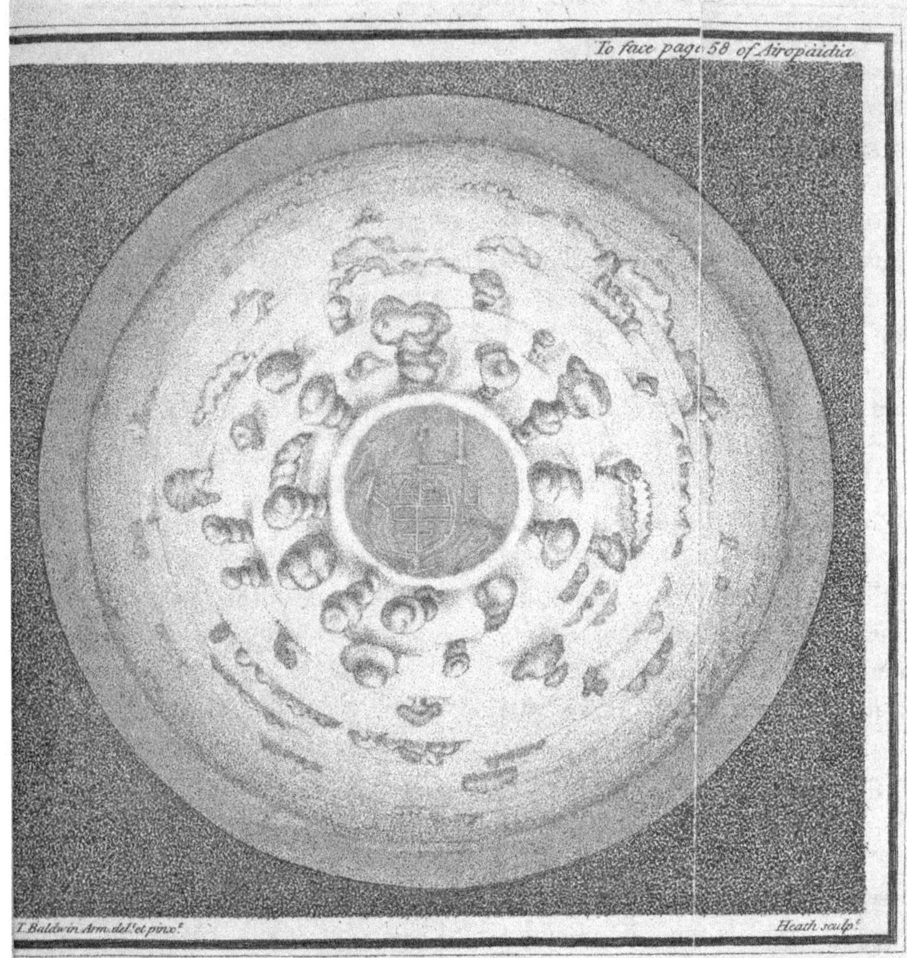

[3.2] *A* VIEW *from the* BALLOON *at its* GREATEST *elevation*, from Thomas Baldwin, *Airopaidia* (1786).

He also notes the changes that the sun's rays effect upon the clouds' colour, making it range from bright yellow to purple, varying according to the density and texture of the cloud and its degree of opacity.[46] Light sometimes makes them appear in '*transparent Blue* like the *Onyx*'.[47] This profusion of detailed accounts adds up to a new way of looking at the earth, an atmospherically based approach that introduces a new dimension – that of light and atmospheric phenomena – which is alien to the tradition of cartographic representation.

The discussion on colours and the enchantment to which they give rise is predominant here: the countryside 'was *continually* illuminated by the Sun's Rays', which render it vibrant and shimmering.[48] Then, as the countryside comes into sharper view, the second engraving shows a perspective of the county from a viewpoint closer to the ground, which Baldwin describes graphically in the caption: '*A Balloon-Prospect from above the Clouds* [...] or *Chromatic* View of the Country between Chester, Warrington and Rixton-Moss in Lancashire'[49] (Figures 3.3 and 3.4). This also gives him the opportunity to showcase his classification of colours.

Baldwin points out the presence of primary colours that, when 'seen from a vertical Situation *only* [...] without *Refraction*',[50] do not mix and, for this reason, can help differentiate the perception of objects from the latter's usual representation.[51] This is fundamental, as objects become defined not by their outline but rather by their colour-suffused shapes. Baldwin's applied classification is made more accessible as he describes it precisely: 'RED Rivers, YELLOW Roads, Enclosures YELLOW and *light* GREEN, Woods and Hedges *dark* GREEN, were the only objects clearly distinguishable'.[52] The world is made anew in extremely 'vivid' colours,[53] while 'Cattle and Corn in the Fields became visible'[54] and the glint of sun-rays in the river and sea dazzled the gaze.[55] The reddish hue of the waterways, the subtle distinction between shades of green (that of the hedges differing from that of the fields), the sinuousness of the roads and the morphology of towns identifiable by the colour and shape of the roofs, all serve to complete the picture.

Aerial vision clarifies the structural nature of things and increases the legibility of land usage. It enables the precise localisation of river curves and the broader understanding of water systems; thus, curiosity prompts Baldwin to investigate the stream 'over which he hung, *admiring* the Beauty of its serpentine Meanders [...] situated to the East of Warrington, and from a peculiar Curve'.[56] One of the bends appears like a knot and this convinces him that the rivulet 'could have been no *other* than the broad Branch of the River MERSEY'.[57] In addition, he can discern the beauty and variety of curves 'into which the Stream had worked the Bed of the River Wever in a Course of *Time*, and in the Compass of a few Miles'.[58] By revealing the form left by the current on the river he spotlights an appearance 'which *demonstrates* the Incorrectness of MAPS'.[59] The aerial

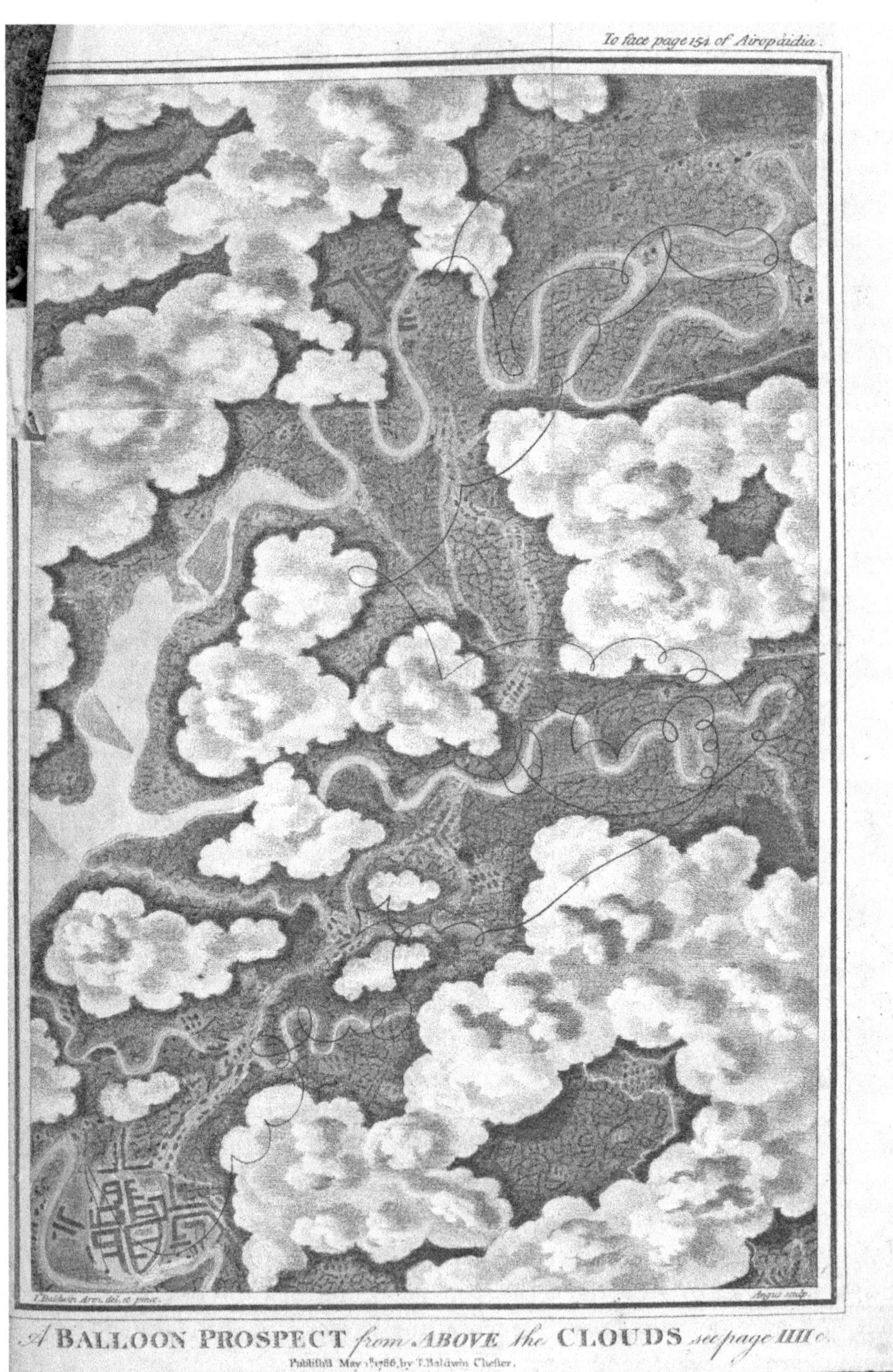

[3.3] *A* BALLOON PROSPECT *from* ABOVE *the* CLOUDS, from Thomas Baldwin, *Airopaidia* (1786).

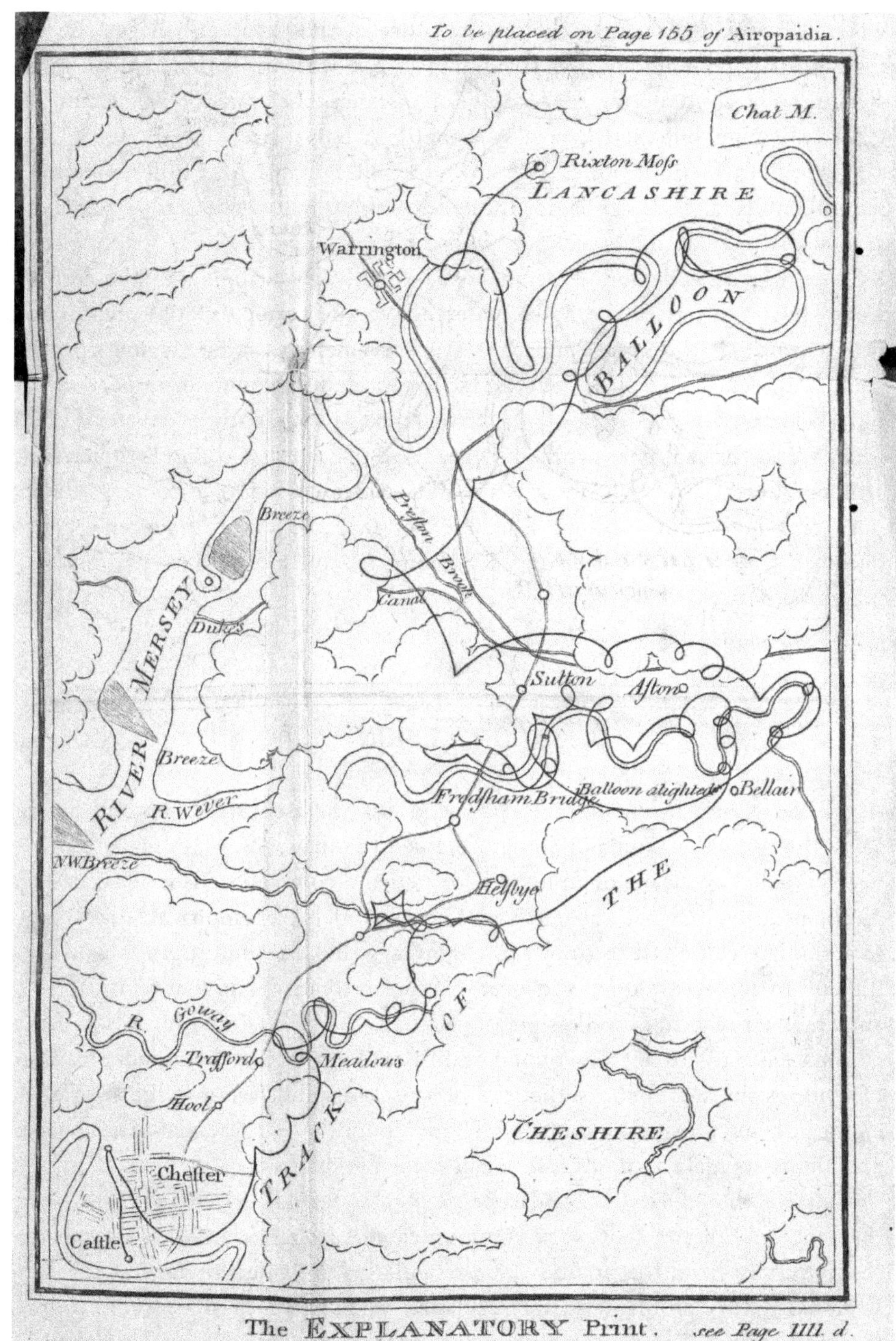

[3.4] The EXPLANATORY Print, from Thomas Baldwin, *Airopaidia* (1786).

view also enables him to make an inventory of the different villages. Beyond their similarity, he emphasises their uniqueness, which is revealed through the specificity of construction materials. For instance, the town of Frodsham, like Chester, is blue, but the town of Warrington, whose plan is 'small, neat'[60] is 'of a *darker Blue,* inclining to *Grey*',[61] an effect attributable to a different kind of slate being used. The gaze is not limited to taking in a single built-up area, but several urban settlements at once, whose relationships the balloonist can then trace within a newly found perspective. Equally, by bringing to the fore the work of art and nature, he makes reference to the famous spatial organisation of enclosures – the great landscaping achievement that left its mark on the eighteenth-century English countryside – and identifies signs of important pre-industrial activity by singling out, for instance, the 'Gunpowder Water-Mills'.[62] It is a world that has been worked by the hand of man that comes into view and, although here scarcely visible, it is a world seen in its own true colours – hence, not a presentation of itself, but a true reflection. Here, nature's 'supreme Pencil' becomes truly alive 'in her highest Colouring', and the aerial view reveals a breathing nature.[63]

CONCLUSION

At the end of an airborne journey that lasted two-and-a-quarter hours and covered some thirty miles, Thomas Baldwin released the image of a landscape that had been revealed by means of an unprecedented and complete sensorial experience. The view from the balloon enabled him to undertake empirical assessments, to formulate rules and to draft the engravings that encoded it graphically. It is difficult to conjecture upon the legacy of such a treatise, one that contributes an authentic aerial gaze as well as an ample analysis of the panoramic view and the chromaticism of vision.[64] It would certainly take its place in the broader tradition of writings that put forward theories of sensations and vision at the turn of the eighteenth and nineteenth centuries, texts responding to the advent of noteworthy and highly sophisticated artefacts, such as the panoramas.

Despite the variety of landscape elements – fields, rivers, villages – and the range of colours that were communicated through a zenithal perspective, seeing nature from the air did not particularly captivate the gaze at the time. Eventually, this problematic was revisited in the twentieth century, through the work of the French sociologist and geographer Paul-Henry Chombart de Lawe, who marvelled at the new powers with which 'the aerial view of the world' could equip the mind in the visual discernment of settlements and rural areas.[65] However, it is urban space, with its buildings, monuments and avenues – rather than the variety of agricultural lands and wooded areas – that takes the measure of the dazzling elevated gaze and contributes to the development of the directly experienced aerial view. As balloon navigators began to bring the first means to mechanically record the perspectives they witnessed aboard their airships, aerial views took shape while cities expanded into suburbs and outlying areas. Whereas in the engravings depicting the Tissandier brothers' ascendant exploits from the 1880s the expansion of greater Paris can be gleaned in the background, Giffard's stationary balloon, to the contrary, placed its vertical gaze right in the heart of the capital, above the Tuileries gardens. The elevated view started with the city, in the midst of the crowds from whom it also progressively distanced itself.[66] This lived aerial view went hand in hand with a burgeoning urban reality, which was at some remove from the sensorial experience provided by the early aerial navigation over the countryside that Baldwin recorded in his treatise.

NOTES

1 Thierry Gervais, 'Un basculement du regard. Les débuts de la photographie aérienne, 1855–1914', *Etudes Photographiques*, 9, May (2001). http://etudesphotographiques.revues.org/index916.html.

2 Stephan Oettermann, *Das Panorama. Die Geschichte eines Massensmediums* (Frankfurt: Syndikat, 1980); Bernard Comment, *Le XIXe siècle des panoramas* (Paris: Adam Biro, 1993); Jean-Marc Besse, 'De la représentation de la terre à sa reproduction: l'invention des géoramas au dix-neuvième siècle', in Isabelle Laboulais-Lesage, ed., *Combler les blancs de la carte. Modalités et enjeux de la construction des savoirs géographiques (XVIIe–XIXe siècle)* (Strasbourg: Presses Universitaires de Strasbourg, 2004), pp.34–59.

3 Nadar, *À terre et en l'air. Mémoires du Géant* (Paris: E. Dentu, 1865).

4 Alain Corbin, *Le Territoire du vide. L'Occident et le désir du rivage, 1750–1840* (Paris: Flammarion, 1988); Fabien Locher, 'De nouveaux territoires pour la Science: les voyages aériens de Camille Flammarion', *Société et Représentations*, 21 (2006): 157–75.

5 Marie Thébaud-Sorger, 'La conquête de l'air, les dimensions d'une découverte', *Dix-huitième siècle*, 31: 'Science et esthétique' (1999): 159–77; and 'La terre vue du ciel: la géographie et les ballons. Les apports contradictoires de l'aérostation aux savoirs géographiques, de 1783 à la première moitié du XIXe siècle', in Jean-Marc Besse, Hélène Blais, Isabelle Surun, eds, *Naissance de la géographie moderne (1760–1860)* (Lyon: ENS éditions, 2010), pp.129–52.

6 Jonathan Crary, *Techniques of the Observer: On Vision and Modernity* (Cambridge, MA and London: MIT Press, 1991).

7 Thomas Baldwin, *PROPOSALS AT LARGE, FOR THE CONSTRUCTION OF A Grand Naval AIR-BALLOON, Furnished with an APPARATUS, corresponding to that of SAILS OARS and RUDDER, to be occasionally applied* (Hoole, near Chester, 1784).

8 Translator's note: in English in the original.

9 Thomas Baldwin, *AIROPAIDIA: CONTAINING THE NARRATIVE OF A BALLOON EXCURSION from CHESTER, the eighth of September, 1785* [...] *TO WHICH IS SUBJOINED, MENSURATION OF HEIGHTS BY THE BAROMETER, MADE PLAIN. WITH EXTENSIVE TABLES. THE WHOLE SERVING AS AN INTRODUCTION TO AERIAL NAVIGATION: WITH A COPIOUS INDEX* (Chester: J Fletcher, 1786), pp.2–3.

10 *Lettre de M. l'abbé Carnus, professeur de philosophie à Rodez contenant la relation du voyage aérien fait le 6 août 1784 sur la Montgolfière 'Ville de Rodez', suivie de la description de la machine* (Rodez: August 1784), in-8° de 30 p,; Jean-François Pilâtre de Rozier, *Premières expériences de la Montgolfière construite par ordre du roi, lancée en présence de leur majesté le 23 juin 1784*, second edition (Paris: imprimerie de Monsieur, 1784), in-8°, p.11.

11 Baldwin, op. cit., Section 155, p.127.

12 Ibid., p.37.

13 Ibid., p.38.

14 Alain Corbin, *L'homme dans le paysage* (Paris: Le Seuil, 2001); M. Thébaud-Sorger, 'La conquête de l'air', op. cit., and *L'aérostation au temps des Lumières* (Rennes: Presses Universitaires de Rennes, 2009), pp. 247–53.

15 Baldwin, op. cit., Section 175, p.145.

16 Ibid., p.46.

17 Ibid., pp.47–8.

18 Stafford, Barbara M., *Voyage into Substance. Art, Science, Nature and the Illustrated Travel Account, 1760–1840* (Cambridge, MA and London: MIT Press, 1989).

19 Translator's note: Such as referred to by Baldwin, first on p.14 ('to try the effects of tastes which have [...] become insipid on the Peak of Teneriffe') and then on p.66 ('found to retain their usual Pungency: contrary to what Travellers have reported to happen on the Peak of Teneriffe.')

20 Jules Duhem, *Histoire des idées aéronautiques avant Montgolfier* (Paris: Nouvelles éditions latines, 1943).

21 Baldwin, op. cit., Section 221, p.172.

22 Ibid.

23 Ibid., Section 128, p.117.

24 Ibid., Section 174, p.144.

25 Ibid., Section 65, p.66.

26 Marie-Noëlle Bourguet and Christian Licoppe, 'Voyages, mesures et instruments. Une nouvelle expérience du monde au siècle des Lumières', *Annales Histoires, Sciences sociales*, 5 (1997): 1115–51.

27 Baldwin, op. cit., Section 50, pp.52–3.

28 Ibid., Section 224, p.175.

29 Ibid., Section 80, p.81.

30 Ibid., Section 76, p.77.

31 Ibid., Section 45, p.43.

32 Ibid., Section 64, pp.65–6.

33 Ibid., Section 224, p.175.

34 Ibid.

35 Ibid., p.176.

36 Ibid.

37 Ibid.

38 Ibid., Section 225, p.177.

39 Ibid., Section 226, p.178.
40 Michel Blay, *La conceptualisation newtonienne des phénomènes de la couleur* (Paris: Vrin, 1983); Elisabeth Lavezzi, *Le Père Castel et le clavecin oculaire, carrefour de l'esthétique et des savoirs dans la première moitié du XVIIIe siècle* (thesis prepared under the direction of M. R. Démoris and submitted to l'Université de Paris III Sorbonne Nouvelle, 1994); J. W. Goethe, *Matériaux pour l'histoire des théorie de la couleur,* trans. Maurice Elie (Toulouse: Presses Univ. du Mirail, 2003).
41 'A View from the Balloon at its Greatest Elevation', plate facing p.58, in Baldwin, op. cit.
42 Thébaud-Sorger, *L'aérostation au temps des Lumières,* op. cit., pp.247–53.
43 Marie Thébaud-Sorger, 'La mesure de l'envol à la fin du XVIIIe siècle. Les premiers ballons: affaires d'opinions ou d'exactitude?', *Histoire et Mesure,* XXI, 1/2 (June 2006): 35–78.
44 Baldwin, op. cit., Section 51, pp.53.
45 Ibid., p.54.
46 Ibid., Section 54, p.58.
47 Ibid.
48 Ibid., Section 79, p.81.
49 Ibid., plate facing p.154; see also Section 130, p.118.
50 Ibid., Section 129, p.118.
51 'The Colours, of which the Ground Work was *principally* formed [...] were four simple and *primary* ones, VIZ. RED, YELLOW, GREEN, and BLUE'; ibid., Section 129, p.117. Baldwin considered green to be a primary colour.
52 Ibid., Section 223, pp.174–5.
53 Ibid., p.175.
54 Ibid., p.88.
55 Ibid., Section 223, p.175.
56 Ibid., Section 190, p.153.
57 Ibid.
58 Ibid., Section 81, pp.81–2.
59 Ibid., p.82.
60 Ibid., Section 82, p.82.
61 Ibid.
62 Ibid., Section 190, p.153.
63 Ibid., Section 3, p.3.
64 Roland Mortier et Hervé Hasquin, eds, *Etudes sur le XVIII siècle: XXIII: Autour du père Castel et du clavecin oculaire* (Brussels: Éditions de l'université de Bruxelles, 1995); Daniel Davalan, 'Le labyrinthe détruit, limites et paysages', *Les Carnets du paysage,* 3 (1999): 57–74.
65 Paul-Henry Chombart de Lauwe, ed., *La découverte aérienne du monde* (Paris: Horizons de France, 1948).
66 Christoph Asendorf, *Super Constellation – Flugzeug und Raumrevolution. Die Wirkung der Luftfahrt auf Kunst und Kultur der Moderne* (Vienna and New York: Springer, 1997).

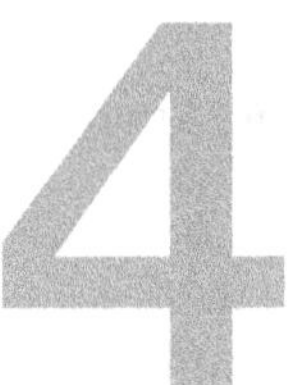

European Cities from a Bird's-eye View

The Case of Alfred Guesdon

Jean-Marc Besse

A new visual culture emerged in Europe during the nineteenth century. Within its ambit landscapes, nature and – above all – cities became the focus of a new way of seeing: a way of seeing that was embodied in the panorama.[1]

Certainly, the panoramic view stays close to the long tradition in which it is inscribed – one encompassing bird's-eye view representations of cities, aerial travels (of a philosophical or literary kind), as well as geographical accounts. It gives expression to a complex intellectual sphere within which science, art and philosophy have merged since antiquity.[2] Nevertheless, following its patenting by Robert Barker in 1787 and its rapid dissemination throughout Europe in the first half of the nineteenth century, we can say that the panorama represented an entirely new cultural device. This device enabled the aerial view to become incorporated almost physically into buildings and into the technical means dedicated to the production and display of this kind of scenic and historical painting. In his book, *Paris and the Nineteenth Century,* Christopher Prendergast highlights specifically the profound effects that the panoramic system had on the conditions and the facets – material, psychological, ideological – of the gaze cast upon urban space and upon the urban imaginary in the nineteenth century.[3] Within this system, cities became theatres for a new genre, or rather a new history – that of modernisation.

The evolution of this urban iconography seems particularly well reflected in the work of the French architect and draughtsman Alfred Guesdon (1808–76), whose artistic legacy extends to some one hundred lithographs of aerial views of

European cities from the 1850s. However, how, and to what extent, did Guesdon's aerial views contribute to the 'panoramic culture' of the nineteenth century? More specifically, did his drawings look upon European cities in a specific way, and – if so – how is this constituted? More to the point, is it possible to discern within them a 'modernising' tendency? These are some of the questions that will be pursued in this paper.

The Life of Alfred Guesdon

Little is known about Alfred Guesdon.[4] He was born at Nantes in 1808 and studied architecture at the École des Beaux-Arts in Paris, in the studio of Antoine Garnaud (1829–32). After graduation he returned to Brittany, but it appears that the professional success he had hoped for eluded him there. Thus he returned to Paris in 1840, where he contributed as a lithographer and illustrator to a number of publishing projects. He belonged to a group of artists who collaborated on works under the direction of Alexandre Du Sommerard (*Les arts au Moyen Âge* [*The arts of the Middle Ages*]), that of baron Isidore Taylor (*Voyages pittoresques et romantiques dans l'ancienne France* [*Scenic and Romantic Travels in Old France*]) and that of Nicolas-Marie Chapuy (*Le Moyen Âge monumental et archéologique* [*The Monumental and Archaeological Middle Ages*]). The drawings he produced at this time tended to be historical recontructions or picturesque scenes.[5] According to his biographer, Charles Marionneau, from 1845 onwards Guesdon started to produce drawings and lithographs depicting views of French and other European cities. During the following 15 years he travelled throughout France, Italy, Spain and Switzerland and produced some 110 bird's-eye views of cities. The majority of the prints were published as thematic series, bearing titles such as *Voyage aérien en France* (*Aerial Journey in France* [1848]), *L'Italie à vol d'oiseau* (*Italy from a Bird's-Eye View* [1849]), *L'Espagne à vol d'oiseau* (*Spain from a Bird's-Eye View* [1853]), or *La Suisse à vol d'oiseau* (*Switzerland from a Bird's-Eye View* [1858]). Some of these images were exhibited at the Salon of 1859. However, it was only the views of Italy that were assembled in a monograph, published in 1849, where they were accompanied by descriptions penned by the writer Hippolyte Etiennez (1813–71), archivist and historiographer of the city of Nantes. Many of the plates drawn by Alfred Guesdon (but not all lithographed by him) were printed in the popular press, such as the weekly *L'Illustration* (*The Illustration*), with which the architect collaborated throughout the period. There, he not only published images of foreign cities, but also drawings documenting various political, military or fashionable society events that the journal chronicled. Nevertheless, after this Parisian interlude, in the 1860s Guesdon returned to Nantes, where he seems to have held the function of President of the Departmental Commission on Patrimony. He died in his native city in 1876.

THE AERIAL VIEW: GRAPHIC CONSTRUCTION AND OBSERVATIONS IN THE FIELD

Guesdon's biographer, Marionneau, provides a detailed description of the method he used in order to create his images:

> by means of a rigorously exact geometric plan (*plan géométral*) which he then transformed into perspective using a very high horizon line, the artist managed to trace within this meticulously set-up chessboard the elevation of houses and monuments of the city, while imagining himself either in a balloon or at a very high point, which allowed his gaze to dive into streets, gardens and courtyards and to represent not only the general, topographic view of a city but also all its buildings and districts. Hence his equestrian – or rather *bird's-eye* – views (*De là ses vues cavalières, ou plutôt à vol d'oiseau*).[6]

The perspectival construction adopted by Guesdon had been used by geometers and cartographers since the sixteenth century.[7] Ideally, this construction follows a four-step sequence. The first phase takes place in the field and involves the measurement of distances and reference points and the sketching of elevational elements. From this initial construct, a global view is then derived: this is what Marionneau terms 'the geometric plan' (it is not unlikely, however, that the geometric plan itself was derived from prior plans that the draughtsman would have perused; nor is it unlikely that Guesdon would have resorted to older views). Subject to changeable projectional methods, this geometric plan is then transformed into a perspectival plan (strictly speaking, into a portrait orientation). Rendered in perspective, this plan then constitutes the so-called 'backdrop' of the view. Finally, against this backdrop, and using on-site sketches and measurements, the city's buildings are shown in elevation and in perspective.

And yet, the views developed by Guesdon cannot be regarded as mere geometric constructions. The plates' captions often include the phrase 'drawn from life'. It is also known that, during his European trips, Guesdon executed numerous sketches on location, which he would then send to various newspapers for publication. During a trip to Spain in 1853, he sent Paulin, the editor of

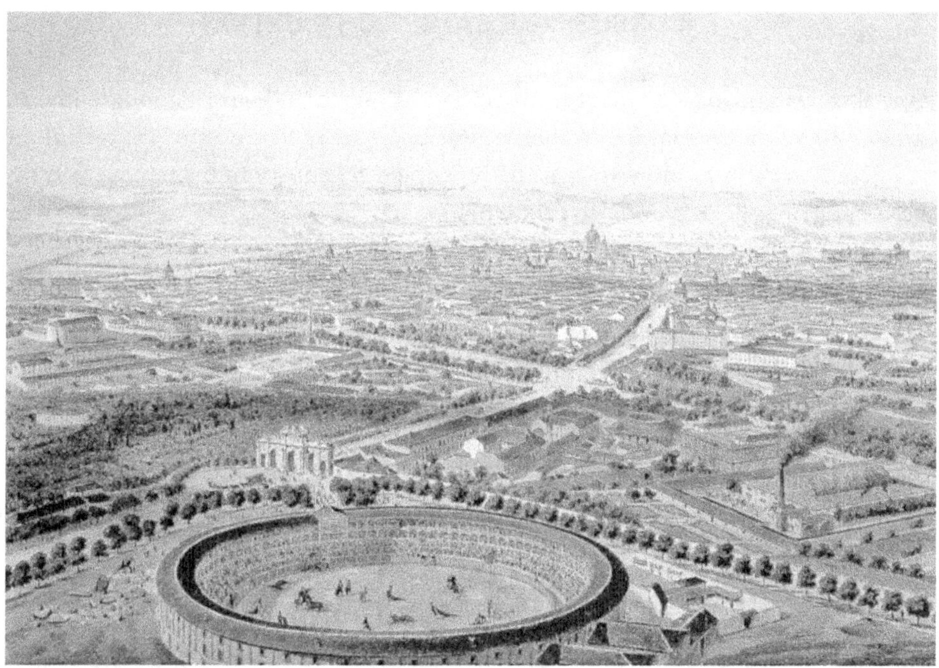

[4.1] A. Guesdon, 'Madrid. View overlooking the Plaza de Toros', in *L'Espagne à vol d'oiseau* (1854).

the magazine *L'Illustration*, drawings he had made in Jerez and Toledo. There are even indications that the artist may have used a hot-air balloon during his trip to Spain, particularly in January 1851, in order to depict a bullfight in Madrid (Figure 4.1). Lee Fontanella has suggested that, while he lived in Madrid, Guesdon worked with the English photographer Charles Clifford, who had arrived in Spain in September 1850, setting up as 'daguerrotypist' and 'aeronaut' soon after his arrival.[8] According to Fontanella, Clifford and his wife Jane worked as Guesdon's assistants in Madrid. However, there is nothing to suggest that Guesdon himself worked directly with a photographic camera.[9]

In other words, even if Guesdon's images are graphic constructions, they are nevertheless based upon direct observations and sketches executed in situ by the artist during his travels. They are interpretations rather than fictions. In actual fact, by using this method Guesdon participates in a long tradition of figurative drawing. As is well known, bird's-eye views belong to a branch of geometric perspective that, since the sixteenth century, has been termed 'catoptic'.

EXCURSUS: THE CATOPTIC TRADITION

Aerial views, and in particular those of cities, belong to the genre of topography. But among all possible topographic representations, these refer to a specific technique. As Père Augustin Lubin wrote in the seventeenth century in his famous *Mercure géographique* (*Geographical Mercury* [1678]),

> This topography can be constructed using either of two drawing techniques: one is to draw up the geometric plan of the site, accounting for all its measurable dimensions that then serve to establish a scale of heights; to this is added a compass star, one of whose cross hairs ends in an arrowhead pointing due North, which cardinal direction aligns doors, avenues and other important features of the site.
>
> The other way to achieve this topography is by means of the elevated or perspectival view, which is of two kinds, and which engravers call 'view of such and such a place', or else *veduta* in Italian, *vista* in Spanish, *Angesicht* in German and *the sight* in English. Or else the draftsman places himself on a plain or at the summit of a very high place – what we call *bird's-eye view*, as birds would see the places they fly over, which is a product of that branch of perspective called *catoptic*, which renders low-lying objects viewed from above.[10]

It is possible that Lubin may have found the notion of the catoptic view in the treatise on perspective written by the Minim friar Jean-François Niceron, *La perspective curieuse* ou *Magie artificielle des effets merveilleux de l'optique par la vision directe* (*The Peculiar Perspective, or the Artificial Magic of the Wondrous Effects of Optics through Direct* Vision [1638]). There, Niceron presents catoptics as one of three possible modes of seeing, or of perspectival construction (which is essentially the same thing): the 'purely optical [view ...] with which we simply look at the horizon [...] the anoptic [view ...] with which we look up above us [...] and the catoptic [...] with which we look down below us'.[11]

This distinction can be found in a passage dealing with anamorphosis. Therefore, it is a matter of – on the one hand – the deformation of features, if not their out-and-out 'deformity', and – on the other hand – the viewpoint that the viewer needs to adopt in order to see clearly a figure or an object which he would otherwise not be able to discern. The latter can be applied in the context of an urban iconography, whereby the aerial view, which is catoptic, enables the viewer to see the urban form quite clearly.

Insofar as the problem that here needs to be solved graphically is concerned, the genealogy of the word is itself revealing. Niceron refers explicitly to a famous compendium, the work of Lodovico Ricchieri (Coelius Rhodiginus), the *Lectionum antiquarum*, first published in Venice in 1516 and subsequently in the posthumous standard edition published at Basel in 1541. In his turn, Ricchieri refers to a Greek optical tradition, but without elaborating upon it. In his *Dictionnaire historique de la terminologie optique des Grecs* (*Historical Dictionary of the Optical Terminology Employed by the Greeks* [1964]), the historian Charles Mugler relates that the word 'catoptic' refers to the action of observing attentively. Specifically, the *katoptes* is the lookout, but also the god who registers an action. Whereas, in pseudo-Aristotle's *De mundo* (391a 8), the expression is used to describe the action of seeing, once the body has left the earth and has ascended skyward.

However, we cannot overlook other possible sources, particularly insofar as the history of perspective is concerned. Thus Giovanni Paolo Lomazzo, in his *Trattato dell'arte de la pittura, scoltura et architettura* (1584), makes a distinction between optic, anoptic and catoptic views when he sets out his reflections on perspective. Somewhat distortedly, he traces this distinction back to Geminus, whose few fragments on the subject he might have read in Proclus's *Commentary* on Euclid's *Elements*. Lomazzo clearly separates these views according to the height of the horizon line, whereby – for instance – the catoptic view, which relates to what Geminus terms 'scenography', is defined by an elevated horizon.[12] The classification of the three modes of seeing can also be found in the chapter on perspective from Pomponius Gauricus's book on sculpture, *De Sculptura* (1504).

Overall, we can say that the concept of the aerial view belongs to a practical and intellectual domain which is highly structured, that of the perspectival tradition; in other words, to an ensemble composed of, on the one hand, studies dealing with mechanisms of vision and, on the other hand, graphic practices related to vision and the construction of images – a conceptual sphere that has evolved considerably in Europe since the fifteenth century. The aerial view is not merely an imaginary view or a literary one, in the vein of *The Dream of Scipio*. It is a graphic construction that follows the rules of perspective and its tenets. Whenever the 'bird's-eye view' is physically impossible to attain, geometric construction allows for an experiential substitution. Hence a constructed – that is to say, virtual – view comes to replace lived experience.

Furthermore, Gauricus provides an interesting directive regarding the *function* of the catoptic view:

> Regarding the bird's-eye view, we must approach it with especial care and diligence, as it is the most frequently used and by far the most difficult. For we resort to this perspective from above whenever the representation of a complex scene is called for: a revolt, such as often erupts among the crowds; battles;

> wars, cities, etc., none of which could be rendered by means other than a bird's-eye view. This is because, in order to eyewitness a great commotion, we always seek an elevated viewpoint. For this reason, if we wish to present the spectator with one of these complex scenes, we need to resort to the bird's-eye view. And whatever comes into view first, from whichever side, would be placed with immediacy in the foreground; that which comes afterwards will be placed in the background, at a greater elevation, such that each element appears well positioned and appropriately spaced in relation to the others.[13]

If, as was frequently expressed in the seventeenth century, topography's purpose is to unfold before the viewer's eyes the stretch of land or the city to be depicted, perspective – and, more precisely, the aerial view – fully achieves this objective, inasmuch as it renders a spatially ordered and therefore clearly readable image of that which the represented area contains.

In the nineteenth century, at the time when urban bird's-eye views became disseminated in the popular press, César Daly, the founder of the journal *Revue générale de l'architecture et des travaux publics* (*General Journal of Architecture and Public Works*), put forward an analogous justification for this representational technique:

> It is only from high above that we can apprehend the volume of the great monuments, that we can read their actual layout, their real character, that we can discern the relationships between all of their parts. It is only from a *bird's-eye view* that we can discover the majestic grandeur of the Alps, the skilful and picturesque parcelling of *terra firma*, the immensity of the ocean. It is by rising high above the dwellings of our cities that we can see their ugliness, detect their hidden faults, and appreciate the beneficial influence that order and a degree of symmetry bring to the distribution of vast urban quarters.[14]

THE EDITORIAL CONTEXT OF ALFRED GUESDON'S ACTIVITIES

Alfred Guesdon did not work in isolation in his capacities as draughtsman and lithographer. Indeed, the production and distribution of urban views were collective activities; therefore commercial partnerships and membership of specialised professional networks were determining factors. As already mentioned, Guesdon belonged to a very active group of draughtsmen, lithographers, printers and editors, all of whom played an important role in the distribution of historical and geographical images of Paris in the mid-nineteenth century. Associated

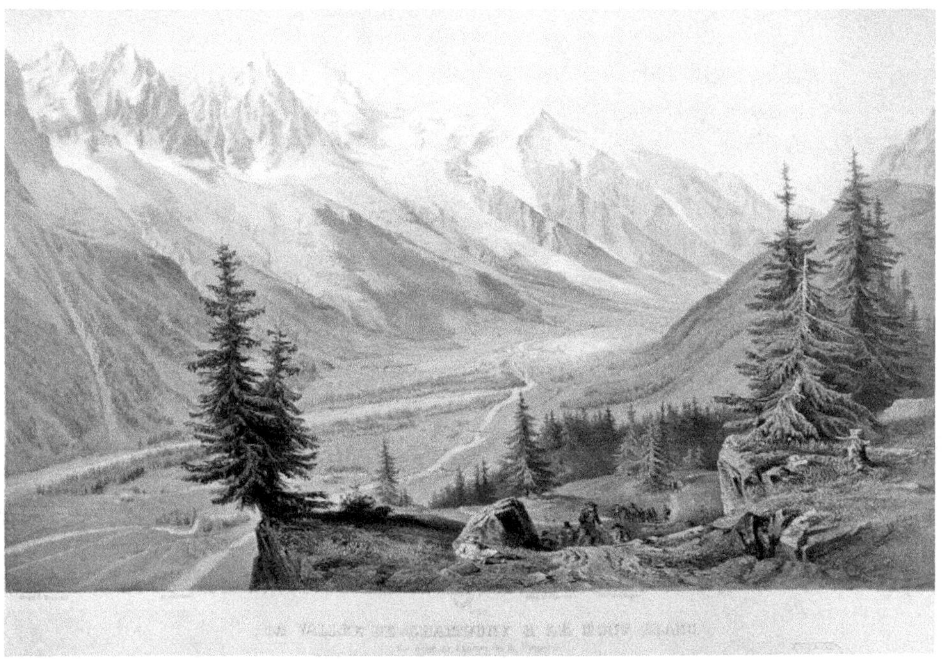

[4.2] A. Guesdon, 'The Valley of Chamonix and Mont Blanc', in *La Suisse à vol d'oiseau* (1859).

with the plates drawn or lithographed by Guesdon are the names of Arnout, Hauser, Dusacq, Lemercier and Delarue.[15] Thus, Guesdon's initial contributions to the field of urban iconography, the plates for the *Voyage aérien en France*, were executed in the context of a larger project, whose leading figure was Jules Arnout.[16]

However, as the publication of a print is a collective effort, this partially drains the authorial interpretation from the very drawing that gave rise to this collective process. For it equally bears the imprint of other mediators of meaning, such as the engravers, the printers and the editors, all of whom work with the drawing and inscribe it with the vectors of their own intentionality. Therefore, what is generally the case also holds true for Guesdon's work: when considering the urban views that he created, one has to take into account the specifics of the way in which they came into being, such as the place where they were produced and the editorial ethos within which they arose. Alfred Guesdon's bird's-eye views were used to different ends, all of which contributed to the creation of a visual culture in the nineteenth century that was thoroughly urban.

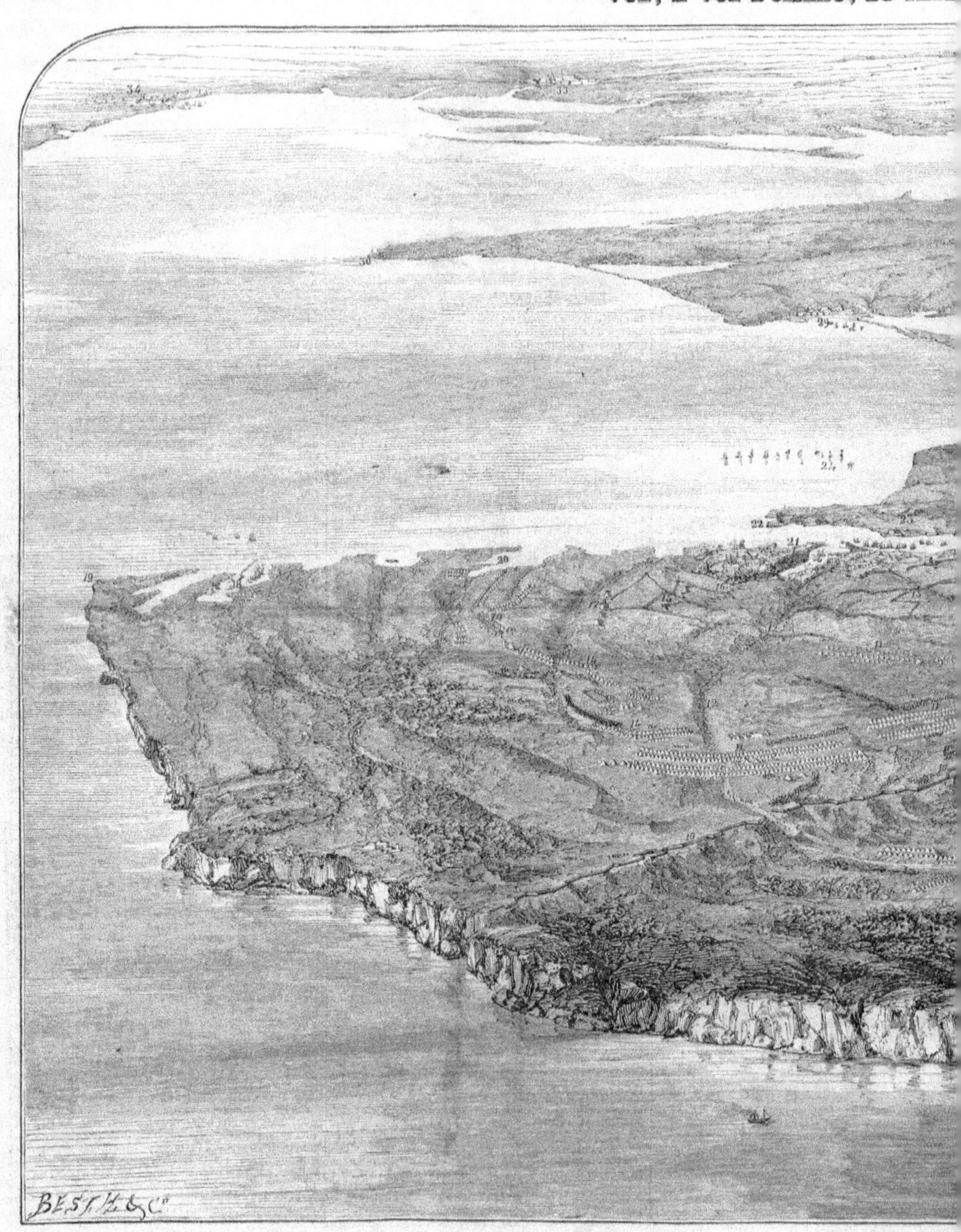

440 L'ILLUSTRATION, JOURNAL UNIVERSEL.

VUE, A VOL D'OISEAU, DU THÉÂ

Nº 1, Balaklava. — 2. Kadikoi. — 3. Camp anglais de Balaklava. — 4, 4. La redoute turque prise par les Russes. — 5. Redoute étoilée construite par les Russes après la bataille. — 6. Village de K
— 12. Grand ravin de Sébastopol. — 13. Attaque anglaise. — 14, 14, 14. Campement de l'armée française. — 15. Attaque française. — 16. 3e parallèle. — 17. Maison du clocheton. — 18
— 26. Baktchisaraï. — 27. Simphéropol. — 28. Rivière Salghir. — 29. Eupatoria. — 30. Cap et phare Tar

[4.3] A. Guesdon, 'Bird's-Eye View of the Theatre of War at the Gates of Sevastopol', *L'Illustration*, vol. XXIV, n.618, 3 December (1854): 440–1.

LA GUERRE DEVANT SÉBASTOPOL.

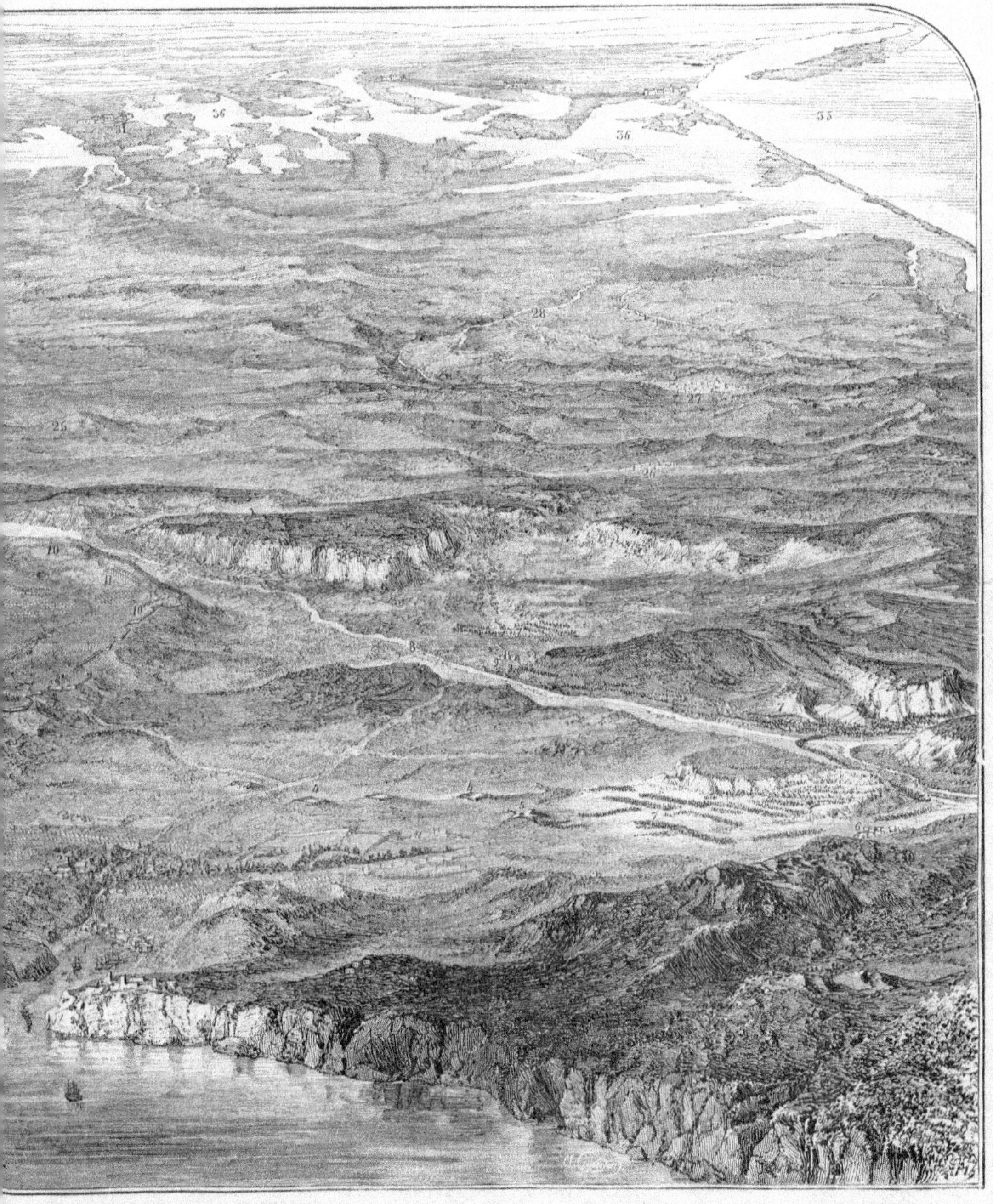

amp russe du général Liprandi. — 8. Tchernaïa (rivière). — 9. Route de Simphéropol. — 10, 10, 10, 10. Retranchement des armées alliées devant Sébastopol. — 11, 11, 11. Campement de l'armée anglaise.
h. — 19. Cap et phare Chersonèse — 20. Baie Kosatchaïa. — 21. Ville de Sébastopol. — 22. Fort Constantin. — 23. Fort du Nord. — 24. Baie et mouillage de la Katcha. — 25. Montagnes de l'Alma.
cop et muraille de défense. — 32. Berislaw. — 33. Nicolaïeff. — 34. Odessa. — 35. Mer d'Azoff. — 36. Mer Putride.

There were three principal domains in which Guesdon's images appeared. First of all, in travel guides, where the views were published at reduced scale. One example is the *Voyage pittoresque sur les bords du Rhin* (*Scenic Journey along the Rhine*), which incorporated a text written in 1856 by the journalist Edmond Texier (who was to become chief editor of *L'Illustration*) and included images of Strasbourg and Nancy that Guesdon had drawn the previous year. Second, Guesdon's images were also reproduced in geographical and tourist travel books about foreign lands, such as the one on Italy, published in 1849, which included 40 bird's-eye views of Italian cities, illustrating a journey that traced its way from the north to the south of the country. Some of the views were annotated with text written by Hippolyte Etiennez about the monuments and other salient aspects of the cities depicted. Here the text functions as a guide to reading the image. In fact, Guesdon himself sometimes contributed geographic and ethnographic descriptions of the cities he illustrated – during his sojourn in Spain in 1853, for example, when he described a wine cellar in Jerez, or else the various stages of sword production in Toledo. These descriptions were subsequently published in *L'Illustration*. Other instances in which Guesdon's drawings were used for tourism and geographical purposes could be found in Adolphe Joanne's book, *Voyage illustré dans les cinq parties du monde* (*Illustrated Travels through the Five Continents of the World* [1849]), to which the artist contributed a view of Brest, or in the series of engravings describing Switzerland, where he presented a view of Mont Blanc and the Chamonix valley (Figure 4.2). And finally, Guesdon's views of Italian cities met with a measure of publishing success during the Italian War of 1859, which pitted the Franco-Piedmontese army against the Austrian troops. For instance, his images of Bergamo, Alexandria, Mantua, Venice and Rome were reprinted by the magazine *L'Illustration* between May and September 1859 to help visualise the incursion of the French army into northern Italy. But Guesdon was also present at other theatres of conflict, notably that of the Crimean War (1853–56). The Siege of Sevastopol enabled Guesdon to publish, again in *L'Illustration* (3 December 1854), a magnificent *Bird's-Eye View of the Theatre of War at the Gates of Sevastopol,* where the panoramic impulse was pushed to its limit, in that the image encompassed the entire terrain, and not just the battle itself. With this, the landscape view became a kind of map (Figure 4.3).

MODERNISATION CAPTURED IN THE URBAN VIEWS

Bird's-eye views of cities in the nineteenth century acquired a heuristic, even moral, justification at a time when a number of architectural theoreticians, such as César Daly, who were inspired by Fourier's and Saint-Simon's ideas, were seeking to articulate tools for a rationalisation of the urban phenomenon. In this respect, the view from above presented those who wished to understand the city with a considerable advantage:

> From atop the towers of Notre-Dame or else from the peak of Montmartre, writes César Daly, the foreigner can better and more quickly see Paris than if he were to walk through its streets. This view of the great city as a whole allows him to better understand its circulation network as well as the placement and relative importance of green spaces and buildings.[17]

Guesdon's drawings contain various pointers to his awareness of the innovations occurring during his time. One can detect, in particular, numerous hints at the process of modernisation that was then sweeping through European – and especially French – cities. His illustrations are replete with trains, factories, as well as bridges, harbours, new buildings and avenues. These unprecedented landscape elements bear witness – at the level of the image – to the expansion of spaces and to discourses pertaining to the fields of economy, industrial revolution, advancements in transportation, and to urban development. Thus smog, factory chimneys, steamships and steam-powered trains, so often dotting Guesdon's images, reflect an emergent landscape of circulation and, more specifically, of energy production throughout Europe. Steam speaks of the machines that produce it. It signifies work energy, the machinic force that transforms urban space, and the sheer power of an industry-based civilisation. Ubiquitous among Guesdon's images, steam heralds the emergence of a new European landscape: that of the technological (Figure 4.4).

The smog, the chimneys, the steam, are all invested by Guesdon with a visual scale and monumentality that are equivalent, in a way, to those of the city's old buildings such as churches and palaces. Frequently, he ushers workshops and factories to the forefront of the image as if to state that, henceforth, modern industry will be accorded the same value as the city's ancient history in the definition of its urban spaces, just as he confers upon the new machinery the same dignity as that befitting the sites of historical tradition. Thus, for instance, in the foreground to his view of Madrid, the factory is brought into proximity with the Plaza de Toros; whereas in the view of Valencia he shows the factory at the city gates, adjacent to a great church.

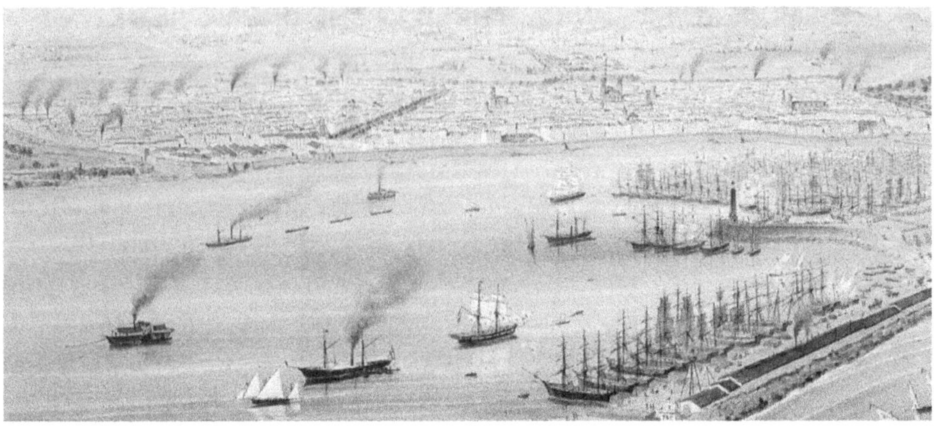

[4.4] A. Guesdon, 'View of Barcelona from Above the Entrance to the Harbour' (detail), in *L'Espagne à vol d'oiseau* (1855).

The railway network constitutes another signifier of the presence of energy in the landscape. As is well known, the nineteenth-century landscape was profoundly transformed by the advent of the railway and the train, and this in the realm of physical realities as well as at the level of perception and representation.[18] Guesdon bears frequent witness to this, by placing rail installations in the centre or in the foreground of his images (as he does for Lausanne and Geneva) and by imbuing them with considerable significance within the ambit of his urban discourse.

In his drawings one can see trains crossing landscapes, going under bridges, exiting tunnels and entering train stations, the latter being shown most frequently right in front of the viewer's eyes. Trains occupy a central position in Guesdon's landscapes, not only visually within the image but also in the pragmatic context of the prevalent industrial conditions: the cities imaged by Guesdon had just acquired train stations, and it is known that sometimes the artist would be present at their inauguration, as was the case at St Nazaire, in August 1857.

However, as Dolf Sternberger has remarked, the march of technology does not eradicate nature. Rather, it gives rise to a new kind of nature. Rivers and mountains join in the technical aspects of the landscape, not as 'the vanquished submitting to the victor but, on the contrary, as a kindred power that fully claims its due prestige in this new environment'.[19] Guesdon subscribes to the search for this harmonious environment in which nature and the economics of industry are in dialogue with each other (Figure 4.5).

But the artist does not content himself with showcasing the train and its railway infrastructure; he gives equal importance to other modernising aspects

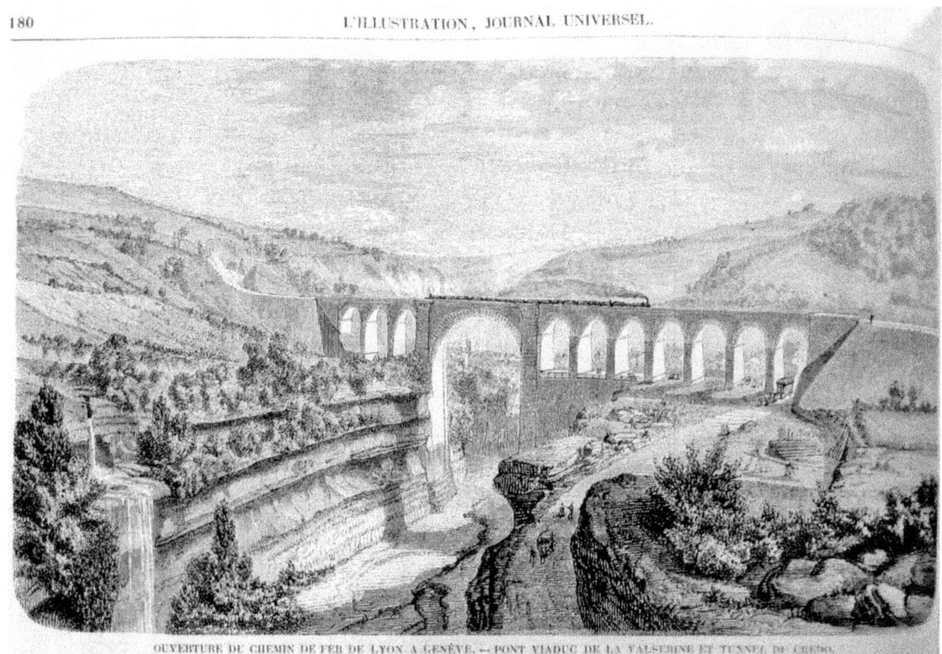

[4.5] A. Guesdon, 'The Lyon-Geneva Railway Line', *L'Illustration*, vol. XXXI, n.786, 20 March (1858): 180.

of the urban landscape. Thus he signals the arrival of new harbour facilities for maritime cities, be they military (like Cherbourg) or commercial (like Marseille). He dwells on the transformations effected in the urban fabric – such as bridges (Geneva), new districts (Plainpalais in Geneva; Marseille; the Bois de Boulogne in Paris), new avenues, new public buildings (specifically the theatres in Paris) – by stressing the aspect of spatial rationalisation brought by these innovations: in these images, the city is presented as somehow better organised and more legible.

Moreover, Guesdon's cities are cities in motion. By virtue of their industrialisation – of the presence of train stations, for instance – historic cities are made to transcend their old limits, as in the case of Geneva, Marseille or Paris. The images hint at future directions that the cities' urban development would follow. They also witness new urban practices that start to take hold within public space: leisure pursuits (as in the print showing the amenities of the Bois de Boulogne in Paris, published in *L'Illustration*) or tourism (as in the view of Boulogne-sur-mer, which captures, in its lower left corner, the ritual of sea bathing).[20]

CONCLUSION

Ultimately, the views created by Guesdon are testimonies to a particular moment during the modernisation of the French landscape, the urban and industrial development of the country that had been promoted by Napoleon III. Note must be made of the fact that Guesdon's drawings were frequently chosen to accompany accounts, published in *L'Illustration*, of imperial travels throughout the country, notably at Cherbourg in August 1858, where the artist witnessed the inauguration of one of its harbours by the Emperor.

More generally, though, Guesdon's work adequately reflects ways of perceiving and representing the urban landscape in the mid-nineteenth century. His images combine the scenic with the descriptive, while they emphasise concrete observations as well as novel aspects of urban space. They accompany and express, in their own way, the general tendency that characterised the nineteenth century, that of 'staging' geographical realities.[21]

And yet, by the end of the 1860s, Guesdon's images had become less and less utilised, perhaps owing to the advent of photography. It is telling that the magazine *L'Illustration*, which had been the major outlet for the dissemination of Guesdon's drawings, increasingly began to use lithographs derived from photographic prints.[22] And so Guesdon's views were dispatched to the deceptive quietude of the archive.

NOTES

1 Stephan Oettermann, *Das panorama. Die Geschichte eines Massenmediums* (Frankfurt: Syndikat, 1980); Silvia Bordini, *Storia del panorama. La visione totale della pittura nel XIX secolo* (Rome: Officina Edizioni, 1984); Ralph Hyde, *Panoramania! The Art and Entertainment of the 'All-Embracing' View* (London: Trefoil, 1988); Bernard Comment, *Le XIXe siècle des panoramas* (Paris: Adam Biro, 1993) (revised and augmented edition: *The Painted Panorama*, New York, 2000); Jean-Marc Besse, *Atlas, jardins, géoramas* (Paris: Desclée de Brouwer, 2003), 3rd part; Ton Rombout, ed., *The Panorama Phenomenon* (The Hague: B.V. Panorama Mesdag, 2006).

2 See especially the collection of essays in J.-M. Besse, M.-D. Couzinet, F. Lestringant, eds, *Les méditations cosmographiques à la Renaissance*, Cahiers V. L. Saulnier n° 26 (Paris: PUPS, 2009).

3 '[T]he panorama had a profound effect on the psychological and ideological forms of urban visuality, on the conditions under which the city was both perceived and fantasized', C. Prendergast, *Paris and the Nineteenth Century* (Oxford: Blackwell, 1992), p.46. See also the writings of Walter Benjamin on panoramic literature and the figure of the flâneur in his *Charles Baudelaire: A Lyric Poet in the Era of High Capitalism* (London: New Left Books, 1973): 'Once a writer had entered the marketplace, he looked around as in a diorama. A special literary

genre has preserved his first attempts at orienting himself. It is a panorama literature. It was not by chance that *Le Livre des cent-et-un, Les Français peints par eux-mêmes, Le Diable à Paris, La Grande Ville* enjoyed the favour of the capital city at the same time as the dioramas. These books consist of individual sketches which, as it were, reproduce the plastic foreground of those panoramas with their anecdotal form and the extensive background of the panoramas with their store of information' (p.35).

4 Charles Marionneau, 'Alfred Guesdon. Architecte, dessinateur et lithographe', *Revue de Bretagne et de Vendée*, June (1876): 1–7; H. Blémont, entry on Guesdon in M. Prevost et R. d'Amat, eds, *Dictionnaire de biographie française*, vol. 17 (Paris: Letouzey et Aué, 1989), p.14; entry on Guesdon in J. Adhémar, *Inventaire du fonds français, graveurs du XIXe siècle*, Paris, Bibliothèque Nationale, Department of Prints, vol. 9 (1955), pp.468–71; D. Stroffolino, 'Alfred Guesdon, *L'Italie à vol d'oiseau* (1849). La veduta a volo d'uccello dalle ali d'Icaro alla mongolfiera', in C. de Seta, ed., *Tra Oriente e Occidente. Città e iconografia dal XV al XIX secolo* (Naples: Electa, 2004), pp.67–76; A. Corboz, 'La ciudad desbordada', in A. Garcia Espuche, *Ciudades: del globo al satellite* (Barcelona: Electa, 1994), pp.219–27; F. Quiros Linares, *Las ciudades españolas a mediados del siglo XIX* (Valladolid: Ambito Ediciones, 1991).

5 Here are some examples. The series 'Scenic Themes' (Bibliothèque Nationale de France, Prints Collection, shelfmark AA-1) contains several lithographs drawn by Guesdon. These are: '1. The well, 2. The lotus flower, 3. The ditch, 4. Fountain of the Virgin, 5. The washerwomen (no. 6 is missing), 7. The font, 8. The kiosque, 9. The sea gate, 10. Calvary, 11. The old manor, 12. The salvation' (copyright registration: 1851). In another folder in the Department of Prints (shelfmark SNR-3) can be found several plates from the 1840s related to the series *The Arts in the Middle Ages*, for instance (plate VIII): 'Sixteenth century. Palace of Fontainebleau. Gallery of Francis I decorated by master Roux (il Rosso) and continued by Francesco Primaticcio. Guesdon draftsman/ lithographer A. Godard'. Several prints drafted by Guesdon belong to ch. IV of Sommerard's book.

6 C. Marionneau, op. cit., p.3.

7 See Lucia Nuti, 'Misura e pittura nella cartografia dei secoli XVI e XVII', *Storia urbana*, 62 (1993): 5–34; Lucia Nuti, 'The perspective plan in the sixteenth century: the invention of a representational language', *Art Bulletin*, LXXVI-1 (1994): 105–28; D. Stroffolino, *La città misurata. Tecniche e strumenti di rilevamento nei trattati a stampa del Cinquecento* (Rome: Salerno, 1999); J. Boutier, *Les Plans de Paris, des origines (1493) à la fin du XVIIIe siècle. Étude, carto-bibliographie et catalogue collectif* (Paris: BnF, 2002); J. Boutier, 'Mesures et triangulation de l'espace urbain. Le lever des plans de Paris à l'époque moderne (XVIe–XVIIIe siècles)', *Le Monde des Cartes. Revue du Comité français de Cartographie*, 172 (2002): 6–18; J. Boutier 'Réduire les villes en cartes', in M. Morel-Deledalle, *La ville figurée. Plans et vues gravées de Marseille, Gênes et Barcelone* (Marseille: Parenthèses, 2005), pp.23–31.

8 Gerardo F Kurtz, 'Charles Clifford aeronaute y fotografo. Madrid: 1850–1852', in Lee Fontanella, ed., *Clifford en España: un fotografo en la Corte de Isabel II* (Madrid: El Viso, 1999), pp.43–69; Lee Fontanella, *La historia de la fotografia en España desde sus origines hasta 1900* (Madrid: El Viso, 1981), pp.57–88; F. Quiros Linares, op. cit., pp.147–68.

9 On the use of balloons and of photography see, *inter alia*, Thierry Gervais, 'Un basculement du regard. Les débuts de la photographie aérienne, 1855–1914', *Études Photographiques*, 9, May (2001): 89–108; Marie Thébaud-Sorger, 'La conquête de l'air, les dimensions d'une découverte', *Dix-huitième siècle*, 31: 'Science et esthétique' (1999): 159–77.

10 Augustin Lubin, *Mercure géographique ou le guide du curieux des cartes géographiques* (Paris: Christophe Remy, 1678), p.8.

11 Jean-François Niceron, *La perspective curieuse* ou *Magie artificielle des effets merveilleux de l'optique par la vision directe* (Paris, 1638), book 2, proposition 3, first corollary. The same distinction can be found in the treatise by Lucas Brunn, *Praxis perspectivae,* published at Nuremberg in 1615.

12 G. B. Lomazzo, *Trattato della pittura... diviso in sette libri ne' quali si contiene tutta la Theorica, & la prattica d'essa pittura* (Milan, 1584). See book V, chapter III (p.254) and chapters X–XII (pp.268–9).

13 Pomponius Gauricus, *De Sculptura,* chapter 4, §3 (French trans. by A. Chastel and R. Klein [Paris, 1969], p.186).

14 Daly, César, 'De la locomotion aérienne', *Revue générale de l'architecture et des travaux publics,* 4 (1843): 17.

15 Entry on Arnout Sr. (Jean-Baptiste) and Jr. (Jules) in J. Laran, *Inventaire du Fonds français après 1800, graveurs du XIXe siècle,* vol. 1 (Paris: BnF, 1930), pp.160–83; Entry on Charles Fichot in J. Adhémar, ibid., vol. 7 (1954), pp.546–55. See also C. Bouquin-Chupeau, *Recherches sur l'imprimerie lithographique à Paris au XIXe siècle: l'imprimerie Lemercier (1803–1901),* doctoral thesis, Paris 1 (1993); as well as K. F. Beall, 'The interdependence of printer and printmaker in early 19th-century lithography', *Art Journal,* 39(3) (1980): 195–201.

16 Mention must also be made of the role played by the technical capacities that lithography was able to put at the artists' disposal. The latter availed themselves very quickly of this technological innovation: 280 lithographic presses were to be found in Paris in the first half of the nineteenth century (cf. K. F. Beall, op. cit., p. 201).

17 César Daly, 'The Daily Chronicle: an interesting question – answer to a reader', *LSG,* XII, 34, 18 February (1888), p.397, cited in R. Becherer, *Science Plus Sentiment. César Daly's Formula for Modern Architecture* (Ann Arbor: UMI Research Press, 1975), p.179. See also M. Saboya, *Presse et architecture au XIXe siècle. César Daly et la Revue générale de l'architecture et des travaux publics* (Paris: Picard, 1991), especially p.246ff., which features a retrospective of the journal's most interesting printed stock. This contained the majority of the artwork that Guesdon had executed by himself.

18 Cf. M. Desportes, *Paysages en mouvement. Transports et perception de l'espace XVIIIe–XXe siècle* (Paris: Gallimard, 2005); and W. Schivelbuch, *Histoire des voyages en train* (Paris: Le Promeneur, 1990).

19 Dolf Sternberger, *Panoramas du XIXe siècle* (Paris: Gallimard, 1996), p.39.

20 Boulogne-sur-mer was at the time a famous spa and, above all, a new rail destination.

21 See for instance J. M. Schwarz, 'The *Geography lesson*: photographs and the construction of imaginative geographies', *Journal of Historical Geography,* 22(1) (1996): 16–45. Regarding photographic expeditions, see also Marta Caraion, *Pour fixer la trace: Photographie, littérature et voyage au milieu du XIXe siècle* (Geneva: Droz, 2003).

22 See Thierry Gervais, *L'Illustration photographique. Naissance du spectacle de l'information (1843–1914),* doctoral thesis, EHESS, Paris (2007).

5

Nadar's Aerial View

Stephen Bann

The aerial view has been a convention in mapping since the early modern period. Jacopo de'Barbari's extraordinary rendering of Venice seen from the air, distinctive by virtue of its convoluted canals, had lodged itself within the mind of travellers. It appears, in a much-simplified version, in the frontispiece of John Raymond's *Voyage through Italy* (1648), to contrast with the earth-bound fortress that is papal Rome.[1] In parallel to such impossible views, of course, there were also the accessible prospects that could be obtained from high buildings such as church towers. When John Bargrave (Raymond's tutor on this earlier journey to France) took up residence in the city of Bourges in 1645, he commemorated one such viewpoint with a sketch in his travel journal. In his entry for 23 July, he notes how he ascended the 'Tour de Beurre' of the cathedral and recorded 'the Prospect of the City as I have figured it in the next page'.[2] Bargrave even inscribed an ironic motto on the 'inside of the pinnacle and steeple': '*Noli altum sapere*'[3] (literally, 'I do not wish to know the heights'). Indeed this memorable visit to a great gothic building was further defined in his journal as a conjoined experience involving both heights and depths: 'I was not then so high, but anon was as lowe. For when we were come downe, we went to the Sepulcher, a church underneath the Quire of the Cathedrall, going through a dark vault to it.'[4]

Doubtless Bargrave had in mind here the moral implications of rising too 'high' above the earth. Throughout the period when tales of aerial travel could only be fictions, their connotations inevitably extended to the sphere of religion and statecraft. Jonathan Swift's *Gulliver's Travels* (1726) places among his hero's adventures the discovery of what he at first perceives as 'a vast Opake body between me and the Sun, moving forwards towards the island'.[5] On himself gaining access to this 'floating island', named Laputa, Gulliver soon discovers that it is a means both of communication and surveillance for the ruler of the state: 'In our Journey towards *Lagado* the Capital City, his Majesty ordered that the Island should stop over certain Towns and Villages, from whence he might receive the Petitions of his Subjects.'[6] He also learns that, as a last resort to quell rebellious subjects, the King could be obliged to exploit his supra-terrestrial advantage to the full by 'letting the Island drop directly on their heads, which makes a universal Destruction both of Houses and Men'.[7]

Bargrave thus allegorises the experience of heights and depths in terms of a moral maxim: 'Noli altum sapere'. Swift, on the other hand, combines the fantasy of aerial surveillance with the political message of Utopian literature. But a new note is sounded later in the eighteenth century, when antiquarians begin to combine a scrutiny of the earth seen from above with advances in the knowledge about what lies under the earth: this being, of course, the developing science of archaeology.

The process can be traced effectively in a sequence of scholarly writings about the remains of the Roman city of Rutupiae, the original entry point to Britain situated on the East Kent coast. William Camden, in his *Britannia*, had seen this site as a *memento mori*: 'Cities as well as men have their fatall periods, it [Rutupiae] is a verie field at this daie, wherein when the corne is come uppe a man may see the draughts of streetes crossing one another.' He also explained a popular myth about the site: '(For, wheresoever the streetes went, there the corne is thinne) which the common people terme *Saint Augustine's Crosse*.'[8] This must be a reference to the cruciform feature which was later identified as the foundation of a Roman triumphal arch. Yet it appears in the aerial views of the site published well into the eighteenth century as if it were indeed a Christian symbol, and as such reminiscent of the arrival of St Augustine to convert the people of Kent in the sixth century AD.

Such an insecurely based folk memory would, indeed, become obsolete when archaeologists began to delve under the ground. The historical reality of the Roman arch would take the place of the figmentary Christian symbol. The looming hill in the distance beyond (so clearly indicated in the prints) would also be given a historical identity. Early sources referred to this feature simply as 'The Mounts', implying that it was an elevated spot from which an overall view of the scene could be obtained. But by 1754, when a minor canon of Canterbury Cathedral, William Gostling, undertook a tour of East Kent in 1754, he was provoked to remark rather testily: 'Had an actual survey of the two Rutupian castles been thought as much to the purpose, surely some notice would have been taken of the remains of an amphitheatre within.'[9] The unusual 'oval or

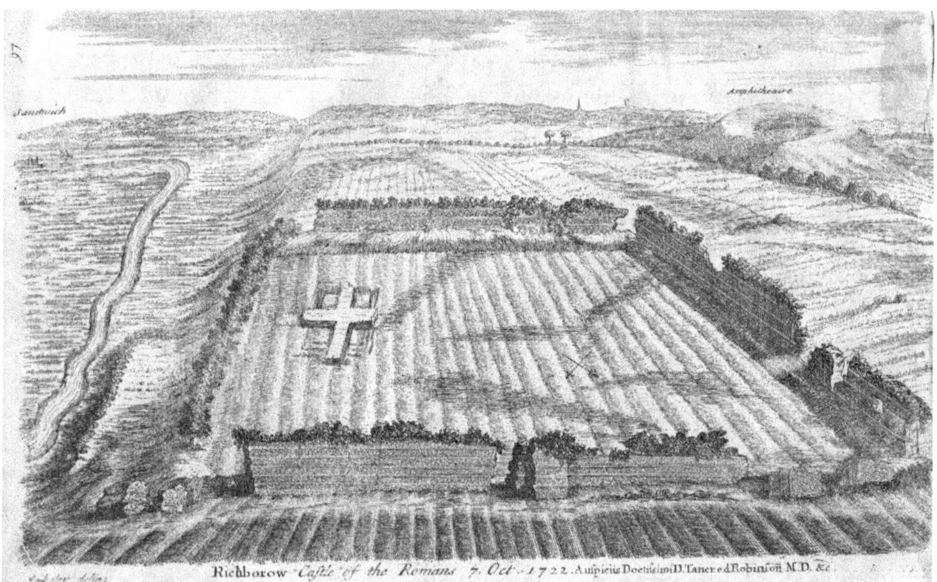

[5.1] Richborow Castle of the Romans, 1722.

circular' raised feature did indeed require to be investigated as a structure that was integral to the ancient Roman city.

These opening remarks touch upon the different discourses into which 'aerial views' were absorbed during the early modern period. By the end of the eighteenth century, the invention of the Montgolfier brothers had made it possible for the earth to be surveyed from a great height. Yet it is noteworthy that the historical culture of Romanticism brought with it a regression from the modern view to a revivalist image of the medieval city as seen from what was traditionally its highest, and most sacred, building. There can be few more memorable evocations of the Middle Ages than Victor Hugo's *'Paris à vol d'oiseau'* ('Paris a bird's-eye view'), which forms the second chapter of *Notre-Dame de Paris*. Hugo has only just noted that the top of the spire of Rouen Cathedral has been destroyed by fire in 1823, when he launches into a description of Paris as seen from the tower of Notre-Dame. However, it is not the Paris of the 1820s, but a medieval city that can only be understood by analogy with the few specimens still extant throughout Europe:

> It was, in fact, when, after having groped for a long time in the dingy spiral staircase that pierces perpendicularly through the thick wall of the towers, you finally came out unexpectedly onto one of the two high platforms, inundated with daylight and air, that there was the beautiful picture that unrolled all at

> once on all sides beneath your eyes; a spectacle *sui generis*, which can easily be imagined by those of our readers who have had the good fortune to see a gothic town entire, complete, homogeneous, as a few of them still remain, Nuremberg in Bavaria, Vittoria in Spain.[10]

All of these previous examples of the 'aerial view', extending over two centuries, appear to be relevant in discussing the contribution of the French photographer, balloonist and memoir writer, Félix Tournachon, generally known as Nadar. For one thing, Nadar was a friend and admirer of Victor Hugo. He acknowledged that Hugo's chapter on 'The Year 1817' in *Les Misérables* was one of the three artistic creations that took him back to the period of his youth. He also visited the poet during his exile in Brussels in 1852, with a view to obtaining *Napoléon-le-Petit*, Hugo's satirical pamphlet directed against the newly elected head of state, Louis Napoleon. This affiliation alone would underline the point that Nadar's 'aerial views' can be appreciated now only through the written accounts that he took such trouble to publish on the subject. These make it amply clear the extent to which the pioneering photographer was deeply absorbed in the problem of how the knowledge that he acquired from aerial photography could be satisfactorily defined and described. They also make it clear that he did indeed proceed through a cognitive threshold: from the description of what he observed in essentially literary terms – and thus in a literary and intellectual tradition – to a definition of a new, precise mode of seeing, capable of being harnessed to further technical tasks. Though the documentation as revealed by the photographs themselves is lacking, the written account provides all the necessary evidence of this decisive shift.

Nadar effected his first ascents in a balloon in 1857, and attempted to photograph the earth from the upper air at the same time. The experiment was unsuccessful, since the gas escaping from the balloon reacted with the emulsion of photographic plates, and the result was a blackened image. Only in the following year, when (by accident) he discovered that this was the cause of his failure to obtain a successful view of the earth beneath, did he find the means to counteract it. This lengthy period between his observations of the earth, and his ability to capture them photographically, is enshrined in the temporality of the essay written subsequently. The first description, then, is reliant on a host of visual cues and literary devices, evoking the vocabulary of games, and of miniaturisation, as well as of Utopian literature:

> Beneath us, as if to do us honour in accompanying our movement, the earth is unrolled in immense carpet without edges, with neither beginning nor end, with varied colours in which the dominant one is green, in all its accents

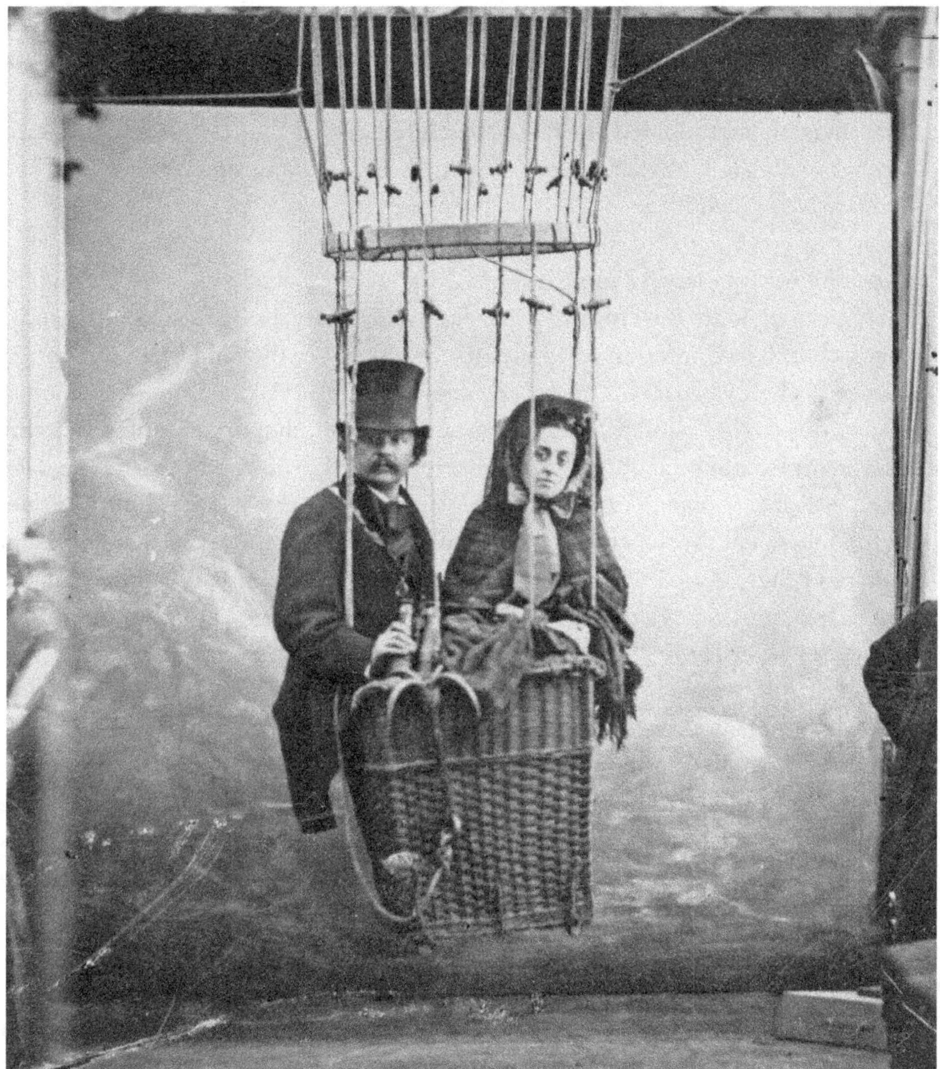

[5.2] Nadar, *Nadar with his Wife, Ernestine, in a Balloon*, *c.*1865.

as in all its combinations. The fields in irregular checkerboard patterns have the air of those coverlets in multicoloured but harmonising pieces brought together by the patient needle of the housewife. It seems as if a bottomless toy box has just been spilled profusely over the earth, the earth that Swift revealed for us in Lilliput, as if all the toy factories of Karlsruhe had emptied their stock. Toys, these little houses with red or slate roofs, toys this church, this prison, this citadel, the three types of habitation that sum up all of our

> present civilization. Even more of a toy this hint of a railway-line that sends up from below its sharp little whistle cry as if to compel our attention, and the dear thing passes along so slowly – yet at its fifteen leagues an hour – on its invisible rail, plumed with its little aigrette of smoke [...] And what is this other whiteish flake that I notice down there floating in space: the smoke of a cigar? No, a cloud.[11]

Quite obviously, there is more than a hint of the social critic here. Nadar's contemporary, John Ruskin, uses the description of a prospect from the most ancient church in Canterbury, St Martin's, to vituperate the modern urban design that places the cathedral 'in distant or despised subservience under the colossal walls of the county gaol'.[12] Nadar's concatenation of church, prison and citadel leaves us in no doubt about his progressive views. But in the main, the passage is a record of the *anomie* induced by the aerial view, which forces him to find a playful equivalent for the effect of miniaturisation. Even the train, that engine of industrial progress, wears its aigrette like a society lady. A cloud seen from above is as inconsequential as a puff from a cigar.

Yet it is precisely in the state of disequilibrium produced by the aerial view that the disinterested optic of the camera becomes necessary: 'The invitation to the lens here was more than a formality, it was imperative; and however intensely we were absorbed to the point of being in the haziness of a dream, in all truth we would have to have never opened the door of a laboratory not to be transfixed straight away with the idea of photographing these marvels'. Nadar sees photography in a certain sense as the antidote to this bewildering new experience of the world. Moreover, the very prospect of photography straightaway summons up the possibility of significant new 'applications':

> As luck would have it, I was apparently the first photographer lifted up under a balloon, and so it befell me to have as priority that could have gone to anyone else.
>
> I had immediately envisaged two extremely interesting applications.
>
> From a strategic point of view, no one disputes that it is fortunate for a general in the countryside to come across a church tower from which some staff officer can conduct his operations.
>
> I carried my church tower with me, and my lens could successively and without limits take positives on glass which I would send directly from my basket to head-quarters, by means of an extremely simple device: a little box that would slide down to the ground along a cord which would come to me with instructions if necessary.[13]

In his description of the floating island of Laputa, Gulliver had already observed the possibility of transactions between the upper air and the earth beneath: 'And to this Purpose, several Packthreads were let down with small Weights at the Bottom. On these Packthreads the People strung their Petitions, which mounted up directly like the Scraps of Paper fastened by School-boys at the end of the String that holds their Kite.' But for Nadar, the analogy with children's games would now be out of place, since it is the hard reality of modern warfare and its need for reconnaissance that has come into question. The second 'application', hardly less well adapted to the conditions of modern life, is in the use of the camera for cadastral surveys, which will hopefully put an end to arduous disputes about landed property.

Yet both of these strategies for the future depend radically on the new vision that the camera can provide. It is Nadar's ability to develop his plates in the balloon – an experiment finally resulting in success – that takes the aerial view to a new cognitive plane, which will be congenial to such important applications. The descriptive passage cleverly shows how the resultant images are not only different in kind from the metaphorical evocations used previously, but provide the photographer himself with a global view of particulars. The gradual emergence of this pristine view from the photographic plate has to be described:

> Wonderful! There is something there! ...
> I insist and force it: the image reveals itself little by little, quite uncertain, quite pale – but then sharp, secure ...
> I take leave of my improvised laboratory in triumph.
> It is just a simple positive on glass, very feeble in this misty atmosphere, all speckled after so many false starts, but what does it matter? It cannot be denied: there they are beneath me, the only three houses in the little hamlet: the farm, the inn and the police station, as befits all of Petit-Bicêtre in good form. You can perfectly make out on the road an upholstery wagon whose driver has come to a halt before the balloon, and on the tiles of the rooftops two white pigeons which have just alighted there.
> So I was right! [...]
> This time, having no gas to lose, I had mounted with the valve *closed*. [...]
> So, at each of previous [attempts], the gushing valve had vomited hydrogen sulphide in floods over my baths: silver salts with hydrogen sulphide, a wicked couple irretrievably condemned to have no children.[14]

As Nadar himself admitted, the expected utility of his aerial photographs did not materialise, at least in the short term. The prospect of ending property disputes, 'even in Normandy',[15] came to nothing. There is even a surprise ending to his essay which concedes that a certain M. Andraud had already published photographs taken from a balloon at the time of the 'Exposition universelle' of 1855.[16] Yet this ballooning experience certainly did not constitute the end of the matter for Nadar. Indeed, at a time when his activity as a portrait photographer tailed off to some extent, his enthusiasm for balloons took a new and revolutionary turn. Now it was a matter of dirigible balloons, and in order for balloons to be dirigible, Nadar argued, it was necessary for them to be heavier than air. On 30 July 1863, he developed this theory at a meeting in his studio, and shortly afterwards published his *Manifesto of aerial locomotion*. He also created a 'Society for the encouragement of aerial locomotion', and founded a magazine, *L'Aéronaute*. Not content with promoting his ideas on paper, he then provided the finance for constructing a balloon of over 6,000 cubic metres in capacity, aptly named *Le Géant* (The Giant), which could accommodate up to 12 people. The ceremony at which this monster was launched, from the Esplanade of the Invalides in Paris, took place in the same year in the presence of around 250,000 spectators.

A near catastrophe soon followed. A fortnight after its launch, the *Géant* went out of control over the Kingdom of Hanover, in northern Germany, and crashed to the ground. This spectacular accident, which certainly increased Nadar's international fame, also gave rise to one of the most mysterious and elliptical texts in *Quand j'étais photographe*: the essay entitled 'The blind princess'. I have written elsewhere at length about the curious implications of this account, which nests the aftermath of the Hanover disaster within a framing story of the appearance of Maria Anna, Princess of Solms-Braunfels, at Nadar's Paris studio.[17] Apart from the light that it sheds on Nadar's studio practice, however, it is strangely revelatory about the equivocal future of dirigible balloons. Nadar tells us that, while he convalesced from the broken leg sustained in the accident, he was visited every day by a young aide de camp, solicitously sent by the King of Hanover. This rising young officer, the Pomeranian Graf von Wedel, himself evinced a passionate interest in the possibility of developing 'heavier than air' dirigibles.[18] By the time that Nadar published his collection of autobiographical texts in 1900, it would have been possible to trace the career of this 'veritable giant' somewhat further, though Nadar does not attempt to do so. After killing the son of the 'blind princess' in a duel, he left Hanover to become a member of the Prussian army, and doubtless took part in the invasion and annexation of that small German state by their powerful neighbour. He certainly took part in the Franco-Prussian War of 1870; finally, in 1907 (three years before Nadar's death) he became military Governor of the occupied provinces of Alsace-Lorraine. No doubt he was also well aware of the testing of 'dirigible balloons' for military purposes by another German count, Graf von Zeppelin, before the end of the century.

Nadar himself showed awareness of the 'experiments' of Zeppelin towards the end of his life, though with a certain prescience he did not rate them as very promising.[19] His ballooning feats had not come to a halt with the wreck of the *Géant*, which indeed was repaired and fitted up for another series of excursions. His strenuous defence of the principle of 'heavier than air' aerial locomotion of course needs no additional emphasis here, since it has become received wisdom. But the mention of the sinister Von Wedel, and his contact with Nadar in 1863, prompts the recognition that Nadar unquestionably found a useful purpose for his ballooning during the Franco-Prussian War of 1870. The time was not yet ripe for the sophisticated system of military reconnaissance that he described as being envisaged in his first round of aerial photography. But the Siege of Paris two months after the start of the war provided him with a valuable mission. Installed in his balloon, he carried post and telegrams across the enemy lines, and even distributed tracts calling for the end of hostilities.

It would be possible to leave this account of Nadar's aerial exploits on this optimistic note. Certainly the theme that runs throughout all his autobiographical writings is a generous commitment to progress. In this respect, he is an authentic child of the philosophy of the Enlightenment and the idealism of the French Revolution. Not for nothing did he frequent in his youth the 'Café du Progrès' that served as the intellectual centre for the Latin Quarter of Paris.[20] Without doubt, the success that he achieved with his photographic practice could be identified with this faith in progress, and in the technological advances that made progress possible. The preoccupation with 'heavier than air' aerial transport was its direct successor, but by no means exhausted Nadar's urge to improve the human condition through diligent research. *Quand j'étais photographe* underlines this commitment literally to the very end, since Nadar added a final postscript above the dateline of 'Marseille, June 99': 'And this very morning, with the certainty of wireless telegraphy by Marconi, what can be the limit to our dreams!'[21]

Yet Nadar had good reason to fear that progress was not a one-way track. French history continued throughout his lifetime with a series of uprisings and changes of government. Born in 1820, he had not witnessed the occupation of France by the Allied troops after the Battle of Waterloo, but, as noted here, he played an active role when the country was once again overcome by a foreign army. His own many-sided and ingenious research sometimes led him to a dead end, or a near disaster. He was always keen to emphasise in his memoirs the role of the accident in human history. For this reason, it is appropriate to end this essay not with the utility of the 'aerial view', but with the symmetrically opposite enterprise that followed up the first experiments in aerial photography. Hardly had he completed his successful aerial photographs of 1858 when he set himself a new challenge: that of photographing by artificial light. His patent for the lighting of subjects through magnesium flares was deposited in 1862, and he immediately set to work on the photography of the Paris catacombs. The record that he later compiled is no less vivid than the testimony from the balloon:

> Here it is. We are penetrating into the ossuary.
>
> Between the pillars of crudely rough-hewn stone, introduced helpfully to protect this part of central Paris from the land-slides that took place all too frequently, are arranged in perfect order (you might say it was a wood merchant's vast and meticulous yard) all the bones collected, after 1785, from the disused cemeteries, the former churches and the excavations that have, under the Second Empire, overturned from top to bottom a large part of the soil of Paris. From the Caesars and the Norman invasions up to the last burgesses and serfs extracted in 1861 from the cemetery of Vaugirard, all that has lived and died in Paris sleeps here, vile multitudes and famous great men, canonised saints and criminals executed on the Place de la Grève. In the egalitarian confusion of death, some Merovingian king keeps eternal silence beside those massacred in September 1792. Valois, Bourbons, Orléans, Stuarts are rotting indiscriminately, lost between the sick from the Cour des Miracles and those two thousand 'of the religion' put to death on the day of Saint Bartholomew.
>
> The men of the ossuary pile up [the bones] in each of the two tipcarts that they push once they are full in the direction of the still vacant archivolts that await their 'filling'.[22]

It is indeed difficult to read this powerful evocation of change and decay without thinking of the earlier examples that have featured in this essay. John Bargrave is driven by an ironically expressed humility to explore the crypt of Bourges Cathedral, after he has witnessed and sketched the view from its highest tower. Nadar proceeds from the upper air to the depths of the earth, and his *memento mori* comes as an irresistible response to the massed detritus of the Parisian cemeteries. However, in the two centuries that divide them, excavation has become a privileged tool of scholars in search of historical data, just as the space underground has become a public resource in ensuring the hygienic disposal of waste. In such complex ways, the earth's surface has ceased to operate so crucially as a limit, and become more like the equivalent of a membrane separating two regimes of possible knowledge.

Two years after the descent into the catacombs, after Nadar had perfected his technique with the use of electricity, a further sortie took place into the Parisian underworld. But once again an accident played its part, and in this case it frustrated his intentions:

> Twice I had to change the technician who had leased us the supply of lighting. Must I speak once more about our disillusionment, our anger, when after several attempts at a difficult point, at the moment when all precautions had been taken, all obstacles removed, or avoided, our purposeful operation was coming to its conclusion – when suddenly, in the last seconds of the shot, a cloud rising from the piping came and misted over our plate – and how we swore at the fine lady or the good gentleman overhead, who had chosen just that moment to release their bath-water![23]

One wonders here at the careful choice of language and incident that so distinguishes Nadar's autobiographical writings from being a mere record. It was 'a cloud' that caused his keen observation of the earth from his balloon to falter. What was the 'whiteish flake [...] floating in space'? 'The smoke of a cigar? No, a cloud.' Here it is a 'cloud' of steam, that intervenes in the course of the inventor's carefully prepared experiment. Hubert Damisch's study, *A Theory of /Cloud/,* looks searchingly at the representational system of Western art since the Renaissance, and identifies the painter Correggio as the first artist whose work is 'linked to the dynamics of an ascensional imagination, and connected, first and foremost, to a *dream of flying*'. Damisch asks: 'does not Correggio seem to be the prototype of a 'vertical' painter, altogether devoted to the aerial element?'[24] If Correggio is indeed the prototype of such an artistic endeavour, with the '/cloud/' as a semiotic operator that leads him upwards into soaring cupolas, he does not lack for modern descendants. Malevich would certainly be one of them, though his Suprematist works, which take leave of earth-bound perspective, also date from the period when the feasibility of air travel was already well known. Nadar, with his airborne camera, was able to achieve a prospect of the earth significantly different from the previous, dream-like visions, that had been elaborated by way of pictorial and fictional representations. For him, nonetheless, the cloud still marked the occurrence of a failure in the system, or at least the necessity to adjust one's perceptions of a world that was still very far from perfect.

NOTES

1 See Stephen Bann, *Under the Sign: John Bargrave as Collector, Traveler, and Witness* (Ann Arbor: University of Michigan Press, 1994), fig. 23.

2 Quoted in Stephen Bann, 'Scaling the Cathedral: Bourges in John Bargrave's Travel Journal for 1645', in Robert S. Nelson and Margaret Olin, eds, *Monuments and Memory, Made and Unmade* (Chicago and London: University of Chicago Press, 2003), p.28.

3 Ibid., p.29.

4 Ibid., p.31.
5 Jonathan Swift, *Gulliver's Travels and Selected Writings in Prose and Verse*, ed. John Hayward (London: Nonesuch Press, 1949), pp.152–3.
6 Ibid., p.159.
7 Ibid., p.167.
8 William Camden, *Britannia or a Chorographical Description of Great Britain and Ireland*, translated by Philemon Holland (London: George Bishop and John Norton, 1610), pp.341–2.
9 William Gostling, *A Walk in and about the City of Canterbury* (New edition, Canterbury: William Blackley, 1825), p.357.
10 Victor Hugo, *Notre Dame de Paris* (Paris: Flammarion, 1967), p.139. My translation.
11 Nadar, 'La première épreuve de photographie aérostatique', in *Quand j'étais photographe* (Paris: Seuil, 1994), p.97. My translation (as in all following texts from this source).
12 John Ruskin, *Complete Works* (London: George Allen, 1908), vol. 33, p.438.
13 Nadar, op. cit., pp.98–9.
14 Ibid., pp.113–14.
15 Ibid., p.102.
16 Ibid., pp.115–16. Nadar even appends what appears to be the title-page of Andraud's book. The copy listed in the catalogue of the British Library appears to have been 'destroyed'.
17 See Stephen Bann, '"When I was a photographer": Nadar and History', in *History and Theory*, 48(4) (December 2009) (Theme issue 48, 'Photography and Historical Interpretation'): 95–111. A major concern in this text is identifying the 'blind princess' beyond doubt, since Nadar does not claim to make things easy for the historian.
18 Nadar, op. cit., p.61.
19 Quoted ibid., p.106.
20 See Bann, op. cit., p.107. The memories of his earlier years are contained in the volume, *Quand j'étais étudiant* (Paris: E. Dentu, 1881).
21 Nadar, op. cit., p.49.
22 Ibid., pp.128–9.
23 Ibid., p.157.
24 Hubert Damisch, *A Theory of /Cloud/*, translated by Janet Lloyd (Stanford: Stanford University Press, 2002), p.21.

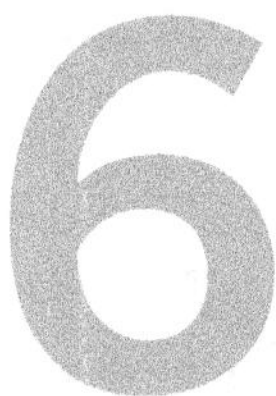

Transfiguring Reality

Supprematism and the Aerial View

Christina Lodder

> The conquest of the heavens, courageous flying records, and looking at the earth's surface from the airman's soaring summits formulated a new love for mathematical idealism, so to speak. This relationship with the infinite space of the cosmos established new values in the psyche of modern man. Forms appear as distant transformations of the idea of objects.[1]

This statement from a lecture that Malevich gave in 1927 while in Warsaw suggests that the aerial view, 'looking at the earth's surface from the airman's soaring summits', was an important inspiration for the artist and may even have been one of the factors that led him to develop, in the early summer of 1915, his first Suprematist painting. Malevich subsequently created a series of works in this new style, all consisting of flat geometric forms in various colours set against white grounds. He described this new style as *bezpredmetnyi*, which literally means 'objectless', but has usually been translated as 'non-objective'. The invention of Suprematism has been attributed to various factors, including a renewed interest in the metaphysical nature of icon painting, philosophical ideas connected with notions of the fourth dimension as developed by the philosopher Peter Ouspensky (Petr Uspenskii), and the poetic theory and practice of *zaum* (the transrational or beyonsense), which acted as 'a supranational, transcendental language of the future', liberating words, syllables, letters and sounds from conventional logic, giving them an autonomy resembling the autonomy of the painted elements in a Suprematist painting.[2] I would like to suggest that the

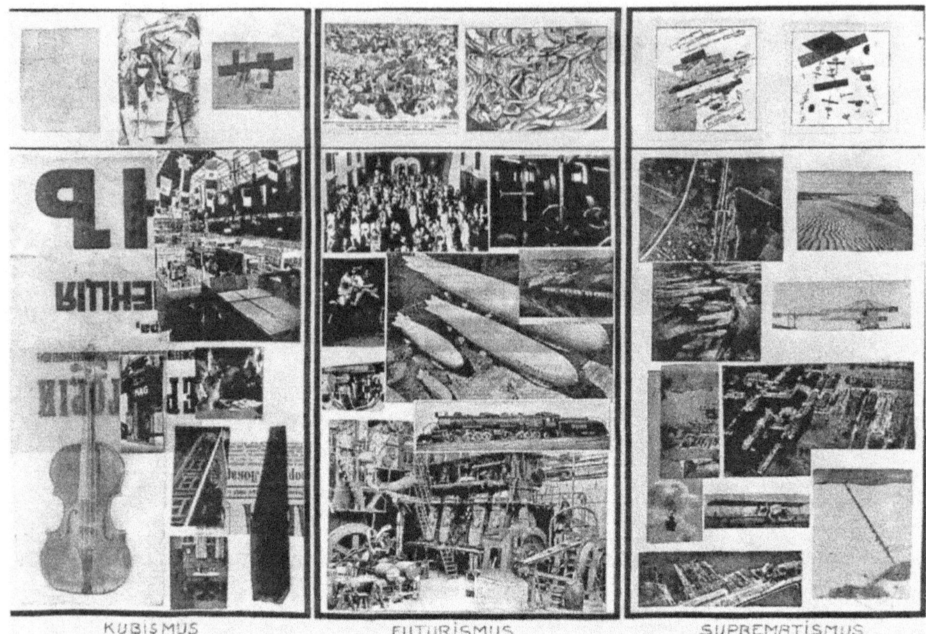

[6.1] Malevich, *Analytical Chart No. 16: The Relationship between the Painterly Perception and the Environment of the Artist (in Cubism, Futurism and Suprematism)*, c.1925.

impact of aerial photographs on Malevich complemented the influence of these various stimuli and may even have reinforced them and so encouraged Malevich to develop objectless painting.

The visual starting points for this hypothesis are two sets of images that Malevich produced in 1926–7. Both sets were connected with the artist's visit to Germany in Spring 1927. Before leaving Leningrad, Malevich prepared his *Analytical Chart No. 16* (Figure 6.1). In this, he presented three different selections of images, referring to three different artistic movements: Cubism, Futurism and Suprematism. He linked Cubism to the world of interiors, exhibitions and the new architecture, while firmly associating Futurism with urban life and the world of machinery, locomotives and zeppelins. In contrast, he connected Suprematism with the world of the aeroplane, the sensation of flying, as well as the new views that could be produced from the air and the world as experienced from it. There are ten images relating to Suprematism, and of these seven are aerial photographs, taken from different positions and angles in space. Six of these photographs represent various urban conurbations and a causeway, while one is a photograph of the desert taken at an angle as if coming into land.

Using a different selection of images, Malevich reinforced and elaborated the importance of this association between Suprematism and the aerial view in his Bauhaus book of 1927, *Die Gegenstandlose Welt,* which is usually translated as *The Non-Objective World,* but might equally be rendered as *The Objectless World.* This text included an extraordinary set of images, displayed across two pages, which Malevich described as 'the environment ("reality") that stimulates the Suprematist'.[3] This environment consists of eight photographs in all: four aerial photographs of cities (Figure 6.2 [figs. 28–30] and Figure 6.3 [fig. 31]), three photographs of aeroplanes flying (Figure 6.3 [figs. 32–4]), and one of a large number of aeroplanes on the ground (Figure 6.3 [fig. 35]). Of the aerial photographs, two are taken at a slight angle to the ground (*c.*60°), while two are taken directly from above the earth. One of these (Figure 6.3 [fig. 31]) is clearly of some kind of fortress; the other (Figure 6.2 [fig. 28]) is marked with lines and Latin letters, evidently intended to identify certain structures.

These two sets of images pose an important question. Was Malevich's connection of Suprematism with aerial photography simply an afterthought, a later explanation, made to appeal to the Germans, who belonged to one of the most highly developed industrial nations in Europe? Or was it authentic? Had these images, or ones like them, actually inspired Malevich in May 1915, when he had first developed the pictorial language of Suprematism? In this chapter, I shall try to answer this question.

Perhaps the first point that should be made is that Malevich could have known about aerial photographs in 1915. Although, as far as we are aware, Malevich never experienced the aerial image at first hand and never actually flew in an aeroplane, aerial photographs had been published in the Russian press ever since the Wright brothers' flying demonstrations in France in 1908. The 'craze for aeronautics', which Wassily Kandinsky observed in Western Europe, was equally marked in St Petersburg and Moscow.[4] During World War I, air power proliferated, and air reconnaissance became a vital element of military strategy. Aerial photographs acquired great importance. They also elicited a great deal of interest in Russian creative circles. In 1914, the writer and critic Ivan Aksenov wrote excitedly that aerial photographs 'introduce the most unexpected combinations of surface with axes and [...] create unprecedented visual sensations'.[5]

Given that Malevich could have known of these images and that they were beginning to be of artistic interest, how might they have stimulated him? One possible and obvious answer is that they provided an utterly new perspective on the real world, producing completely different views of existing reality. As can be

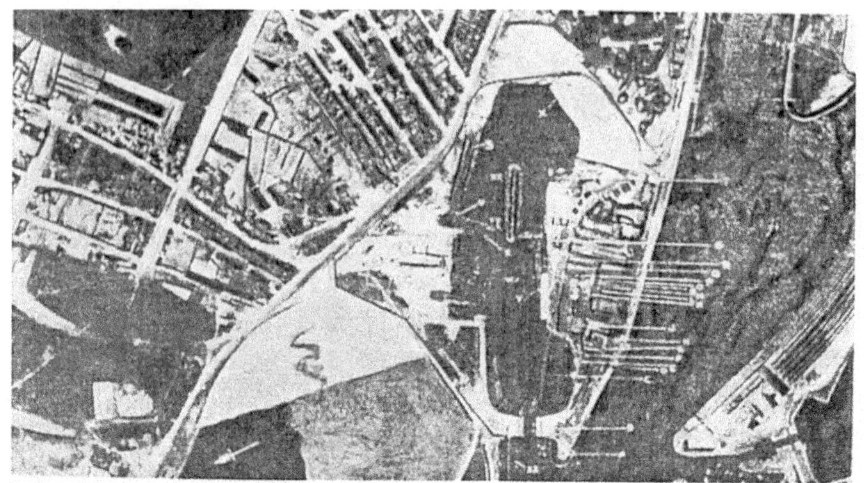

28

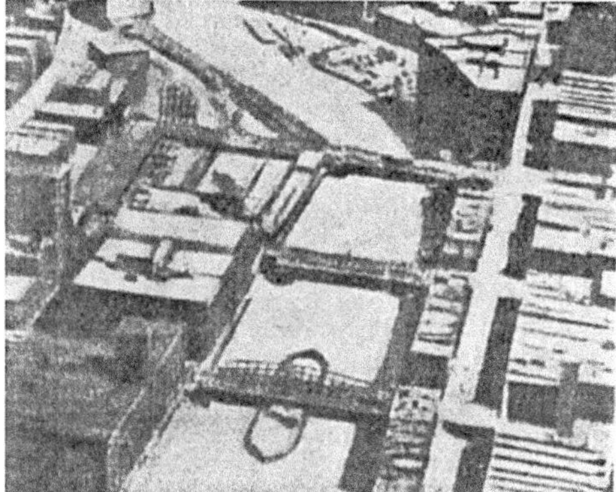

29

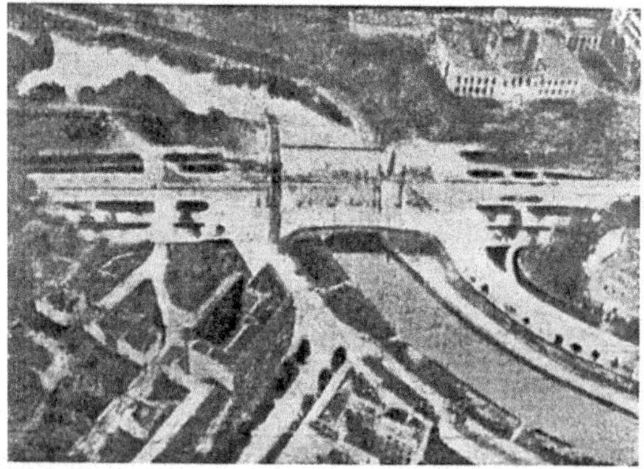

30

[6.2] Malevich, *Die Inspirierende Umgebund ('Realitat') des Suprematisten.*

31

32

33

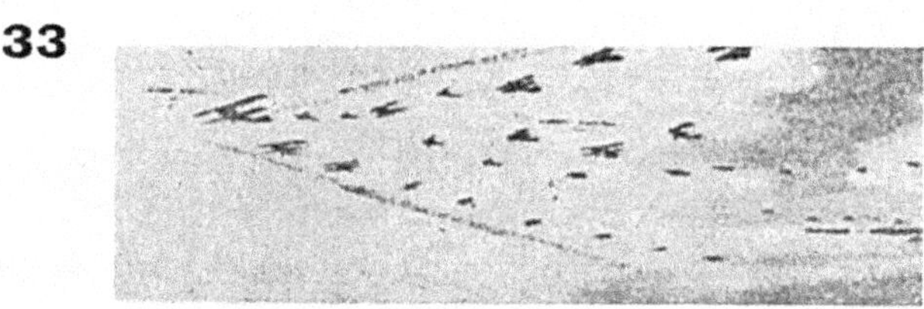

34

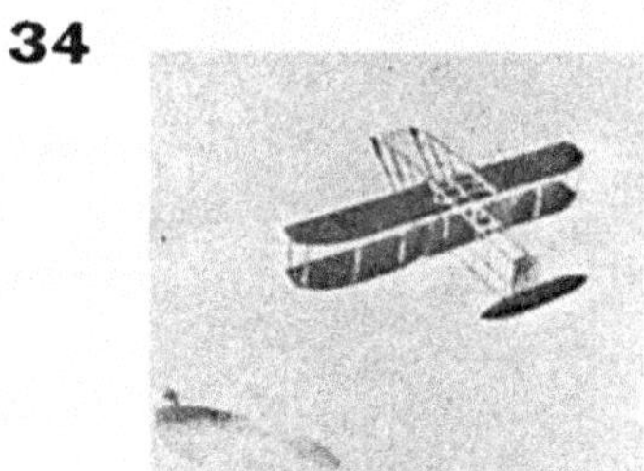

35

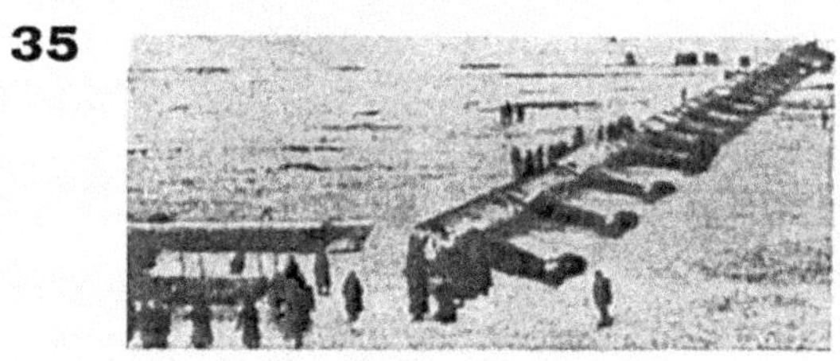

[6.3] Malevich, *Die Inspirierende Umgebund ('Realitat') des Suprematisten.*

seen from the images of urban complexes, the aerial view simplified the structures on the ground making them virtually unrecognisable. As Malevich stated: 'Forms appear as distant transformations of the idea of objects.'[6] The aerial view was rooted in reality, but it was also removed from that reality as experienced by the person on the ground. Aerial photographs de-familiarise the object, stripping it of its three-dimensional earthly identity, and allowing it to become a two-dimensional element.

The technique of de-familiarisation was subsequently identified by Russian formalist critics, notably Viktor Shklovsky in an article 'Art as Technique', which was published in Moscow in 1917.[7] Shklovsky coined the term *ostranenie,* which can be translated as making strange or estrangement, but can equally be rendered with neologisms like de-familiarisation or enstrangement, and was clearly invented to describe the process that endows an image or object with strangeness by removing it from conventional linguistic or visual perceptions.[8] He argued that the technique of de-familiarisation was essential in order to create a special perception or vision of an object. For him, it was this vision, rather than the object itself or its meaning, that was central to the aesthetic experience. He wrote:

> The technique of art is to make objects 'unfamiliar', to make forms difficult, to increase the difficulty and length of perception, because the process of perception is an aesthetic end in itself and must be prolonged. *Art is a way of experiencing the artfulness of an object; the object itself is not important.*[9]

Shklovsky's article appeared more than a year after Malevich had publicly launched Suprematism, but there is no doubt that Malevich would have been aware of this type of thinking. Avant-garde artists and theorists comprised a fairly close-knit group at this time. Malevich himself was very friendly with Roman Jakobson, who was working with Shklovsky in Opoyaz, the literary circle in Moscow. Malevich felt such a strong affinity with Jakobson that he proposed that they visit Paris together, so that he could show his paintings and Jakobson could lecture on their meaning.[10] In summer 1915, Malevich even allowed the literary theorist to visit him in the village of Kunstevo, just outside Moscow, where he was working on his new Suprematist canvases in great secrecy.[11] From Jakobson's memoirs, it is clear that they discussed current literary theories, including *zaum,* and as early as 1913 talked about the move from figurative to objectless painting. Jakobson summarised Malevich's position:

> There was not an abyss between these two concepts. It was a question of a non-representational relation to representationality and of a representational

> relation to non-representational thematics – to the thematics of surface, colour and space. And this corresponded profoundly [...] to my thoughts regarding [...] language, poetry and poetic language.[12]

As Jakobson explained, both men were interested in the structure of the media in which they were working, and were committed to exploring the creative potential of those media in order to develop new languages and meanings. While *zaum* entailed a creative deconstruction of language and narrative into sounds, neologisms and nonsense verse, Malevich was at this time experimenting with Cubo-Futurism and Alogism and subsequently Suprematism, which was predicated on a creative deconstruction of the elements of painting.

In the context of Malevich's experiments, the aerial view might have encouraged the impulse towards deconstruction, simplification and geometricisation. As images, the aerial photographs of cities possess a strange and compelling geometry, which gives the viewer a totally new perspective on the city. We normally walk in the streets and are unable to see the city as a whole. Our visual impressions consist of individual buildings, shop windows, roads, boulevards, squares and pavements. Malevich himself presented such a composite image in *The Englishman in Moscow,* an Alogist painting of 1915 (Figure 6.4). Alogism or an alogical style of painting, which deliberately discarded narrative coherence and conventional logic in the structuring of space and volume, was the manner in which Malevich was painting just before he developed Suprematism and corresponds to what he described as 'a non-representational relation to representationality'.[13] The chronological proximity of the two styles is evident in X-rays of the *Black Quadrilateral* (1915, George Costakis Collection, Thessaloniki), which indicate that the Suprematist composition was painted directly over part of an Alogist composition, without any intervening layer of dust.[14] In *Englishman in Moscow,* Malevich had tried (amongst other aims) to present a mental picture of the urban experience, bringing together various components of the interior and exterior life of the city and its inhabitants (for instance, a diminutive church is juxtaposed with an enormous candle, a fish and a sabre). But the painting is cluttered, and the different objects vie for attention. They do not clarify our vision of reality, but confuse it.[15]

What the aerial photograph does is remove that detail. It gives us an image of the whole. It is a realistic image of the city's totality, but at the same time, one that is completely new and unfamiliar. It is the map of the city made concrete and tangible, in which the various urban structures have become a series of almost abstract elements. The further away the camera, the more abstract the images are, becoming, in Malevich's words 'distant transformations of the idea of objects'.[16] In the largest photograph that Malevich included in the

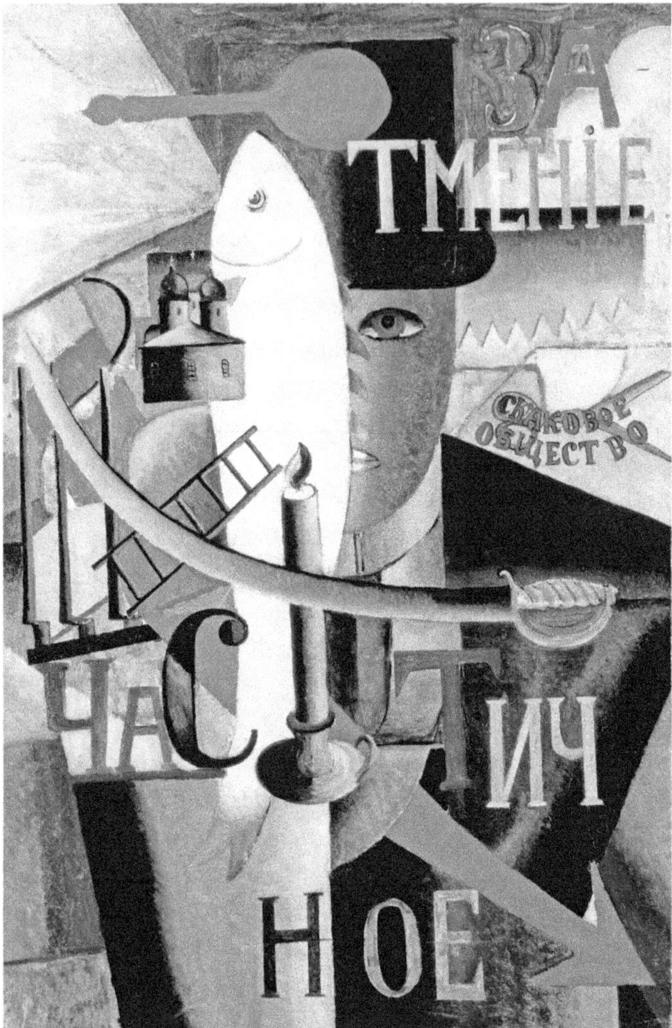

[6.4] Malevich, *Englishman in Moscow*, 1914.

'environment that stimulates the Suprematist' (Figure 6.2 [fig. 28]), the identity of the individual shapes is lost and subsumed within the overall structure. The flattening properties of the black and white of the photographs undoubtedly intensify this effect. The aerial view represents a new perception of existing 'reality' and it is a reality, the perception of which is only made possible by the new technology of the aeroplane.

In the text that Malevich wrote to accompany the launch of his new style in 1915, he wrote:

> It [i.e. academic painting] diverts young forces from the contemporary stream of life, thereby demoralizing them,
>
> Their bodies fly in aeroplanes, but art and life are covered with the old robes of Neros and Titans.
>
> Thus they are unable to see the new beauty of our modern life.
>
> [...]
>
> The new life of iron and the machine, the roar of automobiles, the glitter of electric lights, the whirring of propellers, have awakened the soul which was stifling in the catacombs of ancient reason, and has emerged on the roads woven between earth and sky.
>
> If all artists could see the crossroads of these celestial paths, if they could comprehend these monstrous runways and the weaving of our bodies with the clouds in the sky, they would not paint chrysanthemums.[17]

The way in which Malevich perceived the essence of this new reality is brought out particularly well if 'the environment that stimulates the Suprematist' is compared with 'the environment that stimulates the Futurist' (Figure 6.5). Both relate to contemporary technology: the Futurist environment consists of trains, airships, ocean liners, trams, searchlights, busy city streets, while all the components of the Suprematist environment are rooted in the aeroplane. There is no doubt that Malevich associated Suprematism with the latest technology. But the difference between these two composite images is striking. The Futurist environment is very material – the focus is on the actual products of contemporary technology, their structural details and precise features. In contrast, the Suprematist environment is far less about the actual objects and more about the sensations that are generated by this new technology, and the new view of reality that they reveal, including the aerial view.

A third way in which aerial photographs may have fostered the non-objective style of Suprematism lies precisely in this apparent abstraction of the image. At the time, there was a great deal of debate about the possibility of abstraction. Wassily Kandinsky's text *Concerning the Spiritual in Art*, which had been published in 1912 in Germany, had been delivered in Russia at the Congress of Russian Artists held in St Petersburg during December 1911. In late 1914, just before Malevich developed Suprematism, the text was published in the Congress's proceedings.[18] Kandinsky was concerned to combat materialism through the spiritual content of his painting, but highlighted the danger of abstraction degenerating into pure decoration and losing meaning altogether. Malevich may have had similar reservations. Aerial images of the kind that he chose to reproduce in his Bauhaus book of 1927 might have helped him to overcome these anxieties. In this context, the aerial view provided an interesting

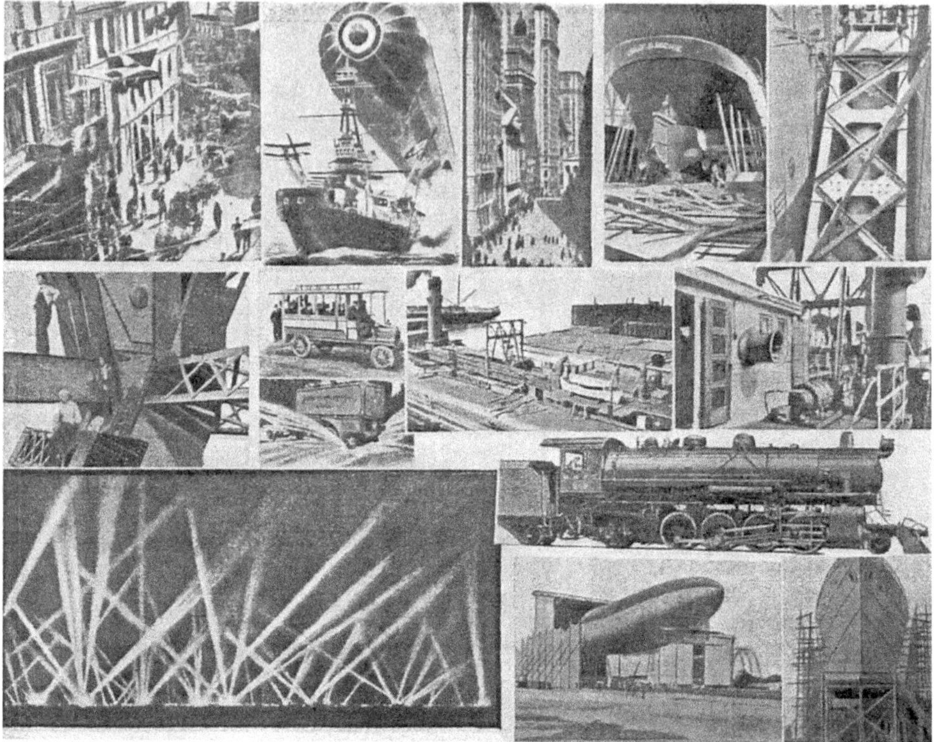

[6.5] Malevich, *Die Inspirirende Umgebund ('Realitat') des Futuristen.*

paradigm and a practical example of the process of abstracting from reality or de-materialising reality; it reduced the complex building or conglomeration of buildings to an abstracted sign or series of signs, which lost their specific identity, creating a new totality or configuration, which at the same time embodied a new vision of reality. In this respect, the aerial view may have encouraged or even facilitated Malevich's move into Suprematism.

Yet when Malevich launched Suprematism in December 1915 he did not connect it with aerial imagery at all or *zaum*, but linked it explicitly with three main ideas: the icon, the fourth dimension and the reality of the elements of painting itself. How did aerial imagery connect with these ideas? I should like to suggest that the aerial view tended to reinforce rather than compete with or undermine these ideas.

First, Malevich positioned his *Black Quadrilateral*, better known today as the *Black Square* across the corners of a room, in the position that the icon was hung in a Russian Orthodox home (Figure 6.6). He thus deliberately connected it with a metaphysical and spiritual truth. He called his *Black Square* 'The icon of

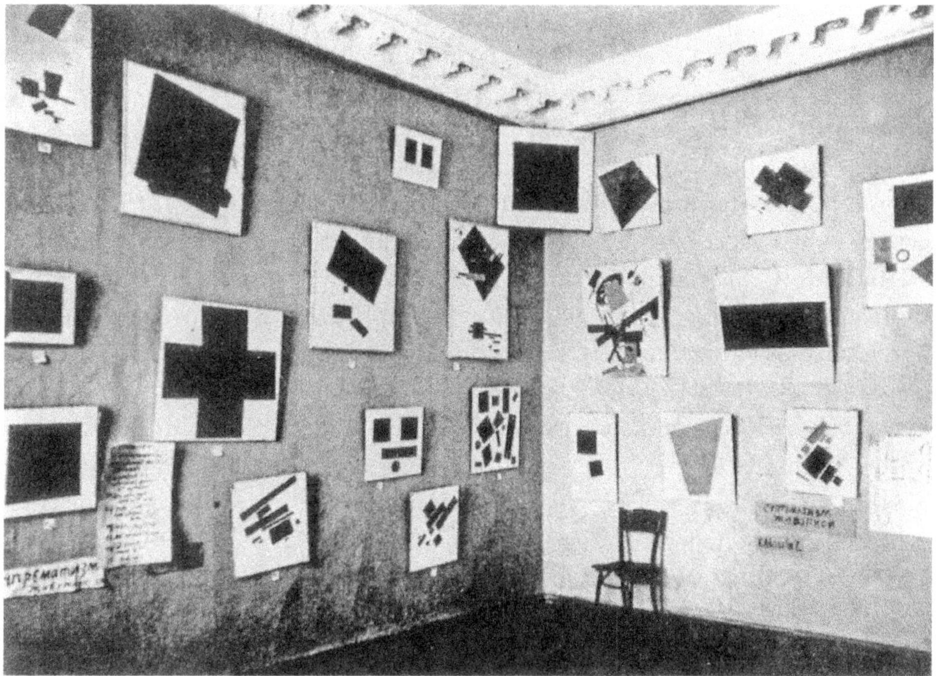

[6.6] Installation photograph of the *Last Futurist Exhibition of Painting 0.10 (Zero Ten)* showing Malevich's Suprematist paintings.

our times'.[19] His action was not lost on his contemporaries, including the artist and critic Alexandre Benois who attacked him for the sacrilege and arrogance of his action.[20] Yet the action was double-edged. While Malevich may have been challenging traditional spirituality, he was also emulating it and harnessing the power of that spirituality to his own work.

At first sight, this reference to the icon seems to have precious little to do with the aerial photograph. The icon did not describe earthly reality, but evoked a higher, transcendental reality. It communicated a spiritual truth and was a direct path to that truth. It produced an earthly image of a heavenly reality, while the aerial photograph produced a view of the earth from the heavens. Yet there are parallels. Both the icon painter and the aerial photographer are elevated above the material world: physically in terms of the photographer – and spiritually in terms of the icon painter. In order to take an aerial photograph, the photographer had to be 'airborne' and thus raised above the detail and trivia that interfered with perceptions of reality on the ground. He could see and experience reality in a different way. The icon painter was equally removed from mundane reality by means of his spiritual enlightenment. He was in touch with a higher reality and responsible for manifesting that reality to his fellow men.

It was clearly no accident that the term that Malevich adopted to describe his new non-objective style was 'Suprematism'. This indicated that it was the supreme form of art and as such distilled an artistic truth. In 1915, Malevich wrote to his close friend and confidante, the artist and musician, Mikhail Matiushin, 'I think that the name Suprematism is the most suitable because it denotes supremacy.'[21] By presenting his *Black Square* as an icon, Malevich was also presenting himself as a spiritually enlightened individual. Although in some ways he was an arch modernist, he had grown up with Symbolism. Some of his earliest works were Symbolist. In one, he depicted himself among a throng of saintly figures, standing out among them.[22] By 1918, he was admitting that he saw himself as a prophet, proclaiming to the world the new objectless truth of Suprematism.[23]

Aerial photographs were taken in an aeroplane from which the pilot, passengers and photographer were able to look down on the people and objects below. They had overcome the physical limitations of gravity and the normal physiological limitations of human eyesight. Like the icon painter who had spiritual vision, they had extended their gaze. Instead of the limited 'ground-based' view, hemmed in by buildings or physical obstructions, they were now able to adopt this god-like view from above the fray. The aerial view gave man the sense of being an Olympian figure, elevating him almost to the status of God. In this respect, therefore, the aerial photograph, like the icon, gave the viewer access to another realm of experience, the sensation of which both types of image sought to convey.

This sense of communicating a normally unattainable truth and a new vision of reality was also evident in the connection that Malevich made between Suprematism and the fourth dimension in the titles that he gave to some of his early Suprematist paintings. Four of his thirty-nine exhibits at *The Last Futurist Exhibition. Zero Ten (0.10)* in December 1915 contained references to the fourth dimension in their titles: *Painterly Realism of a Football Player – Colour Masses in the Fourth Dimension; Painterly Realism of a Boy with Knapsack – Colour Masses in the Fourth Dimension; Automobile and Lady – Colour Masses in the Fourth Dimension;* and *Lady – Colour Masses in Four and Two Dimensions.*[24]

In Russia, Cubism and its pictorial offshoots had been firmly associated with the fourth dimension since early 1913, when Matiushin had connected the two in an important article, written in response to the publication of two Russian translations of Albert Gleizes and Jean Metzinger's *Du 'Cubisme'* (published in Paris in 1912).[25] In his article, printed in the *Union of Youth Journal*, in March

1913, Matiushin combined extended extracts from *Du 'Cubisme'* with long quotations from Peter Ouspensky's writings on hyperspace philosophy, notably *Tertium Organum.*[26] Matiushin declared, 'Cubism has raised the banner of the New Measure – of the new doctrine of the merging of time and space.'[27] The quotes that he chose to take from *Tertium Organum* emphasised the role that art could play in promoting a new perception of the world, and included statements like: 'Art advances in the vanguard of psychic evolution';[28] and

> At the present stage of our development, we possess nothing so powerful as art to be an instrument for understanding the world of causes [...]
>
> The artist must be a *clairvoyant*: he must see that which others do not see; he must be a magician; he must possess the power to make others see what they do not see themselves, but what he does see.[29]

Such statements complemented the quotations from *Du 'Cubisme'* and served to make a firm connection between art – particularly Cubism – and the fourth dimension. Malevich would naturally have read his friend's article. Moreover, the two artists and the poet Aleksei Kruchenykh (who with Velimir Khlebnikov had invented *zaum*) spent some weeks together during the summer of 1913, collaborating on the Futurist opera *Victory over the Sun* which was performed in St Petersburg in December 1913 and for which Malevich produced the sets and costumes. There is little doubt that notions of the fourth dimension were one of the subjects that was discussed by the trio.[30]

For Ouspensky, 'the sphere of three dimensions' was simply 'a section of higher space' and the three-dimensional world was an illusion: 'we are in error in thinking that a three-dimensional body is in itself something real. It is the projection of the four-dimensional body – its picture – the image of it *on our plane.*' [31] He considered that '*this world is the world beyond perceived strangely*',[32] which could only be grasped by a person who possessed a higher state of consciousness. Ouspensky made an analogy between flight (in this instance in a balloon) and the way that man's consciousness could rise above the plane of mundane reality on which it normally operated and overcome conventional notions of time and space:

> Our usual psychic life proceeds upon some definite plane (of consciousness or matter) and never rises above it. If our receptivity could rise above this plane, it would undoubtedly perceive *simultaneously,* below itself, a far greater number of events than it usually sees while on a plane. Just as a man, ascending a mountain, or going up in a balloon, begins to see *simultaneously* and at once many things which it is impossible to see *simultaneously* and *at once* from

> below – the movement of two trains ... two cities divided by a ridge, etc – so consciousness rising above the plane in which it usually functions, must see simultaneously the events divided for ordinary consciousness by *periods of time.*[33]

To a certain extent aerial photographs represent the visual embodiments of this experience. If flight in an aeroplane (or balloon) and the dizzying perspective from which the pilot, passenger and aerial photographer view mundane reality can be regarded as analogous to perceiving the fourth dimension, then the visual trace of this – the aerial photograph – might also be regarded as capturing some elements of the experience of the fourth dimension.

Theorists of the fourth dimension argued that one could catch a glimpse of a four-dimensional body through motion or when it passed through our three-dimensional reality, when it would be seen as a series of segments of a larger body of shifting profile and shape. They used analogies with how a hypothetical two-dimensional being would perceive a three-dimensional body as sections passing through two-dimensional space.[34] Several art historians have convincingly applied this theory to Malevich's Suprematist painting.[35] By flattening three-dimensional reality, it could be argued that aerial photographs themselves provided a visual analogy with the way in which four dimensions could be perceived by a three-dimensional being. From this point of view, it could be argued that in aerial photographs, man had already thrown off the 'fetters of "three-dimensional" logic' and was thus able to perceive a higher, multi-dimensional reality.[36]

Finally, Malevich called Suprematism 'the new pictorial realism' and presented it to the public as such in his seminal text of 1915, *From Cubism to Suprematism: The New Pictorial Realism,* which was published in a revised version in 1916 as *From Cubism and Futurism to Suprematism: The New Pictorial Realism.*[37] Of course, realism for Malevich was not connected with naturalistic styles of painting or descriptive figuration in art, but had a dual importance, embodying a need to convey some perception of reality beyond superficial appearances as well as a need to accept the reality of what a painting was – a two-dimensional surface to which pigments were applied. He wrote:

> The artist can be a creator only when the forms in his pictures have nothing in common with nature.
>
> For art is the ability to construct, not on the inter-relationship of forms and colour, and not on an aesthetic basis of beauty in composition, *but on the basis of weight, speed and the direction of movement.*[38]

Such criteria seem remote from the aerial view. Yet it could be argued that the aerial photographs supplied a visual paradigm to suggest how an object might be perceived as it moves in space and time and thus how it could embody speed and direction. It also destroyed conventional perspective, flattened reality and reinforced the two-dimensionality of the printed photograph. From the air, objects are reduced to their essential geometry. And this is exactly what Malevich did in Suprematism. He reduced objects to (or transformed them into) a geometric configuration.

Malevich stated 'Suprematism is a new non-objective system of relations between elements through which sensations are expressed.'[39] If the way aerial photographs abstracted reality provided one connection between the aeroplane and Suprematism, the new sensation of space that was conveyed by the photographs of aeroplanes in flight provided another. The images (Figure 6.3 [figs. 32, 33 and 34]) demonstrate the way that aircraft enabled man to overcome gravity and his natural, earth-bound limitations and become a spatial element, moving freely in space and being entirely surrounded by it. In other words, the aeroplane made it possible for space to become a new and real medium of human experience. I would like to propose that it is precisely this new 'sensation of space', as manifest in such photographs, that inspired Malevich in the process of developing the pictorial language of his Suprematist paintings. Is it any accident that Malevich chose white grounds to denote space? He deliberately rejected the notion of space as the blue of the sky, instead emulating the white that the sky took on in black and white aerial photographs.

In fact, there is a very strong relationship between the kind of imagery encountered in aerial photographs and specific Suprematist compositions. Charlotte Douglas, for instance, has shown that *Suprematism* (1915; Figure 6.7) is based on a study that Malevich executed earlier that year for inclusion in a new edition of the libretto for the Futurist opera, *Victory Over the Sun* of 1913 (Figure 6.8).[40] Aeroplanes had played an important role in the opera, as Kruchenykh acknowledged: 'The basic theme of the spectacle was the defence of technology, in particular aviation, and the victory of technology over cosmic forces and biologism.'[41] Malevich's drawing, which is now in the Literary Museum in Moscow, indicates the events of an air battle and is annotated in line with aerial photographs of military encounters.[42] He described the drawing in the following terms to his friend Matiushin: 'The monster (just like a louse) is supposed to run over the sun: it can absorb fire, and by eliminating the sun's combustion, it [achieves] a complete victory.'[43] The writing on the drawing indicates features like 'Луна 50,00 А ш' (Luna [The Moon] 50,00 Arshin) and 'огонъ' (ogon [Fire]).[44] The relationship between the two works acquires an added importance and resonance, because Aleksandra Shatskikh

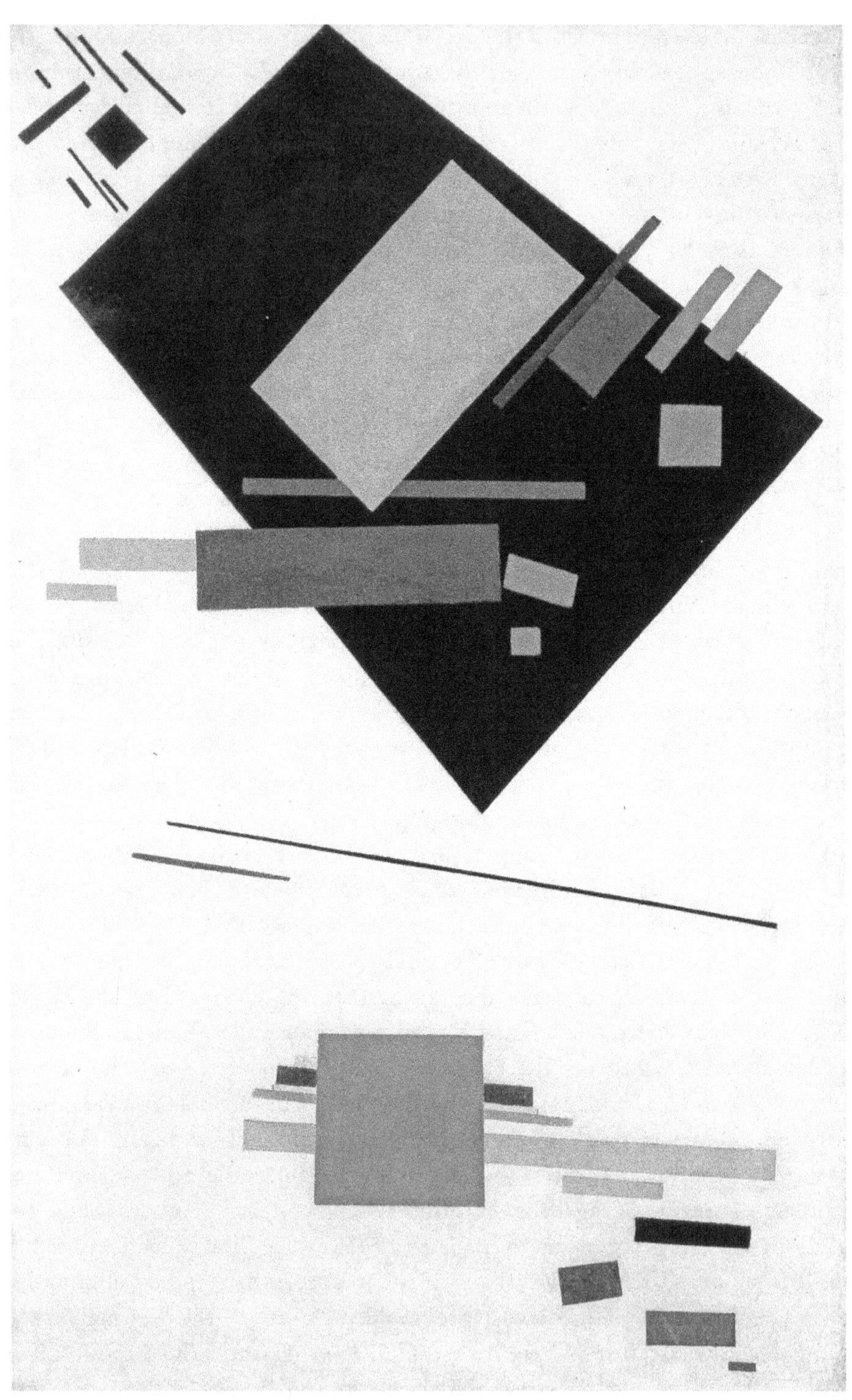

[6.7] Malevich, *Suprematism*, 1915.

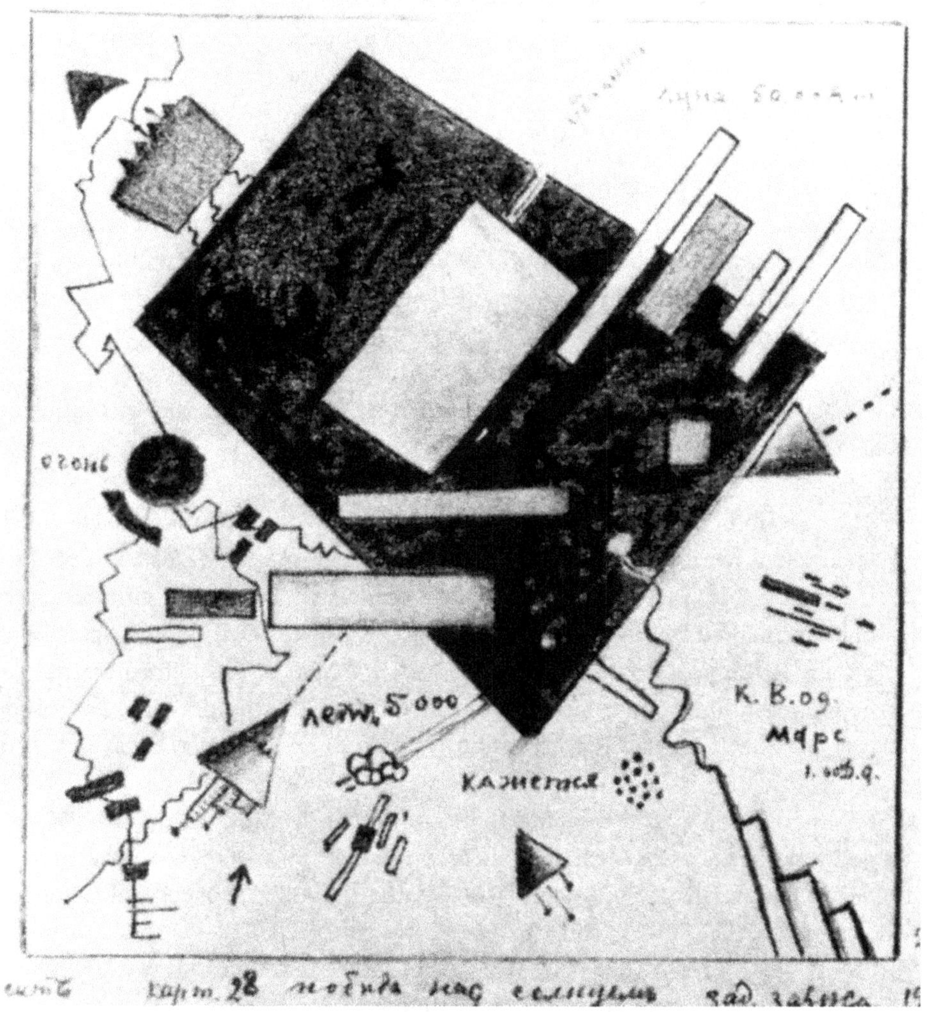

[6.8] Malevich, Stage Design for *Victory over the Sun*, 1915.

has argued that the painting that is based on this drawing may have actually been Malevich's first Suprematist painting.[45] She identifies the drawing as being similar to another sketch (tidied up and without the lettering) that Malevich sent to Matiushin and referred to in his letter of 27 May 1915:

> I would be very grateful if you could include my one drawing of the curtain in the act where the victory took place. I have discovered one project and find that it needs to be placed in the book [...] This drawing will have a great significance for painting. That which was done subconsciously now bears extraordinary fruit.[46]

In a subsequent letter, which accompanied the drawing on its way to Matiushin, Malevich wrote,

> The curtain depicts a black square, the embryo of all potentials – [one which] takes on a terrible strength as it develops. It is the father of the cube and the sphere, and in painting its dissociations bear a wonderful culture. In the opera it marked the beginning of the victory. A great deal that was created by me in [19]13 [for] your opera *Victory over the Sun* has brought me a mass of new [ideas], but nobody noticed [...] It was here, in the drawings for *Victory over the Sun* that the final transition towards Suprematism was made.[47]

Unfortunately the actual drawing that was sent to Matiushin has not yet been found, although it was probably closely related to one that is now part of the Khardzhiev-Chaga Art Foundation at the Stedelijk Museum, Amsterdam, which is inscribed 'Backdrop, second scene the act of the very victory over the sun.'[48] Apart from this inscription above the image, the drawing does not contain any of the verbal, literary or numerical references that are present in the annotated drawing. It may have been from this later, pared down and purified, drawing that Malevich painted one of his earliest, if not the first, Suprematist canvases.[49] The position that the painting occupied, next to the *Black Square* at the *Zero-Ten* exhibition that launched the new style, certainly seems to confirm Shatskikh's hypothesis, reinforcing the notion of its special importance and suggesting that there was a very direct and crucial relationship between aerial photography and the genesis of Suprematism.

The interrelationship between the various stimuli that inspired Malevich and the role of the aerial photograph can be explored further. For instance, one might speculate that the substitution of the *Black Square* for the radiance of the icon might also be related to *Victory over the Sun*. The gilded radiance of the icon is intended to envelop the devotee in its emanation of divine

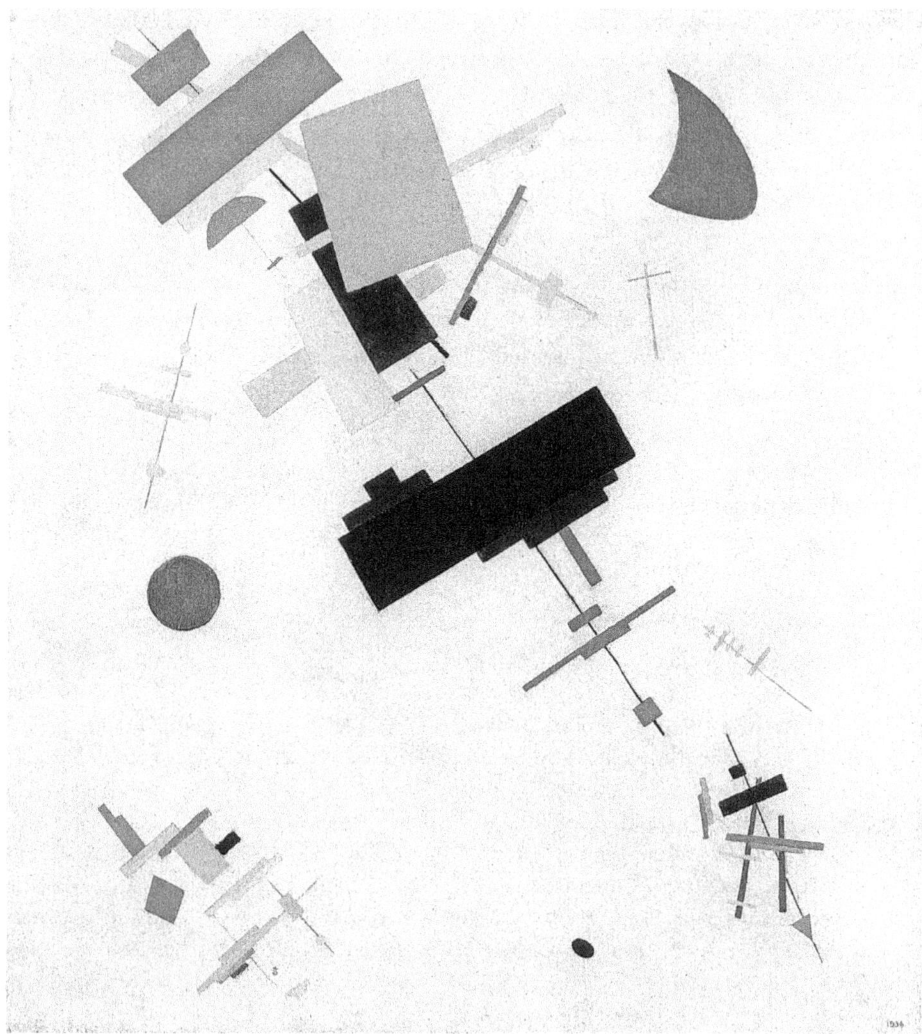

[6.9] Malevich, *Supremus No. 56*, 1916.

light.[50] The *Black Square* – with black representing the pure, non-reflective absorption of light – radically cancels this. From this perspective, the black square seems to play the role of the 'louse' that 'absorbs fire' and eliminates 'the sun's combustion', as it does in the set design for the opera.[51] Of course, to do this it has to climb into the sky and be 'liberated from the weight of the Earth's gravitation', which equates with the elevated corner position of the traditional icon from which it – like the sun – radiates its light downward.[52]

Subsequently the emphasis on flight, space and weightlessness in Malevich's work became more pronounced. Allusions to boys with knapsacks and football players were soon dropped. Malevich simply began to provide titles relating to sensations or to number his works, as in *Supremus No. 56* of 1916 (Figure 6.9). Such paintings were orchestrated to evoke the sensation of experiencing space and culminated in the White on White paintings of 1918. In the summer of 1916, Malevich confided to Matiushin:

> The keys of Suprematism led me to discover what had not yet been realized. My new painting does not belong to the Earth exclusively. The Earth has been abandoned like a house infested with termites. And in fact, in man, in his consciousness, there is a striving toward space. An urge to take off from the Earth.[53]

In feeding that aspiration, the aerial view seems to have played its part.

NOTES

1 J. Centnerszwer, 'Wystawa prof. K. Malewicza (Polski Klub Artystyczny)', *Nasz Przegląd*, 86 (1927): 8; reprinted in Andrzej Turowski, *Malewicz w Warszawe: Rekonstrukcje i Symulacje* (Cracow: Universitas, 2002), p.463.

2 See, for instance, Charlotte Douglas, *Swans of Other Worlds: Kazimir Malevich and the Origins of Abstraction in Russia* (Ann Arbor: UMI Research Press, 1980); and Linda Dalrymple Henderson, *The Fourth Dimension and Non-Euclidean Geometry in Modern Art* (Princeton: Princeton University Press, 1983), pp.274–94. 'Beyonsense' has been coined to convey the essence of the Russian neologism *zaum*. See Velimir Khlebnikov, *The King of Time: Poems, Fictions, Visions of the Future*, trans. Paul Schmidt, ed. Charlotte Douglas (Cambridge, MA and London: Harvard University Press, 1985), p.3.

3 Kazimir Malevich, *Die Gegenstandslose Welt* (Munich: Albert Langen, 1927); English translation, *The Non-Objective World* (New York: Paul Theobald and Company, 1959), p.25, caption to plates 28–35.

4 Wassily Kandinsky 'Footnotes to Schoenberg's "On Parallel Octaves and Fifths", *Salon 2*, Odessa, 1910–1911', in Kenneth C. Lindsay and Peter Vergo, eds, *Kandinsky: Complete Writings on Art* (London: Faber and Faber, 1982), p.94.

5 Ivan Aksenov, *Pikasso i okrestnosti* (Moscow: Tsentrifuga, 1914).

6 Centnerszwer, op. cit., p.463.

7 Viktor Shklovskii, 'Iskusstvo kak priem', *Sborniki II* (Moscow 1917); English translation in *Russian Formalist Criticism: Four Essays*, trans. and ed. Lee T. Lemon and Marion J. Reis (Lincoln, NE: University of Nebraska Press, 1965), pp.3–24.

8 For a discussion of possible translations of *ostranenie* and its meaning, see Benjamin Sher, 'Translator's Introduction', in Viktor Shklovsky, *Theory of Prose*, trans. Benjamin Sher, intro. Gerald L. Bruns (Elmwood Park, IL: Dalkey Archive Press, 1990), pp.xviii–xix.

9 Shklovskii, op. cit.

10 Roman Jakobson, *My Futurist Years*, ed. Bengt Jangfeldt and Stephen Rudy, trans. Stephen Rudy (New York: Marsilio, 1997), p.23.

11 Ibid, p.24.

12 Ibid, p.23.

13 Ibid.

14 For the *Black Quadrilateral*, see A. Zander Rudenstine, ed., *Russian Avant-Garde Art: The George Costakis Collection* (London: Thames and Hudson, 1981), cat. no. 489. The earlier painting *War* (1915) had been cut down and painted over, as revealed by X-rays. See Maria H. Kokkori, 'A Historical Contextualization of Selected Paintings by Kazimir Malevich, Ivan Kliun and Liubov Popova c. 1905–1925' (London: Courtauld Institute, Ph.D. dissertation, 2007), p.155.

15 See, for instance, Christina Lodder, 'To Infinity and Beyond: Kazimir Malevich, Suprematism and the Aeroplane', in C. Lodder, ed., *Constructive Strands in Russian Art* (London: Pindar Press, 2005), pp.77–111.

16 Centnerszwer, op. cit., p.463.

17 Kazimir Malevich, *Ot kubizma i futurizma k suprematizmu. Novyi zhivopisnyi realism* (Moscow, 1916); English translation in Kazimir Malevich, *Essays on Art 1915–1933*, ed. Troels Andersen, trans. Xenia Glowacki-Prus and Arnold McMillan, 1 (London: Rapp and Whiting and André Deutsch, 1971), pp.21, 29.

18 V. V. Kandinskii, 'O dukhovnom v iskusstve', *Trudy Vserossiiskago s'ezda khudozhnikov v Petrograde, dekabr' 1911-yanvar' 1912gg* [Transactions of the All-Russian Congress of Artists in Petrograd, December 1911 – January 1912] (Petrograd: Golike and Vilborg, 1914), 1, pp.47–76.

19 Kazimir Malevich, letter to A. N. Benua, May 1916; reprinted in *Malevich o sebe. Sovremenniki o Maleviche. Pis'ma. Dokumenty. Vospominaniia. Kritika*, ed. I. A. Vakar and T. I. Mikhienko (Moscow: RA, 2004), 1, p.85.

20 Aleksandr Benua, 'Poslednaia futuristicheskaia vystavka', *Rech'* (9 January 1916).

21 Malevich, letter to Mikhail Matiushin, 24 September 1915; reprinted in Vakar and Mikhienko, *Malevich o sebe*, 1, p.69; cited by Evgenii Kovtun, 'The Beginning of Suprematism', trans. John E. Bowlt, in *Kazimir Malewitsch zum 100. Geburtstag* (Cologne: Galerie Gmurzynska, 1978), p.207.

22 See Malevich, *Study for a Fresco Painting (Self-Portrait)*, 1907, tempera on board, 69.3 x 70 cm, State Russian Museum, St Petersburg; reproduced in *Kazimir Malevich* (Leningrad: State Russian Museum, 1988; Moscow: State Tretiakov Gallery, 1988–89; Amsterdam: Stedelijk Museum, 1989), p.32, fig. 13.

23 Varvara Stepanova, diary entry for 8 January 1919, in Varvara Stepanova, *Chelovek ne mozhet zhit' bez chuda* (Moscow: Izdatel'stvo Sfera, 1994), p.62.

24 *Poslednaia futuristicheskaia vystavka kartin 0,10 (nol'-desiat). Katalog* (Petrograd, 1915), nos. 40–41 and 45–46.

25 A. Glez and Zh. Metsanzhe, *O kubizme*, trans. E. Nizen (St Petersburg, 1913); and A. Glez and Zh. Metsanzhe, *O kubizme*, trans. M. Voloshin (Moscow, 1913).

26 Mikhail Matiushin, 'O knige Metzanzhe-Gleza 'Du Cubisme'', *Soiuz molodezhi* (St Petersburg), 3 (March 1913): 25–34; English translation, Matyushin, 'Of the Book by Gleizes and Metzinger *Du Cubisme*', in Henderson, op. cit., pp.368–75. See P. D. Uspenskii, *Tertium Organum: Kliuch k zagadkam mira* (St Petersburg: Trud, 1911); English translation, P. D. Ouspensky, *Tertium Organum: The Third Canon of Thought: A Key to the Enigmas of the World*, trans. Nicholas Bassaraboff and Claude Bragdon (second edition, London: Kegan Paul, Trench Trubner & Co., 1934).

27 Matiushin, op. cit., p.368.

28 Ibid.; from Ouspensky, op. cit., p.83, where it is given as 'Art anticipates a psychic evolution and divines its future forms.'

29 Ibid., p.370; from Ouspensky, op. cit., pp.161–2.

30 A little later, in August 1913 in his declaration 'New Ways of the Word', Kruchenykh copied, with only minor changes, the second sentence and last sentence of Matiushin's first quote from *Tertium Organum* (op. cit., pp.268–369): 'Art marches in the avant-garde of psychic evolution. At present there are three units in our psychic life; sensation, representation, concept (and the idea) and a fourth unit is beginning to take shape – "higher intuition" (P. Ouspensky's *Tertium Organum*)'; Aleksei Kruchenykh, 'Novye puti slova', *Troe* (St Petersburg, 1913); English translation in *Russian Futurism through Its Manifestoes, 1912–1928*, ed. Anna Lawton (Ithaca and London: Cornell University Press, 1988), p.70.

31 Ouspensky, op. cit., p.52.

32 Ibid, p.145.

33 Ibid, p.48.

34 Ouspensky used these analogies in the first few chapters of *Tertium Organum*.

35 See, Douglas, op. cit. and Henderson, op. cit., pp.274–94.

36 Ouspensky, op. cit., p.216.

37 Malevich, op. cit., 1, pp.19–41.

38 Ibid, 1, p.25.

39 Kazimir Malevich, 'Suprematizm' [Suprematism], *c.*1927, ms, Stedelijk Museum, Amsterdam; English translation in Kazimir Malevich, *The Artist, Infinity, Suprematism: Unpublished Writings 1913–1933*, ed. Troels Andersen, trans. Xenia Hoffmann (Copenhagen: Borgen Forlag, 1978), p.146.

40 See Aleksei Kruchenykh, *Pobeda nad solntsem. Opera v 2 deistvakh 6 kartinakh, muzyka M. V. Matiushina, dekoratsii Kaz. S. Malevicha, prolog Viktor Khlebnikova* (St Petersburg, 1914); English translations, 'Victory over the Sun', trans. Ewa Bartos and Victoria Nes Kirkby, *The Drama Review*, 15(4) (Fall 1971), pp.106–24; 'Victory over the Sun', trans. Evgeny Steineer, in A. Kruchenykh, K. Malevich and M. Matiushin, eds, *A Victory over the Sun Album*, 1 (Forest Row, Sussex: Artists Bookworks, 2009), pp.45–99; Rosamund Bartlett, 'Annotated Translation of the Libretto of Victory over the Sun', in Rosamund Bartlett and Sarah Dadswell, eds, *Victory over the Sun: The World's First Futurist Opera* (Exeter: University of Exeter Press, 2012), pp.19–45.

41 Alexei Kruchenykh, *Our Arrival: From the History of Russian Futurism* (Moscow: RA, 1995), p.67.

42 Charlotte Douglas, *Kazimir Malevich* (London: Thames and Hudson, 1994), p.86.

43 Ibid., p.86.

44 An arshin is an old Russian measurement, equivalent to 71 cm.

45 Aleksandra Shatskikh, 'Malevich, Curator of Malevich', in *The Russian Avant-Garde: Representation and Interpretation* (St Petersburg: Palace Editions, 2001), p.149.

46 Malevich, letter to Mikhail Matiushin [27 May 1915]; reprinted in Vakar and Mikhienko, op. cit., 1, p.66.

47 Malevich, letter to Mikhail Matiushin [beginning of June 1915], reprinted in Vkar and Mikhienko, op. cit., 1, p.67; quoted also in Kovtun, op. cit., p.204.

48 *Kazimir Malevich 1878–1935: Drawings from the collection of the Khardzhiev-Chaga Art Foundation, SMA Cahiers, no. 9* (Amsterdam: Stedelijk Museum, 1997), no. 33. Although previously thought to have been sent to Matiushin, it now transpires this drawing was in Malevich's possession in 1926 when it was catalogued. See Troels Andersen, *K. S. Malevich:*

The Leporskaya Archive (Aarhus: Aarhus University Press, 2012), 135, no. 325, i.e. '16t' according to Malevich's schema. Khardzhiev had acquired some drawings from Matiushin, but this clearly came from Leporskaya.

49 The drawing is inscribed with the measurements of the final painting. See Andersen, op. cit., 135, no. 325. The slight compositional differences between the final painting and the drawing suggest that it may have been a study rather than acting as an *aide memoire* for the painting.

50 Evgenii N. Trubetskoi, *Icons: Theology in Color* (Crestwood, NY: St. Vladimir's Seminary Press, 1973).

51 There is also a relationship between the *Black Square* and the set design for Act Two Scene One in *Victory over the Sun*, which consists simply of a slightly curved white triangle in a dark central box, representing the captured sun. See Douglas, op. cit., pp.45–6.

52 I am profoundly indebted to Mark Dorrian for this observation.

53 Malevich, letter to Mikhail Matiushin [June] 1916, reprinted in Vakar and Mikhienko, op. cit., 1, p.89; and cited by Douglas, op. cit., p.26.

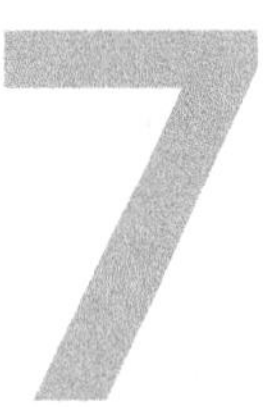

Aerial Views and Cinematism, 1898–1939

Teresa Castro

The history of the aerial view in cinema may be seen as the history of a technical experiment, which coupled the technology of image-making with that of aerial locomotion. It is a history inscribed in the long process of the automation of ways of seeing and the extension of human sight, a process that – since the nineteenth century or earlier – has radically changed our perception of space-time and our modes of vision. It is also the history of a fundamental complicity between the film camera and methods of aerial locomotion, which – as we will see – notably transformed into a quest for 'cine-sensations' of the world, as if aerial vision was itself eminently cinematographic. But cinematographic representation of the aerial view is not solely a matter of vision: due to the movement that constitutes it, often intensified by the film's unwinding speed and the extraordinary mobility of the point of view, it is also a matter of sensation. The feeling of flight is as central to the aerial view as is the enjoyment experienced in observing the earth from an unusual point of view or of visually discovering and dominating it. The particular pleasure of the cinematographic gaze, as far as the aerial view is concerned, lies precisely in the oscillation between visual and kinaesthetic – indeed cenesthetic – perception.

IN THE BEGINNING WAS THE BALLOON: THE AERIAL VIEW AND EARLY CINEMA

Cinematography emerged at a time when the focus was on the conquest of the sky and the emancipation of the gaze from its different types of physical restraints. From the outset the latter displayed an intriguing aerial vocation: as early as 1898, for example, the Lumière Brothers shot a panorama from a captive balloon in an unknown location (View no. 997). The result was a short film that, due to its early production date and affiliation with the Lumière Brothers, acquired an undeniable symbolic value. Three main aspects of this film have been noted as significant: the verticality of the camera angle; the movement both in, and out of, the shot; and the abstraction of space stemming from the disappearance of the horizon-line, whose absence totally eradicates the landscape's conventional dimensions.[1] However, if the verticality of the line of sight was a key feature and distinguished the film from the first efforts of rival production companies (in particular, the Edison Company, who in 1902 shot high-angled views of Chicago from a dirigible balloon), the question of movement was also fundamental, in that the problems of cinematographic aerial vision proved unable to be disassociated from the inter-related couple of perception/sensation. The symbolic importance of this unique film resides in the fact that it reveals, probably for the first time, the concretely kinetic and cenesthetic dimensions of the aerial experience of space. In the 1920s, cinema, with its unprecedented freedom and mobility, became the privileged way of conveying this kind of aerial movement, together with the associated instability of viewpoint.

The verticality of the point of view is at the origin of a strange sort of visual effect, a kind of unique fusion of macroscopic vision and microscopic observation. A well-known optical effect is produced. Contemplating the world from above enables an unprecedented expansion of the field of vision. Aerial vision is thus a macroscopic vision that enables the naked eye to see the extent of a certain territory. Yet the height of the viewpoint is linked to a world that progressively diminishes and loses its characteristic volume. The strictly vertical camera angle flattens and transforms more than any other angle of view, as is seen in the Lumière's View no. 997, where the onlookers are reduced to moving specks, indistinguishable from their shadows. People are turned into 'mass', the world is transformed into a Lilliputian fantasy and the eye acquires Gulliverian dimensions, as seen in a famous lithograph by Odilon Redon (Figures 7.1 and 7.2).

Early cinema has preserved traces of this history that combines the 'I am seeing' of the cinematograph with the 'I am flying' of the flying-machine. The balloon occupies a singular place here, whether in the context of Raoul

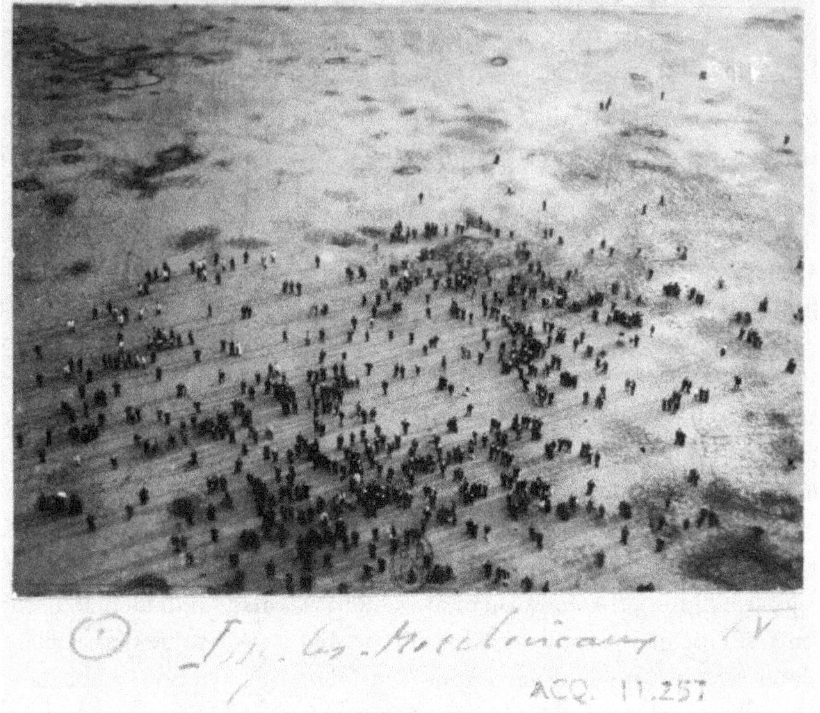

[7.1] View taken from the dirigible Adjudant Vincenot, Issy-les-Moulineaux.

Grimoin-Sanson's Cinéorama scenography, shown at the Exposition Universelle in Paris in 1900, or as part of a set, where balloons were suspended before studio backdrops. However, the domain of balloons and flying-machines is far from being limited to cinematographic representation, but is connected to the wider question of visual culture. The idea dwelt in the febrile imagination of the nineteenth century, before transforming in the first decades of the twentieth into a veritable obsession with images and aeronautic sensations. The aerial iconography of such pre-1914 films as mentioned above are clearly part of a much wider visual context, which included the many images that circulated in publishing and the illustrated press.

Indeed, the film *Les Aventures Extraordinaires de Saturnin Farandoul* (*Le Avventure Straordinarissime di Saturnino Farandola)* (1914) – a series of 18 episodes directed by Marcel Fabre – emerged out of this visual universe. The film features a number of balloons and also shows images that claim to offer the aerial experience, something rarely found in these 'primitive' films for whom the complex and dangerous logistics of an aerostation presented

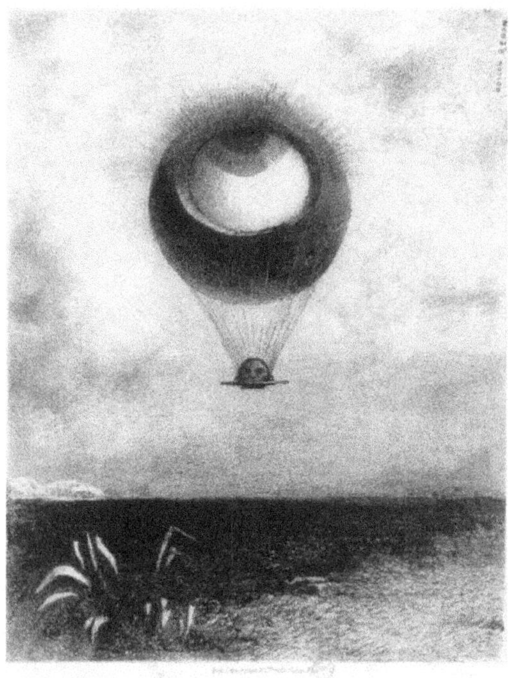

[7.2] Odilon Redon, *L'œil comme un ballon bizarre se dirige vers l'infini*, lithograph, 1882.

insurmountable problems. Three shots magisterially illustrate the endeavour, evoking all the practical difficulties of recreating – in a studio – the radical and exciting effects involved in the height and verticality of the point of view (Figure 7.3). The first of these nicely illustrates the slightly angled vertical point of view that corresponds to Saturnin Farandoul's position leaning out of a dirigible. The angle of the next shot's framing, filmed live, does not correspond to the character's elevated position, yet it is placed in continuity with the first: Farandoul is still looking through his telescope, as the circular mask surrounding the image confirms. The lack of continuity between the shots is striking: in the first, the line of the horizon is absent and the two human figures, literally crushed against the ground (Phileas Fogg's balloon has floundered following a ferocious battle in the sky),[2] evoke the visual effects of verticality that we have already noted in the Lumières' View no. 997. If Farandoul had not been equipped with his telescope, Fogg and his associates would certainly have been reduced to tiny marks on the surface of the earth, as were the onlookers in the Lumière Brothers' film.

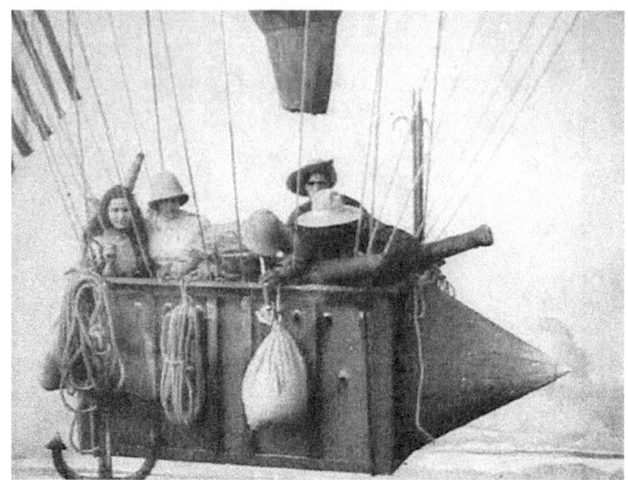

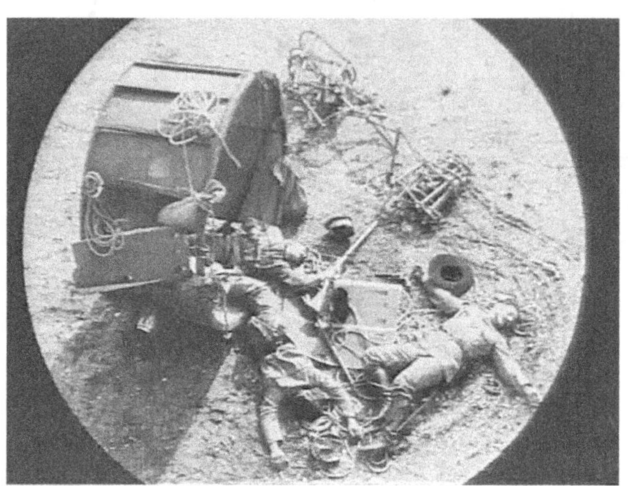

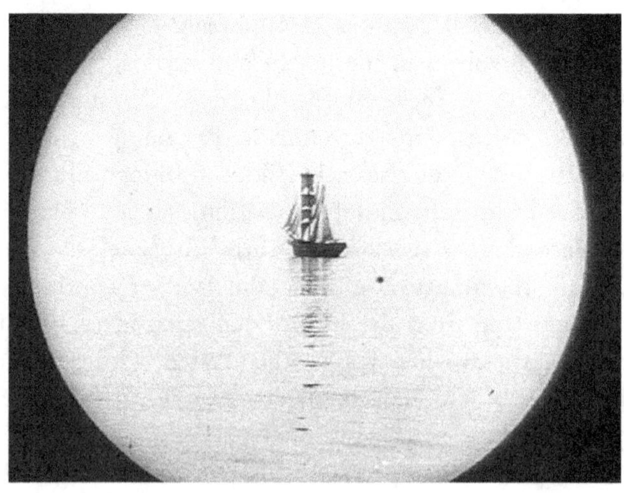

[7.3] Three frames from *Les Aventures Extraordinaires de Saturnin Farandoul*, 1914.

But it is at the heart of non-fiction cinema, particularly after 1914, that the most spectacular and certainly the most significant aerial views are found. Before the war, some camera-operators began to equip airships, then aircraft, with cameras, so as to explore the sensation (typically cinematographic?) of travelling freely through space. In the illustrated press of the time, newsreels attentively followed aviation's progress from the ground, as the weekly publication for the cinematographic industry, *Ciné-Journal,* demonstrates. We find several references, as well as advertisements for 'cinematographic equipment for aviation' ('The Parvo' camera) and images taken from an airship. An article dated 1911, 'Aircraft Cinematography' ('La cinématographie en aéroplane') further attests to the development of aerial cinematography. The author, a certain André Prothin, recounts his filming of a trip from Reims to Mourmelon while on board various mono- and bi-planes. He writes:

> During the course of my flights, I was able to obtain films that are actually very good in terms of their photographic quality, such as their clarity and relief. They are equally as good in terms of their documentary quality, such as visibility, topography and reconnaissance capacity. Yet I was in no way specially equipped. I thus conclude that with slight modification of the usual on-board material, one could do extraordinary things and achieve perfection.[3]

The author goes on to describe his flights in detail and concludes his report with a few practical tips, including advice 'never to take such overly vertical types of shot'.[4] Rather than any radical progress that aerial vision might have facilitated in the field of perception, Prothin was clearly more interested in the conventional panoramic possibilities of such vision, arguing that what distinguished them was their documentary powers, their visibility, their topographic qualities and their evident value for reconnaissance, which is to say their cognitive value. On the horizon of this concept lies a conception of aerial vision that is eminently instrumental and functional, an idea expressed here in relation to its extraordinary expansion of the point of view. In the first decades of the twentieth century, an almost blind and widespread belief in the objectivity of methods of mechanised reproduction – such as photography and cinema – only accentuated the teleological tendency which saw indexical images obtained from the air as the natural replacement for cartographic images. Nevertheless, as Prothin in fact indicates, these indexical images often proved to be less 'readable' than a conventional map. Thus when confronted with Reims cathedral from a strictly vertical line of view, the camera-operator cannot recognise it as such, given that it appears 'in the form of two huge round dining-tables plus another long one'.[5]

1918: *IN AN AIRSHIP OVER THE BATTLEFIELDS*

It was not until the worldwide conflict was over that cinema truly began to show what it could achieve in the field of aerial vision. Naturally, considerable technical progress had been achieved during the course of the war: camera-operators, some of whom had been literally trained in the army, would not forget the lesson in the years to come. One such was Lucien Le Saint who 'managed to attach his camera to the turret of his machine-gun and thus benefited from an ideal "field of fire" and an incomparable flexibility in the shooting of panoramas'.[6] If the allusion refers to the famous analogy between the gun and the camera, Le Saint's experiences most probably explain his participation in one particularly significant project: the production of a series of aerial views taken from a dirigible balloon, undertaken between 1918 and 1919, under the aegis of the Army Cinematographic Service, or ACS (Service Cinématographique de l'Armée [SCA]).

The films, which are known under the name, *In an Airship over the Battle-Fields* (*En dirigeable sur les champs de bataille*), constitute a unique document. Shot at the end of the conflict with the aim of establishing the precise condition of areas destroyed by four years of war, the images fully reveal the enormity of the devastation and also give an indication of the Herculean dimensions of the reconstruction work that was necessary. The production of these images took place in the context of a much wider documentary project, which involved a vast photographic campaign. Moreover, as geographer Emmanuel de Martonne points out, the end of the hostilities was followed by the filming of numerous 'aircraft maps', produced in order to 'rapidly draw up town plans to facilitate reconstruction of devastated regions and to help guide "reallocation" work in areas where the increase in number of fragmented plots was making land exploitation difficult'.[7] This series of views must thus be placed in the context of a veritable programme of visual cartography that aimed to draw up an inventory of the land (through photography, cinema and cartography) in such a way that it, equally, had a powerful propaganda value. The images served to sharpen people's patriotic awareness by simultaneously stressing both the country's martyrdom and its energetic reconstruction work.

The film is organised into four parts and reconstitutes the voyage undertaken by Le Saint and, in all probability, two other cameramen. Several hand-drawn maps carefully position the shots geographically. It is, for want of another definition, a true 'landscape film' which little by little, as the airship flies over the devastated towns and countryside, reveals a country that is profoundly wounded. An analogy between the earth and the body quickly comes to the eye and the mind of the viewer, particularly during the sequence focusing on the battlefields.

The airship flies over them at a very low altitude, enabling close observation of the gashes of destruction. It passes above gutted houses and the ruins of church bell-towers and then floats above fields furrowed by bomb craters. With the exception of one or two accidental shots, the views are neither particularly unsteady, nor vertical. On the contrary, they are invariably oblique, the camera having been placed in the back of the pod to allow easier recognition of what was being passed over. This concern with the point of view was to function from then on as guarantor of the legibility and documentary quality of such images. The journey closes with a panoramic view of Paris, taken at the level of La Porte de la Chapelle, from which it is possible to make out the Sacré-Coeur, the Arc du Triomphe and the Eiffel Tower.

Assembled in the manner of long sequence-shots, these films represent not only a unique panorama of French and Belgian territory affected by the war, but also a remarkable aerial tracking film. Camera movement was already present in the Lumières' View no. 997, but here it is differently explored, with a pan-tracking shot that equally emphasises the documentary value of the images of the world it provides and the unique qualities of the alliance between the 'I am seeing' of the camera and the 'I am flying' of the airship. Only a film such as this can enable both a realisation of the scale – geographical and also qualitative – of the destruction and an assessment of the condition of the land. Moreover, the fluidity of the camera movement acts undeniably as a source of emotion: emotion linked to the pleasure of discovering the earth from a fresh point of view; emotion attached to the sudden recognition of the land as one more wounded body; and emotion, finally, arising from being able to travel freely through space-time. The cinematographic specificity of this film is fundamental, for no assemblage of aerial photographs could possibly convey, so immediately and effectively, the cenesthetic intensity encouraged by the doubled kineticism of the flight and the cinematographic views.

An awareness of the film's virtuosity seems to accompany it, and serves to explain the attempt to simulate the impression of uninterrupted movement: its genius is linked not so much to some realist ideal as to technological progress. Located halfway between the 'primitivism' of the forms that distinguish pre-1914 cinema, and the veritable avant-garde revolution that was gathering, this film 'without author' beautifully expresses the consciousness of cinematographic language's potential. These shots carry with them a 'cine-sensation' of the world, founded in a doubly machinic vision here expressed through the camera-aircraft couple.

Occurring at a time when the exaltation of the values of modernity and praise for 'mechanisation' were growing, aerial movement cinema found a powerful source of fantasy, as if the world's ultimate 'cine-sensation' was that of taking to the skies. If, particularly during the 1920s, the best illustration of the freedom of movement was to consist of a tiny plane performing somersaults above the enthralled gaze of the crowd and an ever-increasing number of cameras, at the same time the mechanical eye of the camera itself was also seeking to 'shoot up', or corkscrew down, according to its desires. The avant-gardists were quick to define the ambition: thus a pamphlet written by Dziga Vertov, dated 1923, declares:

> I am kino-eye, I am a mechanical eye. I, a machine, show you the world as only I can see it. Now and forever, I free myself from human immobility, I am in constant motion, I draw near, then away from objects, I crawl under, I climb onto them, I move apace with the muzzle of a galloping horse, I plunge full speed into a crowd; I outstrip running soldiers, I fall on my back, I ascend with an airplane, I plunge and soar together with plunging and soaring bodies [...] Freed from the imperative of 16-17 frames per second, free of the limits of time and space, I put together any given points in the universe, not matter where I've recorded them. *My path leads to the creation of a fresh perception of the world. I decipher in a new way a world unknown to you.*[8]

Vertov's words, written in the revolutionary environment of the Soviet Union just after *In an Airship over the Battle-Fields* had been made, reveal, despite the difference in context, the full value of the ACS images. The fruit of a mechanical kino-eye, free from the restraints of human fixity, aspiring to a continuity of movement as they lift into the skies then descend towards the earth, they illustrate a new form of perception and a new way of looking at the world.

'CINE-SENSING' THE WORLD (1919–39)

Before the aerial view became a commonplace of filmic discourse, in its form of a conventional shot that sets the scene, it was a subject of particular interest that was stimulated by the intense sensations such a shot procured. A number of films are devoted to these original experiences and stress the unique sensations offered by the camera's aerial vision and motion. Among these are several works that take the city – and urban space in general – as their subject. This was in line with formal research being carried out within a wider artistic project at the time, stimulated by the multiplication *ad infinitum* of points of view. Thus it is unsurprising to find several strictly vertical shots in films such as *The Old Port of Marseille* (*Marseille vieux port*), produced in 1929 by the Hungarian photographer and film-maker Moholy-Nagy, in which the shooting angles and camera-framing clearly enact photographic principles. *Dynamism of the Metropolis* (*Dynamik der Großstadt*), produced by Moholy-Nagy in 1921–2, also contains several sequences that include aerial views. Although Moholy-Nagy's project never saw the light of day, the famous *Berlin: Symphony of a Great City* (*Berlin: die Sinfonie der Großstadt*), made in 1927 by Walter Ruttman, used several themes already announced by the Hungarian in his scenario. As with many of the so-called 'City Symphony' films, here overhead views weave between differently angled shots, most notably taken from below, in a dialectic of high and low-angled shots that was indissociable from avant-garde photographic practices.

In addition, far from being limited to specific experimental projects by a few avant-garde film-makers, the aerial view also featured in current affairs. An impressive example is seen in a sequence entitled *Des 'gratte-ciel' bien élevés* (Gaumont, 1929).[9] Lasting scarcely a minute, the film was made in Chicago. The first shot justifies the enigmatic title 'Some well-brought-up skyscrapers. They bow low to those who look at them from above' ('Des "Gratte-Ciel" bien élevés. Qui saluent bien bas ceux qui les regardent de haut'). The 40 seconds of pure visual and sensory pleasure explore what film-maker Jean Epstein called 'the dance of the landscape' and amply confirm the photogenic qualities of images filmed from a flying-machine.[10] Suspended from an aircraft, a camera sweeps across the city of Chicago, swinging from right to left and creating the impression that the buildings drop to their knees before the camera. This profoundly exhibitionist parade of images demonstrates the dimension of the aerial view that is both cinematic and cenesthetic: their *raison d'être* is no more than to directly stimulate the spectator's senses, not so much through shock or surprise – features characteristic of the 'Cinema of Attractions'[11] – but through viewing angles and the movement of the camera. If the choreographed camera oscillations represented a film attraction, cinema asserted itself as mechanism of the spectacular *par excellence*, capable of demonstrating and reproducing sensations provoked by flight.

Despite the lack of information regarding the origins, aims and reception of this particular sequence, it serves as an excellent illustration of the way in which aerial images assumed significant dimensions within the wider area of cinematographic production during those years. Both Pathé and Gaumont catalogues list newsreels put together entirely around the aerial view; *En survolant New York* (*Flying Over New York*) (Pathé, 1932), is one example, as is *New York sous la neige* (*New York under Snow*) (Pathé, 1934). These two films provide ample affirmation of the fact that the interest shown in the sensory intensity of aerial shooting and the cinematographic conquest of space was not restricted to the avant-garde alone. Moreover, they portrayed the connection between the phenomenon of the modern metropolis and an overhead and hyper-mobile vision, a vision capable of scanning complete areas of terrain, whose ever-increasing complexity rendered their comprehension difficult.

THE 'MASS ORNAMENT' IN HOLLYWOOD: FROM SIEGFRIED KRACAUER TO BUSBY BERKELEY

If the emphasis on aerial vision's sensory aspects constituted the most obvious contribution of the new photographic apparatus to the history of aerial vision and the cinematic gaze, what might have been the problems encountered in the eye and mind of the viewer? In 1927, the German author Siegfried Kracauer devoted himself to the analysis of various popular phenomena; these included dance troupes, among whom the English 'Tiller Girls' were certainly the best known. Kracauer's resultant essay, comprising six chapters, is titled 'The Mass Ornament' (1966). In the twenties, this type of show, originally Anglo-Saxon, had achieved international renown, due in part to cinematographic newsreels. Such 'ornaments' represented what Kracauer called 'surface-level expressions', the study of which – he argued – was capable of providing 'unmediated access to the fundamental substance of the state of things'.[12]

Kracauer identifies the 'mass' as the bearer of the living ornaments formed by the girls: it designates neither the people nor a group of individuals, but a figure, a structure formed by anonymous elements, where 'people become fractions of a figure'.[13] For the theorist Kracauer, these 'living constellations' are stripped of meaning, the ornament being its end in itself. In developing his argument, Kracauer moves towards the concept of the 'ornament' rather than the idea of the 'mass'. According to the author, the ornament 'resembles *aerial photographs* of landscapes and cities in that it does not emerge out of the interior of the given conditions, but rather appears above them'.[14]

The recourse to the aerial view as analogical principle of analysis is not particularly surprising, in that it fits easily into the German visual and cultural context of the time, where aerial photographs were in circulation both in the press and the great exhibitions. Like previous thinkers, Kracauer demonstrated his own sensitivity to this new type of vision and did not hesitate to call upon it – with original critical acuity – in order to discuss his ideas. For Kracauer, the aerial view represented at the same time both a visual phenomenon, able to explain the ornament by analogy, but also the principle of optical and theoretical visibility of the 'surface-level expression'. In other words, far beyond its referential quality, the aerial view provoked fundamental problems of seeing

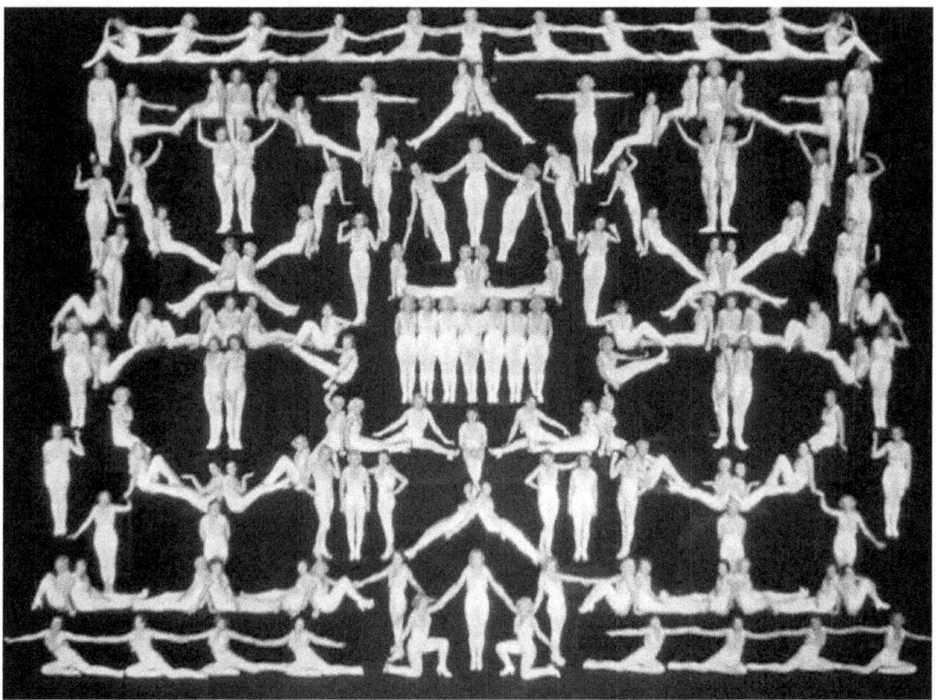

[7.4] Frame from the sequence 'Dames', *Dames* by Ray Enright and Busby Berkeley, 1934.

for its observers. Understood in this way, it not only constituted a revelation of the nature of things in the world that had until then been hidden and unseen, but was also the instrument that enabled access to their content.

Although devoid of meaning in the Weimar Republic, the 'living ornaments' discussed by Kracauer would be later assimilated and mobilised by National Socialism. Given that dance troupes perfectly embodied the Gemeinschaft ('community spirit'), the regime put them to use as powerful propaganda tools. Thus The Scala Girls were advertised as Europas Elitetrupp ('Europe's leading dance troupe'), while The Hiller Girls were to become a national icon (Gordon 2002).[15] In 1939, the musical show, *Wir tanzen um die Welt*, produced by Karl Anton, brought them to the stage, where they executed numbers not far removed from the choreography of the American Busby Berkeley and his famous Berkeley Girls. Indeed, watching Berkeley's films one wonders whether the dances he choreographed might not be linked to the problems raised by Kracauer in 'The Mass Ornament'. In their musical numbers, the dancers constitute the anonymous elements of a living architectural structure, where figures form, then re-form as each scene changes, the one after the other (Figure 7.4). Further, the dancers' sequences are distinctive through the vital role given to the overhead view: the strictly vertical shot is the one shot able to illustrate both the monumental dimensions but also the visual nature of the dance routines. Surely it is pertinent here to pose the question of what, exactly, might constitute this curious relationship and what part does the aerial view play?

Born in 1895 into a show business family, William Berkeley Enos entered the Mohegan Lake Military Academy when he was 12 and graduated in 1914. He volunteered to serve in the American Army during World War I and while there, in the role of Artillery Officer, he organised military parades in France and later, Germany; shortly before the armistice, he attended a course in aerial surveillance. After the war, he began a career as an actor, before moving towards musical show production on Broadway, where he earned his reputation as a choreographer. In 1930, the producer Samuel Goldwyn invited him to participate in Thornton Freedland's *Whoopee!* Two years later, Berkeley signed a seven-year contract with Warner Bros., after which he worked at the frenetic production rate of five films a year, until he joined MGM in 1939.

Berkeley's meticulously planned rehearsals enabled him to film remarkably long and spectacular sequences of shots, mobilising a large group of anonymous dancers inside sumptuous settings. Berkeley mistrusted editing and filmed the sequences with one camera. Able to rise into the air and move about, Berkeley's solitary and mechanical eye took pleasure in overturning conventional perspective: vertical images became his signature shot, assuming a particular symbolic and dialectic role in his film-work. In addition, these vertical views display in all their splendour the 'ornaments' that Berkeley carefully produced. What is striking is the material quality of the image, which is simultaneously flattened and freed from its realist restraints. The image becomes a pure surface that lends itself to the composition of stunning geometrical figures and a whole succession of visual effects. Berkeley did not hesitate to use black backgrounds to highlight the astonishing effects of flattening, reinforcing the idea of a screen-image, understood at the same time as the surface of appearance of the image and a dreamlike projection space. Writing in 1928, Ernst Bloch had already observed that 'the mediating impression produced by a revue is due to the force and visual vivacity of the scenes that have no links between them and emerge the one out of the other, metamorphosing and reaching towards dream'.[16] It is hard not to think of Berkeley and his dreamlike sequences.

Berkeley's experience in the army is often cited as being the inspiration for his rigorously planned choreography. Indeed, the martial discipline of his routines and the recurrence of military motifs are undeniable, but Berkeley's war experience is also linked to his work in another respect. Although his transfer into an army aerial surveillance unit might be incidental, the attraction

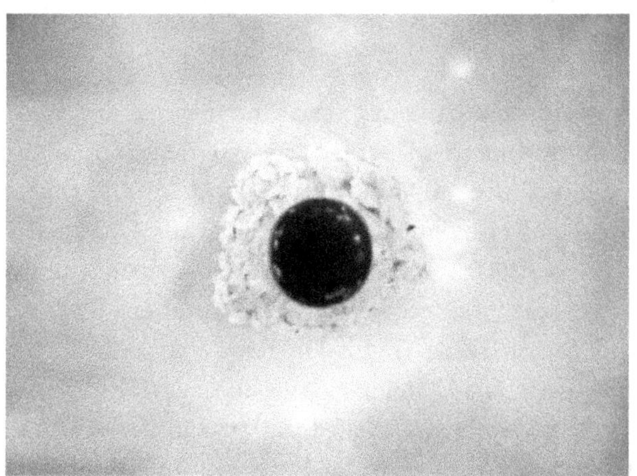

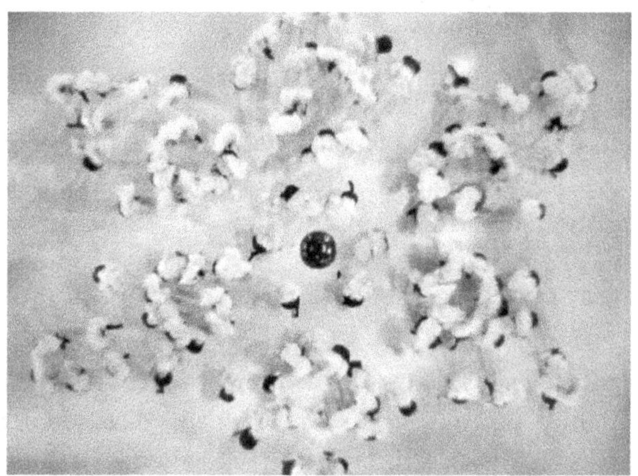

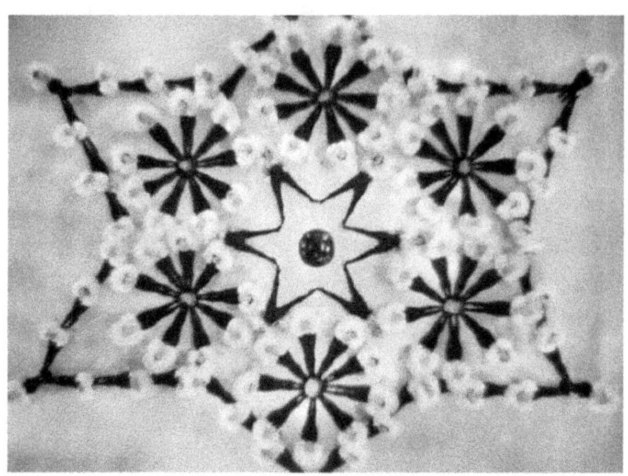

[7.5] Three frames from the sequence 'Dames'. The black ball, which falls like a bomb on the mass of dancers, acts as a pretext for the composition of floral motifs.

Berkeley felt towards the camera's aerial movements and the vertical angles of vision was certainly linked to perceptive experiences tied to the conflict. For it was during, but above all, following, World War I, that shots taken from aircraft and dirigibles circulated in Europe and the US. Such shots enabled not just a view of the world from above, but also a sense of the dramatic variations in scale that are seen in Berkeley's dance numbers. Perhaps aerial views of landscapes and towns seem to be far removed from this type of overhead cinematography, with its kaleidoscopic human constellations and amazing floral figures, yet the problems of abstraction and the aesthetisation of the war are intimately tied. Writing of his experiences in Ethiopia (1935–6), Vittorio Mussolini was able to say: 'I still remember the effect I produced on a small group of Galla tribesmen massed around a man in black clothes. I dropped an aerial torpedo right in the center, and the group opened up just like a flowering rose. It was most entertaining.'[17] As is well known, the elder son of the Italian dictator was passionate about cinema, which perhaps explains his unusual, rather bizarrely cinematographic, memory of the incident. If a sequence by Berkeley perfectly illustrates the visual effect that struck the young Mussolini (Figure 7.5), an observation made by Walter Benjamin, found at the end of his first version of his famous essay, 'The Work of Art in the Age of Mechanical Reproduction', throws an unexpected light on this surprising coincidence: 'This means that mass movements, including war, constitute a form of human behaviour which particularly favours mechanical equipment'.[18] Benjamin's understanding accords with Kracauer's: the aerial view not only resembles such living ornaments, but dictates the very visibility of the phenomenon; the aerial view, in other words, becomes a particular way of thinking about the world.

NOTES

1 Philippe Dubois, 'Le regard vertical ou: les transformations du paysage', in J. Mottet, ed., *Les Paysages du cinema* (Seyssel: Champ Vallon, 1999), pp.24–44.

2 The film's hero Saturnin Farandoul encounters a number of Jules Verne's characters in the film, including Fogg.

3 André Prothin, 'La Cinématographie en aéroplane', *Ciné-journal*, no. 167, 4 November (1911): 5.

4 Ibid., 8.

5 Ibid.

6 Marcel Huret, *Ciné-actualités: Histoire de la presse filmée 1895–1980* (Paris: Henri Veyrier, 1984), p.53.

7 Emmanuel de Martonne, *Géographie aérienne* (Paris: Albin Michel, 1948), p.70.

8 Annette Michelson, ed., *Kino-Eye: The Writings of Dziga Vertov* (London: Pluto, 1984).

9 Translator's note: the French, 'bien-élevé', is used to mean either 'well brought-up' or 'very high'; the film's title puns on the description of 'des gratte-ciel', or skyscrapers.

10 Jean Epstein, 'Bonjour Cinéma', in *Écrits sur le cinéma I* (Paris: Seghers, 1974), p.94.

11 Tom Gunning, 'Cinema of Attractions', *Wide Angle*, 8(3–4) (1986): 63–70.

12 Siegfried Kracauer, 'The Mass Ornament', in *The Mass Ornament: Weimar Essays* (Cambridge, MA,and London: Harvard University Press, 1995), pp.75–86; p.75.

13 Ibid., p.76.

14 Ibid., p.77 (emphasis in original).

15 Terri J. Gordon, 'Fascism and the Female Form: Performance Art in the Third Reich', *Journal of the History of Sexuality*, 11(1/2), January /April (2002): 164–200.

16 Ernst Bloch, 'La forme de la revue dans la philosophie', *Héritage de ce temps* (Paris: Payot, 1978), pp.340–3; p.341.

17 Vittorio Mussolini, *Voli sulle Ambe* (Firenze: Sansoni, 1937). This quotation appears in English in A. J. Barker, *The Civilising Mission: a History of the Italo-Ethiopian War of 1935–36* (New York: Dial Press, 1968), p.234.

18 Walter Benjamin, 'The Work of Art in the Age of Mechanical Reproduction', in Hannah Arendt, ed., *Illuminations* (New York: Schocken, 1969), pp.217–51; p.251.

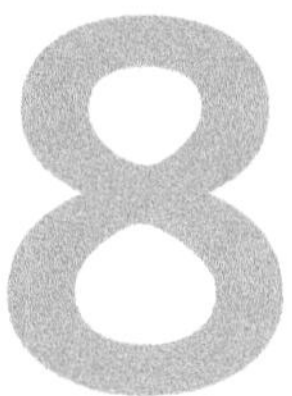

'The Domain of Rrose Sélavy'

Dust Breeding and Aerial Photography

David Hopkins

Histories of modernist or avant-garde photography regularly include among their illustrations an enigmatic photograph, credited to Marcel Duchamp and Man Ray in collaboration, titled *Dust Breeding* and dated 1920. Almost invariably, people tend to read the image as some form of aerial view; possibly an extra-terrestrial landscape or earthwork. Such a view is encouraged by the caption for the work as it was later reproduced by the Paris Dadaists in their magazine *Littérature* in 1922, for there, beneath the image, we find the legend 'Vue prise en aéroplane'.

For the uninitiated viewer, it requires some considerable degree of explanation to establish that this photograph is in fact an oblique close-up view of the lower section of Marcel Duchamp's seminal *La Mariée mise à nu par ces célibataires, même* or 'Large Glass' (1915–23), its surface covered in dust. How, then, are we to interpret this extremely ambiguous image, in which a visionary scene has been conjured opportunistically from what, on the most basic level, constitutes a record of a larger work-in-progress? Was the photograph intended from the outset to have this aerial-view connotation? Or did it later become a 'view taken from an aeroplane' to suit the needs of its authors and their avant-garde associates? And, if we consider the image as a bird's-eye view, what kind of terrain are we surveying? This essay considers such historically specific questions, whilst aiming to establish a new and expanded interpretation of this major photograph.

As already mentioned, the photograph of *Dust Breeding* was first published in the October 1922 edition of the Paris Dada group's journal *Littérature* in Paris. It

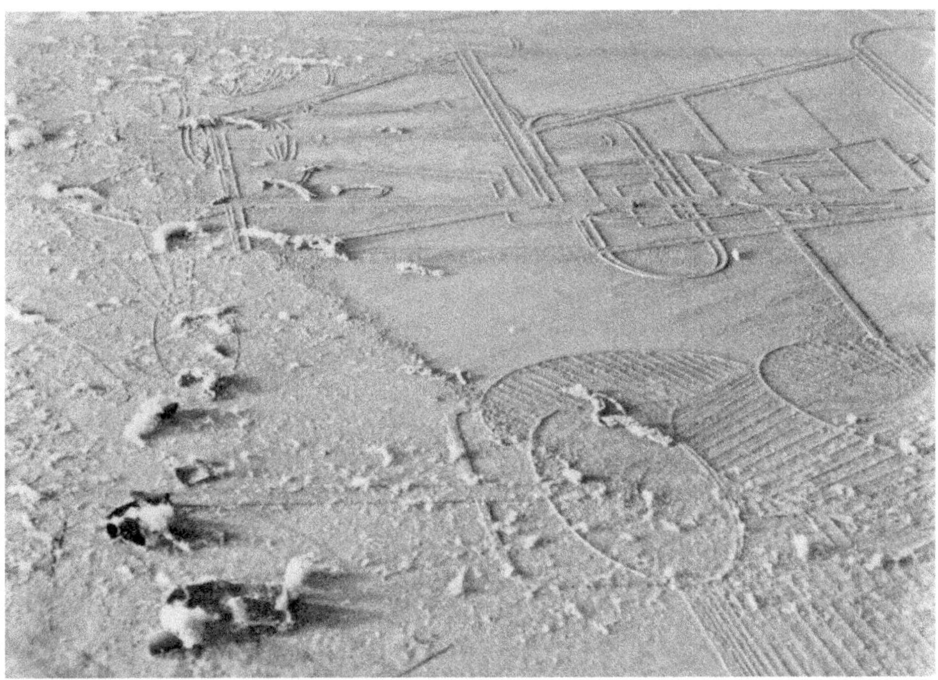

[8.1] Man Ray/Marcel Duchamp: 'Dust Breeding', 1920.

was an image of the build-up of dust on the surface of Marcel Duchamp's 'Large Glass' as the work rested on trestle tables in the artist's New York studio in mid-1920. The photograph seems to have arisen out of a meeting between Man Ray and Duchamp concerning the latter's 'rotary discs' of the period; the two men apparently went out for lunch leaving the camera to take a long exposure of the surface of the 'Glass' in artificial light. In the photograph we see an angled and relatively close-up view of the dust lying on the bottom half or 'Bachelor's Domain' of the work (Figure 8.1). As is widely known, the dust would eventually provide the colouration for the so-called 'sieves' or 'drainage slopes' in this area of the work: having let it settle for some six months, Duchamp wiped away that which he didn't need and fixed the remainder with varnish.

The relation of this photograph to ideas about the passage of time, chance and photographic indexicality, which have been explored by the likes of Rosalind Krauss and David Campany,[1] will not concern me here, and I will return to the thematic of dust shortly. First, however, I want to concentrate on the caption that was appended to the photograph when it was reproduced by the Paris Dada group, and to say a little about their relation to Duchamp.

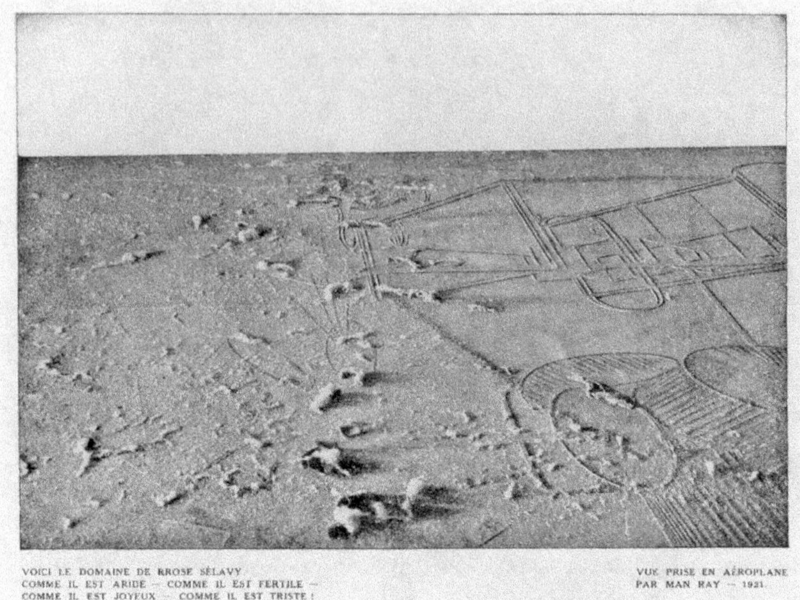

[8.2] 'Dust Breeding' as reproduced in *Littérature*, New Series, no. 5, October 1922.

As we have seen, on its publication (Figure 8.2) the photograph carried the caption 'View taken from an aeroplane' at its lower right, but also bore a more enigmatic epithet at the lower left: 'Here is the domain of Rrose Sélavy – how arid it is – how fertile – how joyful – how sad!' The first part of the caption relates fairly directly to an account that Man Ray would later give of the genesis of the image. He talked of the dust on the work 'resembling some strange landscape seen from a bird's-eye view', and added: 'There was dust on the work and bits of cotton wadding that had been used to clean up the finished parts.'[2] But we should remember that the image was actually produced in 1920, and the caption added by the Paris-based Dadaists – all of them fervent admirers and interpreters of the enigmatic Duchamp – came two years later. Man Ray's description of the photograph as a bird's-eye view, which appeared in his autobiography of 1963, may be a retrospective formulation of ideas that were developed as much by the Paris Dadaists as by Duchamp and Man Ray himself. In what follows I often make the assumption that Duchamp and Man Ray – gazing at the photograph they had produced of the 'Glass' – saw an immediate connection with aerial photography, or actually set up the image in this way, but there is no clear evidence for this. However, looking at the photograph from which the image in *Littérature* was cropped, which has only recently come to light, we get a greater

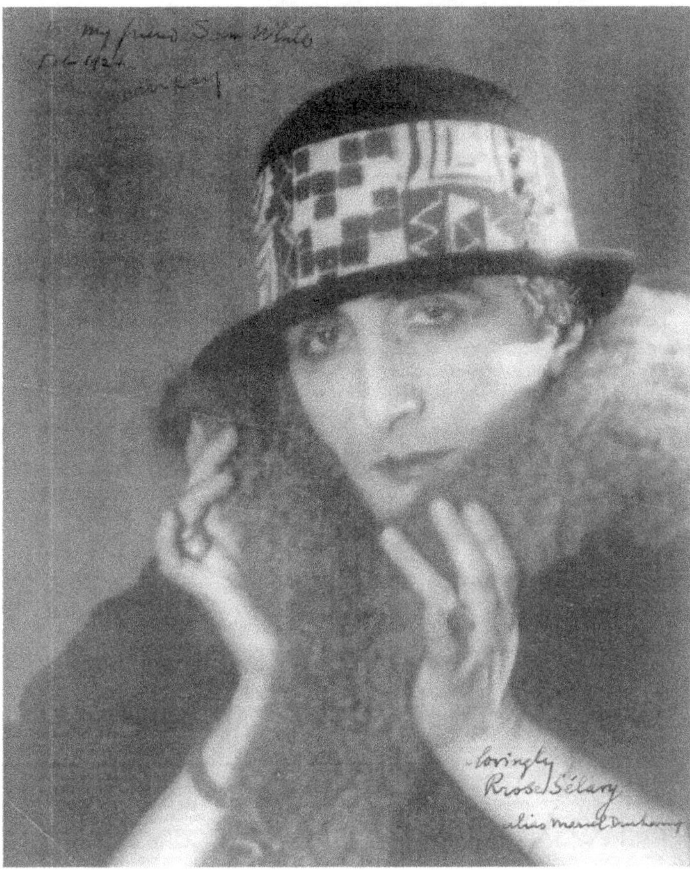

[8.3] Man Ray/Marcel Duchamp: Duchamp as Rrose Sélavy, 1921.

sense of the degree to which the published photograph was manipulated by Duchamp and Man Ray in the photograph as published.[3] In the original image, the templates, which were presumably used to establish the shapes of the sieves in the bachelor's domain, remain in place to provide a record of studio activity. In the final image, however, all of this paraphernalia is eliminated, and the white wall beyond the edge of the table is made to function as an implacable sky above a landscape that ends abruptly at an impossibly straight horizon.

The caption at the bottom left – 'Here is the domain of Rrose Sélavy – how arid it is – how fertile – how joyful – how sad!' – is clearly even more loaded, related as it is to the complex way in which the image was understood by the Dada group in France. 'Rrose Sélavy' was the alter ego Duchamp had invented for himself in a series of photographs and readymade gestures from the early 1920s, in other words from around the time that *Dust Breeding* was created (Figure 8.3).

The Paris Dada group had heard of this mysterious creation of the New York-based Duchamp by 1922, not least from Duchamp himself who had been in Paris in the later part of 1921, and may well have pondered how her name (which, as well as punning on the phrase 'eros c'est la vie' ['love is life'], also suggests 'arrosez la vie' ['water – or sprinkle – life']) in particular resonated with Duchamp's reputation for being a 'dry type'. Hence one way to read the caption is to see Rrose's fertility in counterpoint to the dryness (or dustiness perhaps) of her other half, Marcel Duchamp. It is hardly surprising, in fact, that in his first essay on Duchamp, produced around the time of the *Dust Breeding* photograph, André Breton should talk of Duchamp as 'an oasis for those who are still searching', deliberately playing, no doubt, on these notions of deserts and watering holes.[4] It seems as though the French poets understood the dry Duchamp to have made way for his fertile other half – to have killed off his former self – and this may well be what Duchamp encouraged them to think. I will return again to Rrose shortly, but first let us pursue this deathly inflection slightly differently.

Given that the *Dust Breeding* image was designated at the bottom right 'View taken from an aeroplane', the mournful or elegiac tone of the longer caption at the bottom left further implies an allusion to aerial photographs of battlefields. There has been much research in recent years on the extent to which the Dadaists registered the physical or mental effects of World War I (the key studies being those by Amelia Jones, Brigid Doherty and Amy Lyford),[5] but nothing has been made of the striking links between Man Ray's photographs and the reconnaissance photographs of battlefields which were such a key aspect of the imagery that emerged from the war.

In Man Ray's previously cited description of the photograph he talks about the 'bits of cotton wadding' that had been used to clean up the finished parts of the 'Glass' and, comparing the photograph with a battlefield photograph taken by an American unit headed by Edward Steichen, it is hard to resist the impression that the cotton wads double as plumes of drifting smoke (Figure 8.4). A remarkable jump from close-up to aerial view takes place, such that the bachelor's domain of the 'Large Glass' becomes transformed into a scaled-down war-zone. The trope of miniaturisation seems relevant here. The American literary theorist Susan Stewart talks of a miniaturised 'war game' envisaged by the writer H. G. Wells as a counter-proposition to the war games indulged in by the British army. Wells wrote: 'My game is just as good as their game, and saner by virtue of its size [...] war is [...] a game out of all proportion.'[6] In this context Duchamp and Man Ray assume the personae of boys playing at warfare. It is important here to note that the aerial view (and its implications) was already established as a minor genre within avant-garde art production. The marriage of aeroplane and camera implied in the aerial photograph – the meeting of two technological modes, which was pioneered

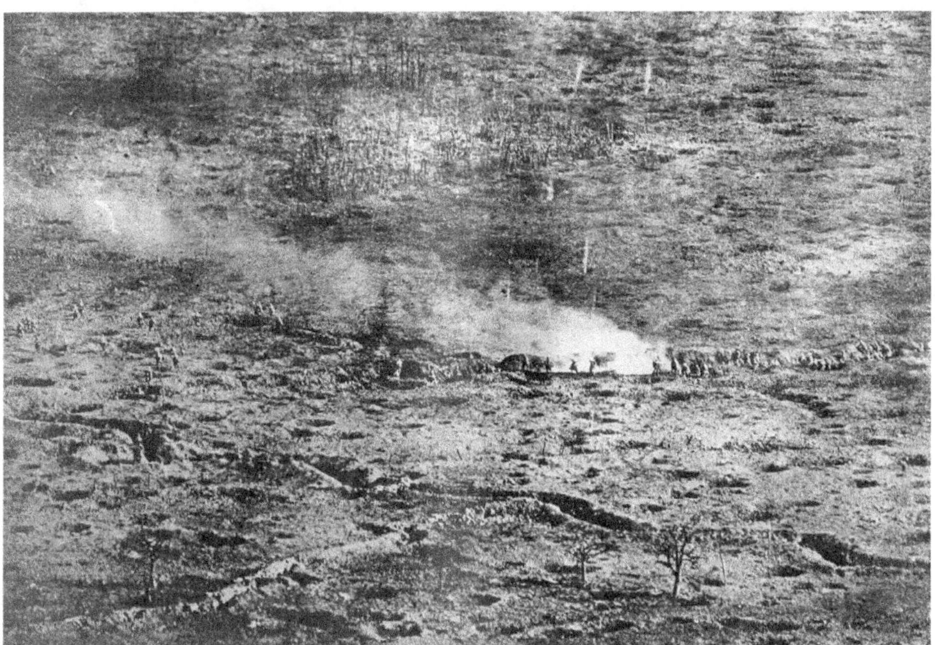

[8.4] Unknown photographer/American Expeditionary Force: Aerial view of Battlefield, *c.*1918.

by Italian pilots in 1911[7] – inaugurated a new mechanised mode of visualising warfare, which we find exploited in, for example, Max Ernst's photomontage *Massacre of the Innocents,* which was produced around the same time as *Dust Breeding.*[8] A nightmarish form of military attrition – aerial bombardment – which had been perfected by the Italians in the bombing of Tripoli in 1911 and which Marinetti had lauded in his Futurist poem 'Le Bataille de Tripoli' – now haunted the imaginations of artists. Even certain visual and textual aspects of Marinetti's 'Words in Freedom' borrowed their impetus from an aviator's viewpoint, as for example in the 'Synchronic Chart' included in his 'Zong Toomb Toomb' that was inspired by events in Adrianople in 1912 (Figure 8.5).[9]

It is worth pausing to assess the enormous psychological repercussions emanating from this annexation of photography to the imaging of the landscape of modern warfare. In a fascinating discussion Bernd Hüppauf has dwelt on the altered modes of perception inaugurated by the alliance of aeroplane and camera. He notes that 'aerial photographs of the front demonstrate pointedly the new perception and expression of a "landscape" hitherto unknown: a landscape of complete destruction and high artificiality in terms of its system of dugouts, trenches, communication lines, supply routes, and so forth'.[10] Expanding on the

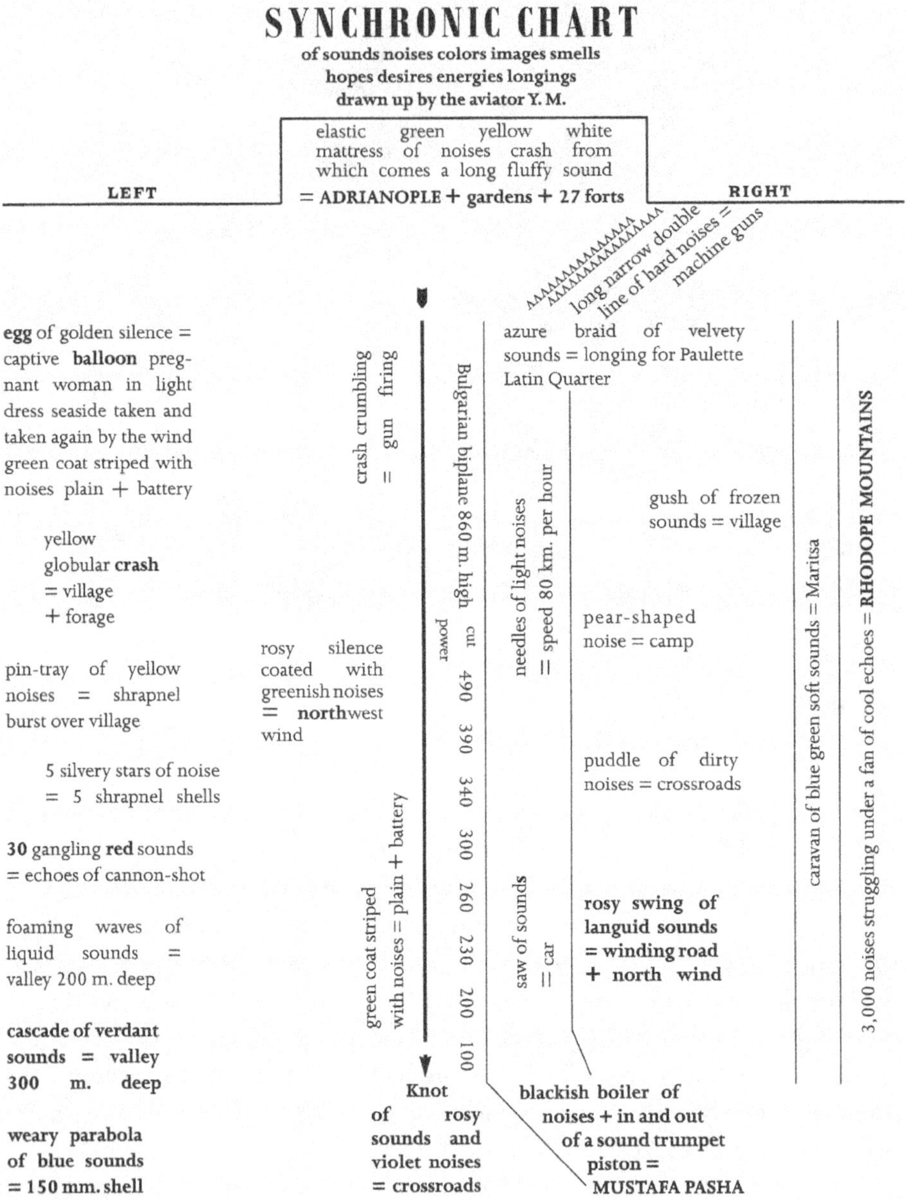

SYNCHRONIC CHART

of sounds noises colors images smells
hopes desires energies longings
drawn up by the aviator Y. M.

elastic green yellow white mattress of noises crash from which comes a long fluffy sound **= ADRIANOPLE + gardens + 27 forts**

LEFT

RIGHT

AAAAAAAAAAAAA
AAAAAAAAAAAAAAA
long narrow double
line of hard noises =
machine guns

egg of golden silence = captive **balloon** pregnant woman in light dress seaside taken and taken again by the wind green coat striped with noises plain + battery

yellow
globular **crash**
= village
+ forage

pin-tray of yellow noises = shrapnel burst over village

5 silvery stars of noise
= 5 shrapnel shells

30 gangling **red** sounds
= echoes of cannon-shot

foaming waves of liquid sounds = valley 200 m. deep

cascade of verdant sounds = valley 300 m. deep

weary parabola of blue sounds = 150 mm. shell

crash crumbling = gun firing

rosy silence coated with greenish noises = **north**west wind

green coat striped with noises = plain + battery

Bulgarian biplane 860 m. high cut power 490 390 340 300 260 230 200 100

Knot of rosy sounds and violet noises = crossroads

azure braid of velvety sounds = longing for Paulette Latin Quarter

needles of light noises = speed 80 km. per hour

saw of sounds = car

gush of frozen sounds = village

pear-shaped noise = camp

puddle of dirty noises = crossroads

rosy swing of languid sounds = winding road + north wind

blackish boiler of noises + in and out of a sound trumpet piston = MUSTAFA PASHA

caravan of blue green soft sounds = Maritsa

3,000 noises struggling under a fan of cool echoes = **RHODOPE MOUNTAINS**

[8.5] Excerpt from F. T. Marinetti: 'Zong Toomb Toomb'.

new alienating aesthetic order brought into being, he notes: 'The morphology of the landscape of destruction, photographed from a plane, was transformed into the visual order of an abstract pattern.'[11] This is obviously suggestive in relation to the choice made by Man Ray and Duchamp to incorporate the angled vision of the bachelor's apparatus from the 'Large Glass', with its enigmatic network of lines, into the *Dust Breeding* image. Is some comment about a new mode of perceptual disorientation being made here?

To offset this, it should be asserted that, rather than expressing the dizzying effects of aerial perception in a grand artistic statement, in the manner of high profile avant-gardists from Marinetti through to Russian artists such as Malevich and Rodchenko – Man Ray and Duchamp deliberately conjure their battlefield scenario out of odds and ends of material, and from a chance perception, a momentary shift of viewpoint. They avoid any pretence of profundity. They assume, as I have argued elsewhere, the attitude of the amateur bricoleur rather than that of the professional modernist artist, and their collaboration is more closely informed by the spirit of boyish camaraderie than by shared experimental zeal: more precisely, their approach is borne out of play rather than moral indignation or aesthetic ambition.[12] And there is, in any case, a considerable degree of ambiguity in the visual conceit they develop. In the past *Dust Breeding* has often been thought to evoke not so much a battlefield as some kind of ancient earthwork or site, and parallels with the 'geoglyphs' drawn onto the surface of the Nazca desert in Peru around AD 300–800 and, significantly, only fully apprehensible from the air, are worth considering.

This element of ambiguity in the image – the way it appears to oscillate between picturing a modern landscape of destruction and an ancient site of ritual significance – also chimes with Hüppauf's thought on the character of aerial wartime photography. Pursuing his sense of the disparity in aerial images of battlefields between the purely aesthetic effect of the images and the horrendous sufferings of flesh-and-blood soldiers that are effectively rendered invisible in them, Hüppauf notes that we are returned to modes of cognition characteristic of primitive art. Hence he writes: 'There too, knowledge was required for the deciphering of shapes and colours associated with events, demons, totems or tribes, and their actions in tribal warfare', adding: 'Visual representation of the modern battlefield in aerial photography is another example of the frequently observed return of archaic structures in the world of modern technology.'[13]

If Man Ray and Duchamp mobilise a kind of entropic metaphor in their photograph, a slippage from the modern to the archaic, this also reinforces the sense of a regressive strategy in their conception of themselves as artists: a reversion to boyishness. And here the male thematic of their play becomes even more poignant. Dust – the material which coats their miniaturised landscape –

is itself evocative of the boy's untidy bedroom, or perhaps more poignantly, the bachelor's habitat. It seems hardly coincidental that the *Dust Breeding* photograph actually isolates the 'Chocolate Grinder' from the 'Large Glass', the part of the work which most closely figures masturbation. Talking about visiting Duchamp's New York studio at approximately the time he was working on the section of the 'Bachelor's domain' pictured in the photograph, the American painter Georgia O'Keefe recalled:

> It was a few flights up in a dismal, draughty building [...] The room looked like it had never been swept – not even when he first moved in [...] the dust everywhere was so thick that it was hard to believe. I was so upset over this dusty place that the next day I wanted to go over and clean it up.[14]

Whatever this might say about stereotypical male and female roles, it is evident that dust was something that Duchamp cultivated just as surely as he cultivated his bachelor status, and we are reminded here, of course, about the way the captioning of the photograph in *Littérature* plays on this dry Duchamp.

In this respect one should mention that the title of the dust photograph clearly derives from a phrase in Duchamp's set of notes for his 'Large Glass', the so-called 'Green Box', which reads 'Élever de la poussière'.[15] Strictly speaking the word 'élever' here means 'to raise' although the added connotation of rearing/breeding was supplied when the title of the photograph became 'élevage de la poussière' which translates more exactly as 'dust breeding'. The implication then is that dust has been coaxed forth, made into an active principle in some way.

We must also of course reconcile this with the fact that dust evokes mourning; ash to ashes, dust to dust. The historian Carolyn Steedman, in a fascinating discussion of dust's role in the gestation of what she calls 'archive fever', dwells on the French nineteenth-century historian Michelet perusing the musty manuscripts at the Archives Nationales in Paris and perceiving himself to be literally breathing-in – via the dust from the documents – the spirits of those who were now, as he said, 'smothered in the past'.[16] As Steedman notes, Michelet particularly longed to inhale the dust of the revolutionary generation of the 1780s and 1790s, along with its nineteenth-century successors, adding that the somatic absorption of such a history was intimately related to the fact that the French catacombs were filled with the bones of the dead from the revolutionary period and that, in the French literary language in which Michelet was writing, the word 'poussière' (dust), rather than 'os' (bones), designated the remains of dead bodies. At a fundamental level *Dust Breeding* is surely about male mourning; it functions as a response to the loss of countless men on the battlefields of Europe, a loss felt acutely by the Paris Dadaists, though rarely expressed by them directly. The archaicising logic of the image, its flip from death to geometry, suggests a degree of male self-alienation, an inability to take in, or deal empathetically with, the overwhelming level of emotional intensity and loss involved, which itself possibly underpins Duchamp and Man Ray's reversion to miniaturisation, and to boyish game-playing.

This discussion of the co-existence of the active and negative registers of dust in the image suggests that it is time we returned finally to the refrain from the caption applied to the *Dust Breeding* photograph by the Dadaists – 'Here is the domain of Rrose Sélavy: how arid it is – how fertile – how joyful – how sad!' and to reflect on how this underlines all that has been said. Although it is hard to square Christian thought with either the Paris Dadaists or Duchamp, the title of the photograph *Dust Breeding* surely has vague connotations of resurrection, and similar imagery percolates through the literature of the period; Eliot's 'The Waste Land', completed around the time *Dust Breeding* was produced, deals with a similarly weird mix of barrenness and the stirrings of new life: 'April is the cruellest month/breeding lilacs out of the dead land', and later: 'There I saw one I knew, and stopped him crying: Stetson [...] That corpse you planted last year in your garden/Has it begun to sprout?'[17]

If, at a certain level, the Paris Dada group seems to have understood Rrose Sélavy in this redemptive way – which would accord with the exalted value they placed on women and the principle of love as means to earthly salvation – it is worth observing that a more ironic deathly subtext had always accompanied Rrose, as far as Duchamp was concerned. Her first appearance in his work had been in *Fresh Widow* of 1920, where her name appeared with one R on the base of the miniaturised French windows, produced by a New York carpenter. It seems likely that the war was obliquely at issue here, since the pun surely derives its impetus from a salacious nod to the sexual availability of newly widowed women in France in the years immediately following World War I. Rrose may well have been a vehicle by which Duchamp mocked his French admirers' obsession with Eros; on the mock-perfume bottle of April 1921, Rrose, in her first visual manifestation in a photograph collaboratively produced by Duchamp and Man Ray, is identified with 'Eau de Voilette' (veil water) and widow's veils are as likely to be at issue as are bride's. In 1921 Duchamp was to produce another work related to *Fresh Widow*, *La Bagarre d'Austerlitz* (*The Brawl at Austerlitz*), which although generally understood to allude to the Gare d'Austerlitz in Paris also throws up another deathly allusion, looking back beyond World War I, to French involvement in the Battle of Austerlitz.

So perhaps, by the time the Paris Dadaists published *Dust Breeding* in *Littérature* in October 1922, Rrose was intimately bound up with their attitudes to the war. What is even more interesting here is the fact that the publication of *Dust Breeding* was being prepared at precisely the moment the French poets were entering into the so-called 'période des sommeils', the trance sessions aimed at eliciting unconscious messages, which had begun late in September 1922 and continued into early 1923 and which derived their basic modus operandi from mediumistic séances. Although, in his essay on the trances, 'Entrée des médiums' of November 1922, André Breton would refute the idea that 'any communication whatsoever can exist between the living and the dead',[18] death was in fact a constant preoccupation of those involved in the trances: the poet Robert Desnos, who adopted the role of medium on these occasions, was frequently asked to predict when or how members of the group would die. During one of the sessions Desnos supposedly received telepathic messages from Duchamp in New York, in which Duchamp adopted the voice of Rrose Sélavy. Revisiting this session in a text in *Littérature* in December 1922 Breton would ask: 'Who is dictating to the sleeping Desnos the sentences we will read and in which Rrose Sélavy is the heroine; is Desnos's brain joined, as he claims, to Duchamp's, to the degree that Rrose Sélavy only speaks if Duchamp's eyes are open?'[19] There is a very strong suggestion here that either Duchamp or Rrose is acting as a medium – and Rrose certainly appears to be mediating in a transatlantic communication between the Surrealists and Duchamp such that her voice almost literally becomes one from the 'other side'.

Seen in this light, and in relation to all that has been said so far, the caption applied to the *Dust Breeding* photograph in *Littérature* evokes the idea of Rrose Sélavy in a kind of mediumistic relation both to the war dead and the absent Marcel Duchamp. Interestingly, Hüppauf, in the essay on aerial war photography discussed earlier, notes that, during World War I, a cult of war pilots emerged, such that the images of flying aces in the popular press had the effect of reconfiguring 'the empty space of aerial photography in terms of individual experience and collective mythology'.[20] This, of course, returns us to the sense of *Dust Breeding* as a battlefield and suggests the emergence of Rrose out of this terrain as a form of compensatory collective image.

In the final analysis *Dust Breeding* appears to allegorise absence in various ways. As a photographic record it shows only part of a larger work. On another level, the build-up of dust that it records is itself an agent of burial. On yet another level, understood as an aerial view, it speaks of the absence of suffering in images of modern warfare. Most of all, though, the photograph allegorises the absence of a person – Duchamp himself. It is, in that sense, a form of portrait; metaphorically akin to one of the 'spirit portraits' that were so much in vogue among spiritualists early in the twentieth century. It 'summons up' Duchamp. But if Duchamp is eerily present in the dusty terrain presented to us in *Dust*

Breeding it is only in so far as this is also 'the domain of Rrose Sélavy'. Hence, as well as being an aerial view, this image also constitutes a portrait of absence, or absence doubled; that of Duchamp and that of his 'other half', Rrose. Duchamp had invented Rrose at some point in 1920, when, shuffling around his dusty bachelor's studio in New York, he presumably reflected on the limitations of his male persona. In giving her life, out of dust, he envisaged himself as capable of a paradoxical male fertility, in an age that had seen the men of his native France slaughtered in their thousands.

NOTES

1 See David Campany, 'Man Ray and Marcel Duchamp: Dust Breeding 1920' in Sophie Howarth, ed., *Singular Images: Essays on Remarkable Photographs* (London: Tate Publishing, 2005), pp.47–53 and Rosalind Krauss, 'Notes on the Index' in *The Originality of the Avant-Garde and Other Modernist Myths* (Cambridge, MA, and London: MIT Press, 1985), pp.202–6.

2 Man Ray, *Self Portrait* (London: Bloomsbury, 1988), pp.78–9 (originally published, New York, 1963).

3 For a reproduction of the photograph with studio paraphernalia see Jennifer Miundy, ed., *Duchamp, Man Ray, Picabia* (London: Tate Publishing, 2008), p.86.

4 André Breton, 'Marcel Duchamp', *Littérature* (New Series) no. 5, October 1922, as translated by Mark Polizzotti; André Breton: *The Lost Steps* (Lincoln, NE, and London: University of Nebraska Press, 1996), pp.85–9.

5 See Brigid Doherty, 'See we are all neurasthenics now, or, the trauma of Dada montage', *Critical Inquiry*, vol. 24 (Autumn 1997): 82–132; Amelia Jones, *Irrational Modernism: A Neurasthenic History of New York Dada* (Cambridge, MA: MIT Press, 2004); Amy Lyford, *Surrealist Masculinities* (University of California Press, 2007), Chapter 2, pp.47–79.

6 H. G. Wells, *Little Wars*, as cited in Susan Stewart, *On Longing: Narratives of the Minature, the Gigantic, the Souvenir, the Collection* (Durham and London: Duke University Press, 1993), p.59.

7 See Sven Lindquist, *A History of Bombing* (London: Granta Books, 2002), section 77, unpaginated.

8 See Werner Spies, *Max Ernst Collages: The Invention of the Surrealist Universe* (London: Thames and Hudson, 1991), plates 36 and 38 (a) and (b) for *The Massacre of the Innocents* (1920) and a related work using aerial imagery, *The Cormorants* (1920).

9 See F. T. Marinetti, 'Zong Toomb Toomb' in *Selected Poems and Related Prose*, translated by Elizabeth R. Napier (New Haven and London: Yale University Press, 2002), p.61.

10 See Bernd Hüppauf, 'Modernism and the Photographic Representation of War and Destruction' in Leslie Devereaux and Roger Hillman, eds, *Fields of Vision: Essays in Film Studies, Visual Anthropology and Photography* (University of California Press, 1995), p.105.

11 Ibid., p.106.

12 See my *Dada's Boys: Masculinity After Duchamp* (New Haven, CT, and London: Yale University Press, 2007), especially Chapter 2.

13 Hüppauf, op. cit., at note 10 above, p.106.

14 Georgia O'Keefe, statement in Anne d'Harnoncourt and Kynaston McShine, eds, *Marcel Duchamp* (Museum of Modern Art, New York, and Philadelphia Museum of Art: Thames and Hudson, 1973), pp.213–14.
15 Marcel Duchamp, *The Bride Stripped Bare by her Bachelors, Even* (*The Green Box Notes*), typographic version by Richard Hamilton, translated by George Heard Hamilton (London and Bradford: Percy Lund, and New York: Wittenborn, 1960) (unpaginated).
16 See Carolyn Steedman, *Dust* (Manchester University Press, 2001), p.27.
17 T. S. Eliot, 'The Waste Land' (1922), from *Complete Poems and Plays* (London: Faber, 1969), pp.61, 62–3.
18 André Breton: 'Entrées des Médiums', *Littérature* (New Series), no. 6, November 1922, translated by Mark Polizzotti, in *Breton: The Lost Steps*, op. cit., p.92.
19 Breton: 'Les Mots sans rides', *Littérature* (New Series), no. 7, December 1922. Quoted in G. Durozoi, *History of the Surrealist Movement*, translated by Alison Anderson (Chicago and London: University of Chicago Press, 2002), p.41.
20 Hüppauf, op. cit., at note 10 above, p.109.

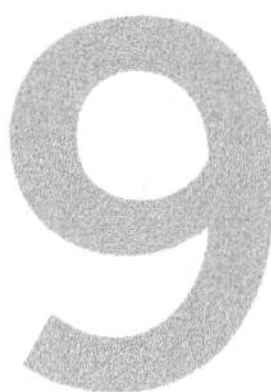

The Aviator and the Photographer

The Case of Walter Mittelholzer

Olivier Lugon

Switzerland offers a privileged terrain for examining the history of the aerial view: the genre has flourished, publications have been numerous and the bird's-eye view has played a major role in imaginary constructions of the national landscape. There are several reasons for this. The country's small size has certainly played a part, since the dream of a totalising visual image – inseparable from the aerial viewpoint – is encouraged by a territory that is limited, as this increases the illusion of being able to embrace it entirely through an accumulation of overhead views.[1] Indeed the very smallness of the country may contribute to an enhanced impression of totality and thus – paradoxically – to the sense of a privileged contact with immensity. In Swiss iconographic production, this dialectic between the small and the great has itself a long tradition, one linked to a second characteristic of the national terrain: its mountainous nature. As Alpine tourism started to develop in the eighteenth century, Switzerland became a country that both contemplated and represented itself from on high. This resulted in a huge production of painted panoramas, panoramic engravings and relief models, while countless viewing platforms and orientation tables were installed within the landscape to provide a pleasure akin to that accorded by an elevated and totalising image.

The development of aerial photography was undoubtedly aided by this tradition, needing only to slightly adjust the language of Alpine representation and extend the market for panoramic mountain views that had already been established. Certainly, as early as the end of the nineteenth century,

Switzerland produced one of the first stars of aeronautic photography, Edouard Spelterini (1852–1931), whose views from an air-balloon helped to maintain the iconography of the Alpine sublime. Nicknamed 'King of the Skies' ('le Roi des airs'), Spelterini became known first as an aeronaut. Dexterously cutting across the various domains of tourism, entertainment, adventure and science and collaborating as easily with a trapeze-artist from the Folies Bergère as a lecturer from the Swiss Federal Institute of Technology in Zurich, Spelterini profited both from balloon passengers who paid to experience the thrills of flight and also from the spectators who watched the take-offs. In addition, he benefited from his enthusiastic involvement in conferences, using colourised photographic plates as illustrations.[2] Thus aerial photography turned out to be rather more than just a portrayal of the landscape: it offered the experience of flight to a wider public and recreated the sensations of the aeronaut-photographer's adventures. In this way, Spelterini launched a spectacle oriented aerial-view economy, which was located at the intersection of sporting attraction and scientific discourse and was based, as befits the rules of the spectacle, on a highly personalised picture production.

THE HERO

It was in the inter-war period that a similar kind of practice propelled the second leading figure in Swiss aerial photography to the foreground: Walter Mittelholzer (1894–1937) (Figure 9.1). Mittelholzer is the aerial photographer who, more effectively than any other, and well before Yann Arthus-Bertrand, succeeded in constructing a true personality cult around himself. His example, like that of Arthus-Bertrand today, contradicted the concept of the aerial view which even now continues to dominate academic thought: that of a photography which is essentially disembodied, anonymous and abstract; that is associated with discourses of rationality and control (such as those of science, political administration, land management and urbanism); and that is thereby linked to supra-individual systems that aim at a form of domination of the world by rationality. By contrast, Mittelholzer's practice demonstrates to what degree the aerial view has also the capacity to be embodied, autographed, individualised and truly steeped in an imaginary of adventure, sporting feat and transcendence. The image produced is not only technical and organised, but also physical and irrational.

In the inter-war period, Mittelholzer's example remained almost unique. While the aerial view occupied a central position in the iconography of the New

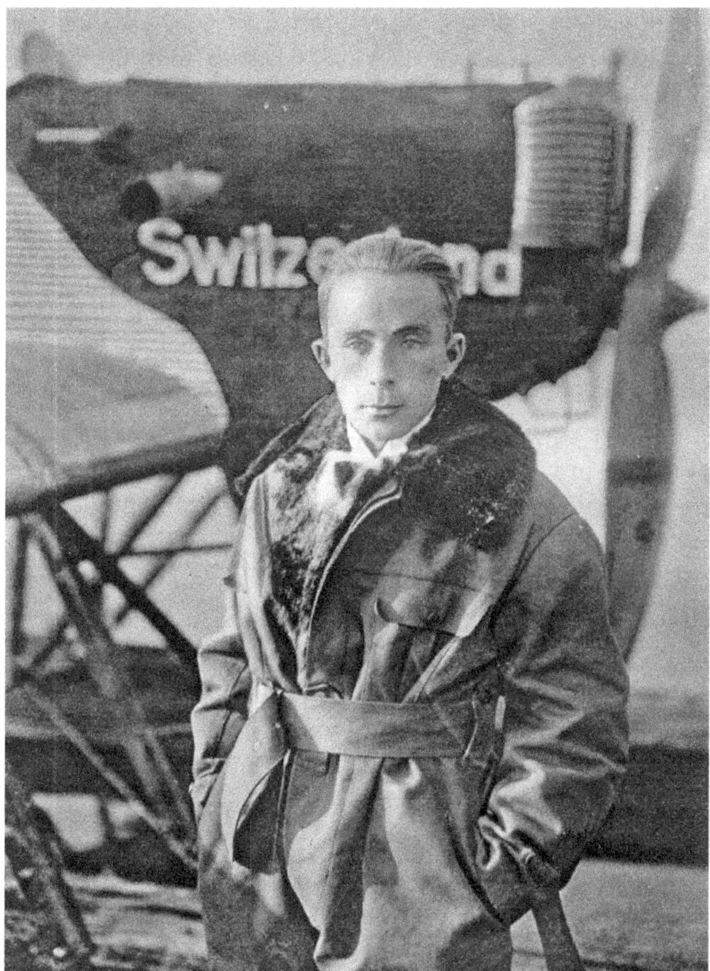

[9.1] Anon., Walter Mittelholzer, *Persienflug*, 1926.

Vision – the modern photography acclaimed by both the avant-garde and the illustrated press – the aerial photographers themselves struggled to achieve the status of authors. In the publications or the exhibitions in which their pictures appeared, photographs were accredited to agencies or state departments, rather than to individuals. The only exception to find a place alongside Mittelholzer was the German, Robert Petschow (1888–1945). Although Petschow was much exhibited by the avant-garde and better represented than either Eugène Atget, Albert Renger-Patzsch or André Kertész in the 1929 *Film und Foto* exhibition in Stuttgart, he nevertheless remained on the artistic and media fringe. Working primarily in administration and allowing his pictures to circulate without any kind of programmatic discourse, Petschow remained far from fulfilling society's expectations of an artist. Very little was known about him at the time and this remains the case today: he remains a paradoxical figure of anonymity embodied in a name.

Conversely, Mittelholzer is in some ways more famous than his images and assumed the status of a national hero between the two wars. According to a magazine poll, he was once the most popular man in Switzerland[3] and after his premature death in 1937, a monument was erected at Zurich airport in recognition of his renown and roads were named after him. The aura surrounding Mittelholzer was greatly enhanced by his mode of transport: while Petschow still used a balloon, Mittelholzer was a pilot and succeeded like no other Swiss in focusing upon himself both the popular enthusiasm for aeronautic adventure and the pride of budding national companies such as Ad Astro Aero (subsequently Swissair) whose name he came to emblematise. His prestige extended to all levels of society, reaching even the champions of modern art. He, too, found a place in *Film und Foto,* as well as in other New Photography exhibitions in Switzerland and Germany; he also caught the eye of Sigfried Giedion, who cited him to illustrate the modern conquest of new areas of perception.[4]

Mittelholzer achieved such pre-eminence through tactics that perhaps anticipate those which lead to the success of Yann Arthus-Bertrand. He managed to endow the aerial view with a rhetoric of elevation in the moral sense of the term and to confer upon the photographer the aura of an 'intellectual of the aerial element' – a kind of 'spiritual aviator', as one journalist wrote at the time.[5] In addition, he mastered the use of diverse types of media, mixing photography with publishing, cinema, radio and theatre talks. He published abundantly: eleven books appeared in his name during his lifetime, translated into six languages.[6] He also worked in close collaboration with journals, regularly supplying them with pictures and stories. In addition, he gave numerous illustrated talks and radio interviews and, as early as 1924, seized the opportunity then offered by cinema, becoming involved in the founding of Praesens Film, a production company of note (he was responsible for several full-length films, each of which simultaneously provided both a narrative and a photographic story, constituting a multimedia event).[7]

Mittelholzer had already shown himself to be a man of images before becoming an aviator. As soon as he reached adolescence, he signed up for a photographer's apprenticeship and, along with many others of his generation, first encountered the aerial view through the war. In 1915 he enrolled in the photographic section of the new Swiss Aeronautic Division; by the following year he was its director and in 1917 he obtained his pilot's licence. Once demobilised, he quickly applied his twin competencies of photographer and aviator to civic ends. In 1919, with his ex-instructor Alfred Comte, he founded the transport and aerial photography business Comte, Mittelholzer & Co., which took the name of Ad Astra Aero in 1920 and in 1931 merged with its competitor Balair to become Swissair. Within every company and in whatever directorial position he assumed, Mittelholzer took charge of anything to do with the image, work which ranged from cartographic photography or commissions for industrial shots, down to the business's own advertising. This image production was key as the companies were first starting out: indeed for several years it was the only sector to reap rewards to the extent that, in 1921, Ad Astra Aero contemplated giving up the transport work entirely.[8] These considerations nicely illustrate the significance that picture production held at the beginning of commercial civil aviation and the paramount role within it that a photographer such as Mittelholzer could play. After the experiences of World War I, where aircraft ultimately acted less as weapons than instruments of reconnaissance and surveillance, it was quite possible to envisage maintaining a fleet with pilots and engineers, whose main aim was to take photographs. At this time, an aircraft was not merely a means of transport, but equally, an instrument for seeing. Similarly, an airline represented a photographic agency just as much as a transportation enterprise.

The image-based slant was doubly important for Ad Astra Aero. Not only did it provide the funds needed to support the rest of the company financially, but it supplied the visual material needed for advertising. Furthermore – in a kind of unique reflective game – the person responsible for producing the publicity material himself became its best vehicle: Mittelholzer managed to personally embody both the sector and the company he was responsible for advertising. When confronted with his iconographic and editorial works, it is therefore often difficult to draw a distinction between para-scientific or technical documentation (the main claim) and commercial advertising or self-promotional material. Similarly, it can be difficult to distinguish between the various roles of photographer, pilot, explorer and company director. Mittelholzer's books and stories produce a conscious blurring of these roles, in particular, those of photographer and pilot: everything in the work leads one to believe that the two activities were fundamentally one and the same; each one of the author's images seems to be charged with aeronautic adventures whose significance its very presence establishes in return. Certainly it was more Mittelholzer's photographs and various publications than his actual feats that made him the aviator *par excellence* in Switzerland. His celebrity put more significant pilots in the shade, despite the fact that he never truly belonged among the elite sky aces and rarely achieved any decisive firsts, either in the Alps or in the Mediterranean and African crossings.

THE PILOT-PHOTOGRAPHER

It is Mittelholzer's books that provide the best opportunity to study closely the interplay between his roles of photographer, pilot and scientific explorer. We will thus now concentrate on them, considering them in their totality: this implies a reading of the images that is profoundly influenced by the texts. With one exception, all works name Mittelholzer as author, whether he had provided the prints, written the text or indeed was rather the book's subject, writing only the introduction or some short chapters. Most of the works adopt a narrative form: the story of an aerial crossing comprises an accumulation of anecdotes and shots, which minutely detail the dangers encountered, the mechanical failures and the moments of exaltation. Together, these elements engender deep ambiguity: while claiming to record voyages of exploration with scientific aims, whose *raison d'être* was to enrich geography, geology and ethnography with their findings, the majority of the texts in fact describe the story of the actual taking of the shots and the 'scientific' analyses themselves remain very superficial. Thus under the cover of a scientific ideal, the aerial view – an image hitherto reputed to be technical and abstract – now became the basis for an adventure narrative that was itself the subject of the pictures.

This reflexive aspect of the photographic expedition is evident also in the plates, where actual aerial views are interspersed with a second type of illustration whose aim is to document the taking of the shots themselves, either through pictures of the expedition team or views of the planes or bases. These supporting pictures give value to the actual aerial views and reinforce their narrative potential. But the very presence of these 'meta-documents' also creates certain ambiguities. Given that all the plates are attributed to Mittelholzer, one might be forgiven for wondering who would have been able to capture the shot of his plane in mid-flight. Similarly, how are we supposed to interpret this or that aerial view where a second aeroplane has appeared? Is Mittelholzer the subject or the author of such shots? Generally speaking, the books themselves take care to leave such ambiguities in place, allowing the reader to remain vaguely aware of the two possibilities.

All is done to ensure that one never stops seeing in the works of Mittelholzer the photographer the achievements of Mittelholzer the pilot, although the two activities are in their nature incompatible: it is not possible at the same time to pilot a plane and take a photograph. Mittelholzer does not conceal this in his accounts: either he is at the controls (in which case he cannot be the true author of the published picture), or he is the photographer (meaning he was not in charge of the plane during this or that historical moment immortalised in the image, such as the first flight over Kilimanjaro). His descriptions regarding the exact methods of picture-taking nevertheless endeavour to minimise the contradiction. In sum, Mittelholzer explains that aerial photography essentially provides an image produced by two people. The photograph emerges through a kind of symbiosis between the pilot and the photographer who work in a close exchange of signals to decide on both the path of the aircraft and the framing of the shot. In his role as mission leader, Mittelholzer was thus able to take credit for control of both flight and picture, wherever he had been located in the aircraft.

When he took the shots that date from the end of the 1910s and the early years of the 1920s, captured from inside biplanes without cabins, Mittelholzer was the passenger, seated just behind the pilot and orally instructing him which manoeuvres to make, according to the image he wanted to obtain. In other words, he was piloting the pilot, who in return assisted in the framing through his manoeuvres. Following the introduction of aircraft with cabins, that relationship clearly had to change, but ways were found to get round it. Mittelholzer recounts that, during the 1923 Arctic expedition, he conveyed his instructions with the aid of a ski stick, which he tapped on the engineer-pilot's left shoulder, helmet, or right shoulder, depending on the direction needed. By the end of the 1920s, aircraft had become even bigger and during the trans-African crossing in 1926–7, the photographer was separated from the cockpit by several metres. But Mittelholzer maintained his boast of perfect control over both aircraft and image. There is no doubt that the contact between pilot and photographer was no longer physical, but the possibility of visual and oral communication remained and the twin-pilot seating facilitated quick switch of flight control. Thus in his account of the flight over Kilimanjaro, Mittelholzer continues to employ 'I' for all decisions taken concerning both flight and photography and manages to sign images documenting his personal adventures as aviator with his own name. Whether piloting the aircraft or taking the shots, he continued to claim he was both aviator and photographer. Even if it had never been his intention, and even if his avant-garde admirers were not aware of his photographic methods, it is nevertheless the case that these methods seem to represent an ideal form of modern creation. Here was a collective work based on the coordination of two types of equipment – the recording instrument and its means of transport – in an interdependence of artistry and mechanical movement.

THE MOUNTAINEER

This way of capturing images – taken, that is, by a cabin-passenger operating through a side-window – defined yet another feature of Mittelholzer's aerial view: the importance of the oblique, or high-angled, shot. This particular aspect of his practice can also help modify prevailing thought on the history of aerial photography, which frequently privileged the vertical cartographic view, as though this alone was the purest and most fully realised form. In reality, verticality had held a minor position for some time, due not only to its being extremely difficult to attain, necessitating specially equipped baskets or aircraft, but also to the fact that it corresponded to an abstraction of the landscape which some had specifically rejected, as had Mittelholzer himself. Mittelholzer held that the vertical image had the disadvantage of flattening relief and diminishing volume unlike the oblique shot, which was able to show the landscape's volumetric dimensions to advantage.[9] Indeed, Mittelholzer's major objective – and his principal field of expertise – was Alpine photography. Here his model was not so much the map, which he saw as less able than photography to convey accurate geological, geographical and economic conditions of a terrain, as the relief model, as he indicates in his best-known work, *Alpenflug*, published in 1928 (translated into French as *Des Ailes et des Alpes* in 1929).[10] With this, Mittelholzer recalls the tradition of cartographical reliefs that had been very popular in Switzerland since the eighteenth century, following Franz Ludwig Pfyffer's landscape relief model of the *Urschweiz* in 1786, the most famous manifestation of the genre.[11] Given this, the question would have been how to develop an aerial photography that would retain the size of the massifs – their 'monumental and heroic nature' – and prevent their becoming frozen 'in a relief without warmth and life'.[12] To achieve this, Mittelholzer favoured a viewpoint that was not only oblique but often completely lateral, with the aircraft slipping between mountains at the same height as the summits, rather than above them (Figure 9.2). For the novice, it is very difficult to distinguish these shots from traditional Alpine representations taken on the mountain-face. At this moment the aerial view constituted less a radically new point of view, abstract and supra-human, than a continuation of established methods of Alpine iconography whereby it comes almost to mimic the mountaineer's viewpoint.

Indeed, Mittelholzer saw the Alpinist's point of view as his ideal model. He had been passionate about climbing as a young man – his adolescence had been spent in mountain and photographic pursuits and it would be in the mountains, not the air, that he would meet his death. *Alpenflug* was aimed specifically at mountain-lovers and mountaineers and the author stressed in the introduction that the shot taken from an aircraft should 'recreate the mountaineer's sensations'

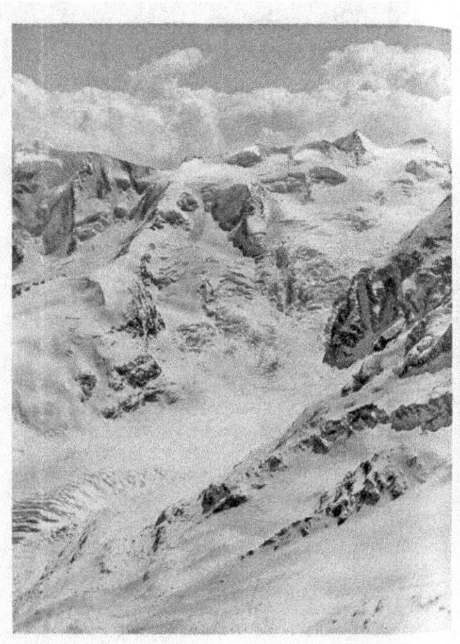

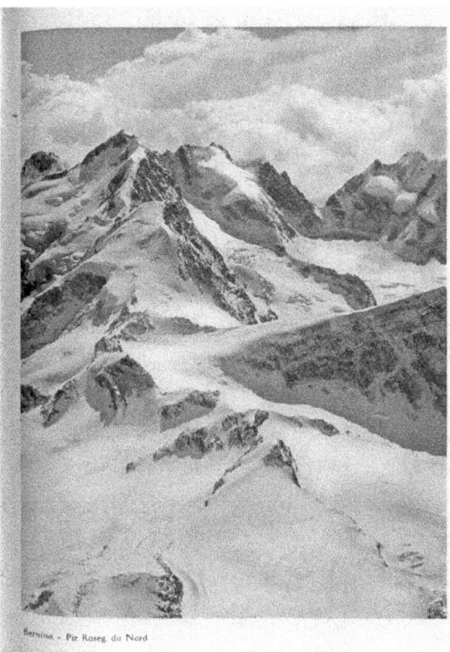

[9.2] Walter Mittelholzer, *Les Ailes et les Alpes*, 1929.

by injecting body into the abstraction of the map.[13] He devoted many long pages to comparing his two favourite activities, in which he never spoke of aviation as surpassing mountaineering or as a technical advance that made the other redundant. To the contrary, the aeronautical project seemed to be a kind of organic extension, driven by the same search for transcendence of the natural forces, the same quest for physical and spiritual elevation. If Mittelholzer came to say that with aviation he missed the physical effort demanded by climbing, the texts nonetheless endeavour to reintegrate that effort into the act of aerial photography itself, where the author repeatedly accentuates its strictly corporeal element. Thus the acrobatic shots presumably taken from an open biplane, the pain-inducing contortions and the 'extreme expenditure of energy' involved in simultaneously hanging on and leaning out in order to capture a shot.[14] Mittelholzer also explains that to prevent a picture from wobbling, the photographer must use his body to absorb the engine's vibrations. Again and again, Mittelholzer imbues what is a seemingly totally disembodied image – a view from apparently nowhere – with a corporality and a very real physical subject, which the shots taken at mountain-height seek to recall every bit as much as do the accounts of the picture-taking.

Although Alpine aerial photography did not radically break away from the language of traditional landscape representation, it added an essentially quantitative component. Photography conducted on foot at peaks of 3,000 or 4,000 metres is self-evidently limited. It would have taken years for a climber to gather the two hundred pictures collected in *Alpenflug*, whereas in a few minutes an aerial photographer could shoot whole chains of summits, varying their relationship and arrangement at will within the framing. Here again, Mittelholzer's example moves against the conventional conception of the aerial view as a synthetic image, as a generic representation of landscape, which gathers into itself all other possible shots, somehow eradicating them at the same time. On the contrary, the work highlights the abundance of different viewpoints of a subject that elevation above the earth permits. This is very clearly seen in the two fine double-pages devoted to Cervin, where different perspectives are arranged to give the impression that the observer is travelling around the summit (Figure 9.3). Such mobility of viewpoint enables an enrichment of the mountain's sculptural might, but it also serves to again remind the reader of the act of taking the shot – of the presence of an aircraft and a photographer, circling around the pinnacle. The presentation of the flight over Kilimanjaro has a similar structure: a sequence of ten or so pictures first chart the progressive approach to the mountain and then the orbital movements of the aircraft around the crater. Many of the illustrations are superfluous, but they nevertheless attest to the exploits involved in the original capturing of the shots: a kind of ceremonial dance around the vanquished summit (Figure 9.4). Once more, despite the deliberately traditional aspect of his aerial photography, at this point Mittelholzer is certainly in step with the precepts of the New Vision, whose works continually celebrate the act of photographic image-capture itself and the body movements demanded by modern framing (those shots favoured by the avant-garde, taken upside-down, off-centre, or alternately diving and soaring). In some ways, his practices bring together two of the main ideals of the movement's theorists, which are at first sight incompatible: the work seems to reconcile photography as scientific document, where the aim was to guarantee objectivity and in which the abstract aerial view constituted precisely one of its privileged incarnations, with photography as an art of the body, produced by physical shot-taking manoeuvres which are thereby inscribed within the final picture. The two poles – the art of the instrument/the art of the body, depersonalisation/embodiment – come together in Mittelholzer in the way that his discourse interweaves scientific claim and sporting endeavour. Indeed, it is precisely this that characterises the photography of exploration, a domain where, as the preface to the work describing the flight over Africa tells us, 'many times have science and sport marched hand in hand towards unhoped-for success'.[15]

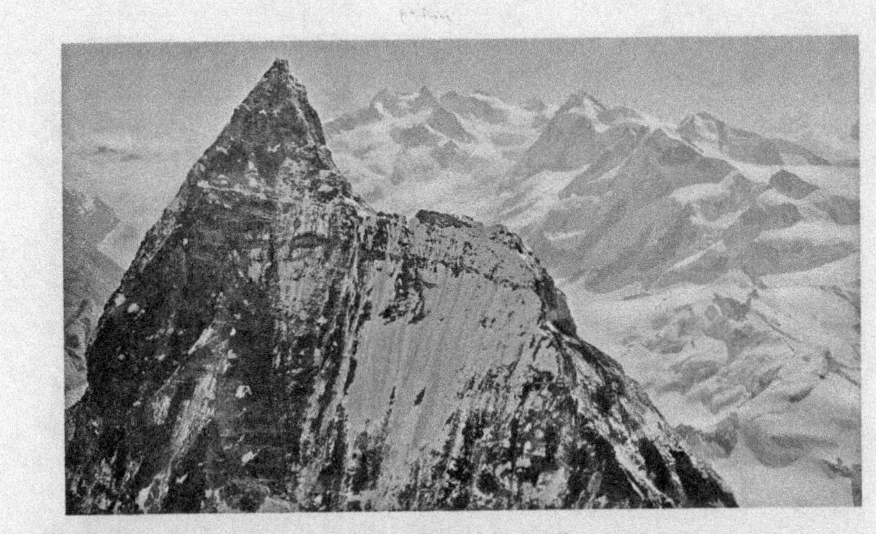

157. Cervin, de l'Ouest. (Pic Tyndall.)

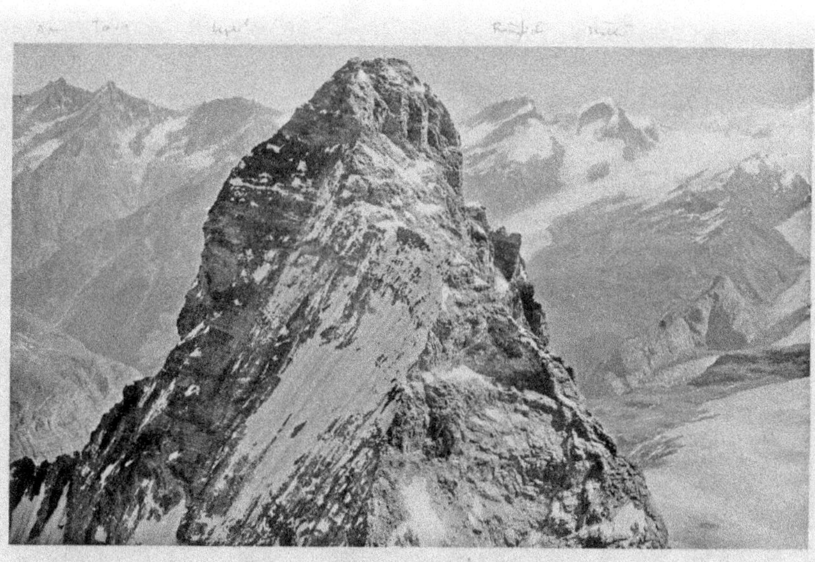

158. Cervin, du Sud-Ouest. (Arête italienne.)

[9.3] Walter Mittelholzer, *Les Ailes et les Alpes*, 1929.

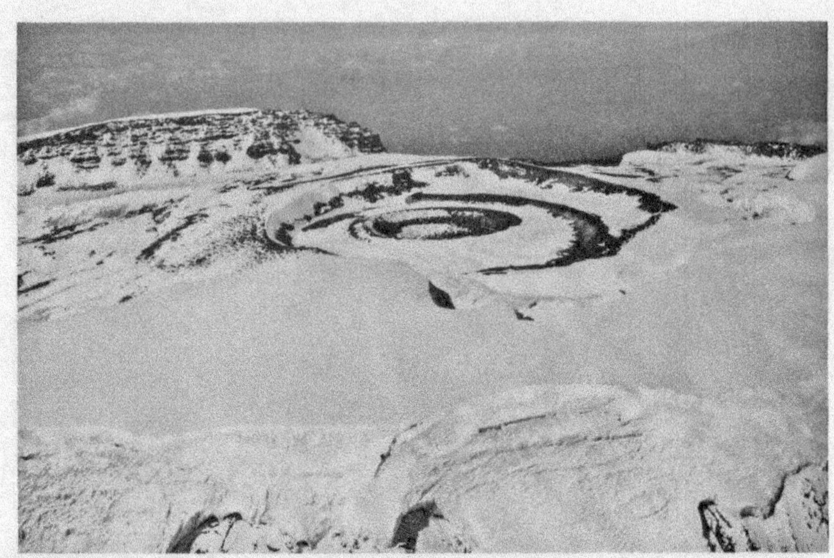

116. Wie ein Riesenauge liegt zu unseren Füssen der Kraterring des Kibo. Flughöhe 6100 m

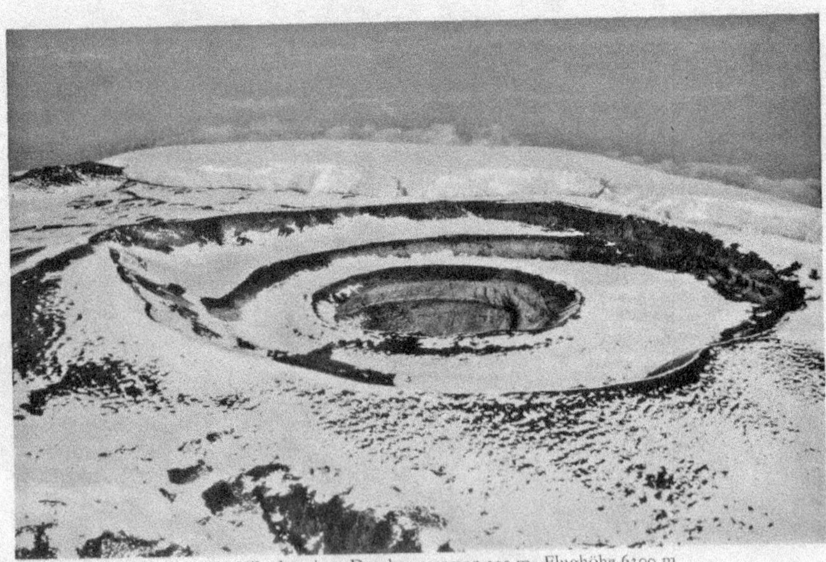

117. Der Einbruchskrater des Kibo hat einen Durchmesser von 500 m. Flughöhe 6300 m

[9.4] Walter Mittelholzer, *Kilimandjaro-Flug*, 1930.

THE EXPLORER

The limitations of such an alliance, however, are well illustrated in the same work, *R-A-S-T. En hydravion de Zurich au Cap de Bonne-Espérance: le raid aérien Suisse-Transafricain (By Hydroplane from Zurich to the Cape of Good Hope: the Switzerland-Trans-African Aerial Crossing)*. It records the first transcontinental crossing of Africa by hydroplane from Zurich to the Cape (the first crossing in a regular aircraft had recently been achieved by the English), together with the 'scientific' findings (geographical, geological, ethnographical) gathered on the expedition. To ensure the trip's scientific element, a writer and African specialist, René Gouzy (the real initiator of the project) and a geologist, Arnold Heim, accompanied Mittelholzer and his engineer, Hans Hartmann. But the trip was primarily a media event and was directly reported as a national sporting venture by the Swiss press, to whom Mittelholzer regularly dispatched his journals. Clearly, the co-habitation of the two dimensions of science and sport was not without problem as in-depth scientific research required lengthy studies of the ground, while the pride of aviator and photographer Mittelholzer focused primarily on the speed of the crossing and the richness of the aero-photographic crop, goals that tended to keep him at a distance from that same ground. Indeed Heim's preface itself expresses some disappointment about the superficial scientific results of the crossing.[16]

This conflict between overhead flight and ground research particularly affected the expedition's ethnographic project. To negotiate the problem, the illustrations alternate aerial views with traditional ethnographic shots (group portraits, village scenes, exotic landscapes, etc.), all of which bear the Mittelholzer signature. Moreover, somewhere between the two, Mittelholzer perfected a unique form of aeronautic-ethnographic image (Figure 9.5) in which crowd scenes or group portraits were taken at a steep angle from the raised aircraft cabin after the plane itself had already landed. These strange framings produced views that came close to fulfilling the rules of ethnographic photography, but were sufficiently elevated to remind the observer of the aeronautic aspect of Mittelholzer's art. For once more, it is the aerial photographer himself who attracts the most attention: the majority of the shots of Africans, as with the narratives they illustrate, do not show much more than the people's encounter with his aircraft and the astonished and enthralled reactions provoked by his arrival. The desire to maintain focus on the aeronautic act undermines any potential ethnographic account, since the moment of discovery of the other is, as it were, turned upside down: here it is more a question of the European observing the admiration of the other. Similarly, all real contact – both in visual and

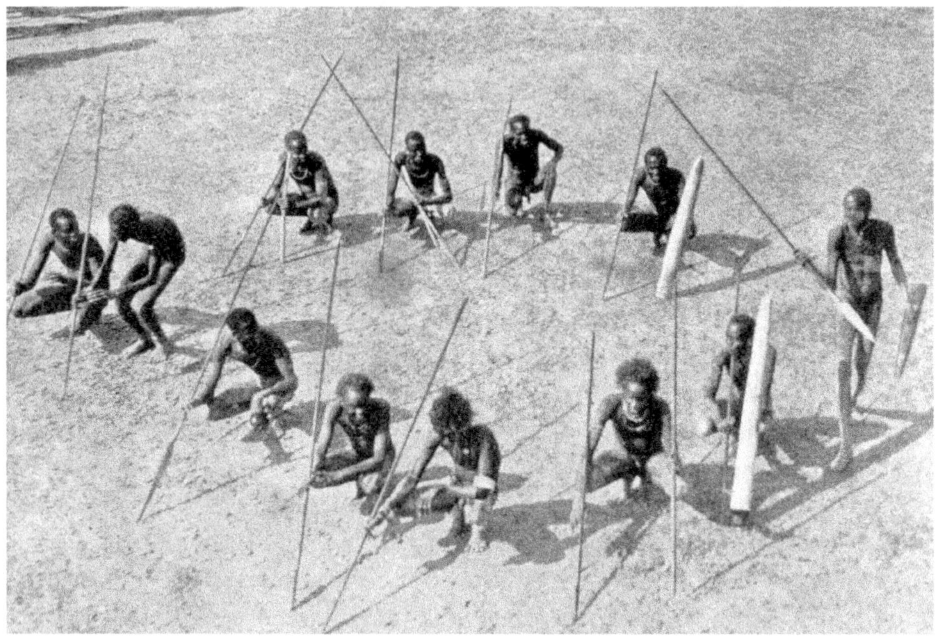

[9.5] Walter Mittelholzer, *R-A-S-T. En hydravion de Zurich au Cap de Bonne-Espérance: le raid aérien suisse-transafricain*, 1927.

relational terms – is thwarted by the overhead position required by the aeronautic model.

For Mittelholzer, then, the photographic and cinematographic narrative seems to have taken precedence over any other more exploratory considerations. He transformed the aircraft into a veritable flying photographic studio, with a dark-room installed in the toilet area and some half-dozen photographic and film cameras on board, despite drastic weight limitations. When on one occasion it proved necessary to lighten the aircraft in order to continue the journey, Mittelholzer decided to dismiss the scientific observers: the geologist and the ethnographic writer were both dispatched, while filming and photographic equipment remained on board. Here again, Mittelholzer had envisaged the airborne expedition as primarily a media enterprise, whose success would be judged by the resultant images. Yet, in his eyes, that did not automatically contradict the scientific value of the shots. As his experience of the war had shown him and as he indicates in the introduction to another of his books, the view from an aircraft does not in itself constitute a research tool, since everything happens far too rapidly to allow direct observation.[17] Only the aerial *photograph*, analysed calmly after the event, can completely fulfil that role. Thus, in Mittelholzer's eyes, an aerial view can at the same time claim to be a research aid, an account of its adventurous creation and a monument to the glory of its maker. It always constitutes a double-sided document that offers an image of both the world and the aviator who glides above it, a photograph in which the very opening onto the vastness of the world holds the potential to celebrate the self.

NOTES

1 Thus, while Yann Arthus-Bertrand takes care to speak in the title of his 2002 work *Une France vue du ciel (A View of France from the Sky)* of being unable to offer anything other than a partial selection from the diverse aspects of his subject, several Swiss works have no hesitation in giving the title, *La Suisse vue de ciel (Switzerland Seen from the Sky)*, rather as though they could effectively contain the country inside a book.

2 On Eduard Spelterini, see his own work, *Ueber den Wolken/Par-dessus les nuages* (Zurich: Brunner, 1928); also the fine catalogues, *Eduard Spelterini. Fotografien des Balloonspioniers/ Photographs of a Pioneer Balloonist*, Thomas Kramer and Hilar Stadler, eds (Zurich: Scheidegger & Spiess, 2007), and *Eduard Spelterini und das Spektakel der Bilder. Die kolorierten Lichtbilder des Ballonpioniers*, Hilar Stadler, ed. (Zurich: Scheidegger & Spiess, 2010). On his 1928 book see Olivier Lugon, 'Über den Wolken/Par-dessus les nuages, Eduard Spelterini, 1928' in *Schweizer Fotobücher 1927 bis heute. Eine andere Geschichte der Fotografie/Livres de photographie suisses de 1927 à nos jours, Une autre histoire de la photographie/Swiss Photobooks from 1927 to the Present. A Different History of Photography*, Peter Pfrunder, ed. (Winterthur: Fotostiftung Schweiz/Baden: Lars Müller Publishers, 2011).

3 Erich Meier, 'Walter Mittelholzer (1894–1937), Balz Zimmerman (1895–1937)', in *Sechs Schweizer Flugpioniere: Henri und Armand Dufaux, Oskar Bider, Alfred Compte, Walter Mittelholzer, Balz Zimmermann*, Schweizer Pioniere der Wirtschaft und Technik collection, no. 46 (Meilen: Verein für wirtschaftshistorische Studien, 1987), p.91.

4 Sigfried Giedion, 'Malerei und Architektur', *Das Werk*, vol. 34 (1949): 36, 39.

5 *B.Z. am Mittag*, Berlin, cited in the advertisement for *Afrikaflug* which appeared in *Alpenflug* (Zurich: Orell Füssli, 1928), without page number.

6 Walter Mittelholzer, ed., *Im Flugzeug dem Nordpol entgegen: Junkers'sche Hilfexpedition für Amundsen nach Spitzbergen, 1923* (Zurich: Orell Füssli, 1924); Walter Mittelholzer, *Persienflug* (Zurich/Leipzig: Orell Füssli, 1926); Otto Flückiger, ed., *Die Schweiz aus der Vogelschau* (Erlenbach-Zurich: E. Rentsch, 1924) (*La Suisse à vol d'oiseau* [Erienbach-Zurich: E. Rentsch, 1926]); Walter Mittelholzer, René Gouzy, Arnold Heim, *R-A-S-T. En hydravion de Zurich au Cap de Bonne-Espérance: le raid aérien suisse-transafricain* (Neuchâtel: Ed. de la Baconnière, 1927) (*Afrika Flug im Wasserflugzeug 'Switzerland' von Zürich über den dunkeln Erdteil nach dem Kap der guten Hoffnung* [Zurich/Leipzig: Orell Füssli, 1927]); Walter Mittelholzer, *Alpenflug* (Zurich/Leipzig: Orell Füssli, 1928) (*Les Ailes et les Alpes* [Neuchâtel: Ed. de la Baconnière, 1929]); Gustav Ehrhardt, Walter Mittelholzer, *Kilimandjaro-Flug* (Zurich/Leipzig: Orell Füssli, 1930); Walter Mittelholzer, *Mittelmeerflug* (Zurich: Rascher & Cie., 1930); Walter Mittelholzer, *Tschadseeflug. Mit dem dreimotorigen Fokker der Swissair durch die Sahara zum Tschadsee* (Zurich: Verlag Schweizer Aero-Revue, 1932); Walter Mittelholzer, *Abessinienflug.*

Mit dem dreimotorigen Fokker an den Hof des Negus Negesti (Zurich: Verlag Scheizer Aero-Revue, 1934); *La Suisse à vol d'avion/Die Schweiz vom Flugzeug aus* (Yverdon: Vautier frères & Cie., 1934); Walter Mittelholzer, *Flying Adventures* (London/Glasgow: Blackie & Son, 1936) (*Fliegerabenteuer* [Leipzig: F.A. Brockhaus, 1938]).

7 Such was the case with *Mein Persien-Flug/Mon vol de Zurich en Perse*, 1924–5; *Mittelholzer's Afrikaflug/De Zurich au cratère du Kilimandjaro*, 1930; *Abessinienflug/Vers l'Abyssinie*, 1934.

8 Meier, op. cit., pp.73–4.

9 Walter Mittelholzer, 'Aus der Praxis der Luftphotographie', in *Alpenflug*, op. cit., p.108. This chapter is not included in the French translation.

10 Ibid., p.108.

11 On this subject, see Andreas Bürgi, *Relief der Urschweiz. Entstehung und Bedeeutung des Landschaftsmodells von Franz Ludwig Pfyffer* (Zurich: Neue Zürcher Zeitung, 2007) and Andreas Bürgi, ed., *Europa Miniature. Die kulturelle Bedeutung des Reliefs, 16.- 21. Jahrhundert* (Zurich: Neue Zürcher Zeitung, 2007).

12 Walter Mittelholzer, *Les Ailes et les Alpes*, op. cit., p.9.

13 Ibid., p.9.

14 Ibid., p.19.

15 Albert Heim, 'Preface', in Walter Mittelholzer, René Gouzy, Arnold Heim, *R-A-S-T*, op. cit., p.10.

16 Ibid.

17 Kurt Wegener, introduction to *Im Flugzeug dem Nordpol entegegen*, op. cit., pp.24–5.

10

From the Sky to the Ground

The Aerial View and the Ideal of the *Vue Raisonnée* in Geography during the 1920s

Marie-Claire Robic

The rare descriptions of geographical methodology published in France at the beginning of the twentieth century held the practice of direct observation carried out in the field in the highest esteem.[1] But although terrain was valorised, it was only one of the terms within which geographers' cognitive experience was constituted. Those practising so-called 'modern geography' would break with a double tradition: that of historical geography, based upon the interpretation of ancient texts; and that of the 'savants de cabinet', intellectuals who directed exploration from a distance in order to synthesise the information gathered. A mixed persona thus emerged, one that combined documentary researcher and interpreter of terrestrial phenomena.[2] The new formula of these geographers, the *vue raisonnée,* captured well the complexity of their approach. The very coining of the expression allowed them to draw attention to a unified, innovative project. Nevertheless, the formula involved a cognitive tension. In fact, their ideal became manifested in a wide range of adopted positions and individual preferences, which ranged from that of the most rationalist of geographers, the adept of the *vue rationnelle,* mistrustful of the visual sense-impressions and reliant on the map, to that of the most strictly descriptive geographer, the enthusiast for terrain and proselyte of the 'concrete'. The epistemological project – which in my opinion partakes of a mixed strategy[3] – manifested itself as an oscillation between the two poles, yet also through a predisposition for composite means of visualisation that combine figural representation with abstraction – such as, for instance, the block diagrams used in geomorphology or the photographic plates used in human geography.[4]

However, the enthusiasm for terrain was to run up against the limits of individual observation, which was both too aleatory in its spatio-temporal unfolding, too fragmentary and too close to the ground to yield firm knowledge. With the proliferation of reliable small and large scale maps, knowledge of locations was largely completed by the end of the nineteenth century. Better still, with the advent of photography – whose realism all geographers, like other intellectuals of the period, proclaimed – objectivity and visual legibility seemed within reach. Infatuated with the photographic medium, geographers attempted to compensate for the limitations of ground-level photography through the panorama and the view from above, which were among their favourite means of visualisation. More broadly, however, their leitmotif was 'knowing how to look': that is, how to choose the right vantage point, capturing the most representative views of a region and shunning the picturesque – in short, exercising a discipline that was differentiated from the practices of tourists and artists. In so doing, the geographer adopted the position of the 'good witness' (*le bon témoin*).[5] Their own experience led them – beyond their professed realism, beyond their intention to be 'level' with the world (to use Olivier Orain's expression [*de plain pied*]) – to construct visual devices that combined photography with maps and diagrams and with text and image, devices that would be used for research and scholarly exchange as well as communicating with the larger public.[6]

In parallel with these developments, the large-scale map had come to be regarded as the best substitute for direct field experience. In France, all geographers extolled the quality of the colour 1:50,000 scale map that the army's cartographic division published in the early 1900s. Apart from accuracy, the map offered completeness and continuity, as if from the viewpoint of an aerial observer. With its meticulous detailing, the clarity of its symbols and its expressiveness, the map was the closest rendition of the concreteness of contact that was sought in the field.[7]

We can consider this topographical map as the concrete avatar of the aerial view, which has fascinated the Western geographical imagination from the figure of Daedalus through to Google Earth.[8] Around the time of its publication, heavier-than-air flight was actualising its implied vantage point with an unprecedented degree of control. This point of view was no longer fictional. Henceforth, the ideal of an absolute seeing eye was possible: the synoptic (the gathering of all things into the same space) and panoptic (all things becoming visible) could merge within the gaze of the aviator or his pictorial double, aerial photography.

How did geographers appropriate the aerial view, whether oblique or vertical? As a document mediating an actual view from the sky, the aerial photograph was aligned with the objectivity and realism that geographers had associated with photography. It was conferred *a priori* with an absolute legitimacy, grounded in an assumption of its transparency and impartiality. At the same time, the view from the aeroplane produced extraordinary scalar and recording effects, with the vastness of aerial coverage and the variety of terrestrial elements captured almost equating to a map. With these images, it seemed that the direct and nearly all-encompassing view of the terrestrial surface – the basis upon which the 'modern' geographers attempted to establish their scientific expertise – could be realised.

What actually happened to geographic practice with the emergence of this technical innovation, when viewing could become aerial, either *in situ* from the cockpit of an aeroplane or via the dissemination of aerial photography? Did this unprecedented experience, this new form of documentation, allow geographers to conduct their programme of a *vue raisonnée* of the earth? Did the aerial view directly achieve their ideal of a convergence of map and terrain?

THE SEDUCTION OF THE MEDIUM: EXPLORATORY USES OF AERIAL PHOTOGRAPHY

The geographical cultivation of the visual and its popularisation

Geographers' infatuation with photography from the end of the nineteenth century onwards, was equalled only by their interest in its use from the air. They incorporated aerial photography early into their publications, whether these aimed at a mass public, were academic textbooks or school manuals. Thus, in 1908, P. Vidal de la Blache[9] included several views, taken from a hot-air balloon, in an illustrated volume of *La France: Tableau géographique* (*France: A Geographical Picture*) (Figure 10.1). The newly illustrated second edition, published in 1911 in the multi-volume collection *Histoire de France*, featured on its frontispiece an aerial view of the centre of Paris, taken from a book entitled *Paris vu en ballon* (*Paris Seen from a Balloon*).[10] After the war, Emmanuel de Martonne published a number of illustrated works on the major regions of France.[11] These also aimed at a wide readership and featured photographs, many of which (18 out of approximately 80) were aerial views. Some of these were laid out in double-spreads, in which views taken from an aeroplane were juxtaposed with ground-level images.

VARIÉTÉS DUES AU SOL

TERRES FROIDES DES ENVIRONS DE LYON : LA DOMBES

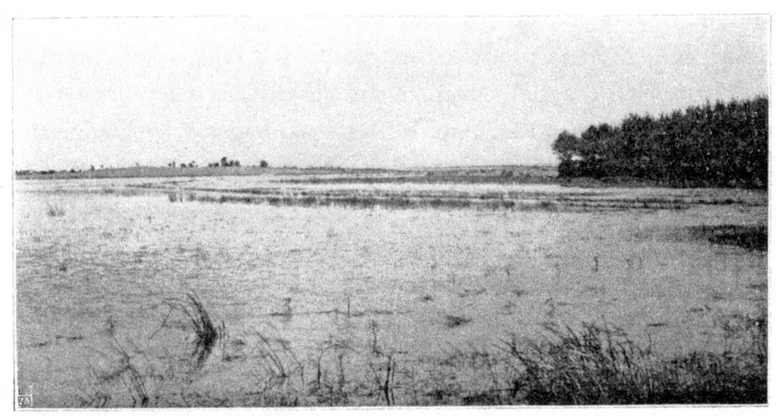

LES EAUX *se sont parfois amassees dans les creux formés entre les moraines, et s'étalent sur le limon argileux qui les retient. La moraine se profile, comme une ride, au dernier plan.* (Fig. 17.)

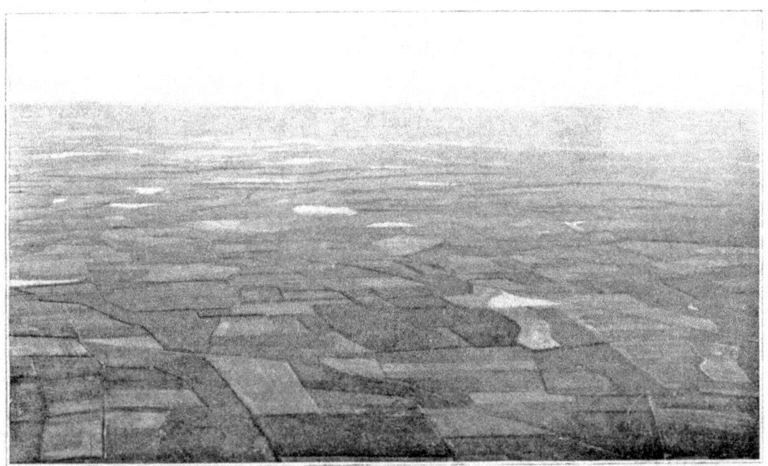

VUE PRISE EN BALLON *sur la Dombes, au-dessus de Villars, vers son extrémité septentrionale : un damier de champs et d'étangs ; ceux-ci pour la plupart artificiels, d'après la régularité de leurs formes. Les routes seules, comme de minces fils, traversent d'un bout à l'autre la surface.* Phot. communiquée par M. Gallois (Fig. 18).

PL. 9

[10.1] One of the very first views taken from a balloon published by a French geographer. From Paul Vidal de la Blache, *La France: Tableau géographique* (Paris: Hachette, 1908).

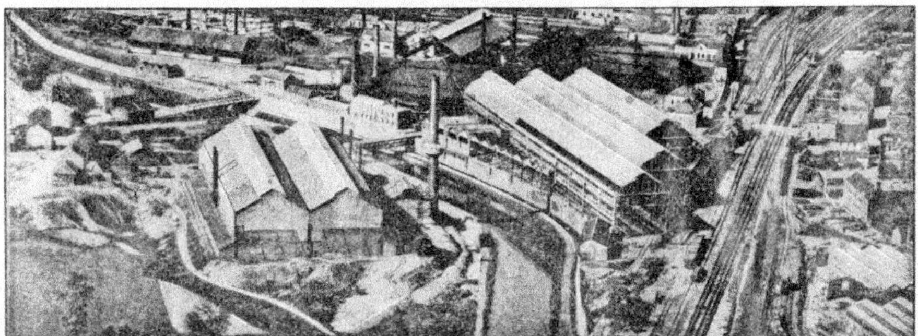

Fig. 37. — Un centre industriel, Louvroil, près de Maubeuge (Nord) ; vue prise en avion, mais en perspective (Cliché Marcel Chrétien).

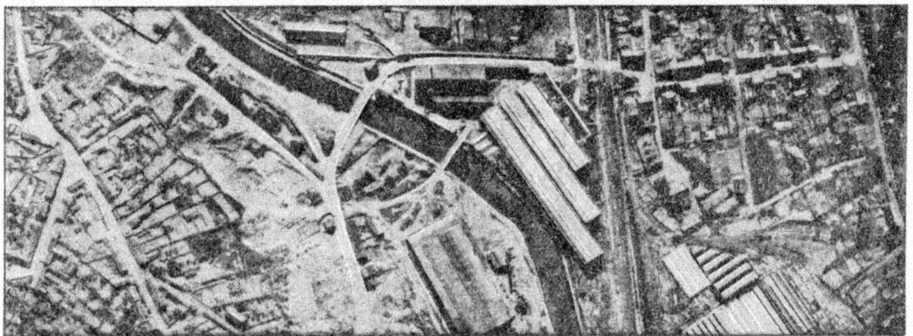

Fig. 38. — Le même centre industriel ; vue prise en avion, droit au-dessus de la petite ville (Cliché Marcel Chrétien).

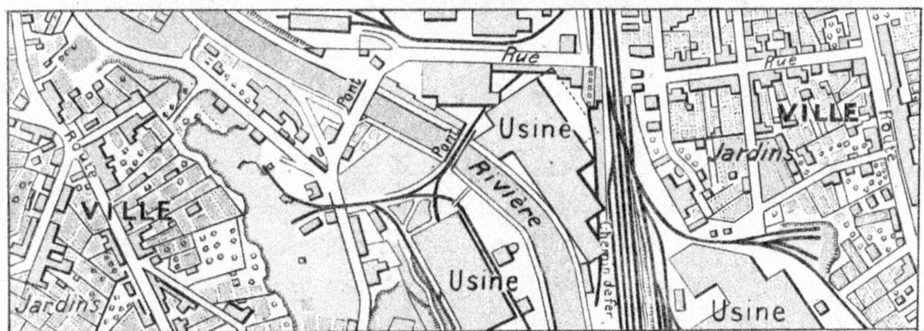

Fig. 39. — Plan reproduisant sous forme de carte l'image entière et exacte de la photographie précédente (fig. 38).

Exercices d'observation. — 1. Que représente la figure 37 ? — 2. Dites ce que vous y voyez. — 3. Que représente la figure 38? — 4. Comment vous apparaissent les routes, la rivière, la ville, la voie ferrée, l'usine ? — 5. Que représente la figure 39 ? — 6. Comment sont représentés les routes, la rivière, les ponts, les maisons, les jardins ?

[10.2] Illustration taken from an elementary school manual from the collection of Jean Brunhes. From Jean Brunhes, *Leçons de géographie à l'usage des écoles primaires, Cours élémentaire* (Tours: Mame, 1924).

The same year, Jean Brunhes included several aerial photographs in the third edition of his *La géographie humaine* (*Human Geography*).[12] He chose several oblique views as well as vertical ones – in all, 13 aerial views out of a total of 278 images (almost all photographs), which accompanied frontal and bird's-eye views taken either in the mountains or from an elevated vantage point.

Brunhes, of all the French geographers the one most particularly dedicated to photographic representation, also published school textbooks that were ahead of their time in featuring aerial representations of the earth.[13] He requested that his books published with Mame be profusely illustrated, colourful and expressive, in order to avoid the prevailing norm of small-scale black and white reproductions that were ultimately 'dreary' for children. He therefore used an illustrator's drawings, but included several aerial views, both oblique and vertical. For a primary school textbook he would combine in one figure an oblique view, a vertical view and a map, this pictorial device illustrating the lesson on 'the representation of the earth' (Figure 10.2).

Infused with a geographical culture of the visual, and wishing to share it with the public, all these authors used the new photographic practices. Fascinated by the contemporaneity of the medium, they competed to demonstrate their modernity through technical and representational innovation.

Geopolitics and development: a full-scale use

As indicated by Bruhnes's textbook, this was also a period of free experimentation, as geographers mobilised the aerial view to solve a multiplicity of problems, to discover various geographical phenomena and to derive field documentation, all at a time before a stable technical know-how had been established. Two little-known examples illustrate this inventive practice.

The first concerns the intervention of a geographer in a territorial dispute, that is to say, in a geopolitical assessment. At the beginning of the 1920s, Emmanuel de Martonne had used aerial photography in rendering this kind of expert evaluation at the request of Colombia and Venezuela:

> This border had been well established by conventions between the two countries; a ridge line separating the beds of certain waterways [...] but there was now some dispute over how to trace the line on a map, as the border was, in parts, covered by impenetrable forests. However, in order to help Mr de Martonne with this Judgment of Solomon, both governments provided him with photographs taken from an aeroplane over the contested areas, thanks to which the expert was able to settle the matter.[14]

The second example comes from the documentary work sponsored by André Cholley in Lyon, from 1923 to 1928. At the Institut d'études rhodaniennes (Institute for Rhone Studies) he promoted an *Atlas photographique du Rhône* (*Photographic Atlas of the Rhone*), which aimed to provide new knowledge about the river and the lands through which it coursed. Consisting of photographs taken from a plane, the work combined vertical views – whose contiguous layout covered a width of 3–4 km of the Rhône valley – and oblique representations, which made possible panoramic views or else 'typical' human and physical data.[15] In keeping with the mission of the Institute, Cholley designed this book with a very general, pragmatic objective in mind, in order to assemble promptly but reliably a 'Rhone documentation', a kind of survey[16] prior to action – documentation that was in fact assisted by the Compagnie nationale du Rhône (Rhone National Company) in the 1930s. For this unprecedented undertaking, Cholley considered it necessary to bring together the geographer and the technician (in the person of the aviator and photographer Seive), while the military's geographic department and other support networks were also involved. This collaborative work seems to have led to a very nuanced understanding of lighting constraints as they related to location and season, and even to the utilisation of the quality of shadows and reflected light to best reveal the landforms that the geographer had chosen.[17] Thus, in his account, Cholley indicated the complexity of the documentary project by emphasising the materiality of interaction between photographic equipment, environmental conditions and the object to be represented, and by showing how this interaction could be instrumentalised. With this, he marked his distance from the notion that aerial photography is a mere recording of the real, a reservation concerning the visible that he was to express throughout his entire career.[18]

From the sky: the revelation of forms

In parallel to this focus on the medium's technical aspects, some of the early geographers who promoted aerial photography pursued the possibilities of the representational forms of this new genre – to use the terms of this book's 'Introduction' by Mark Dorrian and Frédéric Pousin.

In the case of Brunhes, comments accompanying the reproduction of a wartime photograph reveal an inherent enjoyment of vertical aerial vision. This image was incorporated in a plate, published in *La géographie humaine* (Figure 10.3), which brought together two very descriptive photographs: one in close-up, showing a stone-paved street, and the other vertical, which at first sight is enigmatic, intermingling as it does straight, curved and jagged white lines on

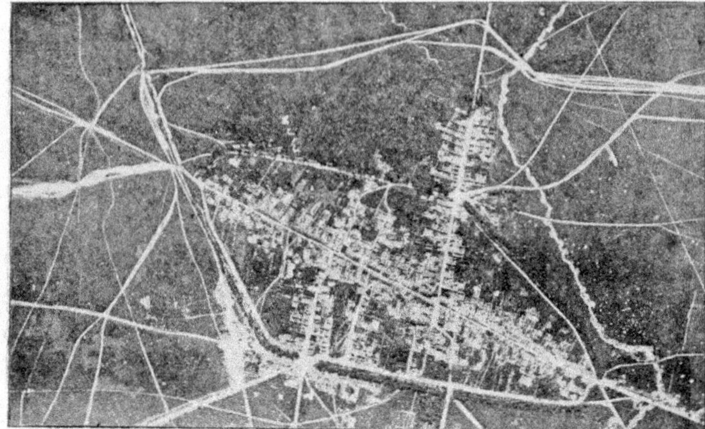

Fig. 56.

La circulation compagne de l'installation.

La ligne dentelée qui va sur la gauche du bas jusqu'en haut est une ligne de tranchées.

Cette vue, prise en avion durant la guerre, représente le village de Bourgogne (Marne), en pleine Champagne pouilleuse, à 12 km. de Reims. C'est l'un des nombreux villages des zones de bataille qui ont été entièrement détruits. Tout le sol et sous-sol est de craie; les moindres sentiers foulés apparaissent de haut comme des lignes blanches sur un tableau noir. — On constate tout à la fois à quel point ce sont des chemins, routes ou rues, qui ont déterminé la structure du village, et à quel point le moindre centre d'installation, surtout en période de suractivité humaine, se trouve enveloppé d'un réseau de circulation. — Ajoutons que moins les lignes de circulation sont perfectionnées, moins elles sont fixes; plus faciles à déplacer, elles se doublent, se triplent, etc., pour redevenir simples en des nœuds de passage qui sont plus ou moins obligés. On a là, *en raccourci*, un symbole de la liaison quasi indissoluble entre maisons et chemins, et même, si l'on veut, une sorte d'image théorique de la circulation sur la terre.

Fig. 57.

Le « pavage » en cailloux roulés de la rue d'une grande ville batie sur une terrasse fluviale : Toulouse.

Il s'agit là de la rue des Chalets à Toulouse dont le pavage a été, depuis lors, amélioré; mais, en 1903, j'ai pu encore en prendre cette photographie tout à fait caractéristique.

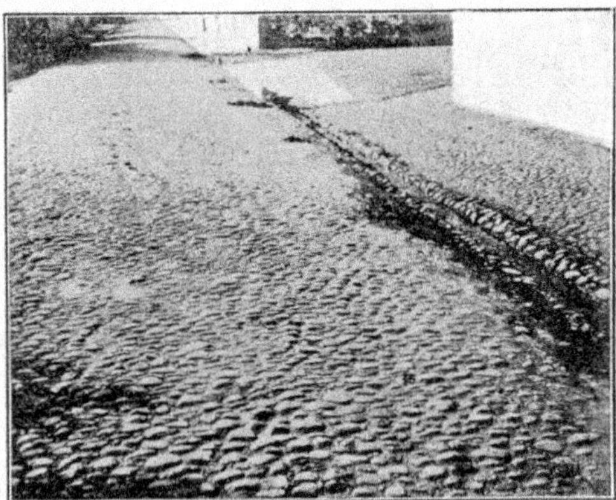

Voir p. 136 et 137.

Cliché Jean Brunhes.

[10.3] The basics of circulation, of atmosphere and of land. From Jean Brunhes, *La géographie humaine*, vol. 3 (Paris: Félix Alcan, 1925).

a dark background. Supplementing the caption 'Circulation as counterpart to settlement', the explanatory comment confers the status of an abstract model on the image: 'Here, foreshortened, one finds the symbol of the almost inextricable link between houses and roads, and also – as it were – a kind of theoretical image of terrestrial circulation'.[19]

The choice of this wartime image, in which a military trench was depicted, dramatised the geographical law that he intended to expound. This was undoubtedly deliberate, as Brunhes was acutely aware of the power of visual communication. However, the image lacks explicitness, despite his having construed it as a teaching example of 'white lines on a blackboard'. Owing especially to the cobweb of roads that it revealed, it was far from expressive, and without his commentary, would have remained indecipherable. In the previous editions of his book, Brunhes had used clearer symbols of the relationship between circulation and settlement, such as the cartographic representation of a city and the radial roads that it polarised. The author therefore overinvested this image, as if this aerial figuration carried its own entrancing value (beyond the attractions of war imagery).

Here it seems that the power of the aerial image had leapt beyond the limitations of method. Indeed, for Brunhes the phenomena of human geography were above anything else the visible facts of terrestrial humanisation. These imprints of human intervention became fully understandable only when they were seen in their true extent, that is – paradoxically – from afar, from above, from the sky. Writing in 1906, Brunhes had established the aerial gaze as a metaphor for geographical method:

> let us rise in a balloon to a few hundred metres above ground; and, with the mind unfettered from everything we know about human beings, let us try to see and record the essential facts of human geography with the same eyes and the same gaze that would allow us to untangle the morphological, topographic and hydrographic features on the surface of the earth. From this hypothetical observation point, what do we notice? Or, better yet, what are the facts of human existence that a photographic plate could capture just as easily as would the eye's retina?[20]

From this fictional observation point he conceived the formal aspects of his object – that is, spatial distributions or geometries (points, lines and surfaces) according to which the phenomena of human geography presented themselves to view:

> Firstly, one of the most visible – a kind of excrescence: the 'house' [conveyed by] all the innumerable and polymorphic givens that dot the earth's surface

> with thousands of tiny points – the red of tile, the grey of slate, the white of marble or limewash, the brown-black of dried leaves [...]
>
> A second fact nearly always and nearly everywhere accompanies the first: it is the 'road' [...] and, from the basket of our balloon, we notice immediately the degree to which – from a geographical point of view – the house and the road are connected.
>
> Other surface stains appear as well, the more numerous the more dense the population: stains with contours that are regular and defined, or of variable shades according to the seasons [...] rendered with a term, still imprecise, that conveys the seen reality – the 'field' or the 'garden' [that] constitute to such an extent positive imprints of human endeavour that they are inscribed on photographs – even if we remain ignorant of by what efforts and what means we here find modified, over such large expanses and in such varied forms, the earth's natural cover of vegetation.[21]

That which the fictional position of the (canonical) aerial gaze allowed him to imagine, aerial photography emphasised by rendering it magisterially visible. Fiction became embodied through aerial photography, and this very embodiment was a source of jubilation.

With his visual sensibility and his way of looking – which was at once analytical and geometrical – Brunhes was struck by the distinctive textures on 'the earth's face' (witness the 'muscle' that he saw described by the rail lines of a marshalling yard). Yet these forms that the aerial image revealed entered his texts as if by stealth, were translated by metaphors and did not affect the methodological constructs or the cognitive projects already developed. The overall spatial figure (the totality of points, lines and surfaces) was neither central to Brunhes' methodology nor to the work he produced following the introduction of aerial imaging. Analysis that was properly *spatial* – particularly the structural study of the totality of points, lines and surfaces that seemed to be prefigured here – played no part in the development of a new geographical paradigm until the 1950s and 1960s.

FROM WARTIME DISCOVERY TO THE GEOGRAPHER-AVIATORS

The geographic journals published between 1919 and 1921 show an explosion of interest in the view from the sky – with which a number of geographers had experimented during the war – and attested to the vistas that aviation opened to geography: exploration and reconnaissance, knowledge production, developmental possibilities, and so forth. In fact, the major French, American and English geography journals simultaneously published richly illustrated articles whose authors (all of whom had been army pilots or assigned to military aerial operations) indicated the suggestive power of this experience of observing the earth, its heuristic scope and its potential for research.[22]

Mountains and marvels

That aims were diverse was shown by three specialist articles published in 1920 in the journal of the Geographic Society of New York, *The Geographical Review*, whose editorial direction was very general in orientation.

One aim, for instance, was to evaluate the possibilites for repurposing the aerial fleet that had become obsolete with the cessation of hostilities. Thus, Lieutenant Leo Walmsley, who took part in missions to investigate the civil uses of the Royal Air Force fleet in the Middle East, described the difficulties and risks associated with the flight between Cairo and Cape Town.[23] Although he felt that the route held no commercial prospects, he concluded with a brief statement on the wonders of Africa seen from the air, 'The Wonder of the African Airscape', 'magical' spectacles that, according to him, no camera could convey and which therefore needed to be personally experienced. While pointing out in his commentaries on photographs their contributions to knowledge of the 'true nature' of the virgin forest or of the population structure, the author also indicated in a heroic manner the difficulties inherent in adventure. His assessment constituted a sort of touristic evaluation of Africa, whereby the aerial journey seemed to further intensify the exoticism to which the continent had been confined by the colonial or orientalist gaze, his 'airscape'[24] bordering on the sublime.

Two other articles showed a more technical usage of aerial photography. One of them concerned cartography, and its author[25] – who had worked with the topographical teams of the Geological Survey – outlined the successive operations (of horizontal reproduction, of photographic montage, of comparison with existing maps) of the experimental technique that was then known as 'aerophotographic mapping'.[26] The other posed the question of aviation's contribution to geography on the basis of tests carried out in hydrography.[27] While the initial test-flight suggested to the author the notion that a 'new world' had opened up to geographers, he nevertheless likened the aerial view to the familiar activity of reading a map: 'The general impression gained from the flight was much the same as that gained by looking down on a map spread on a table.'[28]

The power of the not-seen: the rise of forms and the palimpsest

In other areas of research the aerial view opened up new fields of knowledge. Authors conveyed their enchantment with it (or, at least, their love of its novelty), its powers of revelation – capable of detecting forms otherwise unseen – and the heuristic potency of the tools that derived from combining the aerial view with more conventional ground-level readings (some of which were meant to corroborate an identification).

The main development took place within the field of archaeology. Starting from 1920, the British lieutenant-colonel G. E. Beazeley published in *The Geographical Journal* the results of aerial reconnaissance missions undertaken in Mesopotamia,[29] which led to the discovery of an ancient city, fortifications and an irrigation network.[30] His account suggested two stages in this process: scrutiny of aerial photographs leading to the initial detection of the structures, followed by direct observation through the overflying of the sites themselves. As Beazeley explained, owing to the altitude and therefore to the scale of observation, as well as to the sensitivity of the photographic film to nuances of light and surface, the photographic print revealed forms unrecognisable to an observer on the ground:

> Had I not been in possession of these air photographs the city would probably have been merely shown by meaningless mounds scattered here an there, for much of the detail was not recognizable on the ground but was well shown up in the photographs, as the slight difference in the colour of the soil came out with marked effect on the sensitive film, and the larger properties of the nobles and rich merchants could be plainly made out along the banks of the Tigris.[31]

The French expression *sauter aux yeux* approximates to the English expressions to 'show up', to 'come out at one', to 'make [something] out', all of which emphasise a kind of emergence. The aerial position (and, better, the aerial *image*) created a visual event.

Relying on research undertaken in aerial archaeology in Great Britain, Léon Aufrère was among the first French geographers who, during the 1930s, disseminated the resultant discoveries and therefore demonstrated the potential of the resource. What was revealed concerned especially the overhaul of agricultural systems (Figure 10.4):

> A palimpsest is revealed, within which is inscribed a whole history that had seemed to have vanished without leaving any trace on the ground. Aerial

ANNALES DE GÉOGRAPHIE. N° 250. TOME XLIV. PL. XV.

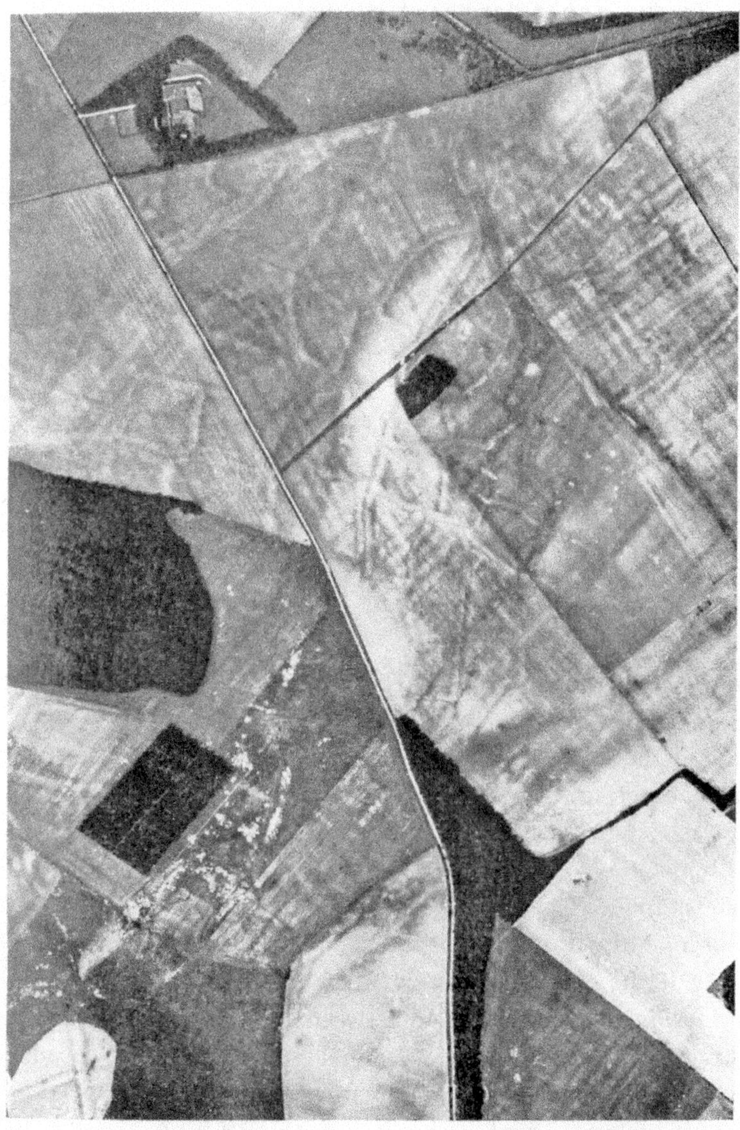

ANCIEN QUADRILLAGE AGRAIRE APPARAISSANT NETTEMENT DANS UNE GRANDE PARTIE DE LA PHOTOGRAPHIE. WINDMILL HILL (HANTS).

Cliché comm. par the Controller of H. M. Stationery Office and the Director General, Ordnance Survey. Crown Copyright reserved.

[10.4] Agricultural archaeology: the palimpsest. From Léon Aufrère, 'The agricultural system of the British Isles', *Annales de géographie*, 1935.

> observation could therefore precede and guide ground-based research, which could contribute an archaeological document.[32]

Other geographers had previously analysed the landscape traces left by past civilisations, the signs of displacement in habitat locations and roads, as well as the temporal superimposition of settlements at selected sites. Ruins were part of the human geography of Friedrich Ratzel and Paul Vidal de la Blache. Through his use of a new medium capable of revealing the historic depth of landscapes upon a single plane, Aufrère was probably one of the originators of the palimpsest metaphor.[33] He showed the 'cognitive qualities of aviation [that] concern also the time of a landscape'.[34] But, whilst he was among the first interpreters of this complex composition of humanised space encompassed within a single aerial gaze, Aufrère combined the advantages of aerial revelation with those of terrestrial exploration. He elaborated an analysis that was much more strictly technical than that of the 1950s authors, such as Pierre Deffontaines[35] and Paul-Henry Chombart de Lauwe,[36] those lyrical aerial discoverers of the earth who were entranced by the human inscriptions seen upon it.

Aerial exploration and geographical knowledge

Research on the detection of objects or movements on the ground and the anticipation of terrain conditions, which had already been partially tested during the war, was systematised by the French military in Morocco over land that was not well known, and particularly over territories belonging to dissident Berber populations. One of the pilots was a young geographer called Jules Blache. As a result of his Moroccan experience, accumulated over several months between 1917 and 1918, he produced strikingly illustrated articles whose argumentation rested primarily on the articulation between descriptions of aerial views and the demonstration by aerial photography – oblique or vertical – produced by the army's photo-topographic division.[37] Furthermore, all of his aerial images were scrupulously annotated and positioned on the page, were explicitly linked to the text (sometimes supplemented by diagrams), and all specified exactly how the views were obtained. Published in France and the United States, his articles aimed to show the relevance of aviation to the three types of research in which geographers were engaged at the time: that focused on the overall region;[38] that based on geomorphology, involving scrutiny of regional landscapes and the identification of typical elementary landforms;[39] and lastly that centred on human geography, where the author attempted to divide Morocco into regions according to the way of life and the habitat of the indigenous population and to pose questions on the relationship between the nomads and the sedentary peoples, as well as on the role played by mountains as places of refuge.[40]

Published for geographers, these articles demonstrated the wealth of this geographer-aviator's experience and the complexity of the processes that he had set in motion (which included the deployment of a talented young scientist who, nevertheless, was only familiar with the alpine domain; working in the field using diverse modes of reading the terrain; and mobilising information already amassed by the military and a few geologists) in order to come up with a sort of 'balance sheet' for an unprecedented cognitive experience.

In his first article, Blache attempted to convey the kind of knowledge that he had acquired and how it had been developed – from the cockpit of a military aeroplane, upon an almost 'empty' map, in a little-known zone in the Middle Atlas mountains. From the outset, his article extoled the virtues of the aerial gaze, which conferred all-inclusiveness and simultaneity (the totality of details seen at the same time):

> The map is pristine, save for a narrow route traced by the marquess of Segonzac in 1905 [...] In this 100km-long stretch, the sight that the plane alone allows one to study, both in its entire expanse and in all of its detail, is extremely varied. Photographs of this landscape, taken at high altitude, have enabled the establishment of a reconnaissance map and represent geographical documents of the highest order.[41]

Moreover, the aeroplane was a mobile observatory that allowed one to follow a particular contour line, to make cross-sections or to draw near to a point of interest for the observer, who was able to gradually build up his knowledge by coming up close to places or overflying them.

In his report, Blache interpreted the forms he saw from on high by occasionally inserting a comparison with the 'ground truth' (*vérité-terrain*) or a reference to the geological map:

> The craters are narrow, hardly prominent, scattered across the lava field. There is no great cone with associated lava streaks; rather, low-lying and isolated mounds, craters devoid of streaks, which one recognises only after having passed them.[42]
>
> Are the volcanic outpourings directly or indirectly responsible for these infillings? It was difficult to estimate without being there, on the ground.[43]
>
> Merged lava streaks, numerous shallow craters, with the volcanic landscape continuing the horizontality of the limestone instead of breaking it up – here are the signs that speak of an extremely fluid lava. This kind of landscape warrants a

> detailed description, as its forms are perfectly preserved, totally untouched by the work of erosion.[44]

The flying geographer undertook from a distance a kind of human and geomorphological diagnosis, which was often expressed in terms of probability or likelihood. In his three articles the images took centre stage, while the text described explicitly what was to be seen in each image, holding the document as witness to the worth of his assertions (Figure 10.5). His reportage of his experiences was undertaken with a great deal of rigour and was substantiated by a plethora of evidence, as provided by the aerial photographs.

And yet sometimes the text veered towards the fantastic. There are two instances of this. The first is when the author seemed to mix together a variety of scales and vantage points simultaneously – wide-angle glimpses from the sky with human-scale views. Such were his descriptions of the giant cedar trees:

> One can see many of them, long after their death, stretch out totally blanched branches of an imperishable wood – just as if they were standing skeletons. Others – a great many of them – lie felled on the ground, often burned by the indigenous people who migrate to the mountains with their flocks during the summer and burn the trunks of trees they want to fell in order to use their branches, which are easier to chop down than the trunk. Plumes of blue smoke, ascending here and there, are tell-tale signs of the logger. But he is impotent before these giants of the forest, whose diameter often exceeds 2m; the oldest of them, whose lower branches have died, at 4m diameter put up gigantic parasols.[45]

The second instance is the shock of alterity, of the *jamais vu*, an indescribable apparition that the observer could only attempt to indicate; such is the case of the High Atlas, on the edge of a Sahara imagined beyond the horizon:

> The mountain crest is perfectly straight. On the slopes, whose gradient doesn't vary, there is no prominent escarpment, no jutting projection to link between the contours of slopes as straight as those of the crest. Here and there, outcrops that are somewhat more rigid trace narrow corniches which get lost in the homogenous paste that formed the mountain [...] Equal-sized ravines descend in parallel like palisades. No scree gathered in the banks, such as those that, in other countries, bring to the starkest landscape the picturesque sight of their sloped, spread-out fan, with the bulkiest boulders arrayed at its base. No vegetation either, except – on the lowest slopes or else in the very middle of the Outat valley – a thin wooded cover, perforated and torn. The rest, which is

PLANCHE IX

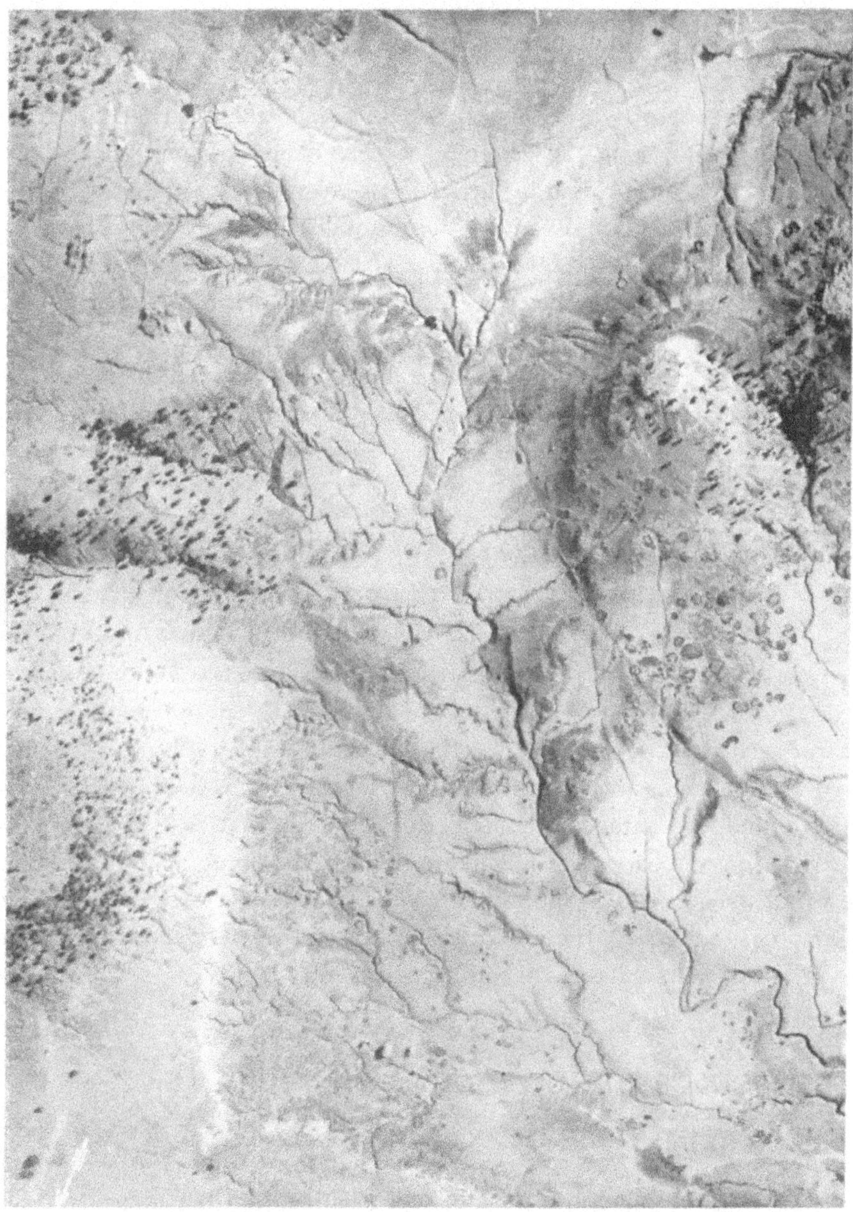

[10.5] Aerial exploration: relief types seen from the air. From Jules Blache, 'Some aspects of the Moroccan mountains', *Revue de géographie alpine* (1920), plate IX: 'A multi-branched network in soft, impermeable soil.'

> devoid of water, trees, grass or colour, traces stiff lines on the inflexible horizon [...] No cliffs, no fallen rocks, no greenery.[46]

In the first of these two instances, despite the potency of the view from the aeroplane, it seems that the geographer merged multiple points of view from the sky and from the ground in such a way as to yield a complex description, to which no single positional vantage point could adequately correspond. In the second case, the narrative description falls short despite the evidence supplied by the aerial view, as it had no previous model to build upon, neither impressions gathered from the terrain nor prior accounts nor sightings. It could only be described by its airborne European observers in terms of what it was not. Beyond aerial vision, was the development of a new vocabulary, visual impressions, or perhaps interpretive diagrams necessary in order to truly see?

THE AERIAL VIEW AND THE GEOGRAPHIC LANDSCAPE

The term 'landscape' (*paysage*) is undoubtedly the conceptual framework which marks, for the French geographers of the interwar period, the new experience of the true aerial view and underwrites their work. Between 1900 and 1925 the term was used with increasing frequency, displacing older terms such as 'physiognomy', 'aspect', 'line' or 'characteristics of place'. It was as if through the emphasis on fieldwork (direct observation), when supported by photography (and especially the aerial images, which appear both 'scenic' and 'concrete'), increasingly led geographers to conceive their discipline as the science of landscapes, as opposed to – say – regional structures or the biological environment.

Representing the landscape accurately

At times the use of the term was rather loose, at other times it was more controlled, even if the author defined neither what a landscape was to him nor what role it played in geography. As suggested by his introduction to the atlas of the Rhone and the captions associated with the oblique views, in the wake of aerial photography's 'vigilant practice' an author such as Cholley was able to direct his attention to landscape. He distinguished between vertical and oblique or panoramic views, assessing both on the types of representation of the terrestrial surface that they enabled, as well as on their usefulness and drawbacks.

Thus, vertical views allowed a faithful rendering in planimetry but had the disadvantage of flattening the relief. Cholley wrote at length on oblique views in relation to these representations' importance for what he terms 'reality' or 'the real' (the ground surface), mobilising a whole gamut of notions related to the landscape view (perspective, basic outline, background, vantage point, angle of shot, lighting, shadow, light).

> As is well known, panoramic views give a perspectival representation of the landscape as it could be seen from an elevated observation point. In general, they are very expressive; the effect obtained is powerful in sharply edged terrain such as the Alps, yet much less assured in the downs and plains, as the undersurfaces become crushed and the backgrounds fade.
>
> Thus, the usefulness of these views depends upon the characteristics of the landscape; it also depends, more than one would think, on the skilfulness of the operator and on his scientific knowledge of the terrain – therefore, on his geographical knowledge. The angle of the shot and the 'point of view' must adapt to each landscape. And the best is that which allows for maximum expressiveness in the translation of the salient characteristics of the region. Is it not as part of a series that a deep and sufficiently wide valley would be best rendered? Conversely, a slightly overhanging view would most felicitously translate the features of high alpine massifs. As regards details, any technician of aerial photography knows very well that his depiction depends upon the contrasts between shadows and fully lit areas. Therefore, a good oblique view demands not only work, but also geographical knowledge and talent.[47]

For him, at the cost of instrumentality, these oblique aerial views reveal landscapes; in fact, the foreword to the atlas mentions that 'the caption that relates to them [...] stresses especially the characteristics of the landscape, whose main geographical features we endeavoured to analyse'. But he was cautious about relying exclusively on the realm of the visible, going so far as to state: 'It is dangerous to take a photograph without having firm knowledge of its object.'[48] All in all, Cholley did not embrace the notion of landscape, instead exalting the region as central to geography. A supporter of 'rational description' (*description rationnelle*), he concurred with those French geographers who privileged the map, by virtue of its realism:

> The map is, in fact, our best document, as it faithfully reproduces reality by showing things in their places and by bringing out their relative value within the composition of the landscape. It clips the wings of imagination and favours the rational description of the region.[49]

Constructing the geographical landscape

A completely different epistemological position was held by Camille Vallaux, who wanted to make the 'geographical landscape' the methodological core of the discipline.[50] His point of departure was to define the object of this knowledge as 'the rational (*raisonnée*) description and synthetic explanation of the mechanism of the terrestrial surface, whether or not inhabited by humans'.[51] For this, two research modalities needed to be combined. On the one hand, the gathering of facts revealed by cognate sciences which produce 'molecular' or analytical data; on the other hand, an overall ('molar') construction that was particular to geography: a work 'that seeks to describe and to interpret the structures that are accessible by visual observation, be it direct, telescopic or ideal' (that is to say, accessible to the naked eye, mediated by an optical instrument, or else virtual, i.e., from space).[52]

The combination of these two approaches produced the 'landscape' or, rather (in the absence of an accepted neologism and in order to distinguish it from its aesthetic and banal connotations), the 'geographical landscape':

> The geographical landscape is the rational (*raisonnée*) description of a given portion of the earth's surface, of the mechanism set in motion by the interaction between the three states of matter – solid, liquid and gaseous – and by the various reactions of the environment on organisms and of organisms on the environment. Geographers construct their landscapes outside the subjective preoccupations of literary hacks and painters, and outside the naturalists' processes of microscopic observation.[53]

It remained to be determined how this particular point of view would be constructed. The centrality of the observer; the privileging of the horizon or *terminateur*; and the schematisation and representativeness of the facts retained were the essentials of this position. Vallaux compared this ideal with conventional means of graphic representation, such as the bird's-eye view and equestrian perspective, which – by elevating the observation point – bordered on cartography. By contrast, what could aerial photography offer? Here, Vallaux also differentiated between the vertical and the oblique view, eventually identifying the latter as the closer of the two to his ideal. In this respect, he tested three vertical photographs, one showing part of the southern coast of France and the others taken in Macedonia. According to him, these shots revealed perfectly those human elements which expressed relief, such as the zig-zag roads that signalled steep terrain.[54] But the major drawback of the vertical aerial photograph was that it masked the topography, which was essential to

Vallaux's conception of geographical landscape. This shortcoming elicited a rather severe verdict from Vallaux, who held only oblique perspective to be useful, after the manner of the old bird's-eye views which he cited as models.

Seeing landscape as human imprint

The diffusion and significance of landscape in geographical enquiry between the two world wars, testifies to the prominence of the (often unfolding) high-level view in the cognitive practices of geographers. The large-scale map already provided this in a basic way, but now its conventionally empty spaces were filled out with the patterning and colours of the earth registered by the field drawing and by aerial photography, which imposed the visual presence of an agricultural marquetry. However, this did not entail an immediate discursive shift. In rural geography the land register remained the preferred tool of study, rather than the cultural fragments that were revealed through aerial photography. Gradually, however, geographers would turn toward the latter.

Another motif linked to the surface visualisation of human activity also emerged in the interwar period, one that overemphasised human creativity on the surface of the earth, and the human being's originality as creator of forms and organiser of space in contrast to an amorphous nature. While this provided an opportunity to celebrate man's greatness, it also discriminated between levels of civilisation. Thus, one of the authors mentioned above, while eulogising the African 'airscape' simultaneously decried the indigenous population's wildness which, in his eyes, was reflected in the savage landscape: 'A civilized country seen from the air is simply a gigantic mosaic, monotonous in its regularity; but the airscape of Central Africa is as untamed and as irregular as that of the moon.'[55]

Especially invasive when it was vertical, the aerial view exhibited in particular the hitherto unknown structures of villages, lands or indigenous cities (Figure 10.6). In a colonial context, it un-covered rebel terrain for the military eye, while to the French geographer it revealed the variety of 'humanised' landscapes.

These endeavours from the beginning of the 1920s indicate that immediately after the war – and, in fact, in the military context for several geographer-aviators – the aerial view became integral to the profession of geographer. For them, it opened up perceptual horizons and the fascination of the true view from the sky, a fascination later shared by other generations that were led to revisit this kind of experience from other aeroplanes, at other speeds and heights, and in the context of other conflicts – Antoine de Saint-Exupéry, Paul-Henry Chombart de Lauwe and Pierre Deffontaines, among others.[56] But, paradoxically, the accounts of these early aerial observers of the face of the earth seem relatively prosaic,

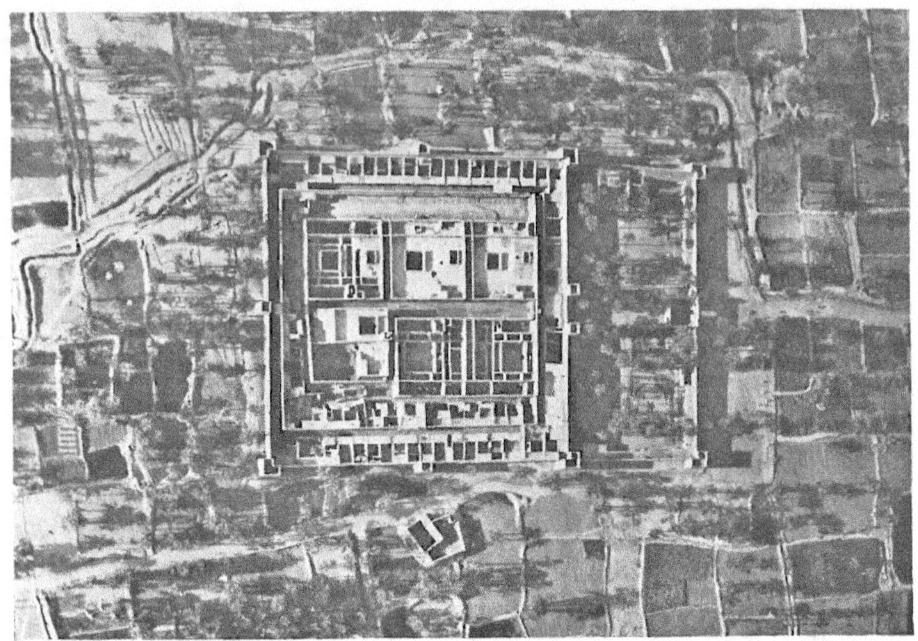

[10.6] The intrusive gaze: aerial view of a Kasba. From Jules Blache, 'Modes of life in the Moroccan countryside. Interpretations of aerial photographs', *The Geographical Review*, XI (4) (1921), figure 12.

compared to the lyricism of their successors, and their projects more focused on the scientific contribution to a particular form of knowledge, even though these were often formulated in a spirit of popularisation or at least of public information. The aerial view was worked through and interpreted.

The aerial view was sometimes immediately folded into a prior knowledge in order to construct canonical tools, such as the map, with which to understand standard objects such as, for instance, types of land contour or water systems. In less defined fields, it was more creative, when the system of reference was little known or inaccessible due to geopolitical reasons, as with the arid morphology of the south of Morocco or in the Rif and Atlas mountains, where a real apprenticeship for Europeans in forms hitherto unseen and unprecedented took place. It was transformed into a tool for specific uses, such as cartography, while the development of a new related technology – photogrammetry – gradually rendered vertical aerial photography the preserve of a specialist corps.

The aerial view participated in the configuration of certain methodological structures of the emerging geography, for which the status of the visible was paramount. But its use faced divergent paradigms that were then being aticulated (such as that which set the analytical Brunhes apart from his colleagues). Finally, its practice had a diffuse effect, marked by the gradual imposition within geographical discourse of the idea of landscape (*paysage*), which displaced – often without challenge – prior notions of physiognomy or characteristics of place. The visual power of aerial imaging seems to have entailed a *paysagisation* of geography in France. However, in a certain sense little changed, because – with their predilection for oblique aerial views and their concern for constructing devices that would combine the verticality of the gaze with the feel of the terrain – French geographers were merely channelling in a different way their foundational tension.

NOTES

1 See Édouard Ardaillon's statement: 'Mr Vidal de Lablache is credited with a remark that is probably not authentic, but is certainly excellent: "With books one can do mediocre geography, with maps slightly better, and very good only in the field".' Édouard Ardaillon, 'Les principes de la géographie moderne', *Bulletin de la Société de géographie de Lille* (1901): 269–90; 285.

2 Marie-Claire Robic, 'The Here and the Elsewhere: The Invention of the Open-air Geographer', in Nicolas Ortega Cantero, Jacobo García Álvarez, Manuel Mollá Ruiz-Gómez, eds, *Lenguajes y visiones del paisaje y del territorio/Langages et visions du paysage et du territoire/Languages and visions of landscape and territory* (Madrid: Ediciones de la Universidad Autónoma de Madrid, 2010), pp.277–86.

3 Marie-Claire Robic, 'La stratégie épistémologique du mixte: "le dossier" vidalien', *EspacesTemps*, 47–48 (1991): 53–66.

4 *Autour du monde. Jean Brunhes. Regards d'un géographe, regards de la géographie* (Boulogne-Billancourt: Musée Albert Kahn/Paris: Vilo, 1993); Didier Mendibil, 'De Martonne iconographe', in Guy Baudelle, Marie-Vic Ozouf-Marignier, Marie-Claire Robic, eds, *Géographes en pratiques (1870–1945). Le terrain, le livre, la cité* (Rennes: PUR, 2001), pp.277–87; Didier Mendibil, 'Dispositif, format, posture: une méthode d'analyse de l'iconographie géographique', *Cybergeo, epistémologie, histoire, didactique* (2008), article 415. http://www.cybergeo.eu/index16823.html.

5 Didier Mendibil, 'Quel regard du géographe sur les images du paysage?', in Anne Le Roux (dir.), *Enseigner le paysage?* (Caen: CRDP de Basse Normandie, 2001), pp.11–26.

6 Olivier Orain, *De plain-pied dans le monde. Écriture et réalisme dans la géographie française au XX*[e] *siècle* (Paris: L'Harmattan, 2009).

7 Paul Vidal de la Blache, 'La carte de France au 50 000e', *Annales de géographie* (1904) pp.21–8.

8 Christian Jacob, 'Dédale géographe. Regard et voyage aérien en Grèce', *Lalies III* (Paris: Presses de l'École normale supérieure, 1984), pp.147–64; Denis Cosgrove, *Apollo's Eye: A Cartographic Genealogy of the Earth in Western Imagination* (Baltimore and London: The Johns Hopkins University Press, 2001); Jean-Marc Besse, 'Géographies aériennes', in Jean-Marc Besse, *Le goût du monde. Exercices de paysage* (Arles: Actes Sud/Versailles: École Nationale Supérieure du Paysage, 2009), pp.71–104.

9 Paul Vidal de la Blache, *La France. Tableau géographique* (Paris: Hachette, 1908).
10 Paul Vidal de la Blache, *Tableau de la géographie de la France* (Paris: Hachette, 1911).
11 Emmanuel de Martonne, *Les grandes régions de la France. Description photographique avec notices géographiques, Région méditerranéenne,* 10 vols, with 61 plates and 3 maps (Paris: Payot, from 1925).
12 Jean Brunhes, *La géographie humaine,* 3 vols, third edition (Paris: Librairie Félix Alcan, 1925 [first edition 1910]).
13 Jean Brunhes, *Leçons de géographie à l'usage des écoles primaires, Cours élémentaire* (Tours: Mame, 1937 [first edition 1924]); Jean Brunhes, *Leçons de géographie à l'usage des écoles primaires, Cours moyen* (Tours, Mame, 1939–1940? [first edition 1925]).
14 Joseph de Joannis, 'La biogéographie. Distribution et migration des êtres vivants', *Études,* 5 December (1925): 586.
15 André Cholley and Fleury Seive, *Atlas photographique du Rhône.* Premier fascicule. *De la frontière suisse à Lyon* (Lyon: Desvigne, 1931).
16 Translator's note: in English in the original.
17 André Cholley, 'L'Atlas photographique du Rhône', *International Geographical Congress, Cambridge, July 1928, Report of the proceedings published by the executive committee of the congress* (Cambridge: Cambridge University Press, 1930), pp.118–20.
18 Cf. André Cholley, *Guide de l'étudiant en géographie* (Paris: PUF, 1942).
19 Brunhes, op. cit., *La géographie humaine (Human Geography);* italics in the original.
20 Jean Brunhes, 'Une géographie nouvelle, la géographie humaine', *Revue des Deux Mondes,* 1 June (1906): 541–74.
21 Ibid.
22 See also the studies on landscape by German and American geographers in Olivier Lugon, *Le style documentaire. D'August Sander à Walker Evans. 1920–1945* (Paris: Macula, 2001).
23 Lt. Leo Walmsley, M.C., late RAF, 'The recent trans-African flight and its lesson', *The Geographical Review,* IX (1920): 149–60.
24 Translator's note: in English in the original.
25 Fred H. Moffit, 'A method of aerophotographic mapping', *The Geographical Review,* X (1920): 326–38.
26 (Translator's note: in English in the original.) The technique developed rapidly, to such an extent that a question on 'aerial topo-photography', raised during the international conference on geography held in Paris in 1931, generated about a dozen papers and the creation of a commission on photo-topography; the first conference on photogrammetry was held at Zurich in 1930, while Emmanuel de Martonne raised a point about the question in 1935. Among the papers presented at the Paris conference was a very technical one by a French geographer on the contribution of aerial photography to the scientific knowledge of dunes (cf. Léon Aufrère, 'Utilisation de la photographie zénithale dans l'étude morphologique et dans la cartographie des dunes', *Comptes rendus du Congrès international de géographie Paris 1931,* vol. I, *Actes du Congrès, Travaux de la section I* [Paris: Armand Colin, 1932], pp.155–63).
27 Thomas Lee Willis, 'Airplanes and geography', *The Geographical Review,* X (1920): 310–25.
28 Ibid., p. 310. (Translator's note: quoted in English in the original.)
29 Aerial agricultural archaeology started in Great Britain in the 1920s with the work of E. Cecil Curwen, O. G. S. Crawford and the campaigns organised by the Ordnance Survery. These works were disseminated in France by Léon Aufrère among geographers and pre-historians, publishing aerial photographs that showed traces of agricultural morphology pre-dating the enclosure of the landscape. Most of the conclusions, especially regarding the interest in

the ground-level view, were reprised and systematised by Raymond Chevallier (cf. his 'Un document fondamental pour l'histoire et la géographie agraire: la photographie aérienne', *Études rurales*, vol. I [1961]: 70–80).

30 Lt-Col. George A. Beazeley, 'Air photography in archaeology', *The Geographical Journal*, vol. LIII, January–June (1920): 330–35.

31 Ibid., pp.330–1. (Translator's note: quoted in English in the original.)

32 Léon Aufrère, 'Les systèmes agraires dans les Iles britanniques', *Annales de géographie* (1935): 385–409; 391.

33 Described by Jean-Marc Besse as a 'hackneyed metaphor': op. cit., p.96.

34 Ibid., p.95.

35 Pierre Deffontaines, 'Défense et illustration de la géographie humaine', *La Revue de géographie humaine et d' ethnologie*, I (1948): 5–13.

36 Paul-Henry Chombart de Lauwe, ed., *La découverte aérienne du monde* (Paris: Horizons de France, 1948); with a preface by Emmanuel de Martonne.

37 Illustrating the *Revue de géographie alpine* was made possible through the generous financial assistance of General Lyautey. In a colonial climate replete with experimentations (as Paul Rabinow has shown), other aerial campaigns produced *surveys* of Moroccan cities, notably an album on Casablanca mentioned by Henry Sellier in 1923 in *La Vie urbaine*.

38 Jules Blache, 'De Meknès aux sources de la Moulouya. Essai d'exploration aérienne du Maroc', *Annales de géographie* (1919): 293–314.

39 Jules Blache, 'Quelques aspects des montagnes marocaines', *Revue de géographie alpine* (1920): 225–38.

40 Jules Blache, 'Modes of life in the Morroccan Countryside. Interpretations of aerial photographs', *The Geographical Review*, XI (1921): 477–502.

41 Blache, op. cit., 'De Meknès aux sources de la Moulouya', 292–3.

42 Ibid., 298.

43 Ibid., 295.

44 Ibid., 298.

45 Ibid., 302.

46 Ibid., 312.

47 Cholley and Seive, op. cit.

48 Cholley, op. cit., *Guide de l'étudiant en géographie*, p.183.

49 Ibid., p.9.

50 Camille Vallaux, *Les Sciences géographiques* (Paris: Félix Alcan, 1925).

51 Camille Vallaux, 'Les paysages de la géographie', *Revue scientifique illustrée*, 20 (1925): 678–84; 678.

52 Ibid.

53 Ibid.

54 Ibid., 681.

55 Walmsley, op. cit., 160. (Translator's note: quoted in English in the original.)

56 Chombart de Lauwe, op. cit.; Deffontaines, op. cit.; Pierre Deffontaines, Mariel J.-Brunhes Delamarre, *Atlas aérien. France*, 5 vols (Paris: Gallimard, 1964).

11

The Figure from Above

On the Obliqueness of the Plan in Urbanism and Architecture[1]

John Macarthur

HOLT

In January 1919, Captain Gordon H. G. Holt RAF, pilot and photographer, wrote in *The Architectural Review* explaining that the techniques of aerial photography, which had been developed during the war for mapping battlefields, would become an important tool for the architectural understanding of cities[2] (Figure 11.1). Holt explains the procedures of ortho-corrected photography for mapping, but also argues for the oblique view.

> Let us suppose that not only the above plan is wanted, but also a more easily understood representation of certain buildings or traffic articulations on the way, such as St Paul or the nodal point known as Trafalgar Square. The ideal representation would clearly be the perspective; by flying round and over it, with a special camera, a bird's-eye view can be taken, showing the ordnance of the square or the 'volume' of the fabric in three dimensions and in their relations to features near by. Characteristic details, anomalous or unusual effects, which with the spectator on the ground would perforce escape attention, reveal themselves instantly.[3]

ARCHITECTURE AND AERIAL PHOTOGRAPHY.

By CAPT. GORDON H. G. HOLT, R.A.F.

IT is, as yet, too early to define with any degree of certainty the relationship that will be eventually established between the two subjects mentioned in the above heading. Still, with four years of intensive warfare at the back of us—a warfare which has brought into existence aerial photography and developed it to a high pitch of excellence—it may not be out of place to adumbrate some of its likely applications to architecture.

To gauge the potentialities of aerial photography, as it might be applied to surveying, archæology, and town planning, for instance, one has but to bear in mind its one overwhelming advantage: it allows objects on or near the ground to be recorded in three dimensions. This statement needs qualifying, but first of all it is as well to indicate clearly what it means.

What is a plan?

It is the representation of certain features or objects in a given area, this area being the result of length × breadth, with the eye of the draughtsman or spectator, assumed to be directly above, in a third dimension, called depth.

Now, in aerial photography, the eye is not assumed to be there. *It is there*, and from its point of vantage it—or rather the lens—merely records everything occurring in this given area, in its three dimensions of length, breadth, and depth.

The qualification might read as follows: It records it as accurately as it will ever need to be; in other words, it will show every single detail to any scale; moreover it does all this in a fraction of a second. Therefore it is bound to affect the method of obtaining the plan or perspective of an actual building, street, or of a whole town. Needless to say, it will never impinge on what, for want of a better term, is called "artistic draughtsmanship." Here we touch a realm of activity calling for the keen interplay of intellectual and æsthetic qualities on the part of the artist, qualities which are denied to the photographer, however ingenious a manipulator he may be either on the ground or high up in the skies.

But it will probably affect many important branches of our profession, for I am hardly committing myself to rash *obiter dicta* when I prophesy that this new form of representation will materially help the architect, the archæologist, and the surveyor, and be increasingly resorted to by them in the near future.

During the War, it soon became evident that a more accurate and speedy method of obtaining information as to the whereabouts of enemy troops and material could not be found than in aerial photography. Consequently, certain types of aeroplanes and balloons were fitted with special cameras having special lenses. These aircraft flew, or were

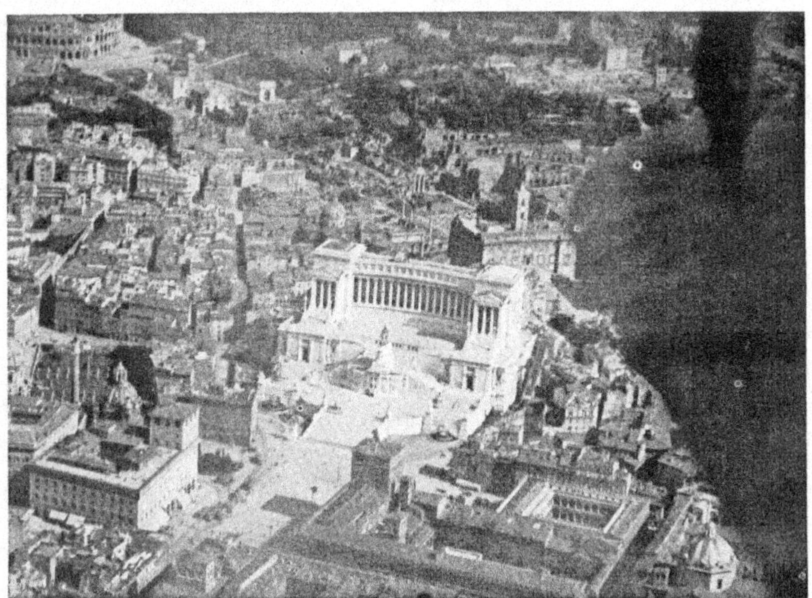

AEROPLANE VIEW OF THE VICTOR EMMANUEL II MEMORIAL AND ITS SURROUNDINGS, ROME.

[11.1] Capt. Gordon H. G. Holt, 'Architecture and Aerial Photography', *The Architectural Review*, 45 (1919).

Holt describes the oblique aerial view as an addition to the survey – 'the complementary data necessary for town planning'.[4] Town planning – in the sense used by Holt – was only ten years old at the time. Preceded briefly by the German *Stadtbaukunst* movement, town planning in Britain officially began in 1909 with the Town Planning Act and the publication of Raymond Unwin's *Town Planning in Practice*.[5] In the progressive tone of Holt's article the new technologies of aircraft and fast lenses and films were to be put to use in this new and powerful way of understanding and intervening in cities.

What the oblique or bird's-eye view shows is the relation of architectural forms. While the vertical view can provide a dimensionally accurate depiction of area, the oblique view adds an impression of depth, which, while it is unable to be dimensioned, is essential to the understanding of the architect and planner. Holt describes what needs to be understood as the 'volume of the fabric', and curiously as 'ordnance' – which normally signifies munitions and artillery, the kind of thing with which Holt had been recently concerned. But this sentence is also coloured by the etymology of the word, which derives from the 'ordonnance' or systematic arrangement of the parts of architecture, as had been described by Claude Perrault in the late seventeenth century.[6]

Unwin's theory of town planning, like that of his sources Josef Stübben and Camillo Sitte, proposed to draw principles from historically developed cities, particularly those of medieval formation that had an urban grain and texture and an identifiable visual character, but little geometric order. Sketches of places widely agreed to be of architectural quality were the staple of these early planning books. Pictorial information is necessary to understand the age of the buildings and the process of accumulation by which the urban character came about. Plans by themselves tend to flatten out this history. Holt's claim is that aerial photographs mark a watershed moment in the development of the planning discipline because of the massive increase in data they make available, but quite what this data can be used for is less clear. Holt's photographs do not place the reader, as Charles Paget Wade's fine drawings for Unwin place one in, for example, Kersey, Suffolk,[7] and the photographs lack the flatness and stable dimensionality which would enable them to be tools for drawing plans for land division and construction. In oblique viewpoint aerial photographs both viewpoint and dimensions cannot be known from viewing the image.

This, however, points us to the great interest of oblique aerial photographs, which is that while they directly represent neither, they connote both the specificities of urban character and the abstraction and instrumental power of the plan. What is more, they suggest that the individual's lived experience of places and the planner's oversight of the whole socio-economic system that a city is, are points within a rotation from vertical to horizontal. The oblique aerial photograph then is a mid-range position that demonstrates this rotation and that makes spatial qualities especially evident. Holt complains of the low viewpoint of most panoramas taken from hills and tall buildings. In these, he writes:

> the monuments are either hiding one another or else confusingly jumbled: a sense of the relative spaces between the several cognate parts is lost [... in] these pseudo-aerial photos. So it comes about that a bird's-eye view, to be professionally useful, should be set at 30°, 45°, 60°, or even 75°. A draughtsman when tackling aerial perspective feels this instinctively.[8]

In a note to this paragraph Holt cites numerous drawn aerial views set at over 30°, starting with the well-known *Britannia Illustrata* of Kip and Knyff of 1708, and proceeding historically to Jules Guérin's views of Chicago. These precedents considerably complicate Holt's claims of modernity, because not only is the bird's-eye view more easily understood than the vertical, but it precedes the dimensioned survey in the history of cartography and human imagination. This is clear when Holt places a flattened vertical aerial photograph of Bruges with a sixteenth-century map that combines plan and elevation into something like two and a half dimensions, the relation of buildings, walls, canals and fields being expressed orthographically, while the buildings are all depicted in a roughly isometric projection of about 75°.[9] This is a map for the identification of places and way-finding, and thus road widths and plot sizes are distorted so that churches and crossroads can be identified. Sixteenth-century surveyors were able to apply mathematics and triangulation methods in the production of mensurable cadastres, but the map that Holt reproduces shows that measurement was a lesser criterion than the appearance and the relations of the parts of the map. In short, its need to be a representation means that it cannot achieve the abstraction of a plan.

What does Holt's comparison of these views mean? The superiority of the photograph does not lie merely in the convenience of its production. In the beginning of the article Holt asks disingenuously:

> What is a plan? It is the representation of certain features and objects in a given area, this area being the result of length × breadth, with the eye of the draughtsman or spectator, assumed to be directly above in a third dimension, called depth. Now in aerial photography the eye is not assumed to be there. *It is there.*[10]

Holt knows perfectly well that a plan is not a view. A view from directly above would be a perspective, not a plan, as those objects further from the centre of the image are also further from the eye. Holt describes the lenses and techniques of overlapping prints that allow the aerial photographer to flatten the images and make them mensurable, effectively removing the specificity of the viewpoint. But in repeating the ancient analogy in which a plan is said to be a view from above Holt draws our attention to another factor with makes aerial photography so compelling: its indexicality.

As Roland Barthes famously argued, the veridical character of photographs is ultimately a matter of touch and presence.[11] The glint of light on the canals of Bruges, which strikes Holt's plate, this same light is fixed on the print, and in its reproduction in the pages of *The Architectural Review,* from whence it reaches our eye. The compelling truth of the photograph lies in our willingness to understand it as an index of the thing photographed. While a draughtsman *re-presents,* conveys to us a Bruges that we cannot see for ourselves, in Holt's photograph it *is* Bruges that we see. To be consistent with his argument Holt should have shown two photographs of Bruges, the vertical and the oblique, which would then have articulated the two aspects that the sixteenth-century cartographer had combined. The vertical photograph would give us the dimensions and the oblique 'a sense of the relative spaces between the several cognate parts', but in fact both of these give us a sense of being-there that is to do with photography not viewpoint. The vertical photograph is corrected from a view to an orthographic plan, and the oblique view contains insufficient information to allow one to place the viewpoint in space. In both cases the viewpoint has been dissipated and dispersed into an above-ness that differs from that of the sixteenth-century map only in being photographic. In fact one could argue the reverse, that Holt's inclusion of the antique map connotes a further dispersion of viewpoint. The indefiniteness of viewpoint in the photographs is like the fictitiousness of a bird's-eye viewpoint in the pre-aeronautic world. The truth of the photograph lies not in the camera having been at a particular point in the sky that could be measured in altitude and azimuth, but rather that the urban photographer has occupied in fact a place only imagined by earlier cartographers.

Holt's preference for high angles of view has further relevance here. All the oblique views that he publishes are so steep as to elide the horizon. With the horizon visible it would be possible to speculate about the altitude of the aircraft and the angle of the lens. With the horizon slid out the top of the picture plane it is not. This makes the oblique images more like the vertical images in their flatness. We might appreciate the receding perspective of buildings and places so as to appreciate the 'relative spaces', but there are no elements that recede to the horizon and unify the view. Even a glimpse of the horizon at the top of the frame would give the photograph a strong orientation

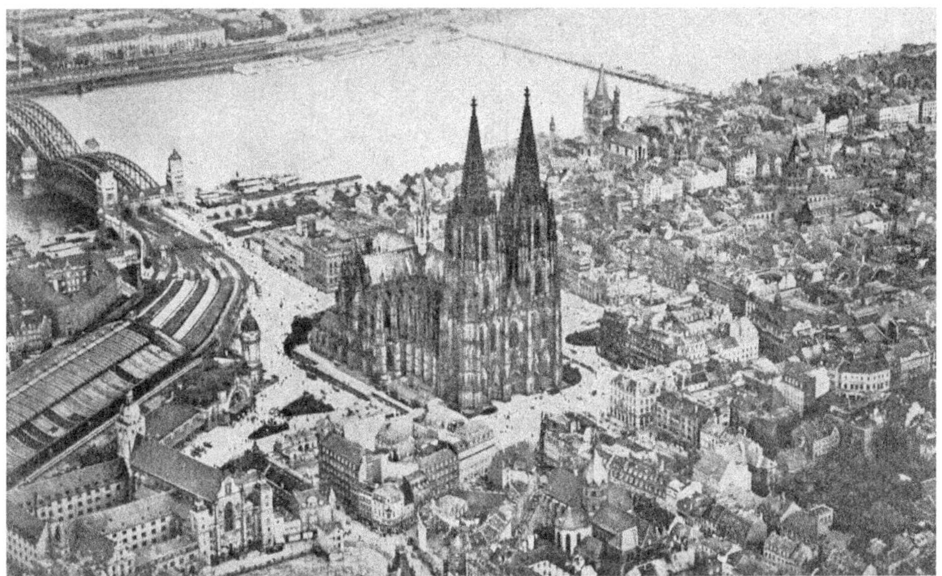

[11.2] Holt's photograph, 'Aeroplane view of Cologne', p.5.

and impression of viewpoint – we would be looking down and out from a notionally upright position seated in the aircraft. Whereas in Holt's images, and so many others like them, the urban fabric is cropped by the frame, and we imagine it extending an unknowable distance out from all four boundaries of the image area (Figure 11.2). These photographs have the 'all-over-ness' as well as the flatness of modern abstract art, and like them an indifference to orientation of the viewpoint (this is a point to which we will shortly return). To see such an image we might be flying laid flat like a bird with our spine parallel to the ground plane.

MARIN

My reading of Holt's article relies on Louis Marin's analysis of the 'utopic' aspects of the city map, and its relation to issues of sovereignty. Marin analyses two maps of Paris, those of Mathieu Mérian of 1615, and Jacques Gomboust of 1652.[12] Mérian's map is very like the sixteenth-century map of Bruges with which Holt illustrates his article in that it attempts to represent each building as a bird's-eye view while giving the general disposition of the city in plan. Marin writes that the image of the city given in the maps forms a 'utopic figure' where a raft of ideologies, in these cases of kingship, seem to be totalised in a single signifying 'figure'. This figure that appears by virtue of the map is nonetheless impossible to locate; it is utopic in its viewpoint:

> The viewpoint is fixed at a totalizing point of view. One can see all. But the eye placed at this point occupies a place that is an 'other' point of view; it is in fact impossible to occupy this space. It is a point of space where no man can see: a no-place not outside of space but nowhere, utopic.[13]

The utopic figure of the map is its no-place between 'geometry and panorama',[14] or vertical and oblique in Holt's terms. This figure of undecidability is then the still point around which are balanced a number of binary oppositions, mutually defining opposed paired terms which Marin arranges in diagrams like the Greimassian 'semiotic square'. These are: narration and description; royal space and the bourgeois community; a flourishing natural world and a powerful cultural centre; and virtue and commerce.[15] Marin is interested in the addressee of the maps – the King. Just as the King's image on coinage shows his power to regulate currency, so the bird's-eye view is also a king's eye. To represent all of Paris, its buildings and also the classes of people represented in their characteristic dress which surround the map in Mérian's print, is to imagine the one point at which this information is properly totalised.

Kingship is divinely ordained, continuous and beyond praise, but there are also kings who win and lose wars, make taxes and public works, compete with their predecessors and attempt to manage their legacy.[16] Mérian's map honours Louis XIII who like all empirical kings has the problem of how, given the limitless virtue of the King, his particular achievements might be known. The making of maps, like the minting of commemorative coins and the commissioning of histories, lies in this conflict of the absolute and the actual. To totalise Paris as a list of its noble families, churches and university, merchants and artisans with their various premises would show the hierarchy on which the King is seated, but to imagine this information and power as a view is to insist on that miracle by which this King is the King. Of course most viewers of Mérian's map are not its addressee. For their enjoyment the map is full of picturesque detail.

> The viewer spectator thus becomes the city's visitor and narrator: a carriage hurriedly makes its way to the Porte Neuve. A rider follows it at a gallop. Three herdsmen keep watch over their pigs [...] There two bandits hang from a gallows, not far from the garden of Queen Margarite. The incidental details have no role other than to give the impression that this representation is like

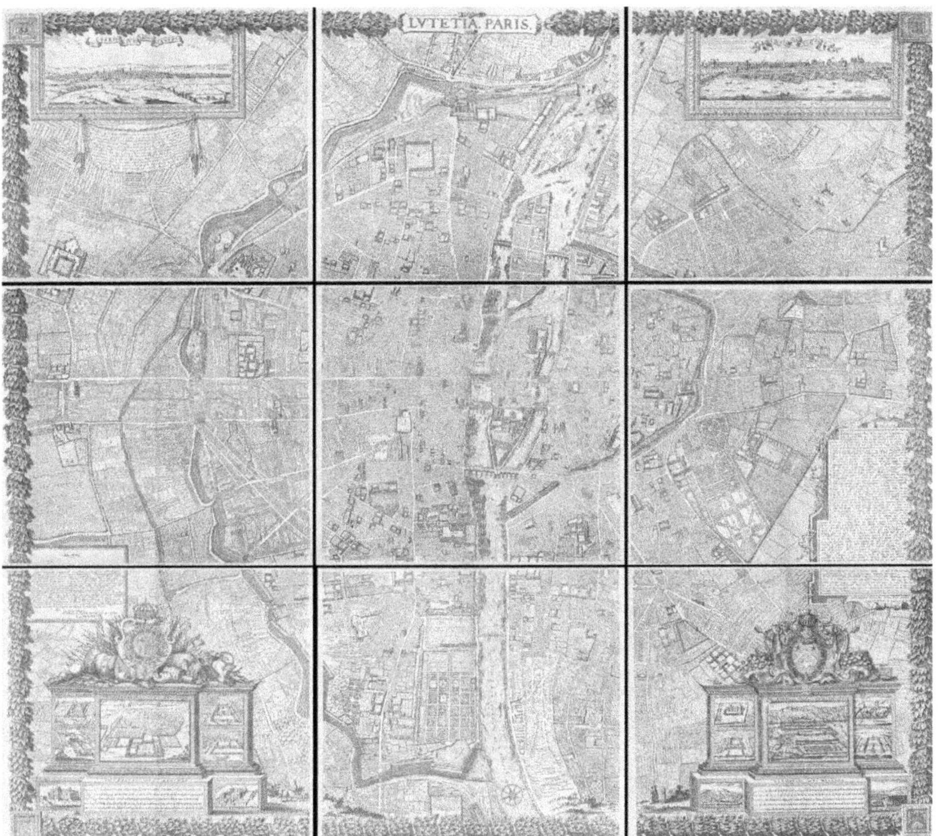

[11.3] Jacques Gomboust, *Lutetia Paris*, 1652 (*c.*1900 Taride reissue).

> reality itself; a narrative meets the eye, just as in reality, in its very unpredictable contingency.[17]

The 'utopic' of the map, for Marin, is this critical equivalence of narration and description. Our drive to narrativise the map, to use it to make an itinerary for an imagined journey into Paris derives from the same verisimilitude that makes it the perfect description – timeless and absolute – of the King who looks down on the map.

Gomboust's plan of 1652 for Louis XIV (Figure 11.3), makes a strong critique of earlier maps on account of their inaccuracy and answers this with a curious and short-lived cartographic technique. Gomboust made the first accurate survey of Paris and the map shows streets and building footprints scaled to various European measurement systems. To achieve this most of the

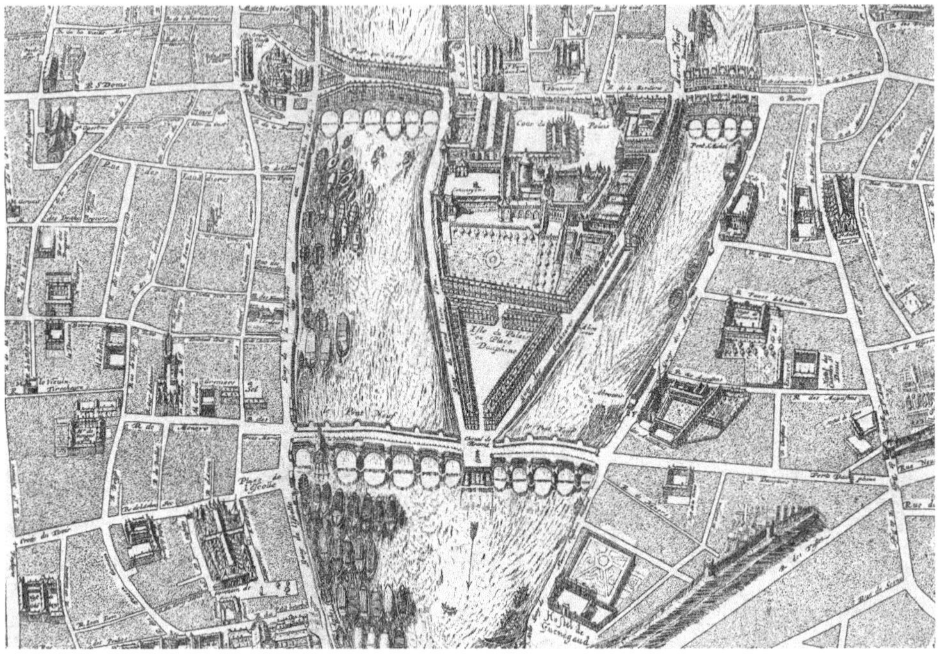

[11.4] Gomboust, *Lutetia Paris*, detail.

buildings are not represented at all, but are merely hatched in by the engraver (Abraham Bosse) in masses that stretch from street to street and without any attempt to delineate the individual buildings or property lines. Gomboust then shows important buildings, palaces, churches, hôtels in isometric-like projection as with the earlier maps (Figure 11.4). Gomboust's claim is that his flattening of the humble buildings into plan view allows the select buildings to be shown accurately in elevation and properly recognised. As Marin points out, this uncomfortable compromise demonstrates an historical watershed. While the figurative buildings show the political matrix of the aristocracy and Church, the dimensioned survey represents the emerging bourgeois and mercantile world, whose relevance for the King (and later the State), lies in its taxable qualities.

In *Utopics* Marin goes on from Gomboust to discuss El Greco's remarkable view of Toledo in which a bird's-eye panorama is represented behind a figure holding flat a geometrical plan, but the present argument will be better progressed if we consider how much of Gomboust's compromise is implicit in a map much more significant in architectural history, Giambattista Nolli's 1748 *Pianta Grande di Roma* commissioned by Pope Benedict XIV (Figure 11.5). This is because of a graphic invention of Nolli's, which has the effect of maintaining an itinerary of monuments within a purely orthographic view. Nolli's map, like

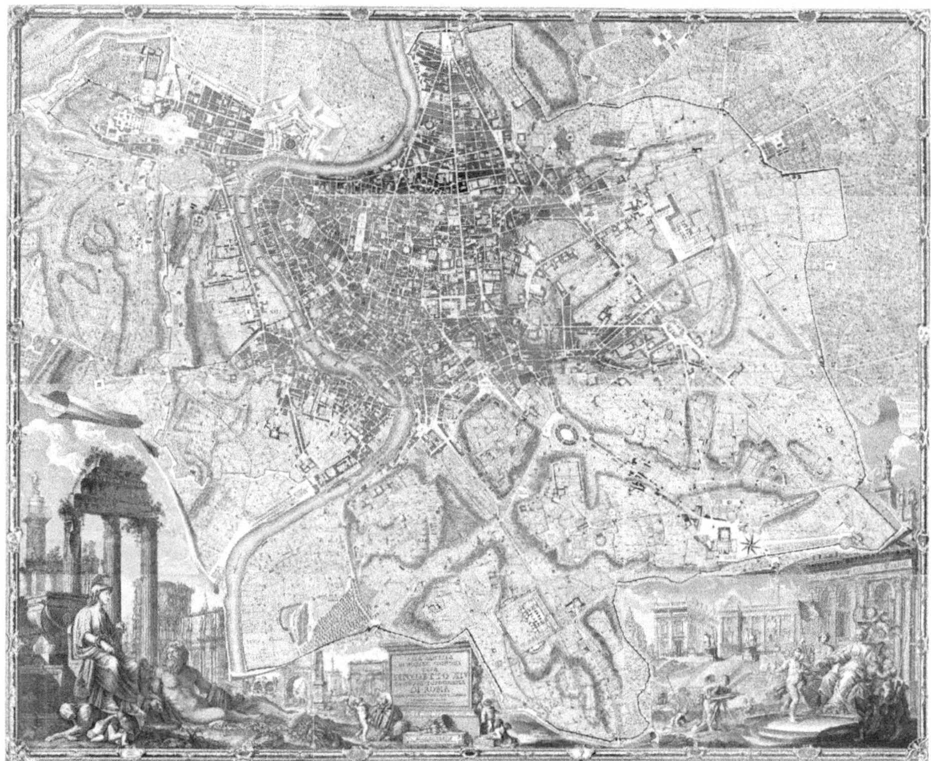

[11.5] Giambattista Nolli, *La Nuova Topographia di Roma*, 1748.

Gomboust's, hatches in the humble buildings without an attempt to describe them. The significant buildings, churches and palazzi, however, have their plans delineated: that is, their walls are solid black lines and their interiors white, like the streets outside (Figure 11.6). The meaning of this device is little different to Gomboust's less successful technique. The monuments of Rome that make up an itinerary for visitors, also depict the domains of the princes of the church, clerical orders and aristocrats who constitute the papal court. Graphically this distinction is so explicit not only because of the figure–ground contrast, but because the important structures have largely symmetrical plans and are thus already figurative. While it is all plan information that we look at in Nolli's map, the churches and palazzi seem to stand out and stand up just as earlier cartographers wished them to do.

The equivalence made by Nolli between the interiors of some buildings and their adjacent exterior spaces suggests that we ought to understand architecture in its urban context. More subtly than this it suggests a complex interaction of

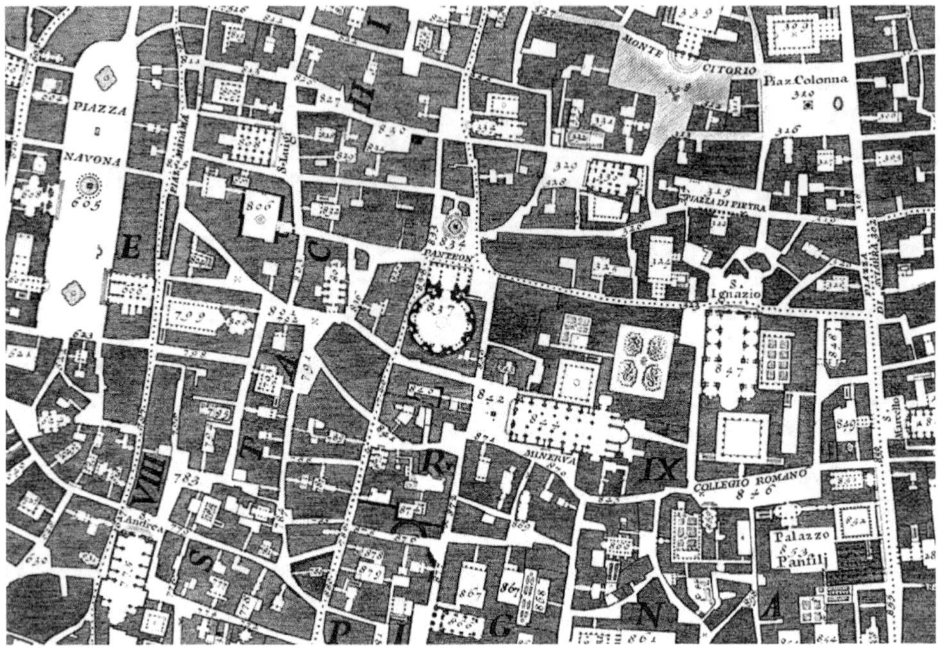

[11.6] Nolli, *La Nuova Topographia di Roma*, detail.

designed and contingent qualities of individual buildings and urban forms. Most buildings and most exterior spaces on Nolli's plan have no observable regularity, they are the results of need and contingency. Yet it is the collision of these mundane matters with intentional design that make many of the most interesting and characteristic places. When a formed piazza is bounded not only by a church facade, but also by houses laid out on ancient and irregular property divisions, this is in some ways more interesting and characteristic than a regular square that complemented the architect's design. Thus Nolli seems to have sublated the desire for recognition within the new primacy of information and in the twentieth century Nolli's plan became the epitome of urban representation in its neutral balance of the demands of orthographic projection and pictorialism. In fact, Nolli allows the utopic of the map to unfold on another axis; while the map might no longer have the imagined viewpoint in the bird's eye, it begins a process of understanding the plan as a figure.

The qualities I describe are implicit in Nolli's map and were widely appreciated at the time and have been since. However, this manner of attending to the formal qualities of urban accretion was first made explicit by Camillo Sitte in his *Der Städtebau* of 1889, particularly in his analysis of the irregular squares of old European towns.[18] Sitte's book, along with Stübben's and the journal *Der Städtebau*, are the foundation of the modern town planning that Holt proposed aerial photography could serve.

Holt's inclusion of the sixteenth-century map of Bruges, contrasted with his orthographic view, is intended to mark out the modernity and the historiographic powers of aerial photography. Holt makes available what had previously only been imagined, and securely positioned in modernity it provides a tool to see urban history. My point in this last section has been to show that the aerial view also has a history. In Holt's insistence that town planning requires the oblique view he is also insisting on the continuing validity of those interests that the older maps served, and recognises the ortho-photo is inadequate in this regard. But that interest itself had also changed. If the assumption of the King's viewpoint was irreducible in the ideology of monarchy, in aerial photography the indeterminate actuality of the viewpoint speaks to a different arrangement of franchise and political sovereignty.

ROWE

Colin Rowe and Fred Koetter's book *Collage City* of 1978 is one of the most influential twentieth-century books on urban planning.[19] And although Rowe (the principal author) neglects to point out his debts to urbanists from Sitte to Rowe's own peers in the Townscape movement, nevertheless the book is a provocative and original treatment of these inherited ideas recast as a powerful critique of architectural modernism (or at least its urbanistic consequences).[20] The book is packed with figure–ground 'Nolli' plans and aerial photographs which are only loosely related to the text, and which can be read as a haphazard atlas of precedents that might interest an urban designer. In this aspect it fulfils very thoroughly what Holt had called the 'complementary data needed for town planning'. While Rowe's argument is that architects should follow the historically developed forms of traditional European cities, he is also concerned to show that seen from the air such cities have the visual qualities of abstract painting. The exteriority of the aerial viewpoint is thus also a temporal relation where modernity can reengage with history. An aspect of the book that many readers find recondite is Rowe's discussion of the political philosophy of liberalism, but it is here that his argument articulates with Marin's discussion of the sovereignty of the aerial viewpoint.

If the totalisation of a city in its maps and views was an ideology of the absolutism of monarchy, Rowe argues that the incomplete and weak urban forms of actual cities arise from ideas freely competing and succeeding one another historically. The value of a 'Collage City' lies in overlapping fragments of attempts to make ideal cities where past and present needs and values are apparent. Rowe claims that utopian thought is required to make cities but it is equally required to fail, productively. His proposed collage city is a compromise between two excesses: first what he sees as the totalitarian utopianism of Modernism; and second, the anti-intellectual popularism of the Townscape Movement. These are, writes Rowe, 'two alternative prisons for the human spirit ... one of them is a fortress with electronic controls while the other is an open gaol conducted on compassionate principles'.[21] Thus one should neither make cities that respond purely empirically to basic needs and tastes, nor should one expect that higher ideals of urban form would ever have more than contingent realisations. The *bricoleur* approach to urban form that he proposed was a kind of compromise, of incomplete, fragmentary and overlapping ideals. It would thus admit the necessity of utopia and abstraction (a.k.a. modernism), but act in the empirical – that is, historical – world. Rowe's compromise is typical of the taste for complexity, ambivalence and genre crossing that drove post-modernism, but within that are linked arguments about formal complexity and sovereignty.

Rowe argued against object-form in building and for formed external urban spaces. The correct formal partnership of architecture and urban design could be achieved if buildings did not attempt to have form as objects but rather acted to form exterior spaces. To demonstrate this he compared a 'Nolli' plan of Parma and Le Corbusier's unbuilt plan for the city of Saint-Dié-des-Vosges.[22] In the latter there are buildings of generic and specific forms sited in a uniform field. Here space is merely displaced around the buildings. In the preferred example of Parma there are again two kinds of buildings, monumental churches and palaces, which are possessed of their own distinct forms, and quotidian buildings for housing and commerce that merely fill out the plots of land on which they are constructed. In Parma, however, there are two kinds of exterior space: the streets and alleys that are relatively formless and have developed through the contingencies of land ownership; and the piazzi that have forms which are as deliberate and intended as the monumental buildings. Rowe's point is that the interplay of the two conditions of exterior space and the two classes of building allow a much richer matrix of formal conditions than the modernist idea of object buildings in an isomorphic field. And while Rowe's insights into the causes of the subtle complexities of urban form are not so different from those of Camillo Sitte or Raymond Unwin, who called such a condition 'picturesque', his explanation of this condition as a structure of oppositions is similar to the development of the Greimassian semiotic square that Marin used to describe the 'utopic' of the city maps in their fragile equation of narration and description, horizontal and oblique, of kingly view and mercantile quantification.

Rowe's account of urban complexity relies heavily on the evidence of aerial views. Theories based on terrestrial viewpoints like those of Sitte and Unwin are happy to stop at 'picturesqueness' as a description of urban complexity. While Sitte, Unwin and other pre-aeronautical urbanists used plans to explain how picturesque qualities were caused, this level of urban structure was planimetric and an abstract representation. Rowe and his readers, as Holt had explained decades before, could palpably see the planimetric character of the urban form, through the veridical character of the photograph. Just as we understand the truth of the photograph to be self-evident, so this indexical chain extends the urban condition: the film is touched by the light reflected from the rooftops, these cover the buildings, the plans of which register the land divisions. When explaining the anti-urban effects of modernist architecture Rowe describes this as a convex spatiality, while traditional architectural urbanism is 'concave'. An example of the latter is the Galleria degli Uffizi which Rowe illustrates alongside Le Corbusier's Unité d'habitation at Marseille, in views that suggest Le Corbusier's slab block would fit the Florentine court like a plug.[23] Rowe's preference for closed and bounded exterior space clashes strangely with this liberal rhetoric, which relies on Karl Popper's polemic against historicism and socialism *The Open Society and its Enemies*.[24] Rowe argues against Le Corbusier's Unité, the product of a democratic republic, on the grounds of its open spatiality and its closed political idealism, its socialist tendencies. At the same time Giorgio Vasari's government buildings for Cosimo de Medici's tyrannical dukedom are held to be the model for the urbanism of an open society. Rowe is supposing the idealism and utopianism of Plato, Cosimo and Le Corbusier can have their hegemonic tendencies limited. According to Rowe urban collage is also a political stance, against both the closed society of the old world, which made the European city, and against the utopian socialists, who would sweep it away and construct a new city with the authority of science. Rowe's position in the air marks his modernity, his necessary distance from tradition, which frees him to reappropriate and collage together the urban forms of aristocratic and/or absolutist societies. He writes:

> Which is to say that, because collage is a method deriving its virtue from irony, because it seems to be a technique for using things and simultaneously disbelieving in them, it is also a strategy which can allow utopia to be dealt with as image, to be dealt with in *fragments* without our having to accept it *in toto*.[25]

By analogy we could say that Rowe's urbanism is a kind of constitutional monarchy. The closed urban forms that Rowe prefers may have been the expression of absolute power, but in collage they become mere images. Rowe wants to maintain what we might call the sovereignty of the city, the idea that the powers that make it have a figurative existence forming significant public spaces. At the same time what is sovereign is the city itself, its own historical continuity that cannot be appropriated by any single individual, interest or principle. Aerial photographs and the actual view of cities allowed by mass air transportion are a perfect continuation of the logic of the kingly view into modern circumstances, but it is only a shell of its former significance. Each of us can occupy that viewpoint that once emblematised the absolute command of a city, but the sovereignty we experience there is vicarious.

The indubitable modernity of a view from aircraft produces one kind of distance for Rowe. The other is the formal qualities of the view taken; for while the piazzi of Rome might look classical and figurative from terrestrial viewpoints, from the air they look like abstract art. In an exegesis of the collage city procedure, a student and collaborator of Rowe's, William Ellis, describes one of Rowe's studio projects at Cornell:

> the Buffalo project takes the Baroque idea of a system of connected nodes and places it under the compositional auspices that typified Suprematist and Elementarist painting. It is the Quirinale complex executed by Malevich, Philadelphia by Van Doesburg'.[26]
>
> [...]
>
> The traditional city is more interesting [than modern cities] as a pattern of buildings and spaces, and with its uniform roof heights, more susceptible to two-dimensional representation. Although figure–ground is a pictorial device involved with *Gestalt* assumptions and procedures, it is not picturesque in the scenographic sense. It suggests the abstract painter rather than the painter of scenes, relationships rather than objects, pattern rather than picture. It betrays Rowe's inclination toward the totally activated field of much modernist painting. Thus it unites two of his great enthusiasms: traditional urban space and certain aspects of modernist art. It also allows him to work with pattern structures at a scale as grand as Le Corbusier's. These patterns are abstract – and anti-picturesque – in a further way: their huge size enables them to be imagined from the plan, but prevents them being seen as pictures in front of the eye.[27]

The Nolli plans and aerial photographs in *Collage City* have the appearance of late modernist painting, characterised by flatness, pattern and an 'all-overness', that imply the painting is not a composition of elements, but an expanse which continues out of view or off the edge of the canvas. The particular marks and the sense of space or event in such a painting are, then, instances of this 'field' condition. These concepts are the basis for the more successful design explorations in *Collage City*, such as Graham Shane's 'field analysis of central London'.[28] What Rowe asks us to admire in an 'aerial' photograph of a model of Hadrian's villa is not the particular arrangement of the buildings and courts; it is rather the compositional tensions that arise in part from the incompatible geometry of the plan-forms and partly from the exigencies of the topography. The varied and contingent causes of the villa have, in fact, formed a general condition that can continue to unfold across a field. There is, however, an issue in Ellis relating the plan and aerial view to 'abstract' painting. He thinks (as does, we can assume, Rowe) that 'abstraction' is a kind of reduction to the essentials of painting, particularly surface and pattern and therefore the aerial view, in its increasing height and distance, achieves a kind of abstraction of the urban condition. There is, however, a different account of developments in post-war painting which emphasises not the 'flatness' of the painting, but its horizontality, and horizontality is a much closer match between art and the aerial viewpoint. The argument that *Collage City* presents to the reader depends, as field painting did, on a rotation of the viewpoint.

HORIZONTALITY AND LANDSCAPE

When Jackson Pollock painted on the floor and then hung the canvas on the wall, a certain horizontal-ness remained in the geometry of the paint dribbles, as well as in the coins, cigarette butts and detritus that were doubly indexical of the horizontal and the floor (Figure 11.7). The viewing conditions of such a painting are like those of any picture, except that canvas is no longer *facing* the viewer. Unlike the upright posture of the viewer, the position of the canvas can only be understood as a convention of the gallery space, not of painting. Formalist proponents of abstraction, particularly Clement Greenberg, celebrated the non-representational aspect of abstract painting as a movement towards purity; as painting addressing matters of its own condition, colour, shape, and the flatness of its surface.[29] In challenging this formalist account, Rosalind E. Krauss developed a different narrative for modern art, one that places greater historical emphasis on surrealism and greater interpretive attention to the phenomenological and psychoanalytic aspects of art.[30] For Krauss, the problematic of surface is an aspect of its horizontality, and it is not a movement towards purity, but rather toward a baseness that underlies human ambitions

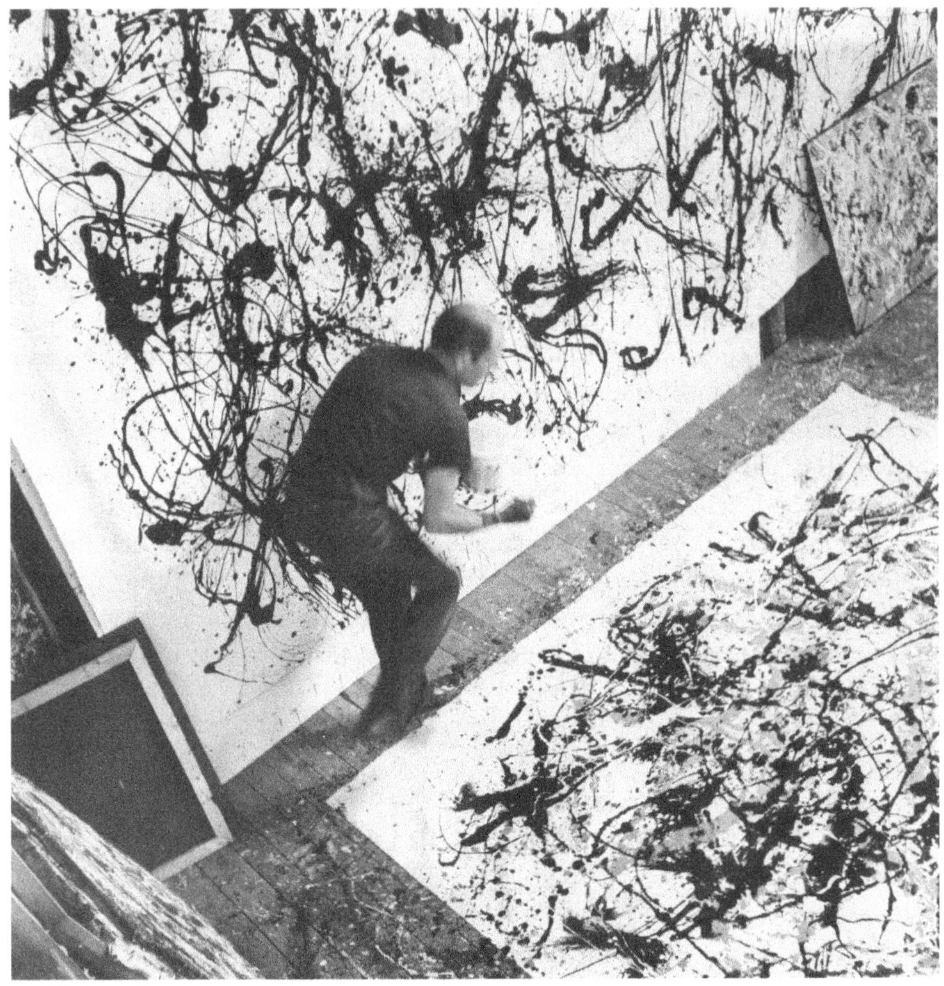

[11.7] *Jackson Pollock*, 1950. Photograph by Hans Namuth.

to 'good form'. Gestalt psychology assumes that a good form is strongly recognisable as a figure outlined against a background. As the analogy implies a gestalt is figurative like a human figure standing up from a 'ground'. Krauss suggests that Pollock and the other post-war artists who were exploring surface were not essentialising the conditions of painting so much as exploring the formal properties of 'ground' and overthrowing the hegemony of good, upright form. Krauss' description of horizontality draws on the ideas of Georges Bataille and Jacques Lacan on the anthropological and psycho-sexual significance of the horizontal which is associated with: 'the vision of animals focused on the horizontal ground on which they and their prey both travel. A vision that is therefore, in certain ways, merely an extension of the sense of touch.'[31] These psychological aspects of 'baseness' may assist in understanding the transgressive aspects of Pollock, and works such as Andy Warhol's 'piss paintings'. However, Krauss's understanding of horizontality fits not at all well with the banal, light wonders of the aerial view and the claims that such views are a kind of natural occurrence of abstract art.

The historical significance of the horizontal orientation of painting in post-war art was argued earlier by Leo Steinberg, and Krauss relies on his insights. Steinberg, however, gives a different account of the relation of the viewer to the angle of the picture plane. Rather than horizontality problematising uprightness and everything that is at stake in 'figure', Steinberg thinks that the horizontal is indifferent to the posture of the viewer, and it is this lack of relation which allows new possibilities in painting. Steinberg's ideas arise from his contemplation of the works of Robert Rauschenberg, which he describes as having a 'flatbed picture plane'.[32] Steinberg chose the term from printing – the horizontal tray in which the type is held – and this has several felicities. It helps him contrast the indifference to orientation in our treatment of printed text compared to painting. The analogy to a shallow tray is also a good description of Rauschenberg's work. Rauschenberg placed found objects, such as a clock or a ladder along with newsprint and photographs, amongst the paint, making both the paint and the painting object-like. As Steinberg puts it: 'The picture's "flatness" is to be no more of a problem than the flatness of a disordered desk or an unswept floor.'[33] Horizontality is not, in the first place, a relation of the viewer to the work, but of the work to the objects within it, which are laid down – a horizontality made apparent through gravity and before any opposition to an upright viewer. This is a mundane flatness of floors and desks, anterior to the specialised flatness of the painting support. The appliqué of the objects is not a transgression of some pure flatness, but the relief any ordinary surface has by being used as such.

We might recall at this point Holt's discussion of the best angle on which to take an oblique view, certainly more than 30°, preferably 60° or 75°. At these high angles, which Holt prefers in his own photographs, the horizon is no longer visible and whatever difference that there is between the oblique and vertical views is no longer apparent in the picture plane, but only in the fragments of the walls of buildings that are visible. The only appreciable difference, as images, between such high oblique photographs and the vertical photographs used to assist in surveying maps, is the relative undecidablity of the viewpoint of the former. The instrumental value of the ortho-corrected vertical image is clear, as is the very real abstraction of viewpoint involved. There is no single body who is privileged to see the fantastic accumulation and rapid dispersal of cartographic information now available, but it is a powerful instrument of government. In the high oblique view the city below is indifferent to the body suspended above it, just as that view, with its dimensionality lost, has no interests at stake nor power to enact them. We could say that the survey is an interested horizontality, whereas the oblique aerial view is not 'un-interested' but *disinterested* in the aesthetic sense.

The angle of view and the height of the horizon in a painting have a history going back to the times of the seventeenth-century maps that Marin discusses. The issue in conceptualising this is, once again, whether this is a binary opposition or a matter of degree. The bird's-eye views, which are the cultural reference in relation to which aerial photography emerges, were also termed 'prospects'. This was a term which stood in opposition to 'landscape' at the time that the latter word came into English. As Henry Wotton wrote in 1624, a prospect was a view from a high place denoting possession and the power to dispose. It was the 'Royalties of Sight [...] which being a raunging and Imperious, and (I might say) an usurping Sense; can indure no narrow circumscription'.[34] The prospect images such as those of Kip and Knyff mentioned earlier were literally topographic portraits of aristocrats' domains, suitably lower in their viewpoint and less encompassing in their extent than the royal city views with which Marin was concerned. Landscapes, by contrast, were essentially genre paintings showing the particularities of rural life. The genre hierarchy between these kinds of views is clear in the height and visibility of the horizon. A prospect usually has a horizon low in the frame and one unbroken by foreground elements. It allows the eye to measure recession of the ground plane in a horizontal plane towards the horizon. A landscape will have much shallower space with a horizon that is high and made up not of the plane of the earth meeting the sky, but rather hillsides, trees and rural buildings, which stand up, like so many screens facing the viewer.[35] Ellis, quoted earlier, stated that Rowe's urbanism was based on abstract art and not picturequeness because of its aerial viewpoint, but in fact it was during the development of picturesque theory and practice at the turn of the eighteenth century that landscape began to be generalised so as to include the prospect. Humphry Repton showed how a designer could take a high viewpoint and, by control of the angle of view and the foreground, give it the compositional values of a 'landscape'. This is an early moment in the the long passage by which landscape has come to mean not only low genre rustic views, but any kind of view taken under aesthetical interests. Coffee table books of aerial photographs are in perfect continuity with the picturesque project. Following Repton's insight, they rotate the viewing angle downward until the vast visual field that would formerly have been called a prospect stands up to face us, its horizonality having become a verticality, or, rather, having that indifference to the body with which we typically treat print media.

THE PLAN

What laypeople see in aerial photographs of cities is the same as what the architect sees, but what they understand of this has diverged and converged historically. What distinguishes the architect from the lay viewer of the aerial photograph is a claim to see through the roof to deduce the internal planning of a building from their knowledge of structure and building types, and, in the arrangement of roofs and streets, to understand the way that land value and transport morphology have caused the distribution of building types and densities. Perhaps mass air transport, Google Earth and, maybe most tellingly, coffee-table books of aerial photographs, mean that the popular experience of cities will increasingy converge with professional understandings. This chapter has argued that architecture should also understand itself in the more general cultural history of viewpoint, should continue to celebrate the productive ambivalence of the view and the plan.

When architects such as Holt, or myself, claim to experience a simple wonder at aerial photographs one might suspect a willed naivety, that the aerial view is merely an occasion to introduce to the public the penetrating insights of the profession. For while the oblique aerial view offers a tremendous realm for the exercise of architectural imagination, to follow those suppositions and test that imagination against the fabric of the city, its constraint and potential, means a necessary shift into dimensioned orthography. To present the dimensioned plan as the inevitable outcome of the experience of the aerial view is to naturalise architectural knowledge by suggesting a natural state of architects' most powerful instrument, the plan. But an unfeigned interest in aerial photography might also be possible for the architect – it is perhaps possible to understand more of the complex history of viewing conventions and drawing techniques by looking at the plan obliquely.

NOTES

1 This chapter is a new presentation of ideas and material that have also been published as: John Macarthur, 'From the Air: Collage City, Aerial Photography and the Picturesque', in M. Ostwald and R. J. Moore, eds, *Re-Framing Architecture: Theory, Science and Myth* (Sydney: Archadia, 2000), pp.113–20; John Macarthur and Rosemary Hawker, 'The city as territory: aerial photography and the everyday', *Photofile*, 63 (2001): 35–9; in sections of John Macarthur, *The Picturesque: Architecture, Disgust and Other Irregularities* (London: Routledge, 2007); and John Macarthur, 'Landscape and Prospect from the Picturesque to Aerial Photography', in Steven Jacobs & Frank Maes, eds, *Beyond the Picturesque* (Ghent:

S.M.A.K., 2009), pp.209–19. My interest in this topic was originally prompted by a studio that I ran with Shane Murray at RMIT University, Melbourne, Australia in 1997.

2 Gordon H. G. Holt, 'Architecture and aerial photography', *The Architectural Review*, 45 (1919): 3–9.

3 Ibid., 5.

4 Ibid.

5 Raymond Unwin, *Town Planning in Practice: An Introduction to the Art of Designing Cities and Suburbs* (London: T.Fisher Unwin, 1909).

6 Claude Perrault, *Ordonnance Des Cinq Espèces De Colonnes Selon La Methode Des Anciens* (Paris: Jean Baptiste Coignard, 1683).

7 Unwin, op. cit., p.300.

8 Holt, op. cit., 7.

9 I have not been able to identify the map but it seems to be a version of the map in that published in the first 'atlas', Abraham Ortelius, *Theatrum Orbis Terrarum*, Antwerp, 1570, and also very similar to 'Brugae, Flandricarum, Urbium Ornamenta', vol. 1, plate 16 of Braun, Georg and Franz Hogenberg, *Civitas Orbis Terrarum*. Cologne, 1572.

10 Holt, op. cit., 3.

11 Roland Barthes, *Camera Lucida: Reflections on Photography* (New York: Hill and Wang, The Noonday Press, 1981).

12 Louis Marin, *Utopics: Spatial Play* (New Jersey: Macmillan Humanites, 1984), chapter ten, 'The City's Portrait in its Utopics', pp.201–32.

13 Marin, op. cit., p.207.

14 Ibid.

15 Ibid., p.214.

16 Here I also draw on Louis Marin, *Portrait of the King* (Minneapolis: University of Minnesota Press, 1988); and Marin's source Ernst Hartwig Kantorowicz, *The King's Two Bodies: A Study of Mediaeval Political Theology* (Princeton, NJ: Princeton University Press, 1957).

17 Marin, *Utopics*, p.209.

18 Camillo Sitte, *Der Städtebau Nach Seinen Künstlerischen Grundsätzen* (Braunschweig/Wiesbaden: Vieweg, 1889) (reprinted 1983). George R. Collins and Christiane Crasemann Collins, *Camillo Sitte: The Birth of Modern City Planning, with a Translation of the 1889 Austrian Edition of His City Planning According to Artistic Principles* (New York: Rizzoli, 1986).

19 Colin Rowe and Fred Koetter, *Collage City* (Cambridge, MA, and London: MIT Press, 1978).

20 See Macarthur, *The Picturesque*, op. cit.; John Macarthur and Mathew Aitchison, 'Pevsner's Townscape', in Nikolaus Pevsner, auth., and Mathew Aitchison, ed., *On Visual Planning and the Picturesque* (Los Angeles: Getty Research Institute, 2010), pp.1–43; and *The Journal of Architecture*, 17(6 – special issue on Townscape edited Mathew Aitchison) (2012).

21 Rowe and Koetter, op. cit., p.98.

22 Ibid., pp.62–3.

23 Ibid., p.69.

24 Rowe refers to Popper's, *The Poverty of Historicism* (Boston: Beacon Press, 1957), and his essays 'Utopia and Violence' and 'Towards a Rational Theory of Tradition' in *Conjectures and Refutations* (London: Routledge and Kegan Paul, 1962). Rowe's terms refer to Popper's earlier, *The Open Society and its Enemies* (London: Routledge & Kegan Paul, 1945).

25 Rowe and Koetter, op. cit., p.149.

26 William Ellis, 'Type and context in urbanism: Colin Rowe's contextualism', *Oppositions*, 18 (1979): 9.

27 Ibid., 7.

28 Rowe and Koetter, op. cit., p.14.

29 Clement Greenberg, *Art and Culture: Critical Essays* (Boston: Beacon Press, 1961).

30 Rosalind E. Krauss, 'No More Play' in Rosalind E. Krauss, ed., *The Originality of the Avant-Garde and Other Modernist Myths* (Cambridge, MA, and London: MIT Press, 1985), pp.42–85; Rosalind Krauss and Jane Livingstone, *L'Amour Fou: Photography and Surrealism*, Arts Council of Great Britain, 1986; Yve-Alain Bois and Rosalind E. Krauss, *Formless: A User's Guide* (New York: Zone Books, 1997).

31 Bois and Krauss, op. cit., p.90.

32 Leo Steinberg, *Other Criteria: Confrontations with Twentieth-Century Art* (New York: Oxford University Press, 1972).

33 Ibid., p.88.

34 Sir Henry Wotton, *The Elements of Architecture* (London: John Bill, 1624), p.4.

35 On these ideas see John Macarthur, op. cit., *The Picturesque*; and op. cit., 'Landscape and prospect', pp.209–19.

12

The City Seen from the Aeroplane

Distorted Reflections and Urban Futures

Nathalie Roseau

How did the invention of flight contribute to the imaginary of the modern city? What influence did it have on the urban fabric? This chaper will explore these twinned questions by examining the representations and practices of *seeing* the city from the aerial vantage point. *Seen* from the air, the city is first of all that which will be unveiled by aerial photography. The history of this view starts well before the beginning of aviation, with panoramas taken from belfries and belvederes, followed by the first aerostatic photographs obtained from a balloon by Nadar in 1858, and by the on-board ascensions devised by Henri Giffard at the Cour des Tuileries in 1878, which enabled people in their thousands to experience the sensation of height.

THE MEDIATISATION OF A NEW VISION

Léon Gimpel, a photographer who had come to attention during the very first major aviation shows, joined the movement initiated by Nadar.[1] In August 1909, during the Great Aviation Week of Champagne, held at Bétheny, hundreds of thousands of spectators came to see the heroes of the air and their exploits. Together with many of his colleagues, Gimpel went along to take the pulse of the event. On the final day of the air show he climbed on board the dirigible Zodiac III with the aviator Hubert Latham and used his camera to pan across the crowds who had gathered below to witness the ascent of the aviators. Instantaneous and airborne, photography took the measure of elevation-induced dizziness, thus intensifying all the more the spectacular nature of the event. The photographs were subsequently published in the journal *L'Illustration,* whose circulation at the time ran to several hundred thousand.[2] The dissemination of the victory over the air was therefore set in motion through diverse media (some in their infancy), which would then rely on these exploits to innovate further. Periodicals, events organisers, sponsors and publicists multiplied images and unprecedented formats in order to disseminate the advancements made by aviation, conveying the unreal in real time. The first newsreels produced in France for the cinematographic news chain Pathé-Gaumont expressed the utterly filmic dimension of aerial navigation.

With his aerial lens trained on urban life, Gimpel would bring legibility to newsworthy events which arose, but whose meaning was not yet comprehensible. From public celebrations to accidents, the photographer would capture all the novel scenes thrown up by the hectic life of the Parisian metropolis. In 1913 Gimpel climbed to the top of the July Column in the centre of the Place de la Bastille and captured the dispersal of the crowds in the wake of the carnival procession that marked the mid-point of Lent. Published as a double-page spread in *L'Illustration,* the photograph bore the following caption: 'From below, seen in vanishing perspective, [the crowds] could give the impression of a multitude; seen from the elevated point where the photograph was taken, the foreshortening of the figures makes the crowds seem strangely rarefied. But how entertaining to the eye is the sheer variety of movements and postures, when studied up close!'[3] Crowds, movement, spectacle: these metropolitan conditions that emerged at the turn of the twentieth century were fastened-down as images, the photographer presenting at a stroke – thanks to aerial detachment – a reality that was otherwise imperceptible (Figure 12.1).

In their turn, painters appropriated this new visual space. When he painted *Tower, first study* (1909), Robert Delaunay reconfigured Parisian shapes from on high. He took inspiration from a photographic postcard showing Count de Lambert's circumnavigation of the Eiffel Tower, which had been executed a short time before. Being quite taken aback, Henri Rousseau, 'Le Douanier', asked him how he achieved the view: 'You went to what street? ... You saw it from which side?'[4] Delaunay pursued his explorations and started working at a bigger scale, experimenting with distortions. He revisited the Eiffel Tower from a variety of angles, from above and from below. The city became panoramic, its roofs composing a Cubist mosaic, and was shown in *The City No. 2* (1910) as a grey-green sea from which the Eiffel Tower and a few dotted red lights emerged. Here, the painter had no longer created an unusual image that baffled his painter

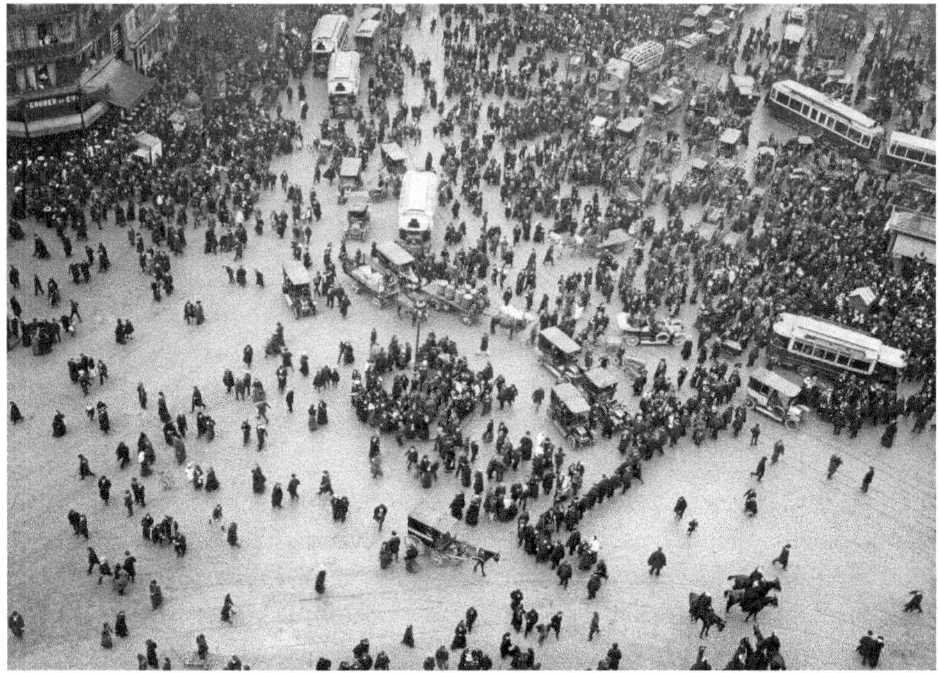

[12.1] Léon Gimpel, 'The Parisian Crowd in the Place de la Bastille', 27 February 1913.

friends, but – inspired by the new times, those of a spatial revolution that celebrated vertigo and instability – had aimed at a reconfiguration of reality.

The radical nature of the aerial view, propelling as it did the use of unprecedented enframings and perspectives, won over the arts in their various movements – Cubist, Suprematist, Futurist. With his *Our Future is in the Air,* a still life painted in 1912, Picasso himself drew up salient parallels between the conquest of the air and the upcoming artistic revolutions.[5] The reduction of depth, the elimination of superfluous detail, the use of simple compositional shapes, the unification of the pictorial field, all these represented – as Gertrude Stein later remarked – so many elements of convergence with the representation of the earth's surface seen from the aeroplane:

> When I was in America I started flying frequently. From the airplane I saw there, on earth, the jumbled lines of Picasso going back and forth, coming into being and dispersing; I saw Braque's simplified solutions, the wandering line of Masson. Yes, all these I saw and understood, once again, that a creative maker always belongs to modernity.[6]

In this creative quest, the Italian Futurists avidly appropriated the aerial theme for themselves in order to put forth new visual representations. Shortly after Wilbur Wright had executed a series of record-breaking flights at Le Mans, Filippo Marinetti published, on the front page of the newspaper *Le Figaro* of 20 February 1909, his Futurist Manifesto.[7] There he exalts the 'roaring car' and the beauty of speed, while at the same time unhinging all academic institutions. Despite its dark tenor, the movement started by Marinetti attracted talented artists; one of them was Umberto Boccioni, who would stress the vertical widening of the aerial gaze: 'The future will continue to increase architectural possibilities, in height and depth. Life will therefore pierce the age-old horizontal of the ground with the infinite vertical scaling of lifts and with the spirals of airplanes and dirigibles.'[8] This zest for the third-dimension revolution was to continue unabated. For the second generation of Italian Futurism, which included the painters Tullio Crali and Cesare Andreoni and spanned primarily the interwar period, these spatial explorations would persist with *aeropittura,* which took into account the dynamism and simultaneity of aerial vision.[9]

THE SEARCH FOR A REPRESENTABLE WHOLE

Broader overviews, foreshortened distances, widening frames of perception: thus the aerial understanding of the world contributed to the creation of a new space of vision. It enabled a new artistic and conceptual reading of the urban environment, whose legibility had been dimmed by its repeated expansions. Triggered by massive-scale industrialisation and its consequent population drain from rural areas, by the increase in circulation and its corollaries – pollution and traffic jams – the expansion of cities after World War I accelerated explosively out of the physical and regulatory corsets that had bound them.[10] Vertical densification and ground-level sprawl defied all limits known until then. Paris continued to grow, to the extent that there was talk of a *Grand Paris* akin to a *Gross Berlin* or a *Greater London.*[11] The first French urban planning law, the so-called Cornudet law, which obliged cities of more than 10,000 inhabitants to plan their further development, was voted in in 1919, at the same time as the decommissioning of the Parisian city walls. And yet, these new legislative measures struggled under the challenge posed by the Parisian metropolis, whose demographic growth had shifted primarily to the peripheries. In fact, the first competition for the enlargement of the capital and the planning of the metropolitan area was launched that same year and was won by Léon Jaussely.[12]

Concurrent with the opening of these new territorial boundaries at the beginning of the 1920s was the dawn of the first campaigns of urban aerial photography. For many large cities this marked the advent of a new cadastral means of representation. In France, through the work of aeronautical companies that were demilitarised after World War I, aerial photography immediately adopted the cause of urban planning, then still in its infancy.[13] On the other side of the Atlantic, the first aerial survey of New York's urban fabric was executed by the Fairchild Aerial Camera Corporation. Beginning with 1921, the company rendered visible through vertical imaging the complete urbanisation of the Manhattan grid. But it was in 1924 that this device revealed its full visual potential, when it realised the Sectional Aerial Map of the City of New York, a photomosaic that showed all five *boroughs* and revealed the new scale of the metropolis.[14]

Crystallised in this way, urban reality – seen both precisely and as a whole – became either celebrated or, on the contrary, *condemned,* as was the case with Le Corbusier's indictment, pronounced in his profusely illustrated book, *Aircraft* (1935). By donning the goggles of the pilot, architects finally acquired the means of reading and understanding the new scales and sizes that were no longer possible to apprehend when seen from the ground or even in plan. In addition, the aerial view acted as a stimulant to their creative imagination. Scrutinising the city from his office balcony, the celebrated New York-based draughtsman Hugh Ferriss rendered it in perspective in his visionary manifesto *The Metropolis of Tomorrow* (1929). This simultaneous process of clarification and subsequent reconfiguration testifies to the vectorial aspect of the aerial imagination, of which Gaston Bachelard wrote in his *Air and Dreams: Imagination in Movement* (1943).[15]

In fact, the aerial imagination enabled architects to devote themselves to rationalisation. The verticality of the aerial dream brought about a principle of order and a law of kinship, as the distancing revealed to the dreamer, in a transparent and simplified way, the concentrated image of his subject. 'At plus 5 miles you turn into a regional planner! For right down there below you is a whole region plain to see, and you can't help wanting to design it, or redesign it. Try, someday, a series of thumbnail sketches in color showing how everything changes and simplifies as you go up'.[16] At the end of the 1940s Hugh Ferriss designed a cartographic vision of the city and its environs, which was prefigured by the scale of the aerial view. 'To draw or to redraw': vision and projection became one, thanks to the limpidity offered by the aerial view. A new dialectic of space was invented. Just like Paul-Henry Chombart de Lauwe, author of *La découverte aérienne du monde,*[17] who interrogated urban space using aerial views, Ferriss also ordered hierarchically and made connections between viewpoint height and projection scale, thus relating detail to whole, establishing correlations between hitherto disparate registers, and further expanding the powers of the architect, who was now able to draw everything.

These facilities made possible by the aerial view would go on to mark out, to this day, the history of city planning and design. From the first cadastral surveys of the 1920s to the satellite images streamed by Google Earth and now at the fingertips of anyone prosthetically equipped with a mobile digital device, the desire for control over a totality whose representability eludes those who roam on the ground would determine the lightning-speed advances in aerial – and then satellite – imaging.

These modes of representation are by no means neutral, for they transform the gaze and prefigure other types of reality, in so doing essaying reconfigurations of our environment. One has only to call to mind the place held by aerial and satellite views in the entries to the most recent international consultation on the future of metropolitan Paris. In that context, which had as its aim to arrive at a global and totalising solution for the future of the French capital, the aerial views, at times lit by images or metaphors, contributed to the attempt to condense a complex reality. These attempts also revive a kind of illusion: that the mastery over problems and their solutions can come from above and, what is more, from a visual representation.[18] For, as others have remarked, there are many nuances and mechanisms that escape those who see from the air. This apparently global gaze of the view from above expunges those scales, those articulations and rough patches that nevertheless give form to the spaces and their attendant practices that are found at ground level. The spatial structures of a megalopolis as approachable and walkable as Tokyo are difficult to seize in plan to a Westerner, and the aerial view of this urban tissue – endless and contiguous, pierced here and there by clusters of buildings and high-rise spears – is no more explicit when it comes to understanding the major forms and structures of the city. As attention to detail (of construction, of connections and linkages, etc.) takes precedence over the quest for a coherent, rationalised and planned totality, the apparent chaos that the aerial view of the Japanese capital conveys actually belies its concealed order and intrinsic urban life.

THE IMAGINARY OF REFORM

This radical vision that marked the aerial view was also active in reflections on how the city might respond to – and be transformed by – aerial mobility. For the city *seen* from an aeroplane was also that assemblage of artefacts that were, from the earliest days of aviation, the projections of urban thinkers. Here again, fantasy writers such as Albert Robida, Jules Verne and H. G. Wells had already accustomed their readers to images of 'aerial cities' criss-crossed by all manner of airships, whose points of reference, uses and designs had acquired new dimensions.[19] The actualisation of steerable flight placed this utopic horizon within the sphere of possibility and, as a consequence, it became incorporated within various projections for cities of the future.[20]

At the turn of last century, professional urbanists published visions of a city as a space that was likely to be recast by the introduction of aerial mobility. These projects were conceived in the wake of major aviation shows, where the mass public was introduced to aerial inventions, particularly as – as already mentioned – the media actively relayed the events that took place there. Urban flights, air shows, exhibitions on the theme of aerial locomotion: the great public spectacles that took place in 1909 celebrated accomplishments and the setting of records, crystallised the unreal in the sphere of the possible and gave rise to a number of urban visions.[21] We are familiar with the predictions of the architect-engineer Eugène Hénard who, in 1910, imagined the 'Cities of the Future' and envisaged an urban future of new horizons.[22]

> Just as man has now managed to mimic a gliding bird, it is by no means inconceivable that he will succeed in imitating an insect. In his *The War in the Air,* Wells had predicted a 'small practical device, easy to drive and easy to handle, suggestive of a bee'. I can subscribe to no higher authority than his and I am fully invested in this enticing science fiction.[23]

This rather optimistic interpretation of Wells's book led Hénard to envisage an urban universe where all buildings would feature lift-garages containing cars and planes, the latter actually termed 'aerial motor cars'. Hénard built up his vision gradually, as if it were an aerial-based system. The 'Cities of the Future' were planned in a ringroad structure. The nature of aerial traffic, from the smallest vehicles to the most grand, determined the respective functions of the inner and outer suburbs. New, quasi-immaterial perimeters, dotted with lighthouse-style towers or else with 'aerial buoys', marked their boundaries and helped orient the aviators. Roof terraces and landing peaks traced a new architecture of urban ridges.

Across the Atlantic, ideas flew freely in New York, advocating this time a vertical stratification of the urban fabric and featuring the roof as a new urban plinth from and on to which airships would take off and land. Here, aerial mobility expanded and enlarged the urban third dimension.[24] A discourse exalting the dream of a freedom of movement that would release from earthly contingencies was being forged. The possibility of air transportation that was either individual or collective was being conceived. Images of tiered cities or of city-regions, sustained by this new means of mobility, proliferated: the city embarked upon the conquest of the air.

Here too the New York visions did not, strictly speaking, invent totally new devices; rather, they legitimated already incubated ideas, which nevertheless had been judged unrealistic up to that point. In other words, the spectacular nature of the feats of aerial conquest lent credibility to those urban ideas that had been deemed merely fantastical. Therefore, the pan of the gaze was no longer literal – it became metaphorical, with a reversal of values engineered by visionary urbanists who would rely on these feats in order to renew the urban imaginary, the aerial metaphor operating here as both guarantee and directional vector for urban reform. Far from vying for the creation of a specific typology, the architects who made the aerial theme their own set in motion a structural transformation of the urban environment. It is therefore not the airport that emerges, from the beginning, as the main material and spatial figure of the intersection between aerial mobility and the urban environment; rather, it is the city, or better yet the city of the future, this finally plausible abstraction that the conquest of the air seemed to make real.[25]

AN AUTONOMOUS WORLD

Similarly to the cities planned from above, the 'aerial cities' traversed by airships and structurally transformed in order to accommodate them raised the question of the tenuous distinction between a totalising and a totalitarian vision. For it is often the case that these visions laid the plans for a global universe, an autonomous world within which mastery would be perfected by the very recovery of this representability.

This panoptical vision was expressed especially in the various networks of systems drawn in the new urban visions. What prevailed in France was Eugène Hénard's structure of aerial roundabouts, access to which was determined according to whether one flew in a 'bee aeroplane' or a 'bird aeroplane'. In the United States, on the other hand, it was the isotropic grid that prevailed. A number of projects conveyed this mode of representation: for example, the global proliferation of *seadromes* that the engineer Edward Armstrong conceived of in 1923 as buoyed relays for oceanic and continental air traffic, at a time when the uninterrupted crossing of the Atlantic was yet to be realised; or the archipelago of urban devices with which New York architects imagined that the city would accommodate airships; or else the fabric of five airports suggested simultaneously by the *Regional*

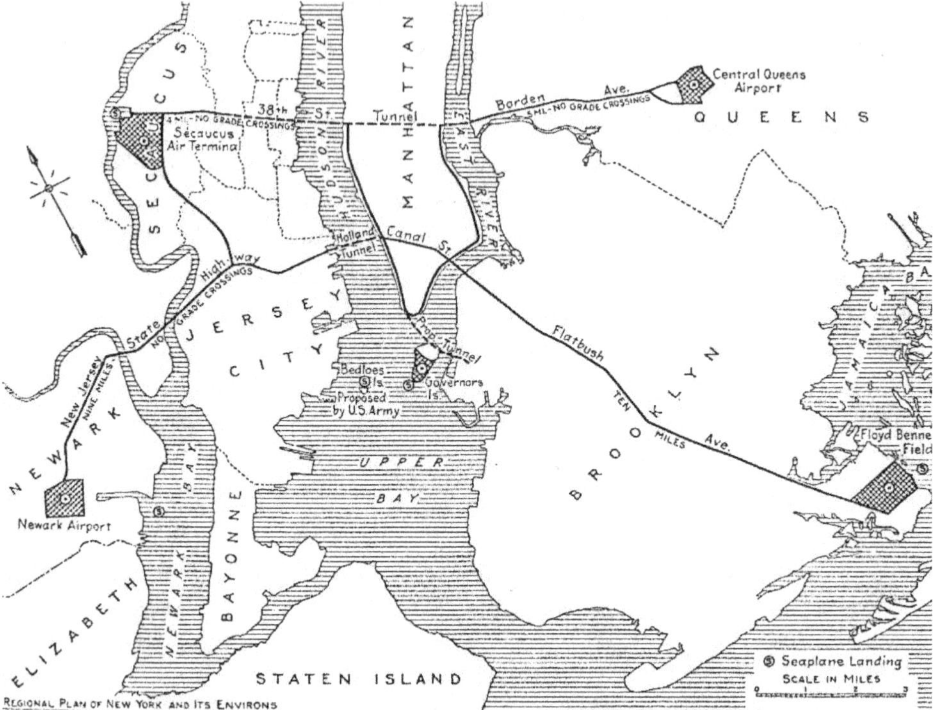

[12.2] 'Important airports, existing and proposed, that would serve the Metropolitan center' (T. Adams, *The Building of the City*, 1931).

Plan of New York (1922–31), and the national chequerboard of 2,000 aerodromes on American soil that was proposed at the same time[26] (Figure 12.2).

An enquiry into this urban imaginary, which has shaped aviation's infrastructure since the invention of steerable flight, enables us to establish relationships and to understand especially the transition between this era, in which aerial transport was imagined as a catalyst for urban transformation on the whole, and the years following World War II when, under the influence of significant changes occurring in the aeronautical industry, the airport became resituated outside the boundaries of the existing city. Far from ignoring the urban question, this shift gave rise to unprecedented places that were conceived as urban experiments, such as Idlewild airport in New York (renamed the John F. Kennedy International Airport) – whose urban design concept of *Terminal City* was commented upon in the architectural press[27] – or Orly airport in Paris, both of which were completed at the beginning of the 1960s. From 'aerial city' to 'airport city', the ambitious and spectacular development of airborne travel, whether private or public, elitist or more routine, would generate countless projects, recreating urban *utopoi*, reviving the idea of an autonomous organism with the capacity to concentrate the complexity of the city into a unique system. The circumscribed isolation of contemporary airports or the use of the megastructure as the dominant architectural typology for an airport's buildings, would prolong the quest for a world that is set apart and within which total control can be exercised.

THE FUTURE AS SPECTACLE

If global and autonomous visions frequently feature in projects and their execution, this is a result of the development of various devices that could accommodate such totality. Seen in this way, the New York international exposition of 1939–40 represented a major turning point in the exploration of diverse media with which the city could be representationally constructed. In keeping with the utopic dream, the exposition devoted a central place to the aerial view. Visitors entering the pavilion entitled *United States Steel* could admire from above the city that the designer Walter Dorwin Teague had fashioned as a diorama, while the iconic Perisphere – a celebrated symbol of the Fair – housed a gigantic maquette of a model city designed by Henry Dreyfuss, 'Democracity', which spectators viewed from elevated walkways (Figure 12.3). Meanwhile, the *Futurama,* designed by Norman Bel Geddes, offered a simulated aeroplane journey by means of an automated train of sound-equipped seats. During a journey lasting some 15 minutes and covering 500 m of actual space, the city was *narrated* to the spectators who were 'flying' over it. The ride unveiled a landscape of farms, bridges and giant motorways stretching out over a vast terrain that was half city, half countryside. Streamlined glass skyscrapers, vast green spaces, rooftops featuring roof gardens or else aircraft docking pads, all created the sense of an Edenic city that the viewers were in the process of discovering from the air. Each day 27,000 visitors were encouraged to imagine themselves inhabiting the scale model they saw during this Wellsian trip by time-machine, stimulated as they were by the pre-recorded narration that kept them on tenterhooks: 'In just a moment, we shall be arriving at this crossroads [...] Entering upon this stage of tomorrow's world [...] the wondrous world of 1960 [...] means leaving 1939 twenty years behind! OPEN YOUR EYES TO THE FUTURE'.[28]

Balconies, dioramas, aerial simulations – all these means were mobilised to make sense, through perspectival distancing, of an increasingly complex city.

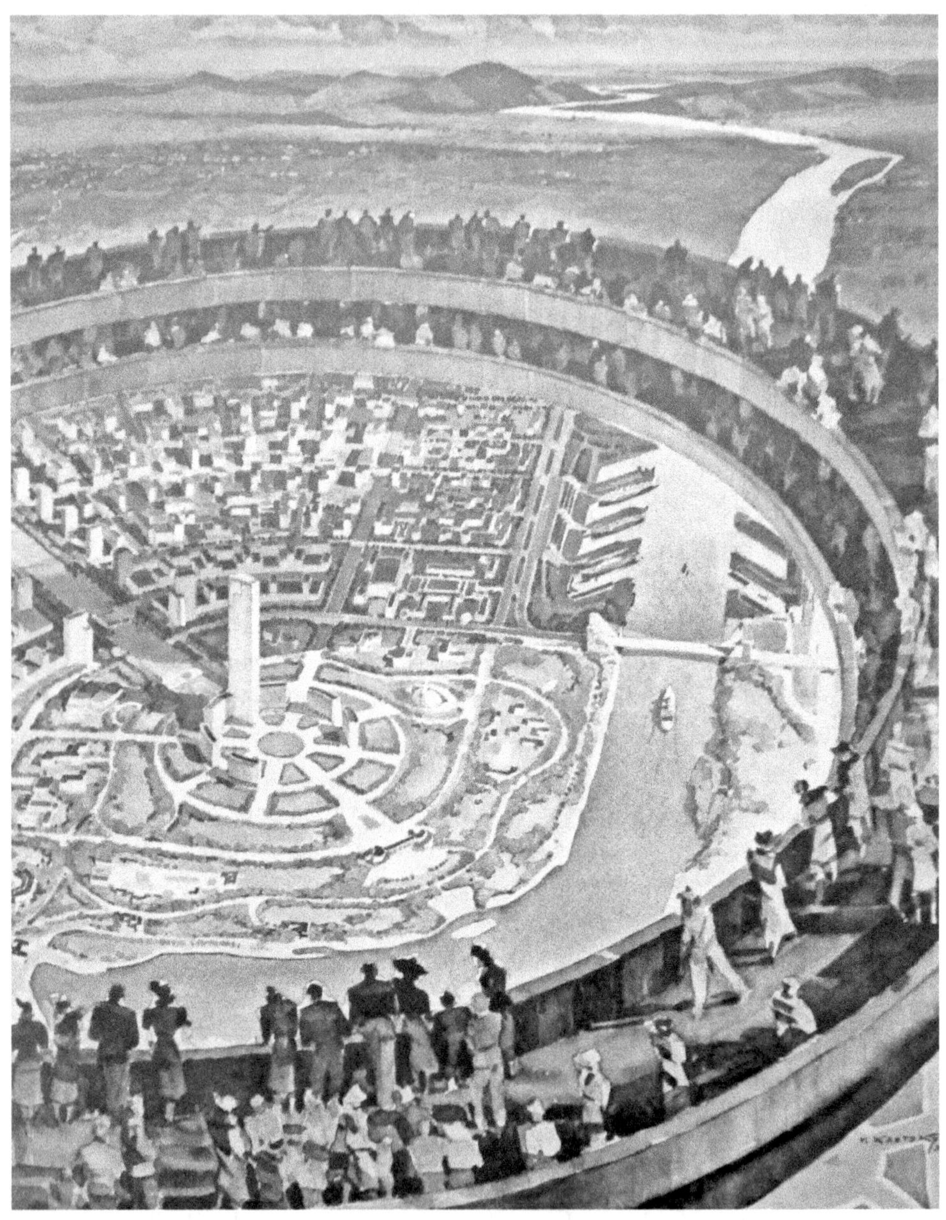

[12.3] Henry Dreyfuss, 'Democracity', New York World's Fair, 1939.

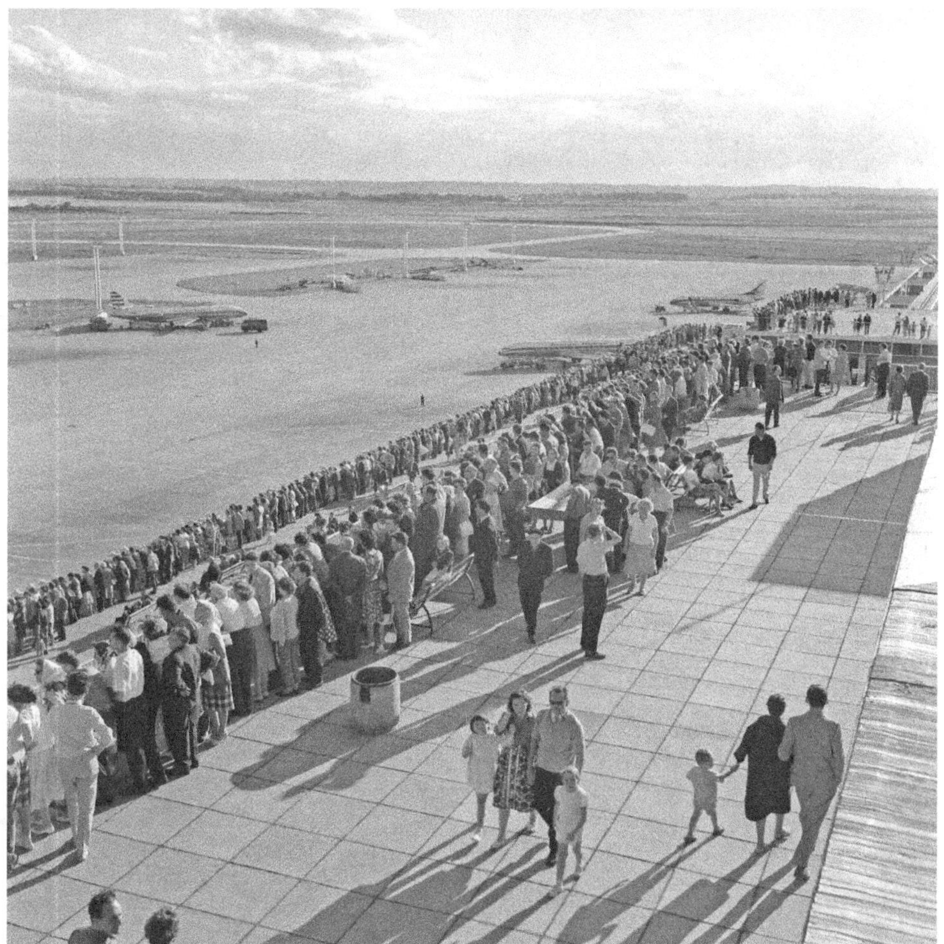

[12.4] Orly Airport, observation terraces, early 1960s.

In terms of aerial infrastructure, the valence of spectacle – present from the very first aeronautical shows – became enhanced by the airport experience. The great airports that had been built in the 1930s proffered the choreography of planes moving on the ground. Le Bourget, LaGuardia, Tempelhof – all of them designed or considerably renovated before World War II and the rapid expansion of commercial aviation – were fitted with observation decks that recalled the pageantry of the epic air rallies. Here, the parallel with the imaginary seemed tangible. The airport viewing platform was a legacy both of the public rally stands from which the spectacle on the ground was surveyed and of fantastic high-level balconies from which the city could be seen from above.

Shortly after the war, the airport itself became the spectacle of modernity. The new Orly South airport is a willowy glass parallelepiped boasting a radical

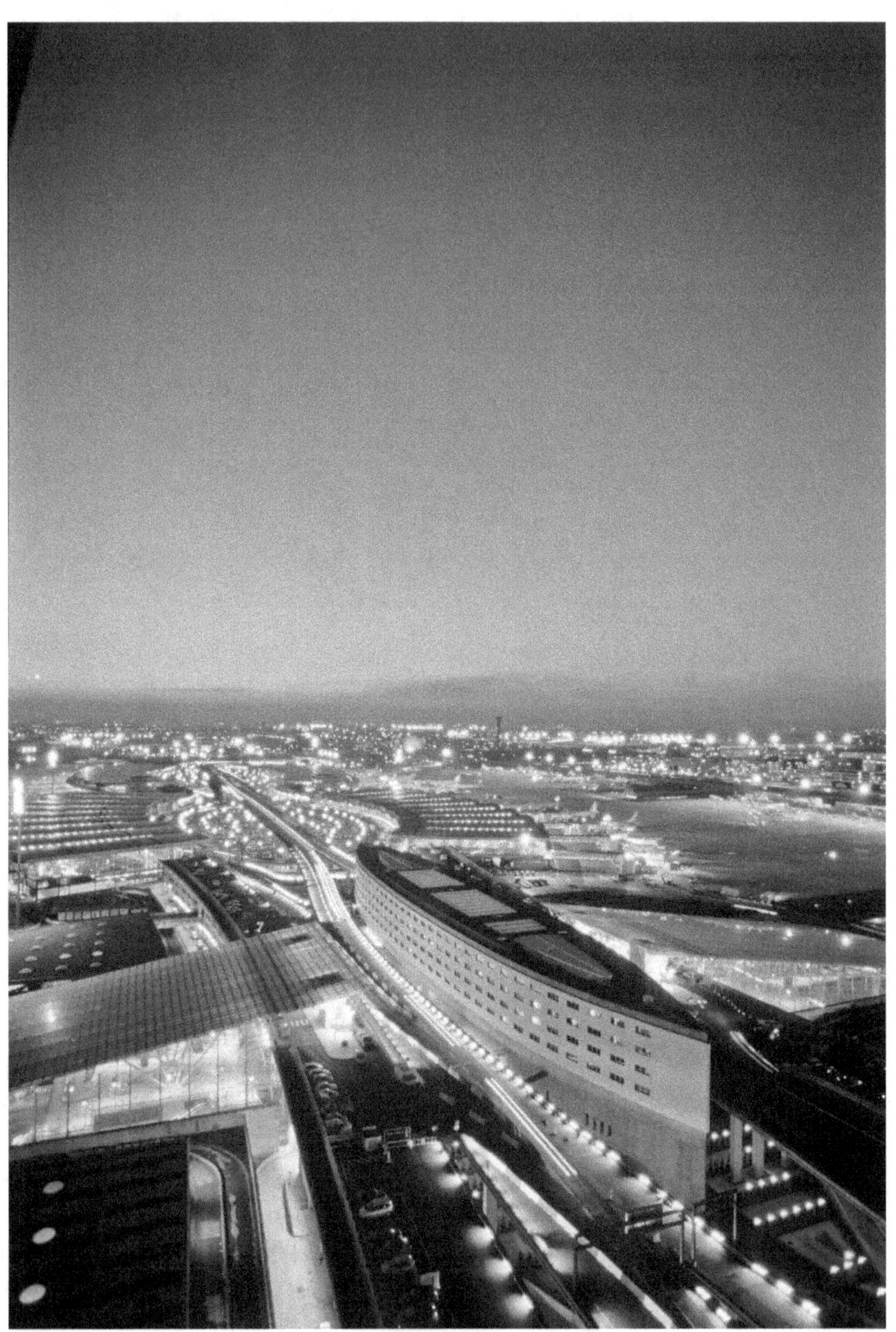

[12.5] Roissy 2, 2003.

scale and aesthetics. The terrace crowning the building is its own world, opening out on to all vistas of the airport (Figure 12.4). Its interior mezzanines, glazed galleries and access ramps enable either vertiginous or panoramic views of the airport's activity. With its string of jewel-like terminals, the Idlewild airport in New York stages its own performance of itself. It is a continuous show: celebrities stride by, journalists commentate, inaugurations follow one another. And the media disseminate these spectacles. *Skyrooms*, walkways, *observation decks*, elevated terraces and restaurants, a whole gamut of scenographic props helps to stage this urban show of an unprecedented kind.[29] The burgeoning of 'showcase' airports also gave rise to a staggering number of scenarios written at the behest of airport officials. The airport resorted to film in order to narrate itself. These screenplays presented the airport's activity as an extraordinary adventure taking place in a fantastical universe.[30]

The spectacular character of the airport did not disappear, however, when – towards the end of the 1960s – the figure of the visitor became progressively displaced by that of the passenger. In a certainly more catastrophic vein, novels such as *Airport* (1968), which was later adapted for film, depict a dramatic plot in an airport that is seen as a closed entity.[31] This figure of the script in fact echoes the many films that were shot either partially or entirely in airports. *Stand-by, The Terminal, Tombés du ciel*[32] – all these films turned the airport into their spatial and temporal unit of measurement, the backdrop as well as the very subject of the plot.[33] This screenplay vision of the airport – which would warrant its own study – is another connection to the fundamentally cinematic function of the aerial view.

Spectacle also continued through the emblematic devices designed and built in the space of the contemporary airport. Access ramps and gangways, balconies and mezzanines, glazed galleries and concourses, all speak of a dramatic vision of space inside the terminals. Outside, the curves and overhangs of infrastructural elements create the notion of a dynamic passage through space that visually captures the entire site. Arrival at the airport by car is frequently designed as a staged sequence of events.[34] The view from the aircraft of the airport's lights as night falls offers a vision that is almost magical (Figure 12.5).

MIRRORING THE EVOLVING CITY?

The imaginary of the airport *cum* city stands in relationship to the city planned from the air. Indeed, the upward motion – that of aerial panning to rediscover and rationalise – and the downward motion – that of the view from above that draws up new shapes and boundaries – produce specific figures that can be compared to the models on which the space of aerial mobility was fashioned.

The shift from the spectacularisation of the city, via the aerial view, to staging the airport itself as urban spectacle, originates with the incremental consolidation of a field of visual representations generating a metropolitan culture for which the city of the future is understood in spectacular terms. A constant tension marks out this blend of the spectacle with the real: the spectacle of the city that unfurls when seen from the aeroplane; the spectacle of the airport that mimics yet leaves behind the city, without being able to completely portray it; the reality of a vision finally recovered from the urban totality; the reality of an artefact that exacerbates the expectations of our contemporary societies. Ascending from it the better to observe it and redesign it, getting closer to it the better to understand and transcend it, the city *seen* from the aeroplane, literally or figuratively, is defined by reference to the existing city in a play of mirrored reflections, imaged in the figures of thought that we have touched upon here: representability, clarification, rationalisation, panopticism and the construction of the spectacle. In other words, the city *viewed* from an aeroplane reproduces and projects, condenses and deforms, delays and anticipates the city it constantly looks at, all at the same time. In this dialogue between the city that is served by the airport and 'its' aerial counterpart, between the subject and its representations, studying these complex distortions offers us keys to unlocking the construction of our contemporary urbanity.

NOTES

1 Thierry Gervais, 'Un basculement du regard, les débuts de la photographie aérienne 1855–1914', *Études photographiques*, 9, May (2001): 102–8.

2 'La grande semaine de Champagne', *L'Illustration*, 3471, 4 September (1909): 153–64.

3 *L'Illustration*, 3654, 8 March (1913): 198–9.

4 Cited in Robert Wohl, *A Passion for Wings: Aviation and the Western Imagination, 1908–1918* (New Haven, CT: Yale University Press, 1994), p.183.

5 Béatrice Joyeux-Prunel, 'Jouer sur l'espace pour maîtriser le temps. La géopolitique des avant-gardes européennes (1900–1914)', *EspacesTemps.net, Textuel*, 28 November 2006 (http://espacestemps.net/document2118.html); Gerald Silk, 'Our future is in the air', in D. A. Pisano, ed., *The Airplane in American Culture* (Ann Arbor: University of Michigan Press, 2003), pp.14–15.

6 Gertrude Stein, *Picasso* [1938] (Paris: Christian Bourgeois, 2006), p.91.

7 Between September and December 1908 Wilbur Wright set more than eight records at Le Mans. It was not until the competition at Bétheny that these records were broken by the French aviators.

8 Umberto Boccioni, 'Architecture futuriste, manifeste' [1913], in *Le Futurisme, 1909–1916* (Paris: Musée national d'art moderne, 1973), p.162.

9 Tullio Crali, *Incuneandosi nell'abitato (In tuffo sulla città)*, 1939, Museo d'Arte Moderna e Contemporanea di Trento e Rovereto.

10 A. Sutcliffe, ed., *Metropolis 1890–1940* (Chicago: University of Chicago Press, 1984); Richard Guy Wilson, Dianne H. Pilgrim, Dickran Tashjian, eds, *The Machine Age in America, 1918–1941* (New York: Harry N. Abrams, 2001), pp.22–41.

11 Greater Berlin (*Groß-Berlin*) was started in 1920, when the eponymous law (*Groß-Berlin-Gesetz*) was passed; while Greater London, after many decades of development, was officially recognised by the *London Government Act* of 1963, which came into effect on 1 April 1965.

12 Jean-Louis Cohen and André Lortie, *Des fortifs au périf. Paris, les seuils de la ville* (Paris: Picard/Éditions de l'Arsenal, 1991), pp.120–5.

13 Jean-Louis Cohen, *Le tour de Paris, les promenades aériennes de Roger Henrard* (Paris: Paris-Musées, 2006), p.11.

14 'Aerial survey of Manhattan Island', *Fairchild Aerial Camera Corporation*, Library of Congress, Washington, DC, 4 August 1921; 'Sectional aerial maps of the City of New York', 1 July 1924, *Fairchild Aerial Camera Corporation*, New York Public Library; See also Paul E. Cohen and Robert T. Augustyn, *Manhattan in Maps: 1527 – 1995* (New York: Rizzoli, 1997), pp.156–7.

15 Gaston Bachelard, 'Le rêve de vol', in *L'air et les songes, L'imagination en mouvement* [1943] (Paris: José Corti, 1994), pp.27–78.

16 Hugh Ferriss, 'Random thoughts of Hugh Ferriss', undated text (likely from the end of the 1940s) from the archives of Hugh Ferriss, Box 7, Second file, Avery Drawings, Columbia University, New York. (Translator note: in English in the original.)

17 Paul-Henry Chombart de Lauwe, *La découverte aérienne du monde* (Paris: Horizon de France, 1948).

18 Frédéric Pousin, 'Aerial views and the future of metropolitan Paris', *New Geographies*, 4, Harvard University Press (2011): 64–2.

19 Jules Verne, *Robur-le-Conquérant* (Paris: Hetzel, 1886); Albert Robida, *Le XXème siècle* (Paris: G. Decaux, 1883); Herbert G. Wells, *The War in the Air* (London: G. Bell and Sons, 1908).

20 Nathalie Roseau, *Aerocity, Quand l'avion fait la ville* (Marseille: Éditions Parenthèses, 2012). This work traces the history of the relationship between urbanism and the developments of aerial mobility in the contexts of Paris and New York.

21 Nathalie Roseau, 'Reach for the skies: aviation and urban visions circa 1910', *The Journal of Transport History*, 30, December (2009): 121–40.

22 Eugène Hénard, 'Les villes de l'Avenir', paper delivered at the Town Planning Conference held at the Royal Institute of British Architects on 14 October 1910, subsequently published in *L'Architecture*, 13 November (1910): 383–7.

23 Ibid., 386.

24 Several drawings from the first decade of the century illustrate this vision of a city that is thoroughly suffused with air traffic. Cf. Archives of Harvey W. Corbett, Box 4:1, Drawings and Archives, Avery Architectural and Fine Arts Library, Columbia University, New York.

25 Nathalie Roseau, 'Les métamorphoses de l'infrastructure, New York et l'imaginaire de la ville aérienne', in C. Prelorenzo and D. Rouillard, eds, *Le Temps des infrastructures* (Paris: L'Harmattan, 2007), pp.57–70.

26 'Seadromes', 1929, source: Musée de l'Air et de l'Espace, Le Bourget, France, Ref. 4B9576; Thomas Adams, Harold M. Lewis and Lawrence M. Orton, 'The Making of the City', in *The*

Building of the City, Regional Plan of New York and Its Environs, vol. 2 (New York: Committee on the Regional Plan of New York and Its Environs, 1931), pp.265–73.

27 See in particular 'New Aerial Gateway to America', *Architectural Forum,* February (1958): 79–87.

28 Folke T. Kilhstedt, 'L'utopie réalisée, Les expositions universelles des années 30', in Joseph Corn, ed., *Rêves de futur, Culture Technique,* 28 (1993), pp.102–17.

29 'Your weekend guide visits: Idlewild Airport', in *The New Haven Register,* 25 August (1962), p.32; On the aspect of spectacle regarding Idlewild Airport, see Nathalie Roseau, 'The obsolescence of the monument: the future of airports icons', in D. Van den Heuvel et al., *The Challenge of Change: Dealing with the Legacy of the Modern Movement – Proceedings of the 10th International DOCOMOMO Conference* (Delft: IOS Press, 2008), pp.87–92.

30 For instance, 'Number 1 World Way', screenplay for the Los Angeles airport by Cate and McGlone Films, 6 March 1963, source: Archives Aéroports de Paris, Box 143, slip n.2005308; and another, for Orly airport, 'Projet de scénario sur l'aéroport de Paris', scenario for a film by Louis Pauwels and Robert Menegoz, 22 September 1960, source: Archives d'Aéroports de Paris, Box 141.

31 Arthur Hailey, *Airport* (New York: Doubleday, 1968).

32 Translator's note: literally, *Fallen from the Sky,* yet with the English title of *Lost in Transit.*

33 *Stand-by,* directed by Roch Stéphanik, 2000; *The Terminal,* directed by Steven Spielberg, 2004; *Tombés du ciel* (*Lost in Transit*), directed by Philippe Lioret, 1993.

34 Teresa Castro, *Le cinéma et la vocation cartographique des images. Questions de culture visuelle* (*The Cinema and the Cartographic Calling of Images: Issues in Visual Culture*), PhD thesis, Université Paris III, 2008.

13

Vectors of Looking

Reflections on the Luftwaffe's Aerial Survey of Warsaw, 1944

Ella Chmielewska

> Memory is not an instrument for the exploration of the past but rather its theatre [Schauplatz]. Memory is the medium of what has been experienced, as the earth is the medium in which dead cities lie buried in debris [...] facts of the matter are only deposits, layers which deliver only to *the most meticulous examination* what constitutes the true assets hidden within the inner earth: the images which, torn from all former contexts stand – like ruins or torsos in the collector's gallery – as the treasures in the prosaic chambers of our belated insights.
>
> Walter Benjamin[1]

A Warsaw address: 36 Smolna Street. An artist's studio/archive hidden in an annex of a century-old tenement.[2] The building, bombed in the last weeks of 1944, in one of the final acts of the urbicide, retains the memory of its past trauma, its front sheared and its back annex reduced to a single storey. The studio, built into the ruin after the war, supports the disfigured structure from within, offering a sense of architectonic coherence that is not visible in the exterior – a solidity of a place set against the material vulnerability of the site. Outside, the trajectory of a falling bomb – registered in a hideous scar on the party wall and in the futility of a staircase that once led to now-absent floors – outlines an architectural section of destruction.

The extent of the damage, however, the sense of the larger trauma, the tragic topography of the mutilated urban surface, can only be seen in a plan view. The consequences of the aerial attack six decades prior, of a targeting view from above, remain scored in the landscape.

Stored in a desk drawer in the studio is a collection of century-old glass negatives featuring portraits of Warsaw landmarks. One of the negatives is damaged, its glass sheet shattered into seven shards that originate from a small point of impact: a sharp, sudden blow that gouged the centre, radiating fractures across the brittle plate. Pieced together, assembled on a flat surface, the glass fragments form a disquieting image-object.[3] Archiving the photograph within its splintered body, the negative cannot be held up to the light. Only when supported by a horizontal plane, only when viewed from above, can this broken object be regarded as complete – a potentiality of an image. I pick up a sharp glass segment from the table, holding it above the stone floor of the studio and feel a sudden vertigo, a realisation of vertical distance, of vulnerability to impact that this fragment materialises along the vector of my gaze.

A print made from the fractured negative renders the image whole, not whole *again* but whole *anew*. Neither the composition nor serenity of the pictured scene is disturbed. As the puncture coincides with the water surface along the horizontal axis, the symmetry of the view is retained. Gentle ripples only underscore the disjuncture between the forces affecting the surface of the glass and those impacting the scene. The image can no longer be what it would have been before the negative's damage. The residue of the past trauma is now sealed in the photograph, located in the place of material absence, where the missing piece joins long cracks and hairline fractures. This point simultaneously indexes the memory of the originating site, the momentary co-presence of the glass surface and the action of photography – the photographer's gesture and the camera's object of focus. The place of damage, now incorporated into the image, holds the memory of impact and points to spatio-temporal dimensions of looking. The photograph is mute about its trauma, though: the violent event remains obscure and cannot be revealed by the material memory alone. The surface only retains the consequences.

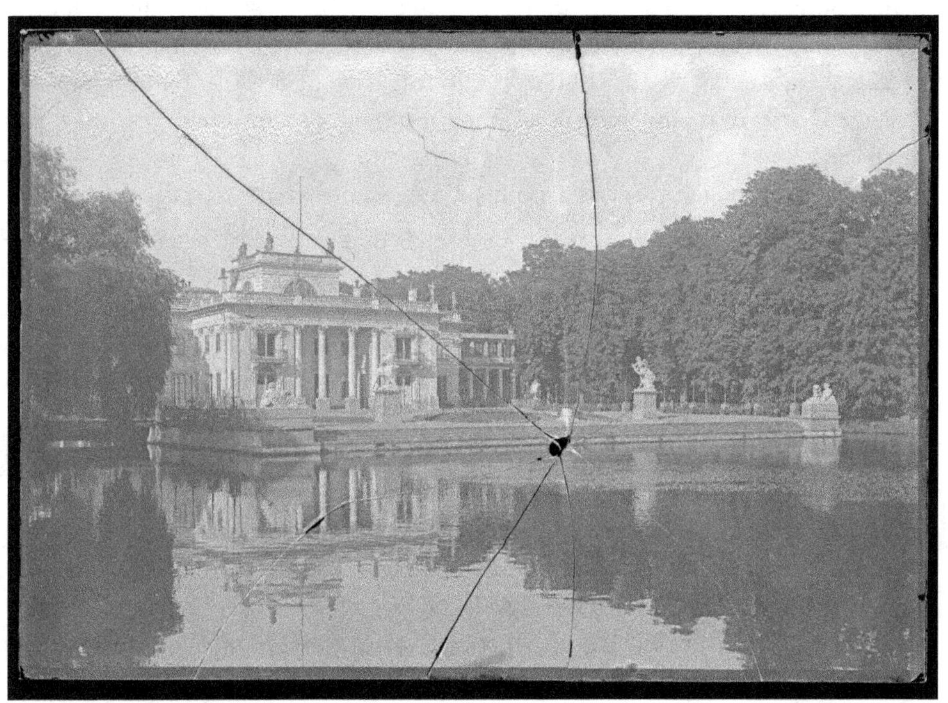

[13.1]

The eighteenth-century Palace on the Island in the Łazienki Park, which is recorded in the cracked negative, sustained serious damage in the last weeks of 1944 but was carefully reconstructed immediately after the war, as were many of Warsaw's palaces and churches.[4] There is nothing unique about the particular image stored in this negative: little memorial value resides in the captured scene alone. Photographs shot from the same angle, with a similar scenographic framing, abound in albums showcasing Warsaw's history. What is, however, both critical and poignant here is the materiality of the negative, which points to further – if inevitably unknowable – stories. This fractured glass, simultaneously so mute and so eloquent, remains a rare material witness of the past, surviving, as I find it, in this fragment of a building in this damaged city. It is an emblem of the ruination of time held within a ruin of space.

I take this image-object as a point of entry into a reflection on the memory of the city as registered in a set of aerial photographs. It is to act as a (re)minder of the privilege given here to images over texts as a source of insight. For Walter Benjamin, whose words open this essay and will guide it through some junctures, memory is a substance within which 'facts of the matter' are accumulated, just as earth is a medium that holds the remains of dead cities. Uncovered, these deposits come to attention as images, as fragments of our understanding. But dead cities also remain on surfaces, in a flotsam of scattered image-objects. These images, 'ciphers of history written in visible forms' assert, as Jacques Rancière tells us, their 'raw material presence'.[5] Retaining the process of ruination, they both document and destroy. They come into (new) visibility, Edward Casey insists, in a specific *where*, 'on and through surfaces of [their] presentation', 'wherever we may be'.[6] Pointing our attention toward directionalities of looking and the location of points of view, the injured image-object at which we look asks specifically for a consideration of surfaces where actions are felt, where consequences are registered and where viewing is inscribed into the material. Surfaces disclose points of impact, refract vectors of looking. In singularities of contact, they retain memories of seeing and being seen. These vectors of looking will be closely examined here in a sequence of photographs that resulted from aerial views that immediately preceded the violence inflicted upon the specific address in which I sit, the place that still now, in its vulnerability, in singularities of its objects and surfaces, holds memories of the damage –'belated [material] insights'.

FOCUSING

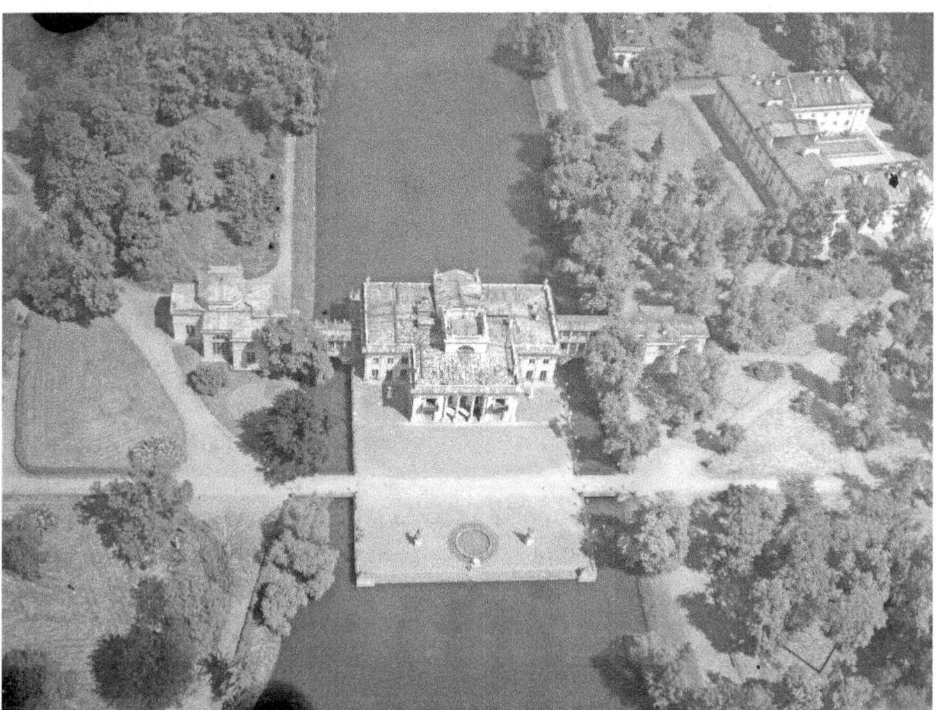

[13.2]

Surveying occupied Warsaw in the Focke-Wulf FW189 Eule (The Owl) aircraft on a bright summer day in 1944, a Luftwaffe photographer captures this view of the Palace in Łazienki Park.[7] In the carefully composed aerial close-up, the palace seems desolate against the lush trees, its roof a blotchy pattern of tiles. (Is glass missing from the front windows or are these just deep shadows?) The ensemble looks intact, unaffected by the war. The grounds are well tended, grass mowed. Lush trees cast dark shadows on the still waters of the lake. Portraying this fine symmetry of the palace ensemble, the photograph could be an illustration for a tourist guidebook. What does this image tell me, though, if it is a product of military reconnaissance?

The framing of the shot fuses the skills of the pilot and the discernment of the photographer. The flight path is aligned with the axis of the palace and the camera angle precisely aimed at the specific view. The directed looking deployed in navigation of the weapon is coordinated here with the field of vision of the photographing machine; a definite aesthetic accomplishment of the preservation of a target through a military sighting apparatus.[8] This is a consummate 'target acquisition technique' as Paul Virilio points out, 'the deadly harmony between the function of the eye and the weapon'.[9] Aided by its agility, 'The Flying Eye', with its almost fully glazed fuselage and camera mounted in a special socket of the floor, was both a superb seeing weapon and a high-definition recording device; a combat apparatus designed to optimise both vision and firing arcs.[10] Here, however, the FW189 is flying at a chillingly low altitude over the safe territory of the occupied city, over what is at the time the German section of Warsaw. Its target is hardly of military importance: a small palace and still water around it.

The image alone is mute about its provenance. Nothing in the photograph reveals the military plane pointing the camera, nor the contiguities of the aircraft's controls – the machine-gun trigger next to the camera's shutter release.[11] Not even the obvious proximities of gestures of the photographer-navigator-gunman-pilot are visible here, even if the synchronicity of actions is evident in the execution of the shot. Taken in the fifth year of the occupation, a year after the annihilation of Warsaw's Ghetto, shortly before the outbreak of the 1944 Uprising and the subsequent punitive destruction of the city, the image – in its focus on composition and aesthetics – is mute with respect to *the photographed time*.[12] Although a product of a Luftwaffe sortie, its details – which carry no apparent military significance – do not speak of the city outside *the photographed space*. The image alone does not disclose the adjacencies involved in its recording: conjunctions that complicate both the photographic act and the resultant document are external to its surface. Here, these proximities to other images need to be carefully considered.

Benjamin tells us that '[e]very present is determined by those images that are synchronic with it: every Now is the Now of a specific recognizability'.[13] Read in context, then, the image in the specific Now, carries 'the imprint of the perilous critical moment on which all reading is founded'.[14] The reading in the Now of this photograph is made possible by a chance discovery, and a subsequent act of protection fused with the deliberate destruction. Found in 1980 in an attic of a private house in Osterode, and deposited in Bildarchiv Foto Marburg, the set of negatives that included this image was like an unexploded bomb.[15] The highly flammable nitrate-based film had to be destroyed and the negatives preserved in copies.[16] Now, only the adjacencies of other frames thicken the meaningful surface of the image, specifying the context, the Now of my reading. A set of 110 negatives from the Luftwaffe's 1944 survey of Warsaw is included among the records of over 3,000 aerial views of German cities from the years 1941–4. The Luftbildarchiv Deutscher Städte, as described on Bildarchiv Foto Marburg's website, was part of the inventory created for the 'Arbeitsstab für den Wiederaufbau der deutschen Städte nach dem Kriege' (Task Force for the Reconstruction of German Cities After the War) led by Albert Speer.[17]

Warsaw is included in the Luftbildarchiv Deutscher Städte alongside the German cities bombed by the Royal Air Force in 1942–4 such as Lübeck, Hamburg and Frankfurt on the Main, as well as those, like Dresden, whose destruction in Allied raids was to come later. Many of the photographs are studies of specific landmarks, in some cases showing the buildings with the adjacent ruins. Warsaw is an odd component of the archive, the only city in the inventory that had been bombed by Luftwaffe itself. Curiously, its photographs form the largest sub-set, with the images of the Łazienki Park accounting for a quarter of the whole grouping. The Warsaw photographs seem different in content as well. They include what seems like attempts at obtaining desired views with repeated approaches to targets, shots taken from various altitudes and angles, and experiments with framing. Among portraits of buildings there are images that look like studies of the morphology of ruins. This material registration differs in content and organisation from typical military aerial photographs, such as we find, for example, in the massive archive of Luftwaffe military intelligence images captured by the Allied forces in the last days of the War and designated with the code name 'GX'.[18] Typical reconnaissance photographs either gather details of intended targets or document the ruinscape and thus the extent and effectiveness of the military action.[19] Reconnaissance photographs can be relied on for military intelligence, for details of scale and altitude, orientation, camera specifications and positions, coordinates of the targets and details of the specific mission.[20] Compared with the GX inventory, the images gathered in the Luftbildarchiv Deutscher Städte resemble pictures from a (wartime) tourist guidebook or illustrations from an album on architectural history rather than documentation from a military survey.[21]

FRAMING

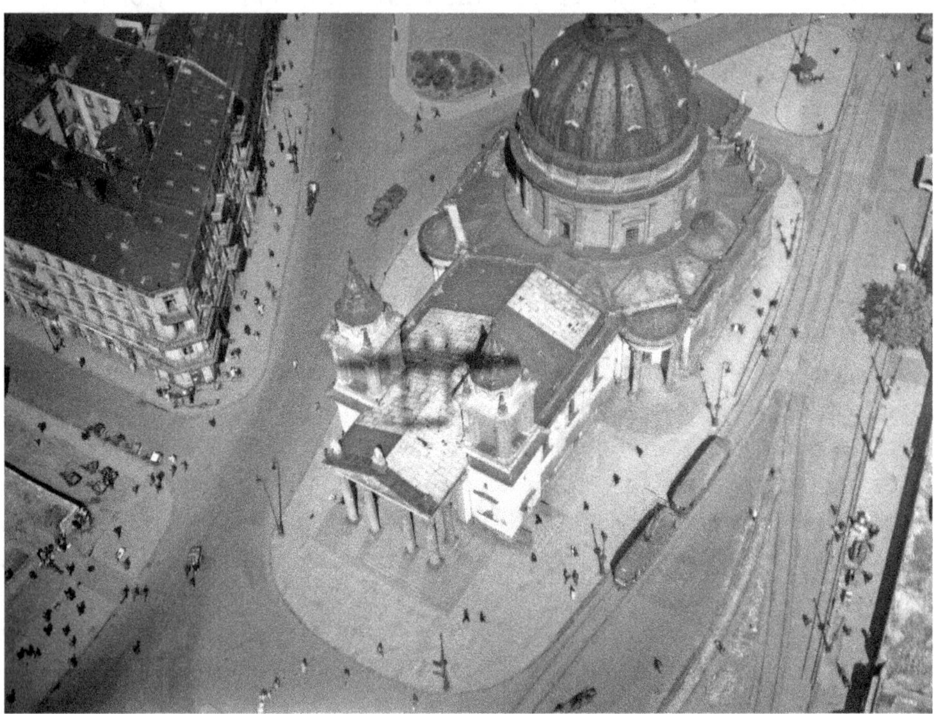

[13.3]

Heading north-west from the Łazienki Park, The FW189 flies low over the Plac Trzech Krzyży, its distinct shadow marking the Church of St Aleksander. As if bridging the bell towers, its wings span across the surface collage of roof tiles crudely patched up after earlier damage. (A fire caused by the 1939 Blitz?) At a safe distance from the trajectory of the shadow, a woman in a bright dress walks toward a tram. On the lower steps by the bell tower, the bulky figure of a beggar sits, whose shadow has – a moment earlier – been spared from momentary absorption by the wing of the plane. To the left, along the tenement, a man in a trench coat, briefcase in one hand, strides hurriedly down the sidewalk, as if keeping ahead of The Eule, his right arm bent in front of him in a recognisable gesture – he is checking the time on his wrist-watch. At the bottom of the photograph, at the edge of the paved isle, directly within the flight path, a single observer faces the sky. A moment earlier, in a 'perilous critical moment', the left wing of the aircraft touched him with its shadow.[22]

Used extensively on the Eastern Front, the FW189 was known on the ground as 'Rama' (The Frame), a reference to the characteristic shape of its tailboom that facilitated visibility.[23] Here, focused on the Church of St Aleksander, the airborne camera is tightly cropping the context out of the space of the photograph. The damage to the square evident in the large sections of cleared ruins, which testify to the 1939 aerial attack, are only vaguely indexed by the fenced-off emptiness at the edges of the image. The signature shape of the aircraft, an ominous shadow marking both *the photographed space* and *the space of the photograph*, scores not only this image but it touches every image from the sortie, simultaneously marking all Warsaw's surfaces. A superb cropping instrument, the airborne Frame, framing the ruins, frames the Now of my looking.

Viewed within a set of photographs gathered for the album entitled *Warszawa – Ostatnie Spojrzenie. Niemieckie fotografie lotnicze sprzed sierpnia 1944 roku /Warschau – Der letzte Blick. Deutsche Luftaufnahmen aus der Zeit vor dem Warschauer Aufstand August 1944* (*Warsaw – The Last Glance: German aerial photographs from before the August 1944 Uprising*), the image is framed by a sense of premonition.[24] The stillness of the scene registers the looming contrast with what is to come later that summer – the violent rapture of the Uprising and the imminent urbicide.[25] Nothing in the photograph, though, tells me that the city is going to die.[26] This intuition resides in the adjacencies of the image-object, in the Now of its reading; I read this sense of foreboding *into* the image. Staged by the wording, the photograph abides by the dictum of the book's title.

Selected as the cover image of the album, the photograph is transformed from a presentiment into the testimony. It becomes an indication of the (imminent) Future placed in the past Now. Capturing the marking of the place with the menacing shadow, in its specificity the photograph makes vivid the precise moment of looking. The *last glance*? Whose glance is it? Mine, the image's reader, is expected to return. Mine is not a quick look either. The image demands, as Benjamin noted, a meticulous examination, a scrutiny then, rather than a glance: I am intently enquiring, asking questions of this photograph. It is a 'bound glance', as Casey would tell me, 'vigilant in a way pertinent to orientation'; it 'fastens on particular things and places' and directs me toward the orienting surfaces and objects.[27] In its mobility, the glance choreographs proximities, it 'also signifies [...] that what it captures in its visual net is *sudden* in its appearance'.[28] In the flash of realisation, I see my looking reflected in the pilot-photographer's scrutiny of the city surfaces.

Is it perhaps *his* glance then? His aerial 'stroll' around Warsaw on a summer day? A tourist glancing around for the best views to capture with his high-tech camera? Is this image a snapshot in a set of 'souvenirs' from the Eastern Front?[29] I have a sudden recognition of the pilot-photographer's urge to frame his own shadow marking the surface of the image. Here, his (playful?) glance facilitates my looking at the not-yet-completely-destroyed Warsaw's past, the past thus preserved by the Luftwaffe, the very apparatus of its ruination. The building framed by the shadow, will have been destroyed in a few weeks' time, but then rebuilt right after the war, substantially altered, corrected to obtain a more desired look.[30] But the city was no longer whole at the time of this capture, it was already a horribly fractured image-object. Only the view from above still holds it together in one image. On the ground its shattered surfaces resist completeness, voids gaping with incomprehension.

There is a sense of disquiet in the proximity of the aircraft to the city's surface, in the deliberate framing of the scene. But I take shadows as the key points of disquietude, of indeterminacy, allusive and shifting points of attachments for the vectors of looking and of being seen. In the images that follow, I will track three shadows then, each anchoring a different point of seeing. One is fastened to the pointed silhouette of the aircraft ominously indexing the tenement's courtyard. It acts as a poignant deictic object, foreshadowing the destruction to come, the 'will have been' of the trauma of the ordinary spaces of the city. Another is attached to the irregular scar of the flattened ghetto, the achingly bare 'had been', the acute outline of emptiness indexing the future condition of absence. They both amplify the force of the third vector. Tethered to a specific address, attached to a shadow of a building bombed soon after the aerial documentation, it shifts my direction of looking, forcing me close to the surface, reminding me to consider the material traces of seeing and being seen, to locate the specific places of the consequences of the view from above.

MULTIPLE EXPOSURE

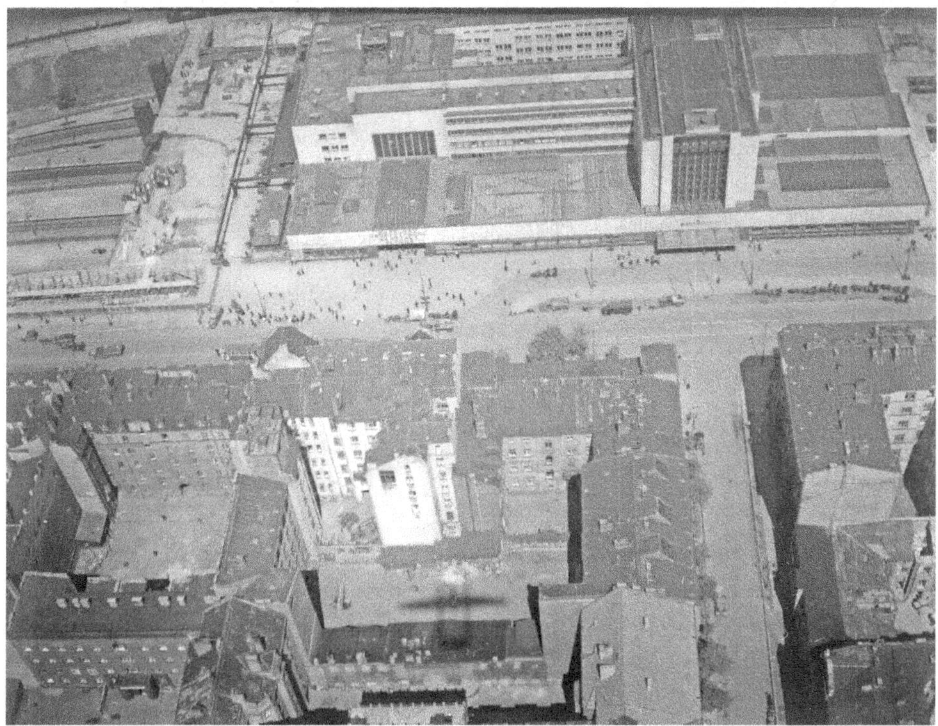

[13.4]

Flying north – now along a different path – approaching the train station Warschau Hauptahnhof / Warszawa Główna along Aleje Jerozolimskie, the FW189 photographs its shadow pausing inside a tenement's courtyard. A moment before the plane slides its silhouette over him, a young man in a dark jacket, hands in his pockets, makes eye contact with The Flying Eye. From the small house behind him – an odd-looking cottage pressed against tall party walls – other observers spill out. There are two figures near the front porch on the right, two standing by the low shed at the foot of the towering white wall, one more nearly touching the tip of the fuselage. Facing the sky, the whole group suddenly stills in its singular focus while the object of their gaze marks the courtyard with a dark stain of obstructed light.

Guiding the aircraft, the shadow confronts me here with a 'raw presence' that Rancière believes is to be found in the captured moments of indeterminacy.[31] It is a mark of both concealing and exposing. It specifies vectors of looking and those of apprehension. In the shadow, the momentary presence of the aircraft is witnessed in the courtyard simultaneously by the photographer/camera and the (chance) photographed subjects/spectators. It is a 'haunting presence' that Casey speaks of, experienced when the photograph, suddenly 'captures a glance that issues from the subject toward the photographer'.[32] It arrests the spectator's witnessing of the photographic act, and of the very act of looking. The courtyard's surfaces register the silhouette of the aircraft at the moment of fixing this event in the material of the film. The glance of the photographer (here, a complex apparatus extending human action) calls out for that of the 'spectator' (the city enclosing human presence). It captures 'the dialectic of looks'. The pictured 'object' or the revealed 'event' is now 'looking out toward us as its current viewers' and in this looking, Casey writes, 'through the physical photograph that presents it', it perdures.[33]

Located in the spatio-temporal relationship to its object, the shadow constitutes a peculiar index. It extends the object through a hinged-like adjacency and a mobile deictic positioning, yet loyal to the time alone, it disregards the place while locating the coincidence of presence. Despite their attachments, shadows 'keep distance', Herta Müller tells us; they do not wholly belong to their objects, 'just like the shadow of a wall does not belong to the wall. The shadows have abandoned objects they belonged to. They belong entirely to this afternoon that is about to end.'[34] Unstable, whether in their presence or absences, they cannot be relied upon for remaining in place. In their marking of discrete events, though, they anchor vectors of looking, activating or intensifying memory. Touching the ground, pointing to the strange assembly of buildings hidden in the courtyard, the shadow of The Frame exposes a manifold of vulnerabilities. Already at the moment of taking the photograph, the tiny cottage encircled by tall tenements is an odd survivor in the centre of the city. It comes into visibility with its set of material memories, clinging onto the surfaces of the courtyard, protected, as it were, within the impossibility of casting its own shadow. Tall walls to the north, the distances between the 'crushed shadows' of the tenements flanking the courtyard, and a low (abandoned and boarded up) annex closing it along the south edge, all shelter this diminutive building while ensuring its access to light. Only the airborne shadow, only a presence from above can touch it. Only the aerial view can expose its precarious condition.

In the traditional morphology of Warsaw tenements, the courtyard was an intimate territory, a node in the networks of movement, the system of localised commerce and the infrastructure for social relations. In a few weeks after the taking of this photograph it will become a centre of the violence inflicted on the city: a place of shelter, of battle, of prayers between aerial attacks and of quick burials. Later still – as a result of the destruction that is to ensue – the courtyard will become a critical tool in the ideological battles of the new regime where the condition of light between the buildings, the shadows cast by the tenements, will be deployed in the post-war urban reconfiguration.[35]

Elaborating the relationships between violence and architecture, Andrew Herscher contends that a 'violent alchemy must take place in order to transform a building into a target into a ruin. Part of this alchemy is discursive; certain stories about architecture guide and legitimate these transformations.'[36] These are stories of spatial legitimacies and privilege: the discourse on hierarchies of reconstruction, the legality of violence enacted through and against the urban fabric, the events of dislocations and dispossessions under the condition of *occupation*. Here the memory of past transpositions and conversions – and the premonition of the transformations still to come – are indicated in the specific condition of the ordinary tenement's courtyard. Violence targeting cities, Herscher continues, is enacted by denying the ordinary places and buildings their singularity, denying them a consideration as architecture, as 'objects and spaces for living, for the living', and positing them instead as generic objects in historical discourses.[37] Exposed in the single moment of the captured aerial view, the curious dwelling hidden in the courtyard carries radical dislocations and transformations already abstracting the city. It is not in a photograph of an iconic building – whether a palace, a church or other historical landmark – that complexities of city memories are found. Rather, it is in the ordinary surfaces and places of dwelling, singular glances of chance spectators, and objects of spatio-temporal vulnerability that give testimonies that require the kind of meticulous examination of the memorial debris demanded by Benjamin.

OVEREXPOSURE

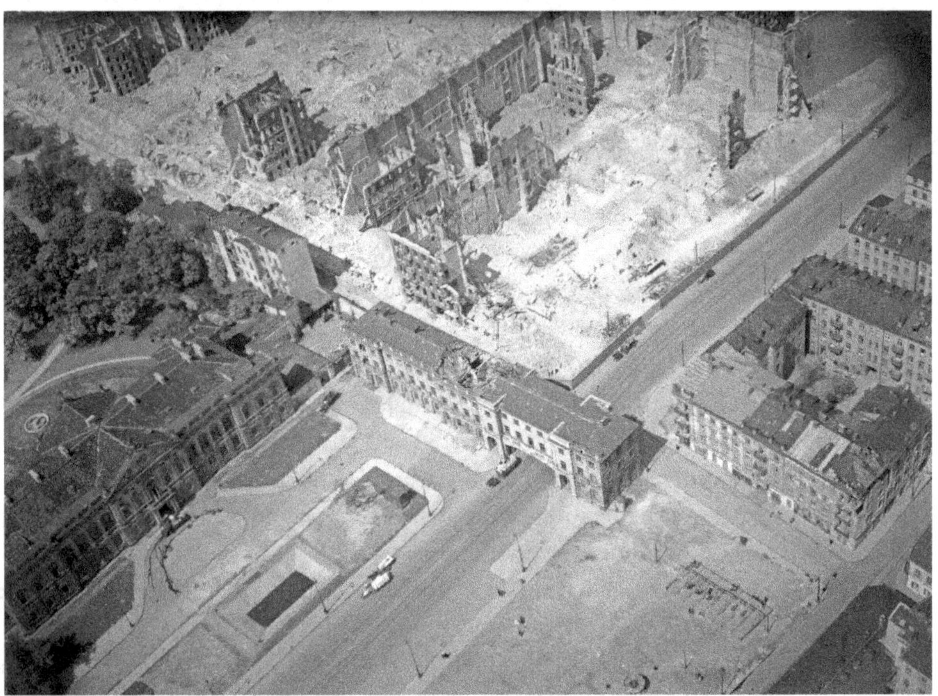

[13.5]

Over Plac Krasińskich, at its northern edge where Świętojerska Street intersects with the square's central axis, Bonifraterska, the airborne camera captures a formal composition of diagonals. Each segment of the photographed space, a distinct morphology of ruination: a completely obliterated targeted section of the city, a spot-damaged traditional tenement block, an empty space cleared of rubble from the earlier bombardment, and an imminent ruin – a still intact palace with its gardens. The axes of the image converge in a deep gash in the precariously sited building in the centre. The puncture in the roof of the annex of the palace (of 'collateral target damage'?) highlights the precision of the violence enacted on the bordered space at the top section of the photograph, the 'liquidated' Ghetto adjacent to the square. The crisply drawn wall, uninterrupted by damage, is now a redundant outline of the space clearly marked by the mutilation of its surface. Within its boundary, the wall contains the city turned into a scarred plane punctuated by sharp verticals of still-standing fragments of facades and party walls. At a glance, the total destruction is registered as an unvarying brightness, unbearable intensity, overexposure.

In the photograph, the tragedy of that which 'had been' and the foreshadowing of the 'will have been' come to a heightened visibility in the signs of the ordinary that are adjacent to the Ghetto wall. The damaged tenement on the right, its front still marked with a signboard of a furniture store (MEBLE), overlooks the vast space of a bleak playground on whose cleared surface traces of removed buildings are still visible. Five swings are in use at that moment, and a group of schoolboys, their heads raised, look up right into the camera. At the lower edge of the image, a round shape (a carousel?), its reading predicated upon recalling Czesław Miłosz's poem 'Campo dei Fiori'.[38] On the left, the water reservoir in front of the Krasiński Palace, a premonition of its futility in fighting the fire of a few months later, a pointless figure considering the scorched terrain nearby.

With its contiguity severed, the annex of the palace is now an absurd 'porte-cochère': no longer connecting buildings across the square, it is a divider between the spaces it overlooks. Still allowing passage into the voided city to its north, pinned down in its position by the vertical puncture, it is now a material witness to death and survival. In the summer of 1944, a year after the 'liquidation' of the Ghetto, the building remains an immobilised onlooker, it is still unable to reconcile the disjuncture of its split vision, the impossibility of experiencing the simultaneously opposing directions of seeing. In the Now of this photograph, this former court building remains a material witness to the wartime tragedy of its location. With a prospect across Świętojerska, the views from one side of the building registered the physical construction of the racial division within the city, marking the spaces as 'Jewish' and 'Aryan', and the subsequent erasure of the part of Warschau designated and enclosed as the Jewish quarter. It witnessed the city deployed as a tool for annihilation of one third of its inhabitants, and its total destruction within the area marked as the space of the Other. (The city will remain fractured ever since.) Toward the square, the bombing of the tenements in the Blitz of 1939 would be seen, as would the weapons piled up high after the surrender,[39] and the subsequent clearing of the ruined buildings for the make-shift playground. The building witnessed the turning of the city into an instrument of occupation: a massive process of relocations, dispossessions, annexations and conversions that took place in order to claim spaces as 'Nur für Deutsche' and those designated for the others.

Along Świętojerska Street, the lone tenement at the edge of the palace garden overlooks the field of destruction. The building's sharp shadow, folding itself over the divisive wall, enters the space of the raw memory of the Ghetto. It touches the absence of the house across the street. Facing the walled-in section of the city, its shadow routinely crossing to the other side, the tenement has been a witness to looking, a witness to witnessing. Now, its shadow points to absent surfaces of past seeing. It outlines the memory of being seen. If seeing is visiting, as we learn from Michel Serres, then an act of seeing demands coming forward, crossing roads, assuming positions.[40] But seeing also issues from immobility, from a fixed stare, the denial of movement, from disregarding the glance coming from the object being looked at. The shadow moving over the wall of the Ghetto, crossing to the other side, marks the place where the vectors of looking are attached, where the memories from before the city's forced segregation and those of the city's complicity in death and survival are located.

The sharp mark of the tenement's crossing points out that the overexposed space voided from the city is not empty. On the bleak planes of ruination, shadows index sudden presences in signs of human activity. A figure marked by a vertical line (a gun swung over the shoulder?) is guarding a group at work: a few men carrying, lifting, piling up material against the wall. Along Bonifraterska, neatly stacked, sorted, piles of objects of similar shapes lie prepared for collection. The material of the 'liquidated' ghetto is being segregated, sorted out. Is it for the reconstruction of the German cities? For Albert Speer's 'Arbeitsstab'? Herscher insists that 'damage transforms a building from an object with precise uses and meanings into a treasure trove of materiality, into heaps of stuff and clouds of smoke, that easily, even necessarily serve as substantiation for violence'.[41] Here, the designated area of separation first became an instrument of dehumanisation. In *the time of the photograph*, still raw from the violence of destruction, it is being de-materialised through segregation. It will soon become a sign of absence. The Ghetto wall – an instrument of violence performed on the city – will later take on a memorial significance, while the city within its boundary, its architecture, 'the space of living for the living', would be confined to oblivion, its insight denied.[42]

THE PENSIVE SURFACE

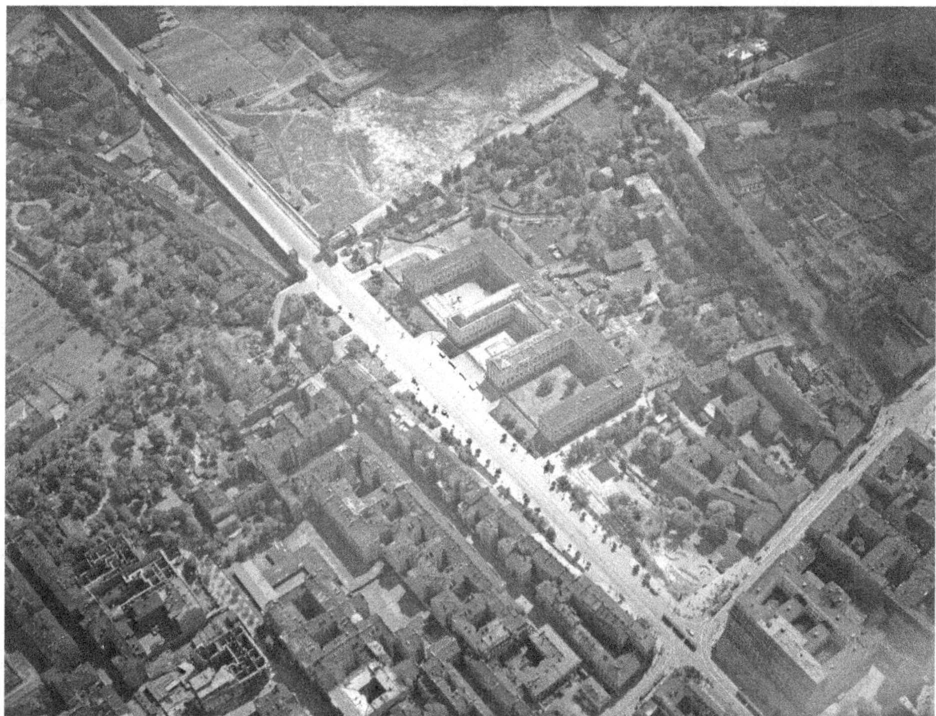

[13.6]

In the last photograph that I will consider here, the FW189, gaining height and turning south, is flying right above Smolna Street. It does not register anything worthy of close scrutiny. It seems focused on the rigid geometry of the National Museum and on the compositional diagonals of the image. The axis of the photograph, along Aleja 3-go Maja (then Bahnhofstrasse) intersecting with Nowy Świat at the lower right and with the line of the Escarpment in the upper left corner, frames one of the key sites of Warsaw. Here, beside the Museum, the Communist Party headquarters will be built soon after the War asserting a new spatial regime for the city, the tenements along the street cleared to ensure visibility across new parade grounds. In the time of the photograph, Smolna, the narrow street parallel to Bahnhofstrasse is still intact and only the houses along the nearby Foksal reveal extensive war damage, their rooftops missing, floor plans exposed to scrutiny from above. Before the summer ends, the rooftops of Smolna will be similarly opened up by fires. The aerial attack shearing the tenement at number 36 and reducing its annex to a ruin will come later that year.

Inside the studio, I am examining this photograph in the album *Warsaw – The Last Glance*. I am looking at the cluster of shadows cast by the back annexes of Smolna. In a sudden moment of realisation, one rectangle of blocked light hinged on the blind party wall, becomes the point of singularity. In the Now of my reading, it is a shadow of the absence of the house, of the missing storeys above the studio space. In recording the building's past presence, the photograph makes visible the present absence. The shadow affirms the place's spatial memory, linking the Then of the image with the material vulnerability of this site in the Now of my looking. It becomes a *punctum* in Rancière's sense, a tangle of indeterminacies, a point of tension between the known and the unknown. It extends the notion, however, into the materiality of *puncture*, a point of impact, an index of loss where the 'unthought thought' resides.[43]

While Rancière seeks pensiveness in art images, I am tracking the insights of the surfaces viewed by the airborne weapon. In their indeterminacies, these surfaces anchor vectors of looking and those of seeing. They cohere objects, directing movements, specifying positions and distances. They frame places, locating and affecting their viewing and their views. Through the shadows cast upon them, surfaces mark time. In singularities of contact, points of impact, memories come into view, sudden moments of insight surface to attention. These moments are marked by a vertiginous disquiet: a whirl of details, a vortex of local histories, 'a vertigo of things that attention [...] compels us to follow'.[44] Vertigo, Mark Dorrian notes, is not about the height or looking down, but a 'certain ungrounding', a sense of imminent fall.[45] It is dizziness triggered by a sudden awareness of distance or proximity, a sense of anxiety set off by changing the axes of viewing and sensing a pull of a spiraling force. Vertigo is a surface condition of visibility, of transparency: not just looking through but a sense of falling through the surface, 'breaking through' the surface tension of the Now.[46]

With the higher altitude, moving from a 'low oblique' toward a 'high vertical', the aerial photograph becomes thinner in surface detail, its abstraction increases. The unsettling gazes from the ground are no longer registered. The sense of transparency heightens. Ernst Jünger, recalled by Virilio, described glass-like transparency of the aerial landscape viewed as a high vertical.[47] Antoine de Saint-Exupéry likened his looking through the glazed cockpit to examining objects through the glass case in a museum.[48] Reflecting on looking at the aerial image, Dorrian points to the different directional modes of aerial views, each focused on a specific interpretation of the visible. For Saint-Exupéry, the oblique view, the mode the pilot normally engages with, was linked to a sense of coherence, while the vertical view, required for the task of a military observer, was about as Dorrian writes, the 'vertiginous itemization of series of objects'.[49]

In looking in the Now of historical aerial photographs, however, our modes of viewing are negotiated differently. In these images, the vertigo is set off by conflicting temporal dimensions of the views: the vertical for the topography of destruction, patterns of death and survival, and the oblique in which the detailed texture of places comes to attention.

Benjamin sees memory as a stage, a place where images severed from their context arise into visibility in the Now of understanding. In his metaphor, the buried city is simply a city of the past, its debris accessible through an archeological procedure of recovery whereby the deposits are brought out as insights, but no major trauma is registered. What if, however, as is the case in my examination, the urban memory is that of the catastrophe, of the 'piling ruin upon ruin' witnessed by Benjamin's later figure, that of the Angelus Novus? What if the Angel of History were both the witness and the instrument of destruction (now blind and weighted down by the symbolic debris as in Anselm Kiefer's 'Angel of History'?)[50] Would coming to visibility not require a different procedure for the memory of urban trauma? Dorrian suggests a possible figure for such a city. He finds her in a photograph of a child in Warsaw, who in the aftermath of the War is shown drawing her house on a blackboard. 'Poised on the edge of the vertiginous spiral' of her chalk drawing, depositing line upon line of troubled memories, the girl confronts him both with her stare and with the catastrophe beyond history.[51] As a figure of absence I place this image within the frame of our looking, in this sequence of photographs of aerial views of Warsaw.

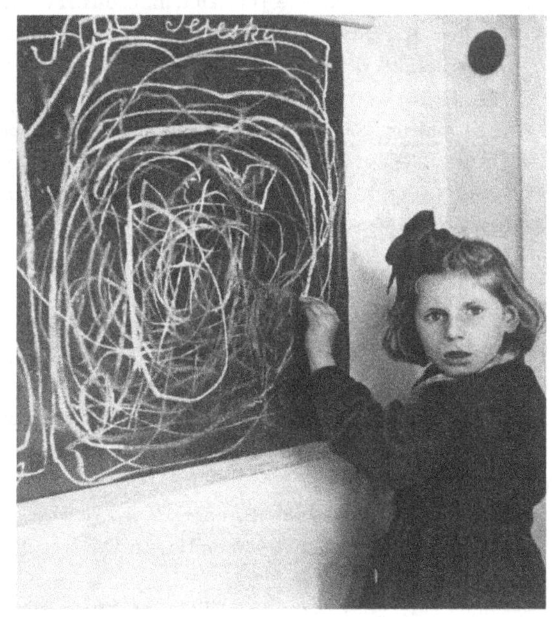

[13.7]

I am indebted to Mark Dorrian for his belief in and encouragement of this project and for his critical advice at key moments of writing. Thank you for conversations and comments to Jerzy Elżanowski, Sebastian Schmidt-Tomczak, Manuela Antoniu and Marco Rasch, and to Katy Bentall for the inspiration of her Studio and her work on place.

NOTES

1 Walter Benjamin, 'Berlin Chronicle', in *Reflections*, trans. Edmund Jephcolt, ed. Peter Demetz (New York: Harcourt Brace, 1978), p.25 (emphasis mine).

2 For the discussion of Katy Bentall's Pracownia, see Ella Chmielewska et. al., 'A Warsaw address: Smolna 36', *The Journal of Architecture*, 15(1) (February 2010): 7–11.

3 I am following Edward Casey's articulation of the 'image-thing', an entity that is constituted by surfaces, but imbuing the term with a potential for resistance, objecting. Edward S. Casey, *The World at a Glance* (Bloomington: Indiana University Press, 2007), p.389.

4 'Łazienki w odbudowie' [Łazienki in reconstruction] *Stolica*, 1 December 1946, No. 4: 4–5.

5 Jacques Rancière, *The Emancipated Spectator*, trans. Gregory Elliott (London and New York: Verso, 2009), p.115.

6 Casey, *The World at a Glance*, op. cit., pp.387, 398.

7 See multimedia Herder-Institut Marburg, *Waschau – der letzte Blick*: http://www.herder-institut.de/warschau/indexpl.html [accessed 10 March 2010].

8 Paul Virilio, *War and Cinema: The Logistics of Perception*, trans. Patrick Camiller (London and New York: Verso, 1989), p.68.

9 Ibid.

10 William Green, *The Warplanes of the Third Reich* (London: MacDonald, 1970), p.188. George Mellinger and John Stonaway, *P-39 Airacobra Aces of World War 2* (Oxford: Osprey Publishing, 2001), p.73.

11 Virilio, *War and Cinema*, op. cit., p.20.

12 I am following Eduardo Cadava's nuanced differentiation between the space and time of the photograph and that of the photographed. Eduardo Cadava, '*Lapsus imaginis:* The image in ruins', *October*, 96 (Spring 2001): 35–60, 36.

13 Walter Benjamin, *The Arcades Project*, trans. Howard Eiland and Kevin McLauchlin (Cambridge, MA, and London: Harvard University Press, 1999), p.462.

14 Ibid., p.463.

15 Bildarchiv Foto Marburg at Philipps Universität Marburg is the German documentation centre for art history containing over 1.7 million images. The Luftbildarchiv Deutscher Städte (previously called Kieler Luftbuildarchiv) aerial photographic archive contains medium format negatives donated by Professor Lars Olaf Larsson, who had found the collection of negatives in Osterode in the Harz mountains, in the attic of a house belonging to the aunt of his father-in-law. See http://www.fotomarburg.de/bestaende/uebernahm/kieler [accessed 10 April 2010]. See also, Christian Bracht, 'Das Marburger Luftbildarchiv deutscher Innenstädte', in Christian von Fuhrmeister, Stephan Klingen, Ralf Peters and Iris Lauterbach, *Führerauftrag Monumentalmalerei. Eine Fotokampagne 1943–1945* (Köln:

Böhlau, 2006), pp.163–72; Marco Rasch, 'Frankfurts Stunde Null. Kontroversen um den Wiederaufbau nach dem Krieg', in Ingo Herklotz and Hubert Locher, eds, *Marburger Jahrbuch für Kunstwissenschaft* (Marburg: Philipps-Universität Marburg/Lahn and Bildarchiv Foto Marburg, 2011), pp.335–51.

16 With time, the cellulose nitrate film used in aerial photography of the time becomes highly explosive when subjected to increased temperature. See HSE, *The Dangers of Cellulose Nitrate Film*. 08/2003. http://www.hse.gov.uk/pubns/celulose.pdf [accessed 10 April 2010].

17 Speer-lead 'Plannungsstab für den Wiederaufbau der Deutscher Städte nach dem Kriege'. See http://www.fotomarburg.de/bestaende/uebernahm/kieler [accessed 10 April 2010].

18 GX (Luftwaffe) Reconnaissance Imagery, Royal Commission on the Ancient and Historical Monuments of Scotland (RCAHMS): http://aerial.rcahms.gov.uk/isadg/isadg.php/refNo=GB_551_NCAP/19 [accessed 10 April 2010].

19 See for example Davide Deriu, 'Picturing Ruinscapes: The Aerial Photograph as Image of Historical Trauma', in Kirsten Moana Thomson and Roger Hallas, eds, *The Image and the Witness: Trauma, Memory and Visual Culture* (New York: Wallflower Press, 2007), pp.189–206.

20 GX (Luftwaffe).

21 Ibid.

22 Walter Benjamin, *The Arcades Project*, op. cit., p.462.

23 The aircraft might not have been well known on the Western Front. See Virilio, *War and Cinema*, op. cit., fig.36 where what appears to be an American copy, The Hughes XF11 is shown as a prototype developed in 1944. For details on the FW189 see George Mellinger and John Stonaway, *P-39 Airacobra Aces of World War 2* (Oxford: Osprey Publishing, 2001), p.73.

24 The Warsaw section of the Luftbildarchiv Deutscher Städte (Kieler Luftbuildarchiv) was discovered at Bildarchiv Foto Marburg in 2003 by a Warsaw art historian Marek Barański who presented the photographs in a special exhibition in Warsaw for the 60th anniversary of the 1944 Uprising. The exhibition was accompanied by an album and an extensive online presentation developed by Herder-Institut Marburg. The album describes the photographs as taken 'last days before the annihilation'. Marek Barański and Andrzej Sołtan, eds, *Warszawa – Ostatnie Spojrzenie. Niemieckie fotografie lotnicze sprzed sierpnia 1944 roku /Warschau – Der letzte Blick. Deutsche Luftaufnahmen aus der Zeit vor dem Warschauer Aufstand August 1944* (Warsaw – The Last Glance: German aerial photographs from before the August 1944 Uprising). Muzeum Historyczne Miasta Stołecznego Warszawy, Bildarchiv Foto Marburg, Herder-Institut, 2004. See http://www.herder-institut.de/warschau/indexpl.html [accessed 10 April 2010].

25 The material surveyed by Zygmunt Wałkowski for the exhibition, *Patrząc z góry. Looking from Above* (Warszawa: Dom spotkań z historią, 2009).

26 See the discussion of Barthes' *punctum* in Rancière, op. cit., p.114.

27 Casey, *The World at a Glance*, op. cit., p.108.

28 Ibid.

29 The relationship between wartime photography and tourist adventure was shown at the onset of the War by the American journalist and photographer Harrison Forman. His images from the first days of the September 1939 Blitzkrieg of Warsaw were published in *Travel* magazine. http://www.umw.edulibrary/digilib [accessed 10 February 2010]. See also Danuta Jackiewicz and Eugeniusz Cezary Król, eds, *Warszawa 1940–1941 w fotografii dr. Hansa Joachima Gerke* (Warszawa: Rytm, 1996); *Warszawa w obiektywie nieznanego Niemca w czasach okupacji, 1943–1944*, Archiwum Państwowe m.st. Warszawy. http://www.warszawa.ap.gov.pl/dtland/index.html [accessed 10 March 2010].

30 Robert Bevan, *The Destruction of Memory: Architecture at War* (London: Reaktion Books, 2006), p.182.

31 Rancière, op. cit., p.115.

32 Casey, op. cit., p.408.

33 Ibid., p.399.

34 Herta Müller, *Lis już wtedy był myśliwym* (Der Fuchs war damals schon der Jäger) (Wołowiec: Wydawnictwo Czarne, 2009), p.21 (translation from the Polish is mine).

35 On clearing of the rubble, clearing the ruins see Ella Chmielewska, 'Sites of Display', in Peter Martyn, ed., *City in Art* (Warszawa: Instytut Sztuki, 2007), pp.135–52.

36 Andrew Herscher, 'Warchitectural theory', *Journal of Architectural Education* (2008): 35–43, 42.

37 Ibid., 42.

38 Czesław Miłosz, 'Campo dei Fiori': http://www.poetryfoundation.org/archive/poem.html?id=179942 [accessed 10 March 2010].

39 See images from the square from September 1939. http://www.warszawa1939.pl/strona.php?kod=krasinskich_a [accessed 10 March 2010].

40 Michel Serres, *Five Senses: A Philosophy of Mingled Bodies (I)* trans. Margaret Sankey and Peter Cowley (London: Continuum, 2008), p.305.

41 Andrew Herscher, 'The language of damage', *Grey Room,* 07 (Spring 2002): 68–71, 71.

42 Ibid.

43 Rancière, op. cit., pp.114–15.

44 Mark Dorrian, 'The aerial image: Vertigo, transparency and miniaturization', *parallax,* 15(4) (2009): 83–93, 87.

45 Ibid.

46 Ibid.

47 Virilio, op. cit., p.72.

48 Ibid.

49 Dorrian, op. cit., p.87.

50 See Rita Valencia, 'Sitting with Anselm Kiefer's Angel of History and Zim-Zum (1989), *Times Quotidian,* 5 July 2009. Anselm Kiefer, http://www.timesquotidian.com/zim-zum [accessed 10 March 2010].

51 Mark Dorrian, 'Introduction: Tracking the city', *Journal of Architecture,* 15(1) (February 2010): 1, 3.

14

The Aerial View and the *Grands Ensembles*

Frédéric Pousin

The period of reconstruction in France following World War II provided a propitious context for the development of the aerial view. Technological advances, in part driven by wartime industries, came to revolutionise not just methods of communication, but also modes of flight and photographic techniques and, in parallel, town and country planning entered a phase of planned developments. It is the connection between the two that will be examined here. What precisely is the relationship between the emergence of 'New Towns' – known in French as 'les grands ensembles' – and the development, distribution and what one might even describe as the *banalisation* of aerial photography? To discuss this, we will examine the case of Firminy-Vert, in the Loire, a town that won the 'Grand Prix de l'Urbanisme' in 1961. In doing so, we should note that the representation of this town is very closely associated with the work of the talented, yet little-known photographer, Ito Josué.

Several aerial expeditions were launched in the early post-war period, giving rise to great enthusiasm for this new way of acquiring information. A good example is *La découverte aérienne du monde* (Figure 14.1), published in 1948, a work which brought together several well-known names under the editorship of Paul-Henry Chombart de Lauwe. In the book the aerial view becomes a metaphor for knowledge:

> Aerial discovery, even limited to direct or recorded vision, has a boundless sphere [...] As a method it serves many sciences, principally those which

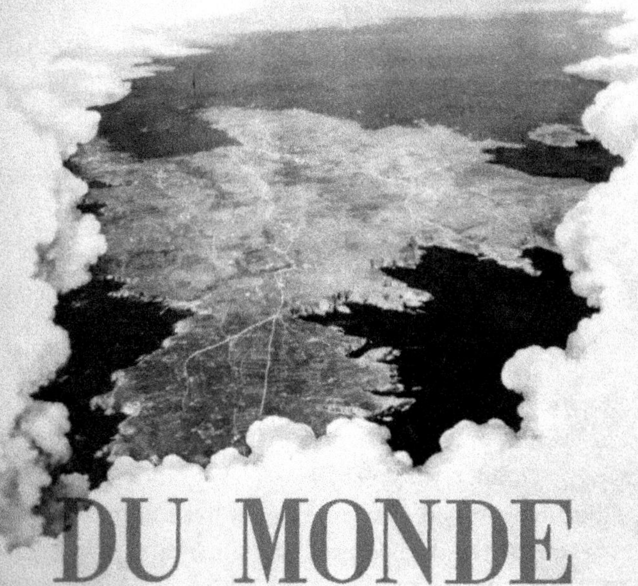

[14.1] Paul-Henry Chombart de Lauwe, *La découverte aérienne du monde* (Paris: Horizons de France, 1948).

> observe the surface layer of the ground and the phenomena that occur upon it. It extends scientific possibilities and opens up new horizons. Moreover, rather than simply providing a certain fact, it drives discoveries by hypothesis, control, comparison and synthesis. Its principal significance lies in a vision of things seen from new and variable angles.[1]

This metaphor was already present in modernist discourse, particularly in architecture, where the aerial view could reveal the building's fourth facade[2] or offer the distance required to reveal the 'formal chaos' into which cities had descended, thereby justifying the urgency of urban planning interventions.[3] This heroic vision of the aerial would, however, came to be tempered, both by the advancement of urban research accompanying French post-war reconstruction and by the doubts to which it would give rise, particularly with respect to the 'grands ensembles'. Michel Parent, curator of the Musée des Plans Reliefs in Paris, was already moderating the general enthusiasm evident in *La découverte aérienne du monde*.[4] In his contribution he analysed the significance of the aerial photograph for the study of towns, arguing that its scientific value is not innate, but that it emerges through its comparison with other documents. He distinguished three categories of documents: very low oblique views that can be compared to prints of urban sites; oblique views taken at medium altitudes; and vertical views, which can be scaled.

The idea that aerial photography constitutes a global photographic document, a corpus from which analytical and interpretive readings can be drawn, is an important idea, well worth emphasising. Interpretation and contextualisation are essential in giving meaning to an aerial photograph. Independent from the technical dimension of interpreting vertical views, Parent shows that aerial photographs reveal the structure of an urban system – of a morphology – and allow the logic of a settlement, which shows the relations between building and environment, to be read. As necessary, the image can highlight the coherence or incoherence that the continued existence of ancient buildings generates in the organisation of more recent constructions. Above all, aerial photography permits perceptive calculations, which are impossible from ground level. Throughout his interpretive and pedagogical analysis of examples, selected for their representative qualities, Michel Parent does not consider, or considers only little, the aesthetic dimension of photography, which is valued only for its documentary role.

THE AERIAL VIEW AND POST-WAR RECONSTRUCTION IN FRANCE

Photographic reporting on new towns was for the most part conducted by state-sponsored agents funded by the Ministère de la Reconstruction et de l'Urbanisme (the Ministry of Reconstruction and Urbanism) and then the Ministère de la Construction (the Ministry of Construction). This significant endeavour of photographic documentation needs to be resituated within the more general context of photography's role in planning. Here, the aerial view is a supreme aid. It is the instrument of a strategic vision of the land, not simply through the high level from which a shot is procured, but also through the documents it helps to produce. Emblematic of this contribution is the important work by the topographical department of the Ministère de la Reconstruction et de l'Urbanisme (MRU), followed by that of the Division Topographique of the Ministère de la Construction. The Division was made up of some 55 people who were responsible for commissioning the topographical maps, essential preliminary documents for any town planning project. The Division itself undertook the fundamental tasks of obtaining the aerial views and preparing the photogrammetric work. In doing this, it created new scientific methods and techniques, which it tested and disseminated, having already trained surveyors and building contractors in the new and emerging discipline of interpretation that had been announced by Chombart de Lauwe as early as 1948.[5] The Division also oversaw the drawing-up of the topographical plans themselves by various companies and technicians. These topographical urban maps, whose scales vary between 1:20,000 and 1:500, are documents that describe and express the visible and three-dimensional state of the ground and its superstructures. They were required to meet the needs of town planners and the different types of technicians involved in construction. Between 1943 and 1965, more than 450,000 very large-scale aerial photographs were produced (usually at a scale of 1:5,000) of 6,500 construction sites over a period of 10,000 hours of flight.[6] As the town development that characterised this period proceeded, existing plans had to be extended and old plans updated: an urban plan is valuable only in terms of its accurate updating. Depending on the required detail of the plan, the photographic document was taken from flights so that the scale varied between 1:20,000 and 1:2,000.[7] To resolve the difficulty of updating plans at 1:2,000, the Division developed a specially adapted photogrammetric method, known as the 'orthophotoplan'.

Thus aerial photography documented the land in the most literal sense of the term. Plans drawn up with reference to vertical aerial photographs were more or less precise, depending on the method of execution and the reliability of the

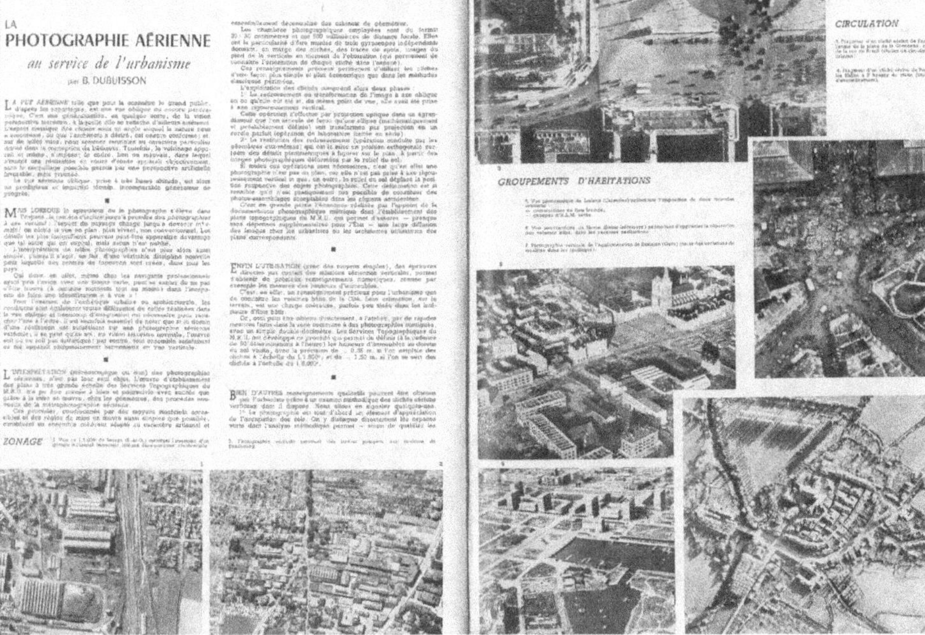
LA
PHOTOGRAPHIE AÉRIENNE
au service de l'urbanisme
par B. DUBUISSON

ZONAGE

CIRCULATION

GROUPEMENTS D'HABITATIONS

[14.2] *Urbanisme*, 1–2 (1952): 44–5.

measurements (Figure 14.2). In the jargon of the period, 'expedient' plans of town planning groups were distinguished from 'regular' plans of urban and suburban areas, which were required to give precise measurements. Finally, very large-scale plans were known as 'particular' – a prerequisite for the execution of certain planning projects.[8]

Due to the abundant information aerial photography revealed about land use, it also played a documentary role in areas which ranged from hygrometry through the description and measurement of planted spaces, to the management of traffic, crucially important to planning. In addition, urbanism profited from vast amounts of information, as Michel Parent's work demonstrates. Photographic documentation held in the 'Photothèque' of the Ministère de la Reconstruction et de l'Urbanisme constituted an invaluable source of information for architects and engineers involved in planning.[9]

Independent of the collection established by the Division Topographique, another photographic source exists, established from the work of different ministries from 1945 to 1979. Rarely studied, this constitutes an impressive iconographic enterprise that consists of 320 albums. Dominique Gauthey, the first to attempt an analysis of the whole collection, emphasises the strategic dimension of photographically documenting the land.[10] He shows how in this

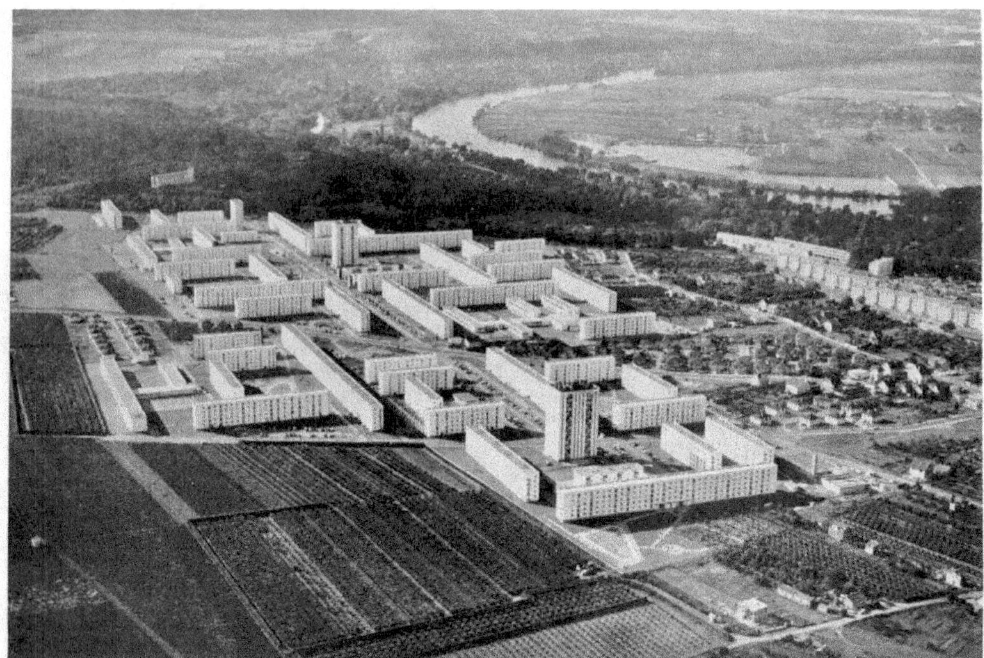

POISSY. — 2.200 logements. Architecte : G. Stoskopf.

Photos " Spirale "

LES MUREAUX. — 1.300 logements. Architecte : G. Stoskopf.

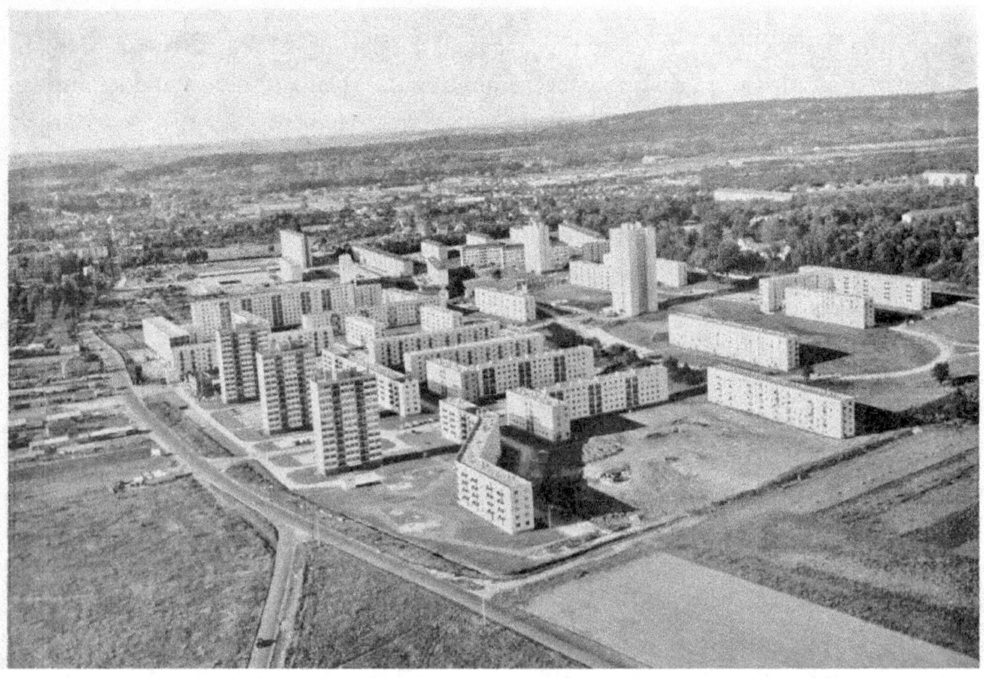

[14.3] *Urbanisme*, 75–76 (1962): 164–5.

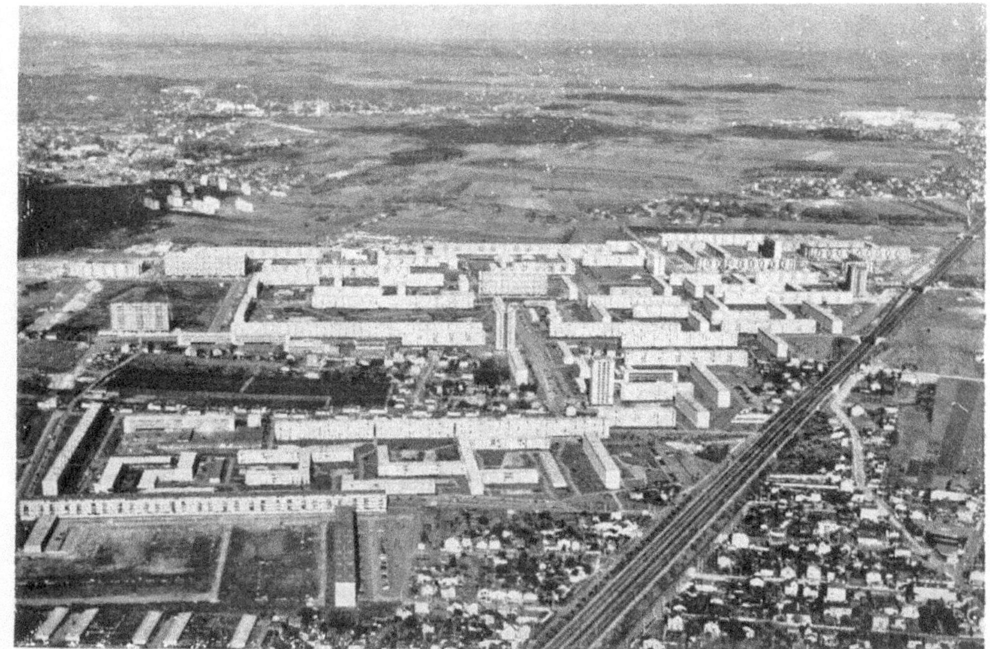

SARCELLES. — 10.000 logements. Architectes : R. Boileau et J. Henri-Labourdette.

VERNOUILLET. — 800 logements. Architecte : G. Stoskopf.

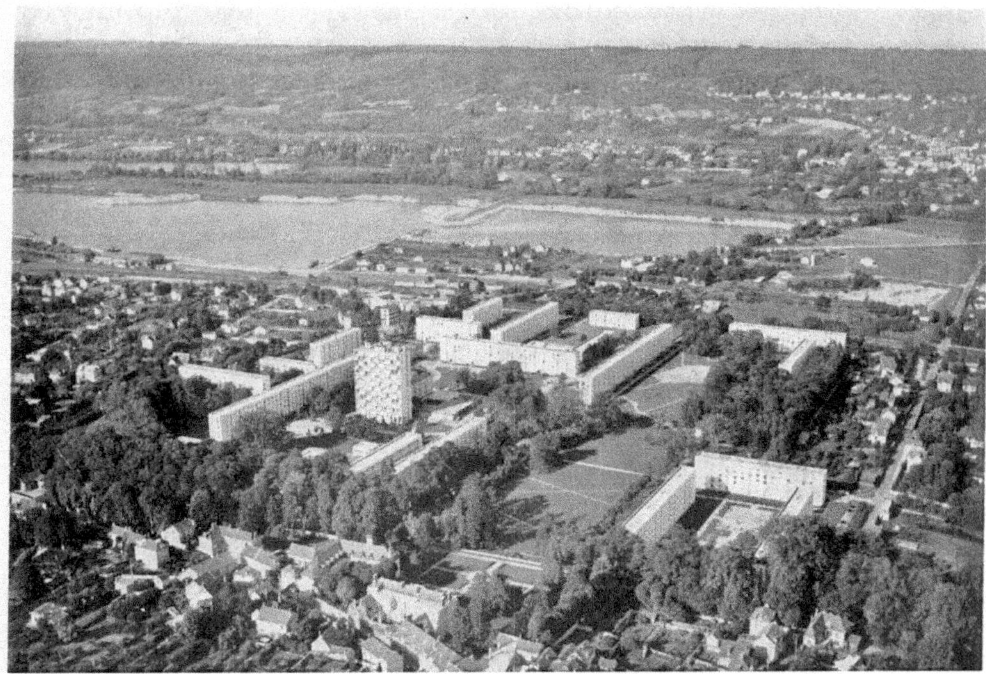

collection relationships are established between iconographic documents through an interlinking of cartographic scales from the regional to the national.

> In the recovery of post-war towns, the photographic image becomes a tactical weapon in the hand of a strategic vision. The aerial view establishes the operational map, while detailed plans, biopsies of the urban tissue, constitute all the evidence required to convince each and every person to wage this just war.[11]

The photographic albums demonstrate the local effects of national policy: the prints serve as much to illustrate the major political axes as they do the specific manifestations that derive from them.

Among these albums, Gauthey distinguishes two main series. The larger of the two, which covers the period 1950 to 1957, mainly consists of reports and assessments of the destruction and reconstruction work. Photography of the areas most heavily affected was prioritised and the reports extend until the end of the reconstruction period. A second series of albums, classified by 'département', or region, covers virtually the whole of the country from the end of the 1950s to the 1970s. This geographical series brings together all the various types of project: housing, with shots of construction sites, sections of motorway, bridges and industrial equipment. The big industrial 'départements', modernised during the 1950s and provided with high density housing during the 1960s, feature very strongly in the collection.

The photographers who were asked to produce the documentation were machine-operators in the full sense of the terms. First of all, the Ministry's few photographers – five in all – did not all have a formal training in photography.[12] Three of them were trained as technical draughtsmen and were appointed to the Planning Department and the two others had a basic certificate in aeronautical naval photography, or in engineering photography for the Air Force, which provided earlier opportunities to develop photographic skills. Lastly, the Ministry's photographic output was also increased by administrators in regional offices, who, while not professional, were good photographers.

From at least 1959 onward, these MRU photographers were regularly sent to different regions with instructions to draw up an inventory and highlight noteworthy state projects (in areas such as education, the 'grands ensembles', public health, public works, scientific research, etc.). Their prints were sent to the regional offices for identification. The MRU's images were thus produced within a strict documentary structure and according to precise demands from the chain of command. The role of the photographer as a machine-operator is here undeniable. In this case, the photographers were the executors of orders from the state.

Throughout the 1960s, there was a reduction in photographic coverage. This was accompanied by real change in the types of photograph taken: an account of the reconstruction effort and the monitoring of the main construction sites was replaced by an 'updating of photographic documentation', that consisted of a 'permanent inventory of buildings worthy of reproduction'.[13] The documentary strategy developed on a daily basis and, as the photographic collections show, also gradually transformed – via various exhibitions intended to promote the country's modernist politics – into a propaganda machine. The MRU's photographs may give a full account of the recovery of French territory, yet, paradoxically, they reveal the emergence of a landscape that was indeed new, but also remarkably banal (Figure 14.3).

Professional publications placed this rather striking banality into circulation, a banality that was itself a clear reflection of the strictly documentary strategy. Thus we find MRU images serving to illustrate journals such as, most notably, *Urbanisme*. While remaining independent, under the editorship of architect Jean Royer during the 1950s, the journal was very closely allied to the MRU. During the period of reconstruction it was the organ of information with respect to regulatory changes and the promotion of developments in France and abroad. The 'grands ensembles' occupied a central place here. It was *Urbanisme* that published the results of the commission of inquiry into life in the 'grands ensembles',[14] which made it difficult to express critical views in the same journal.[15] The images of the reconstruction thus convey a fundamental ambiguity: they testify, rather paradoxically, to both the banality of the created landscape, but also to a fundamental rupture in the process of town formation.

A PRESTIGIOUS DEVELOPMENT: FIRMINY 1953–71. A MAYOR, AN ARCHITECT, A PLANNING TEAM, A HERITAGE

The full value and meaning of the aerial view during the 1960s emerges from an analysis of a project considered exemplary both in its own time and today.[16] Firminy-Vert, near Saint-Étienne, was awarded the 'Grand Prix de l'Urbanisme' in 1961 (Figure 14.4) and, as one of the major sites of Le Corbusier's architecture, is today a candidate for UNESCO World Heritage status. In fact, this modernist town possesses more works by Le Corbusier than any other.[17] The plan for Firminy-Vert was not designed by Le Corbusier himself but by a young team of planners and architects, all of whom were influenced by him: Charles Delfante, André Sive and Marcel Roux. By that time, Le Corbusier had become a controversial figure and the Mayor of Firminy, Eugène Claudius-Petit (elected in 1953), a

PRIX DE L'URBANISME 1961

FIRMINY - VERT

Urbanistes et Architectes : André Sive †, Marcel Roux, Charles Delfante et Jean Kling.
Bureau d'Études : O. T. H.
Maître d'ouvrage : Office public d'H. L. M. de la ville de Firminy. Président : E. Claudius-Petit, Maire de Firminy.

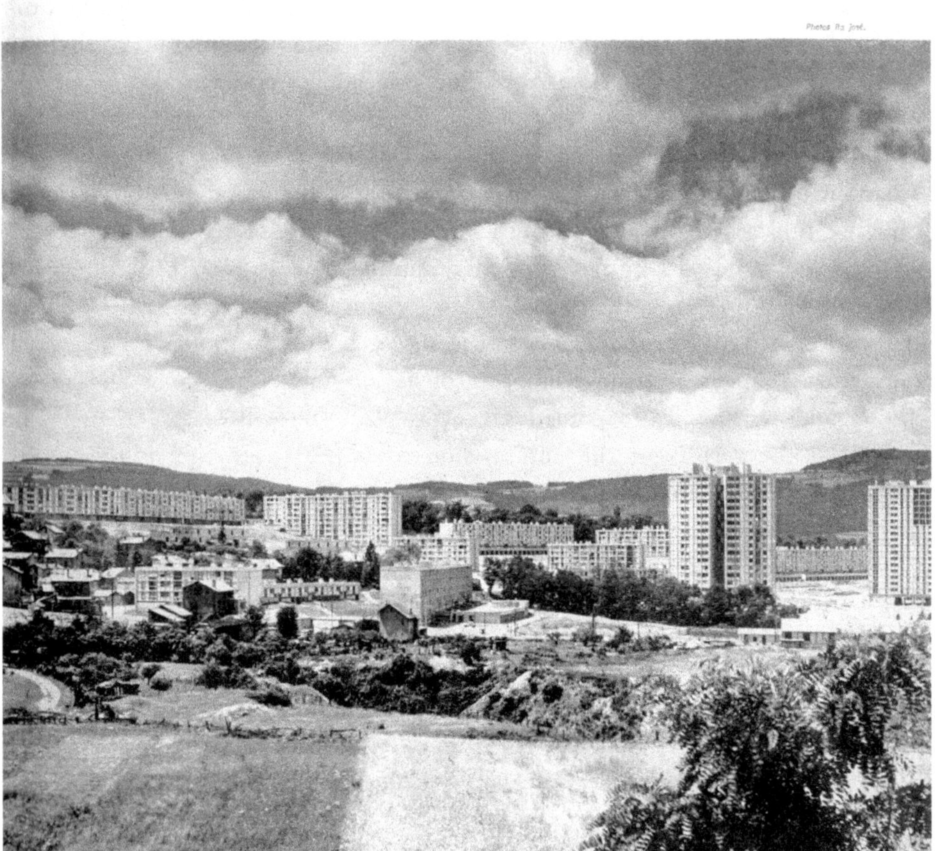

[14.4] *Urbanisme*, 75–76 (1962): 7.

friend of Le Corbusier and former minister of reconstruction in France (1948 to 1952), preferred a younger team. Claudius-Petit was a fervent champion of both modern architecture and planning and also its underlying ideals, most notably the need to reconcile the town with nature. He called on Le Corbusier as soon as he could and placed him in charge of various amenities: a stadium, a cultural centre (begun in 1960), as well as a housing-block, the first stone of which was laid in 1965, the same year as Le Corbusier's sudden death. This modern town was fully completed at the beginning of the 1970s.

In Firminy's case, the vertical view did not play the same role as in many other reconstruction projects, namely that of a documentary technique used to provide an accurate topography of the site and to develop an urban plan. Charles Delfante's account of the years when the first plans were being drawn up, reveal that, while enthusiasm and conviction were not in short supply, the tools were rudimentary and the plans put together in an incontestably empiricist fashion:

> But the condition of Firminy in 1953 was such that we could not make do with makeshift measures and we could not limit ourselves to trying to obtain a possible extension, or to improving the available equipment. The urban analyses developed a rather traditional form; they were both sketchy and precise, scattered yet directed. They provided very uneven knowledge of the town and the problems it presented.[18]

Similarly, later on, Le Corbusier, who was preoccupied with his travels to India and Boston, had no greater recourse to the aeroplane in order to study the positioning of his buildings. No records exist of either flights or sketches – in contrast to the process for the UN headquarters in New York – which would permit analysis of the role played by the experience of flight and aerial perception in the decision to establish a building on a particular site.[19] On the contrary, in the case of Firminy, it is known that Le Corbusier chose the precise site for the housing development by surveying the area on foot, finally somewhat displacing the one chosen by the planners and in doing so, substantiating the reputation of the architect-creator.[20] It was thus rather to introduce the modern town of Firminy and enable it to be understood that the aerial view was called upon. Certainly, both the planners and the architects needed the skills of the photographer to communicate the colossal transformation of Firminy and to make it comprehensible. They appealed to photography, not so much as to document one of the major projects of the 1960s, but to render visible and transmit its architectural, urban and territorial values.

It should be noted that as far as Claudius-Petit was concerned, Firminy offered a positive counterpoint to the 'grands ensembles', which had been heavily criticised as of the late fifties. Indeed, it was conceived with the facilities, most notably cultural ones, which other 'grands ensembles' so sorely lacked. And above all, it came with a genuine landscape plan, prepared by the urban planners in charge of the project. (Moreover, between 1963 and 1965, Claudius-Petit organised various conferences on Firminy all over the world, most notably in the USA,[21] but also in Canada and Brazil.)

As early as the 1960s, exhaustive photographic missions to document construction sites were set up, accompanied by a qualitative change that derived from different approaches to commissioning. The system of documentation on a national scale, which had prevailed in the previous decade, was abandoned, in favour of a more personalised relationship between those commissioning the photographs and those taking them. This change carried the effect of promoting photographic authorship, which in turn bestowed a connotation of landscape on the 'grands ensembles' and modern town developments. The aim was to create an image for new towns. Also at this time, companies specialising in the production of postcards began to record new towns, just as they had recorded the picturesque cities of the past.

A NOTEWORTHY PHOTOGRAPHER

Claudius-Petit contacted the Saint-Étienne-based photographer Ito Josué, who already possessed a certain artistic notoriety. Originally from the Basque region of Spain, Ito Josué, like many photographers of his generation in France, had – although trained in portrait photography – practised as an industrial photographer. Between 1948 and 1963 he worked for the theatre, the Comédie de Saint-Étienne, under the directorship of Jean Dasté and he also took on work from the arms industry and the company Manufrance.[22] It was because of his reputation as a photographer that the architects and planners of the region around Saint-Étienne turned to him. In 1960, Charles Delfante hired Josué to produce a report on the reconstruction of Firminy. This commission was given to Ito Josué in his capacity as an artist, to document an architectural planning project that had just begun to take shape. This was no longer the domain of machine-operators, as discussed earlier, but that of artists. The distinction is important, in that artists are expected explicitly to introduce elements considered to be aesthetic.

What kind of gaze did Ito Josué cast on Firminy's modern architecture? One that was resolutely modernist and wholly consistent with the beliefs of his employers. In his 1951 article, 'Pour des maisons réconciliées avec la nature' ('Towards reconciling housing with nature'), Claudius-Petit stated:

> Now, even in a desert of stone, those who build our cities design them with greenery and do not think twice about digging up the ground to find the sites necessary for such installations. They realise that the city of today, of tomorrow, must reconcile man with nature; it must welcome trees, man's eternal companions, at its centre, so that from his own window he can see the seasons turn and the birds returning to nest.[23]

Although Ito Josué produced compositions reminiscent of constructivism, highly structured in their organisation of mass and interplay of lines, he developed in parallel an eye for scenery, which found expression both in overhead and aerial shots. Ground-level, 'pedestrian' views include vegetation in a 'Japoniste' style, while shots from above and aerial views place the new town in a geography whose scenic and perceptible characteristics are revealed: a blurring of a background, for example, creates a strikingly pictorial effect. The images show the insertion of functional urbanism and modern architecture into a non-urban landscape, one shaped by humans, but nevertheless composed of cultivated fields and stretches of forest. Ito Josué's aerial views do not show a particular attachment to the industrial town. They lean deliberately towards a relationship with the landscape and nature, revealing the formal logic of lines and the interplay of mass and space as it is delimited by the frame (Figure 14.5). In this respect, the images appear completely consistent with the thinking of the planners and architects. It is worth noting that in the 1950s, composition, the interaction of mass and site and the constructions' silhouettes were considered fundamental by the planners of the 'grands ensembles', who were wrestling with the dimension of landscape and scenery.[24] Similarly, aerial views of Le Corbusier's housing block in Briey show it to be isolated in the middle of a forest: this is entirely coherent with the overall plan, where hatching is employed to represent a dense mass of vegetation.[25] The scenic element of Ito Josué's photographic expression demonstrates an aesthetic that can only be fully understood when placed in dialogue with the architectural and urban project it is serving.

The themes behind Josué's photographic expression, which is remarkable in terms of framing and use of light, are clearly seen in his photographic albums, made up of distinct series.[26] These albums, which are intended to convey a summary of his photographic output, are much more than mere photographic contact sheets. They are an unusual and original work by a photographer who is in genuine dialogue with those commissioning the shots. Initially, the viewer is struck by their rather crude appearance: the title is handwritten on a plain neutral-coloured cover and the album is made of card, bound by plastic spirals. But the quality of the layout and the selection of images soon become apparent. Different print formats are presented alongside one another on the page, thus providing an overview of the photographed sites. Those series devoted to major projects such as Firminy-Vert function through the use of a visual logic sometimes reminiscent of cinematic montage. The albums provide an original medium in which to analyse the relationship between aerial views and other photographic reporting used in the course of an urban development (Figure 14.6).

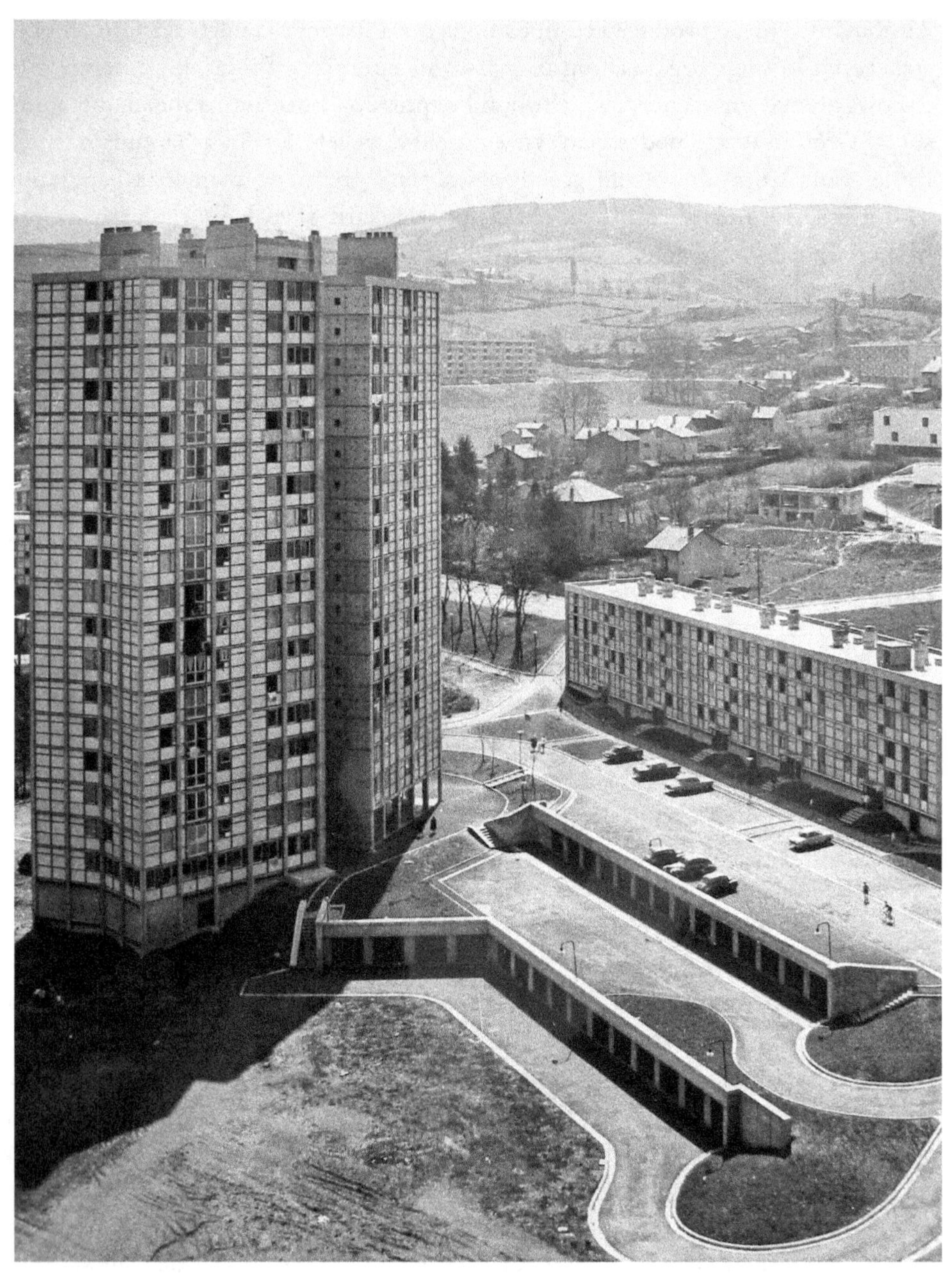

[14.5] Ito Josué, Firminy.

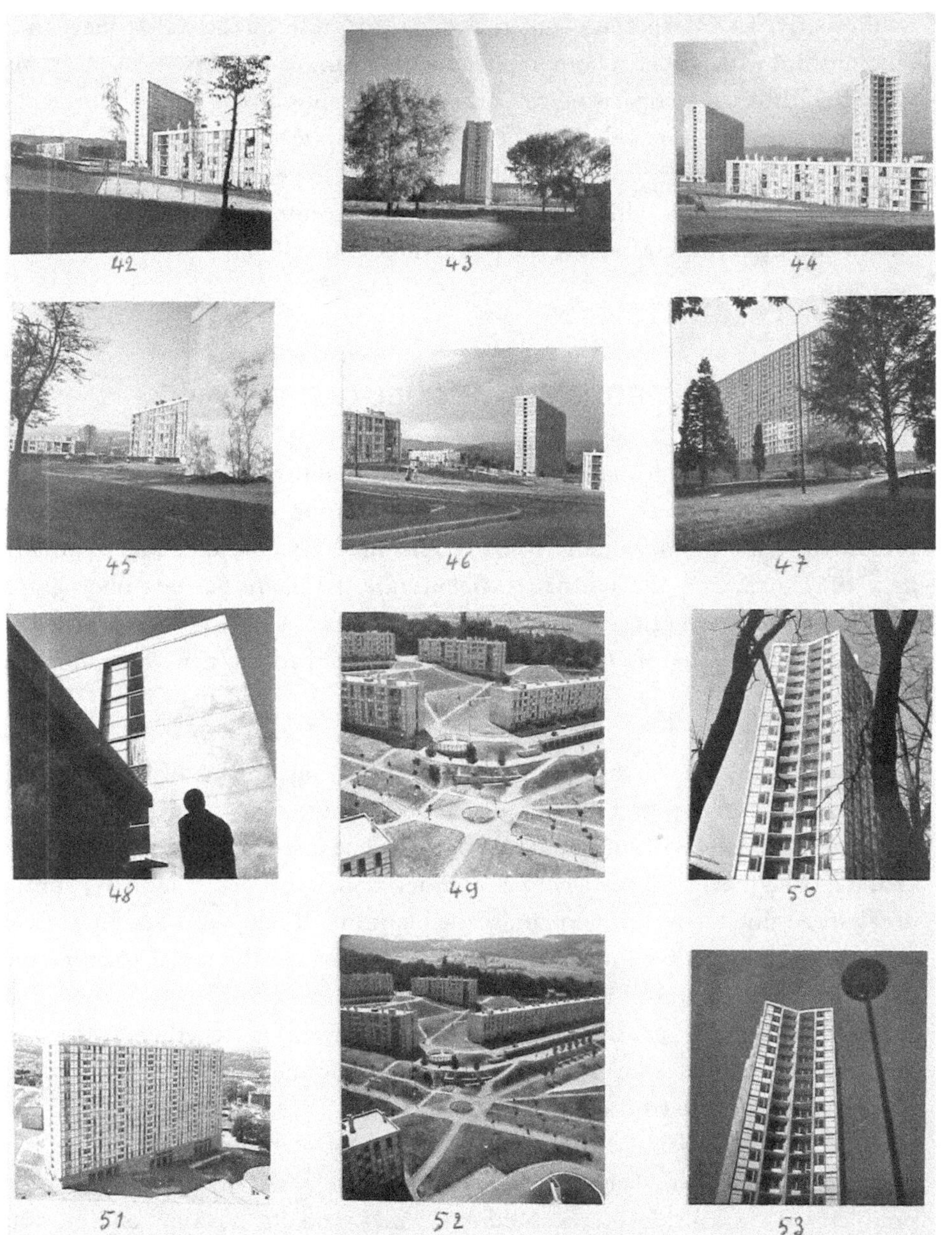

[14.6] Page of an album by Ito Josué.

Similarly, an interpretation of the value and role of the aerial view in its relationship with other photographs documenting an urban project is also permitted through comparison with other photographs by the same photographer that are found, in particular, in the specialist publications. Our analysis must now turn to the different media in which the aerial experience features and, more significantly, through which this experience is communicated in professional circles and more widely, within the public domain.

PROFESSIONAL PUBLICATIONS

A fair number of Ito Josué's photographs were published: in the 1962 issue of *Urbanisme* that focused exclusively on the 'grands ensembles', they feature prominently in the presentation of the Firminy-Vert development.[27] Similarly, in a 1962 article in the journal, *L'Architecture d'Aujourd'hui,* his photographs illustrate Claudius-Petit's article on Firminy-Vert.[28] Following Le Corbusier's death, a special issue of *Urbanisme* in 1968 devoted to the new town, included many photographs by Josué.[29]

Precisely in this 1968 issue, we find a canonical use of the bird's-eye view: an oblique aerial view is used to characterise Firminy, in this instance through its industrial activity, and a low-altitude aerial view also captures its market's communal activity. By 1968 aerial photography had lost the heroic aspect that had characterised it even 20 years before: now aerial views were common in planning dossiers. Architects working in landscape planning developed the habit of flying over sites and were even able themselves to undertake the aerial photographic coverage of a site upon which they were working.[30]

The 1968 issue of *Urbanisme* places aerial views together with other documents: this was unexceptional practice, one found in every special edition of *Urbanisme* devoted to the 'grands ensembles'. Thus, the oblique aerial view taken by the Lyon-based company CUYL, is associated with a map in order to convey the geographic setting. Here we see the inscription of the new town's perimeter on a hillside in the Ondaine valley and its position on the outer edge of the old town, at the intersection of agricultural land and woodland. This view, taken prior to the construction of Le Corbusier's cultural and sporting facilities, emphasises their strategic significance, in that they were to be built at the intersection of the old and new towns. A vertical view, probably produced by the National Geographic Institute, reveals the urban structure prior to the construction of Firminy-Vert.[31] A plan of the projected new town, at approximately the same scale, allows the reader to superimpose the two in his or her mind and acquire a real sense of what the project would become. The aerial view is a representation of the territory on which the imagined project is inscribed. This function as an imaginative aid can also be fulfilled by an oblique view.[32] On page 23 (Figure 14.7), an oblique view without horizon taken at a low altitude is allied with a photograph of an architectural model and an aerial view taken from a high vantage point, again without horizon. Due to its clear 'Japoniste' influence, there is no doubt that the first photograph is by Ito Josué. The latter might also be attributed to him, given that it represents the Firminy-Vert construction, while the tight framing valorises the interplay of the built mass and landscaped green spaces, notably the Cours des Maronniers. The association of these three images emphasises the analogy between the oblique aerial view and the scale model. It is known, incidentally, that Ito Josué produced a number of photographs of models for the architects and planners with whom he collaborated.[33] The overhead and oblique views fulfil the same cognitive function as that provided naturally to the observer of the scale model, in that they convey a similarly overhanging perspective. This analogy between the oblique view and the scale model photograph is further confirmed on the following page.

It is not only the relationship between a project and its realisation that is at stake here, but also the relationship between fictional and real points of view. On another page composed of Ito Josué's images (Figure 14.8), the overhead views constitute a commentary on the project's relationship to the topography and landscape. The almost square format of the photographs has been cropped and the landscape in the background, including the horizon – a key element in the original image's composition – has been cut. Nevertheless, this re-framing does not constitute a contradiction in sense, since the page layout is such that the two images together produce an inverse zoom effect, whereby the horizon is reintroduced virtually into the shot. These overhead views of landscape developments and traffic circulation illustrate the concept of green space (as seen in the plan on the facing page) and their direct link to the town's facilities – always the Achilles heel of urban developments. The photographs stand as testament to the three elements of modern town planning: green space, traffic circulation and amenities.

Aerial views of housing developments figured prominently in construction companies' publicity material and were often used by contractors for advertising in specialist journals. In the eyes of those who used them, the aerial view undoubtedly conveyed quality and modernity, which immediately reflected back upon them. Thus an oblique aerial view of Firminy, showing the whole of the new town, served as a valorisation of the local office responsible for social housing and the projects it managed. The accompanying inscription

1

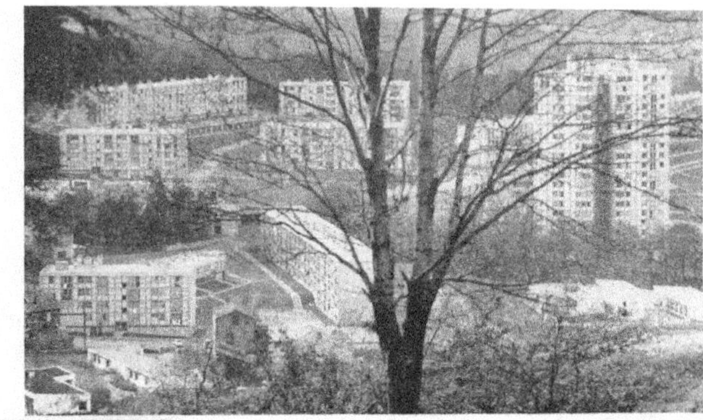

2

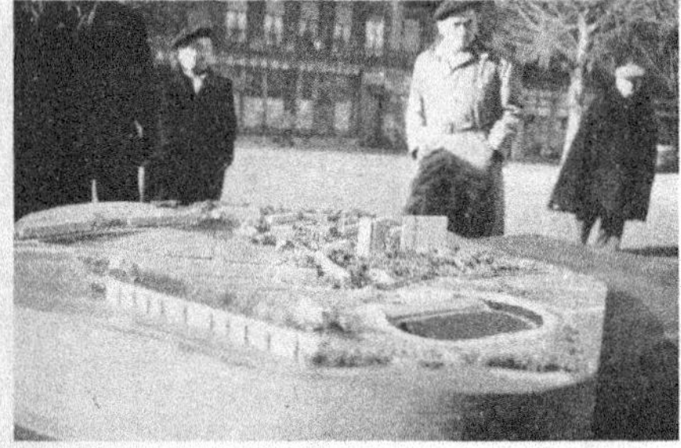

1 - Vue partielle de Firminy-Vert.

2 - La maquette exposée dans la rue.

3 - Vue d'ensemble de Firminy-Vert et la ville ancienne au second plan.

3

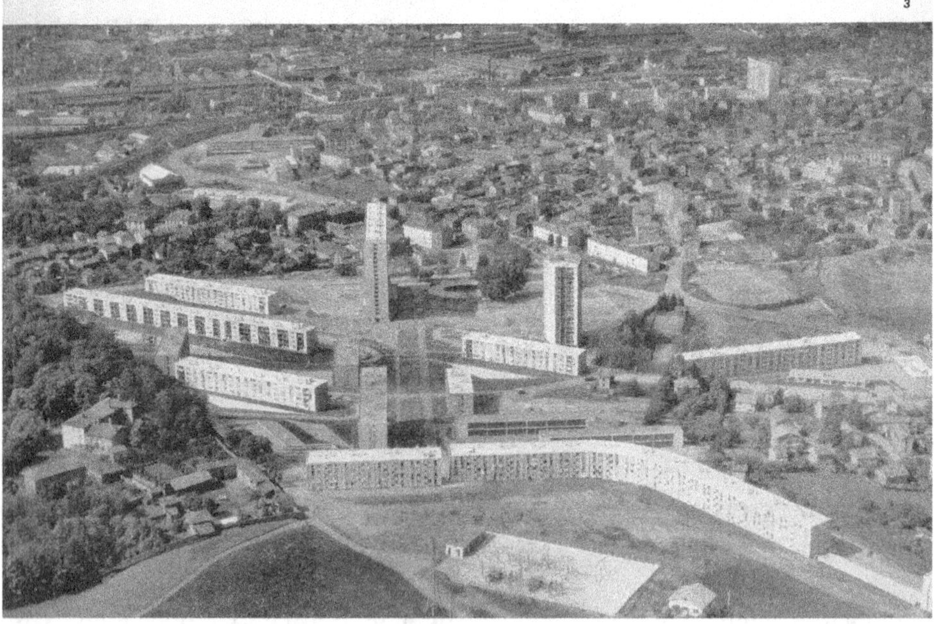

[14.7] *Urbanisme*, 104 (1968): 23.

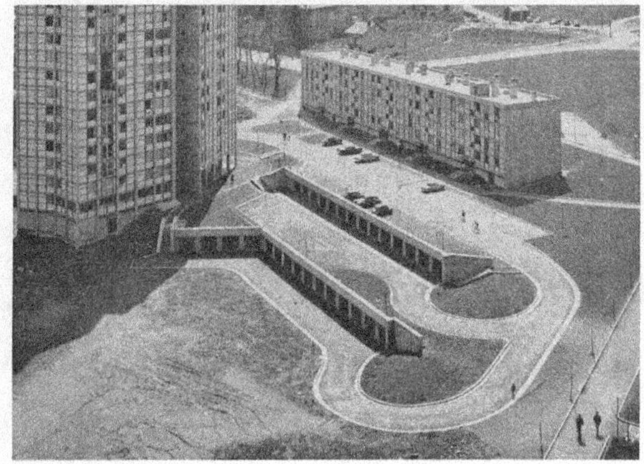

Utilisation des dénivellations du terrain pour dissimuler les garages.

UTILISATION DU TERRAIN

Les dénivellations du terrain, en pente du Sud vers le Nord, ont été utilisées notamment pour la construction de garages.

On retrouve du reste le même principe pour les bâtiments d'habitations. Les entrées ne sont pas nécessairement au même niveau. Dans les immeubles situés près de la Place de la Corniche, par exemple, on entre au Sud de plain-pied depuis la Place dans un hall précédant un couloir, mais à l'extrémité de ce dernier, on se trouve au 4e étage du bâtiment qui a donc quatre niveaux au Sud et huit au Nord.

CIRCULATION

Firminy-Vert fut un des premiers ensembles à connaître une circulation différenciée pour les piétons et pour les véhicules.

Les voies carrossables, horizontales ou peu pentues, suivent en général les courbes naturelles du terrain et encerclent l'espace aménagé. Les voitures peuvent accéder à tous les bâtiments sans traverser le cœur de Firminy-Vert qui reste libre pour les piétons et la verdure.

Contrastant avec ces routes périphériques, la perspective droite du Cours des Marronniers, véritable colonne vertébrale de Firminy-Vert, grimpe en haut de l'ensemble par un jeu d'allées et d'emmarchements qui touchent au passage chaque bâtiment ou chaque groupe de bâtiments et qui permet ainsi aux piétons d'emprunter des parcours calmes et très discrets.

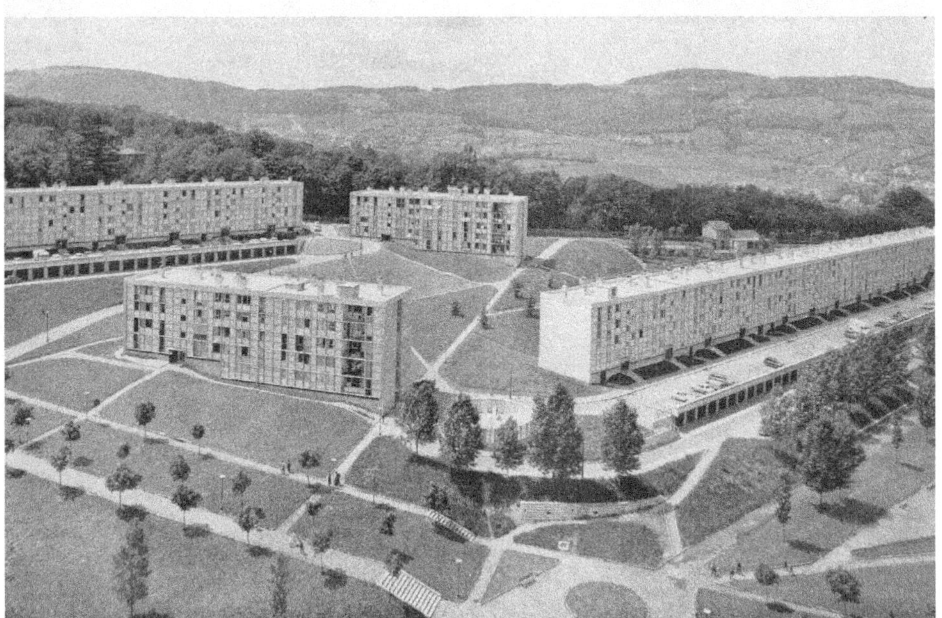

[14.8] *Urbanisme*, 104 (1968): 28.

OFFICE PUBLIC D'H.L.M. DE FIRMINY

Président : **M. Claudius Petit,** Ancien Ministre, Député-Maire de Firminy. *Directeur :* **M. André Baudie**

1954 : 32 H.L.M construits
1963 : 1.524 H.L.M. construits
1967 : 2.258 H.L.M. construits
609 en construction
429 en permis de construire
876 en projet

de l'Abbé Pierre... au Corbusier
l'urbanisme d'avant-garde
une rénovation audacieuse
une politique d'aménagement
bien équilibrée

Firminy-Vert, Grand Prix d'Urbanisme : **1.300 logements**
▼ **5.200 habitants**

Un centre social, une maison de la culture, 52 classes, une laverie autom collective, 372 garages et parkings, 62.500 m² d'espaces verts et ai jeux, un centre commercial, un jardin public et un stade en construction

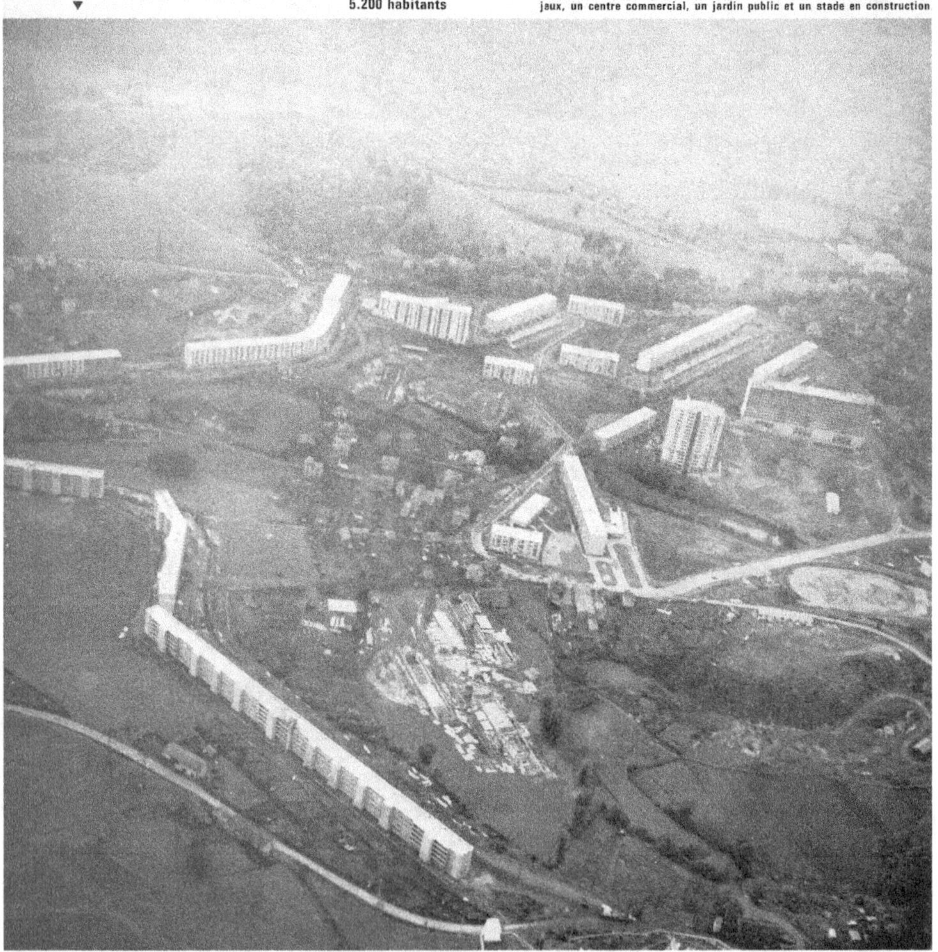

[14.9] *Urbanisme*, 104 (1968): xiv.

reads, 'From l'Abbé Pierre [...] to Le Corbusier: avant-garde urbanism, daring renovation and a balanced policy of town planning'[34] (Figure 14.9). The Stribick company, principal constructors of Firminy-Vert, included in its promotional material an oblique aerial view produced by the Lyon-based photographers, CUYL, showing the new town as an extension of the industrialised town. The inclusion of aerial photographs in the companies' press material can perhaps also be explained by the popular appeal of these kinds of images. Indeed, in the 1960s, postcards of the 'grands ensembles' – particularly featuring their aerial views – were increasingly in circulation. These images show the stereotypical 'grand ensemble'. The oblique aerial view restricts the framing of the shot and thereby fails to show how the project relates to its environment. The new town emerges as detached from its environment in order to stress the geometry of its composition and its monumental scale. On these postcards, it is the whole town that is principal monument. This kind of characteristic representation is seen in a 1962 issue of *Urbanisme,* in the form of a series of four images on a double-page spread, with no caption other than the name of the 'grand ensemble' plus its architects (Figure 14.3).[35]

In addition, the archives of the social housing office in Firminy contain aerial view postcards published by the companies CIM and CUYL. These come in two forms: views of developments taken at medium altitude and low-altitude shots, focusing on particular spaces within the town with their inhabitants. These two types of images are similar to those we have already identified as characteristic of the portrait of Firminy-Vert conveyed in *Urbanisme*'s 104th issue.

AERIAL VIEWS AND POSTCARDS

Unlike Ito Josué's aerial views, which reveal a deep understanding of urban planning and the architectural culture from which the projects arose, aerial views that were published as postcards were produced by organisations whose first priority was to highlight the country's 'modernisation'. This can be observed in the output of a company such as CIM, which had specialised in postcard production since the 1920s.[36] It was this company that was able to seize the post-war opportunity to produce postcards carrying aerial views (Figure 14.10). To do so, it bought aviation equipment used by the USA during the Normandy landings, which could be used for low-altitude flying, together with photographic equipment used by military staff for mapmaking. Thus CIM set about the epic task of photographing France from above, made possible by an experienced crew in which the roles of pilot and photographer were closely intertwined. The images produced of towns

PRISES DE VUES AÉRIENNES ET SOL, COULEUR ET NOIR SUR TOUTE LA FRANCE SUR DEMANDE, (TROIS AVIONS). PHOTOTHÈQUE A DISPOSITION DES PRINCIPALES VILLES DE FRANCE ET AFRIQUE DU NORD : SOL DE 1900 A 1940 - SOL ET AÉRIENNES DE 1940 A CE JOUR.

COMBIER, IMPRIMEUR - MACON — Tél. 0.42

[14.10] CIM – Combier Imprimeur (printer), Mâcon, France.

fall into two categories: oblique views of developments taken at medium altitudes, which reveal urban projects in their various forms and low-altitude shots which capture the detail of urban structure, its facilities and the activities taking place in and around them. With the postcard, the aerial photograph emerged as the dominant way of depicting its subject, but it also could not deviate too far from a natural perspective. Thus very high views were less favoured than close-ups, which allowed easy identification of what was photographed. The company's operators perhaps took risks in flying, to get as close as possible to their subjects, but unlike artistic photographers, they took no risks whatsoever in the aesthetic domain. Nevertheless, their chosen perspectives are not without merit, especially in terms of the manipulation of space and light. Postcards play an indisputable documentary role and allow continuities to show through. They bear witness to the many changes and developments carried out across the country, assuring the continuation of the kind of photographic project embarked upon by the camera-operators commissioned by the Ministère de la Construction. Postcards were produced by publishing houses with a national scope, such as La Cigogne or Yvon, but also by regional publishers like CIM or CUYL, or even local publishers who served a particular community or département. The apparent neutrality

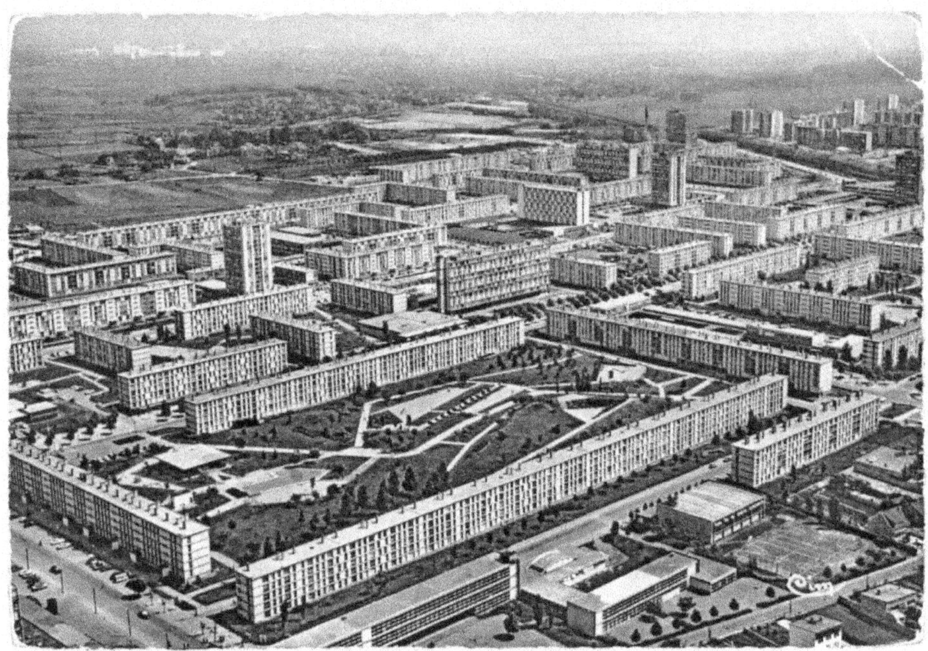

[14.11] Sarcelles-Lochères, 95 (Val d'Oise), aerial view, postcard, CIM (Combier printer).

of the postcard, the cropping of the image by selective framing, as well as the monumental quality conferred on the photographic subject were characteristics adopted by photographers towards the end of the 1960s, who integrated them into their own artistic procedures.[37]

The cards were often in black and white, given that the technology for printing coloured images was slow to develop. Colour bromide printing was used from the 1950s until 1973, when the technique was dropped indefinitely due to the shortage of silver and the rise in costs. In fact, the colourisation was not credible and somewhat clumsy. The postcards seemed to oscillate between photography and painting, or reality and utopia. The success of these images was short-lived.

These stereotypical views of new towns from the 1960s, in particular the aerial views, are today collectors' items and artists such as Mathieu Pernot, studying the significance of the qualities of 'modern urbanism', are keen to acquire them (Figure 14.11). In his book *Le grand ensemble,*[38] Pernot compares outmoded colour photographs with contemporary black and white images that show the collapse of 'les grands ensembles' and signal the end of a utopia. Clouds of smoke dominate the image: a housing tower, then a large block of council flats, disappear in a fraction of a second and with them disappears the story of those who inhabited them. Pernot reports the voices of some of the inhabitants of these 'grands ensembles' in his book; messages written on postcards read: 'Greetings from Argenteuil, where all is well. Our building is the one marked with a cross. Mickael is very happy, he can play outside in the sand-pits and has lots of friends.'[39] These are fragments of existence, captured via daily life, and bearing a promise of uncomplicated happiness. Peoples' pictures emerge from within the cards and imprecise human forms spring from out of the frames. Such people are both real and generic. Thus it is not only what the aerial photograph records which is open to interpretation, as argued by Chombart de Lauwe and his collaborators in 1948, but also what belongs to the medium containing the photographic document – here the postcard itself: the printed narrative and its conveyed messages.

During this period of intense construction, vertical and oblique aerial photography served different purposes and facilitated urban development in two particular ways: on the one hand technically, by enabling the rapid production of large-scale urban plans; and on the other hand symbolically, by permitting a wide circulation of images of the entire fabric of new towns. Aerial vision illustrated radically new ways of organising the use of land, as well as a certain number of intentionally striking urban and architectural achievements. However, in contrast with the revelatory role that it played in areas such as archaeology or ethnology, in urbanism, the aerial view was the tool of a government with firm planning intentions, one that covered the country with housing developments and extensive facilities, thereby breaking with the past. The photography reveals the country's radical transformation, which finally reveals itself as highly uniform. This uniformity is explained by the very extent of the operation, in terms of both reconstruction and modernisation (the whole country was affected), as the government's exhaustive documentation project itself shows. The uniformity also certainly results from the size and speed of the developments, made possible by the construction industry's industrialisation. Finally, the sense of regularity cannot be completely separated from the media through which images were diffused, as I have tried to show. In the first place, the professional publications which circulated aerial views of the 'grands ensembles' were very closely linked to the state: this was particularly the case for *Urbanisme*, but was also true of the journal, *Technique et Architecture*, created under the Vichy government to communicate the national reconstruction effort. Of course, the state's desire to promote exemplary projects led it to approach professional photographers, who could lend an aesthetic perspective to the developments. However, that particular kind of photographic production remained secondary to that of the postcard, which emerged as the principal means by which the country's reconstruction and modernisation was conveyed to the wider public. The aerial view figures prominently here: first, because it represented a symbol of modernity, but also because the postcard industry itself turned increasingly to modern landscapes. The postcards, produced by photographic companies, depict a stereotypical vision: through the framing of the main object, they contribute to the idea of a building as monument.

This clichéd view subsequently became one of the hallmarks of modernity, notably amongst photographers who proclaimed themselves as 'topographic' photographers.[40] However, this group turned away from the aerial view, and instead sought to appropriate the aesthetic and social values of the postcard. The format of – and subject matter presented by – the postcard must be understood as a mode of municipal self-representation, an understanding that Stephen Shore would draw upon in his famous report on the 'monuments' of the town of Amarillo in Texas.[41]

The perspective on the Firminy development constructed by Ito Josué is altogether different. His work represents the meeting between industrial production and a landscape rooted in a still tangible rurality. His gaze is that of a humanist who valorises industrial construction and a modern use of space, as much as the hopes and the new functions that were borne by the recent developments and facilities. These ideas were at the core of Firminy's projects and amenities, which, in its creation as a 'green' town, aimed to replace the image that had been blackened by its mining past.[42] Ito Josué's gaze is founded on a complicity with the commissioners of his work and his photographic production tends towards an aesthetic of familiarity rather than the banality produced by mass production. It is perhaps this tension between familiarity and banality which today continues to intrigue an observer of Ito Josué's 'pastoral' aerial views, with their play of lines and delicately balanced values; or indeed when one places the printed aerial photograph alongside postcards with messages written on their backs:

> Here's a card showing the building opposite us. The crane has gone and has been replaced by beautiful lawns. Young people live there. The cross marks where the shop "Nova service" used to be; now it's a temporary nursery.
>
> Epinay sur Seine (Seine) Cités d'Orgemont. Youth centre[43]

I wish to extend my sincere thanks to Martine Dancer, heritage conservationist at the Saint-Étienne Museum of Modern Art, and also to Yvan Mettaud, heritage conservationist of the town of Firminy, for the help that they have given me in this research on aerial photography, and in particular with the Ito Josué collections. Equally, my thanks go to Fabrice Bunuel, photographer, who led me to discover the work of Ito Josué in the course of some research on urban landscape that we previously undertook for BRAUP. I am indebted too to Olivier Josué, Marc Combier and Mathieu Pernot and to the journal Urbanisme *and the Nicéphore Niépce Museum, who gave permission for the reproduction of images from their collections.*

NOTES

1 Paul-Henry Chombart de Lauwe, 'La vision aérienne du monde', in *La découverte aérienne du monde* (Paris: Horizon de France, 1948), p.25.
2 José Luis Sert, *Can Our Cities Survive?: An ABC of Urban Problems, Their Analysis, Their Solutions; Based on the Proposals Formulated by the CIAM* (Cambridge, MA: Harvard University Press, 1942).
3 Le Corbusier, *Aircraft* (London: The Studio, 1935).
4 Michel Parent, 'Les civilisations vivantes, les villes et leurs structures', in Chombart de Lauwe, op. cit., pp.281–326.
5 The International Society for Photogrammetrics acknowledged the leadership of the Topographic Division of the Ministry of Construction in the field of techniques and methods for mapmaking. From 1948, it made it responsible for the sub-commission of urban maps. Cf. Bernard Dubuisson, 'Nouvelles applications françaises de l'aérophotogrammétrie au Ministère de la construction', *Urbanisme*, 87 (1965): 71–80.
6 Dubuisson, op. cit., 73.
7 For maps of 1:5,000 the flight was at 1:20,000; for maps of 1:2,000 the flight was at 1:8,000; and for maps of 1:500 the flight was at 1:2,000.
8 M. Laqueuille, 'La topographie au service de l'urbanisme', *Urbanisme*, 35–36 (1954): 47–51.
9 See Bernard Dubuisson, 'La photographie aérienne au service de l'urbanisme', *Urbanisme*, 1–2 (1952): 44–6.
10 Dominique Gauthey, 'Les archives de la reconstruction (1945–1975)', *Etudes photographiques*, 3, November (1997): 103–17. See also the exhibition catalogue: Danièle Voldman and Didier Mouchel, *Photographies à l'oeuvre. Enquêtes et chantiers de la reconstruction (1945–1958)* (Cherbourg-Octeville/Paris: Le Point du Jour/Jeu de Paume, 2011).
11 Ibid., 104.
12 Ibid.
13 Ibid., 108.
14 'La vie dans les grands ensembles', *Urbanisme*, 62–63 (1959): 30–94.
15 Charles Delfante, in Thierry Paquot and Frédéric Seitz, eds, *Histoire d'urbanisme 1932–2002* (Paris: PUCA, 2002), vol. 2, *Témoignages*, pp.9–22.
16 The Firminy-Vert project experienced a period of intense controversy and conflict between 1971 – the date of Eugène Claudius-Petit's defeat in the municipal elections – and 1987, the date of the Le Corbusier centenary celebrations, which began a new era of recognition under the growing influence of cultural heritage. See Gérard Monnier, *Le Corbusier. Les unités d'habitation en France* (Paris: Belin Hersher, 2002), chapter V, 'L'unité d'habitation de Firminy', pp.147–57; and Vincent Veschambre, 'L'unité d'habitation de Firminy, Le « Corbu » en héritage: entre contraintes et atouts', in Xavier Guillot, ed., *Firminy, le Corbusier en héritage* (Saint-Étienne:

Publications de l'Université de Saint-Étienne, 2008), pp.53–71.

17 See Guillot, op. cit.

18 Charles Delfante, 'Le point de vue de l'urbaniste', *Urbanisme*, 104 (1968): 51.

19 See Jean Louis Cohen, 'Moments suspendus: le voyage aérien et les métaphores volantes', in *Le Corbusier. Moments biographiques* (XIVe Rencontres Le Corbusier) (Paris: Fondation Le Corbusier/ Éditions de la Villette, 2008), pp.144–57.

20 See Le Corbusier, *Carnets 4, 1957–1964* (Paris: Hersher/Dessain et Tolra, 1982), pp.61–2.

21 See Benoît Pouvreau, *Un politique en architecture, Eugène Claudius-Petit (1907–1989)* (Paris: Le Moniteur, 2004), p.222.

22 Delphine Millo, *Ito Josué, photographe de la Nouvelle Architecture de Saint-Étienne et de Firminy*. Masters dissertation, University of Paris IV, Sorbonne UFR Art History and Archaeology (2005).

23 Eugène Claudius-Petit, 'Pour des maisons réconciliées avec la nature', *Urbanisme*, 11–12 (1951): 7.

24 Hélène Jannière, in Frédéric Pousin, ed., *Saisir le paysage urbain. Du rôle des publications, figurations architecturales, des pratiques photographiques et cinématographiques dans les décennies 1960–1970*, research report for the interdisciplinary research programme 'Art, Architecture et Paysages' organised by the Ministry of Culture and Communication (2007), pp.29–32.

25 See Sandra Parvu, *Journal de bord de quatre chantiers. Grands ensembles en situation* (Lausanne: Métis Presses, 2010), p.54.

26 Fabrice Bunuel, in Pousin, ed., op. cit., pp.207–11.

27 *Urbanisme*, 75–76 (1962): 7–10.

28 Eugène Claudius-Petit, 'Firminy-Vert', *L'Architecture d'Aujourd'hui*, 101, April–May (1962): 58–61.

29 *Urbanisme*, 104 (1968).

30 Isabelle Estienne notes that in the case of OREAM North (Organisation d'Etudes d'Aménagement des Aires Métropolitaines), the architect Pierre Delcourt organised flights over the site; and in the case of the Organisation d'Etudes d'Aménagement de la Loire Moyenne, the geographer Pierre Falaise, a former military pilot, undertook aerial photographic coverage on behalf of the landscape architect Pierre Dauvergne. Isabelle Estienne, *L'intervention du paysagiste dans la ville, de 1960 à aujourd'hui: pertinence et enjeux pour les architectes et les urbanistes. Le cas de la métropole lilloise*. Doctoral thesis in Geography and Planning, under the supervision of Didier Paris, Lille University 1 (2010), p.311.

31 Estienne, op. cit., p.20.

32 See the image published in *Urbanisme*, 62–63 (1959), dedicated to new town facilities, showing a guiding diagram superposed on a photograph of the town of Mourenx (p.149).

33 See the interview carried out in July 2006 at Saint-Étienne's Museum of Modern Art with photographer Yves Bresson.

34 *Urbanisme*, 104 (1968): xiv.

35 *Urbanisme*, 75–76 (1962): 164–5.

36 See Marc Combier, *Un siècle de cartes postales. CIM-Combier Imprimeur Mâcon* (Paris: Éditions Alternatives, 2005) and Marc Combier and Laurent Chabrol, *La France des années 60 vue d'en haut* (Paris: Desinge & Hugo & Cie, 2011).

37 Cf. Stephen Shore in the USA and later photographers such as Pierre Joly in France.

38 Mathieu Pernot, *Le grand ensemble* (Paris: Le Point du Jour éditeur, 2007).

39 Flight over Argenteuil 95100 (Val d'Oise). La ZUP. Vue Générale. Ibid., p.131.

40 See Robert Adams, Lewis Baltz, Bernt and Hilla Becher, Joe Deal, Franck Gholke, Nicholas Nixon, John Scoot, Stephen Shore, Henry Wessel Jr., *The New Topographics. Photographs of a Man-Altered Landscape* (Rochester, New York: International Museum of Photography, George Eastman House, 1975).

41 See Stephan Schmidt-Wulfen, 'Stephen Shore's Uncommon Places', in *Stephen Shore: Uncommon Places* (London: Thames and Hudson, 2004), pp.7–15.

42 See the remarks made by Eugène Claudius-Petit on the subject of the street that connects Firminy to Rive-de-Gier, quoted by Charles Delfante: 'It must be remembered that Firminy, in 1954, was no more than a slum crossed by what Claudius-Petit called "the joyless street" and I described as a street lined with buildings made of coal-industry sandstone, a soluble material which disintegrates into dust, blackening objects and people'. Charles Delfante, *Souvenirs d'un urbaniste de province* (Paris: Éditions du linteau, 2010), p.88.

43 Mathieu Pernot, op. cit., p.130.

15

Robert Smithson and *Aerial Art*

Gilles A. Tiberghien

The interest of artists in the aerial view goes back to ancient times and long pre-dates man's ability to fly. Nevertheless, a moment occurred towards the end of the nineteenth century and, more particularly, at the beginning of the twentieth, when this particular perspective was transformed into the symbol of modernity.[1] From the 1960s on, artists' interest took a fresh path, one linked to theoretical issues emerging out of new technical devices, particularly in the world of painting. The most famous examples probably include Jackson Pollock's 'drip' paintings – popularised by Hans Namuth's film and still photographs – and Robert Rauschenberg's 'flatbeds'.[2] Also significant was Maria Reiche's 1964 publication of new theories regarding the Nazca lines, which formed patterns visible only from an aircraft (and upon which Robert Morris proposed to walk in 1975).[3] Nevertheless, despite this burgeoning interest, the originality of approach of an artist such as Robert Smithson has to be noted: Smithson saw this kind of vision as a material and an intellectual challenge and it was to mark his entire work.[4]

In June 1966, the architect Walther Prokosch, then employed by the architectural firm, Tippetts-Abbett-McCarthy-Stratton (TAMS), attended a lecture given by Robert Smithson entitled, 'Art in the City'. The lecture was part of a conference held at the *Yale Art Association* on the theme 'Shaping the Environment: the Artist and the City'.[5] Prokosch suggested to Smithson that he become consultant on a construction project for Dallas regional airport; more specifically he asked Smithson to consider the actual meaning of an airport, with a view to participating in the project later on. And that is exactly what the artist did over the next year and a half. He found the questions of scale, size and

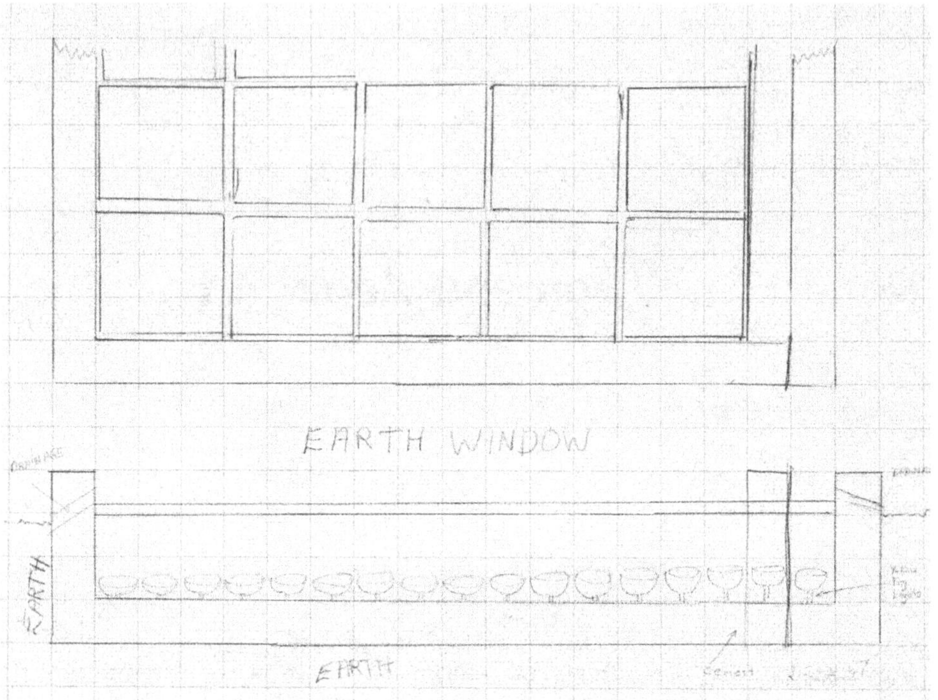

[15.1] R. Smithson, *Earth Window*, 1966.

general perception to be crucial. The architects worked out the calculations and plans for the runways and Smithson finally offered them something he called 'aerial art'. This he described as '*earthworks* on the fringes of the airfield that you would see from the air'.[6] On his personal copy of the master plan drawn up by the agency, Smithson noted various instructions from which it can be deduced that he had planned four different types of *earthwork*: a square of red rocks, a rectangle of yellow rocks, a spiral of blue rocks and five circular mounds of white sand. According to Smithson's instructions, the height of each construction was not to exceed about one and a half metres.[7]

On numerous occasions the artist was to state that this study was at the origin of his ideas for *earthworks* and that it was at that time that he

> developed an interest in the mapping situation, and an interest in finding new sites outside of the white walls of the gallery or museum. The non-sites really come out of a comprehension of limits; they set up a dialectic [...] The *earthworks* I had planned for the outer edge of the airfield had to be transmitted back to the airport, so I thought of setting TV cameras out there to do this.[8]

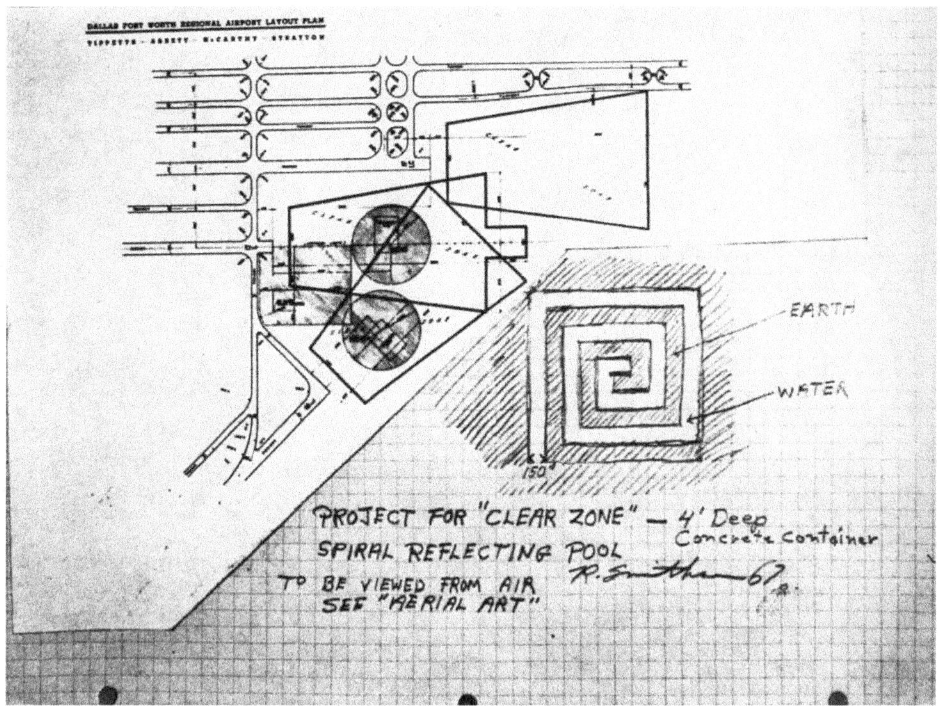

[15.2] R. Smithson, *Project for 'Clear Zone' Spiral Reflecting Pool*, 1967.

The visibility of the works was therefore double: it was possible to both view them from the ground, in a 'museum' – *The Terminal Museum* – situated in the airport building itself, through cameras that transmitted the image onto monitors, and also from aeroplanes at the time of their take-off and landing. But Smithson also drew up other projects. Among these, as can be seen from sketches that have been preserved, was an installation, between runways, consisting of 'windows' turned towards the sky, which Smithson named *Earth Windows* (Figure 15.1). A drawing entitled *Three Earth Windows Under Broken Glass* (1967) shows a series of grids of diminishing size, corresponding to shallow boxes buried in the ground and intended to contain rows of broad 'yellow fog-lights' or 'baseball game lights'. The intention was to place glass panels on the works that would be level with the ground and piled with pieces of broken glass.[9]

In a document entitled *Project for 'Clear Zone' Spiral Reflecting Pool,* which came out of the TAMS agency plans, Smithson drew a spiral that was intended to be constructed as a canal, four feet deep and filled with water (Figure 15.2).

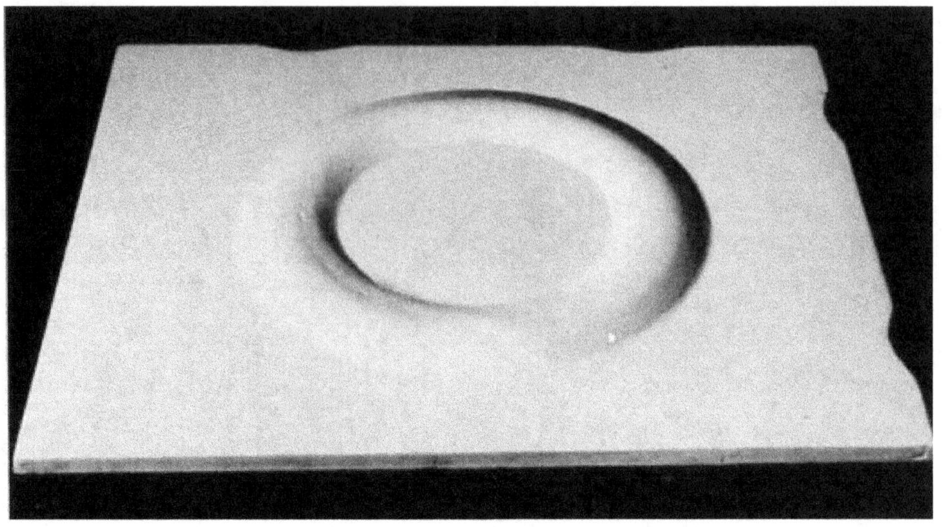

[15.3] R. Morris, *Model for Project in Earth and Sod*, 1966.

The ground between the hard construction materials is indicated as being earth. Under Smithson's signature it is possible to read, in his hand, 'To be viewed from air/See "Aerial Art"', the latter making reference to an article published under that title in 1969, two years after the project's conception. Or again, on the drawing entitled *Wandering Earth Mounds and Gravel Paths,* a series of earth hillocks are sketched between the runways, their forms oblong and supple, like writhing worms. The graphic aspect of these projects is striking.

These barely elevated forms were intended to be viewed from the sky according to what Smithson understood to be 'aerial art'. When he was asked why he chose the term 'aerial', he replied

> well I used that mainly to make that clear to the architects that that was the proposal. I did want to accent the idea of getting above in an airplane and viewing things in that way, and it was the only term I could think of. It is a kind of rubric, but at the same time it connotes a certain kind of scale consciousness which I wanted to get across.[10]

In the article 'Aerial Art', mentioned above and published in the February–April 1969 issue of *Studio International,* Smithson described a project whose completion necessitated the collaboration of three other artists. Robert Morris suggested constructing a circle of earth of about one metre high with a

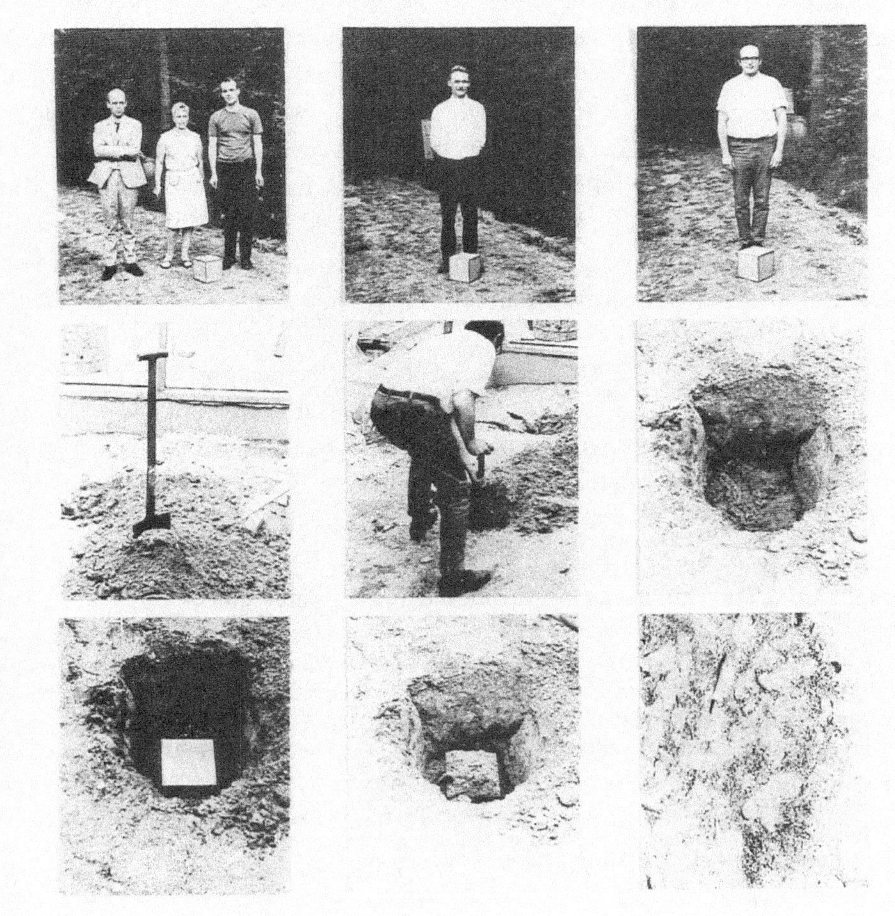

[15.4] Sol LeWitt, *Buried cube containing an object of importance but little value*, 1968.

trapezoidal section following a 45° slope and covered in grass. 'Its radius could extend to up to 330 metres – easily visible from planes as they landed or took off'[11] (Figure 15.3). Carl Andre's intention was to drop a one-ton bomb from a 3,000-metre altitude, or else 'plant an acre of "blue bonnets" (*Aquilegia hybridia* – the state flower of Texas)'. Sol LeWitt's project, located in an area that was not to be revealed, was to construct 'a small cube with unknown contents cast inside a larger cube made of concrete', that was to be buried in the ground (Figure 15.4). Smithson concluded the presentation of this project by stating that Sol LeWitt 'emphasized the "concept" of art rather than the "object" that results from its practice'.[12]

Smithson's own project as described in 'Aerial Art', a text that seems to connect to his most advanced projects, involved the construction of a vast aerial map (*Aerial Map*), a huge flat spiral formed of geometric components that would be visible from the sky. His model, made of mirrors, was shown in the article but corresponded to a construction that was to be produced from triangulated slabs of concrete. Their layout followed the internal development of a hexagon rolling up on itself through an angulated rotation around a void, in the manner of certain salt crystals. In 1968, Smithson created *Gyrostasis,* the three-dimensional version of his proposal for the Dallas airport project.

> The title *Gyrostasis* refers to a branch of physics that deals with rotating bodies, and their tendency to maintain their equilibrium. The work is a standing triangulated spiral. When I made the sculpture I was thinking of mapping procedures that refer to the planet Earth. One could consider it as a crystallized fragment of a gyroscopic rotation, or as an abstract three-dimensional map that points to the *Spiral Jetty,* 1970, in the Great Salt Lake, Utah. *Gyrostasis* is relational, and should not be considered as an isolated object.[13]

Aerial Map can thus be seen as anticipating *Gyrostasis* which itself presaged *Spiral Jetty.* These three works appear as structures embedded in time, the first two playing for the third the role of a temporal, as opposed to a spatial, *non-site.*[14] At the same time as he had envisaged exhibiting the results of his research at the Dwan gallery – which he never actually did – Smithson created his first *earthwork* at another airport in the Pine Barrens of New Jersey:

> This place was in a state of equilibrium, it had a kind of tranquillity and it was discontinuous from the surrounding area because of its stunted pine trees. There was a hexagon airfield there which lent itself very well to the application of certain crystalline structures which had preoccupied me in my earlier work [...] Initially I went to the Pine Barrens to set up a system of outdoor pavements but in the process I became interested in the abstract aspects of mapping, At the same time I was working with maps and aerial photographs for an architectural company and I had very easy access to those.[15]

In fact, according to Virginia Dwan in an interview with Ann Reynolds, Smithson discovered the site some time after his first trip to Pine Barrens, when consulting a map to see where they had been, because the isolated airfield was difficult to find.[16] *A Non-Site, Pine Barrens, New Jersey* (1968), which at first had been entitled, *A Non-Site (an outdoor earthwork),* took a hexagonal form, suggested by the layout of the landing strips. When Smithson described the project in 'A

Sedimentation of the Mind: Earth Projects' he wrote: 'The map of my *Non-Site #1 (an indoor earthwork)* has six vanishing points that lose themselves in a pre-existent earth mound that is at the centre of a hexagonal airfield in the Pine Barren Plains in South New Jersey. Six runways radiate around a central axis. These runways anchor my 31 subdivisions.'[17] Smithson himself would say that the *Non-Site* was a 'three-dimensional map of the site'. As Ann Reynolds writes,

> because it is mounted on a low platform, the primary orientation when viewing this map is aerial, as if the spectator were in an airplane hovering over the Pine Barrens, in preparation for landing. *A Non-Site (an indoor earthwork)* refers back to all the visual conditions of the airport – the relationship between inside and outside, views from the air and on the ground, and two- and three-dimensionality – as well as to the material processes used to construct the airport.[18]

It is clear that this non-site was one in a group of works that, at about the same moment, attempted to subvert the conventional system of linear perspective.[19] Without examining each of these, we can nevertheless focus on one in particular so as to better understand Smithson's approach.

In 1966, seven years after Virginia Dwan had settled in Los Angeles, where she opened her first gallery in 1959, she opened another in New York's East Side. As early as 1967, in a group exhibition called *Show 10*, Smithson exhibited for the first time the enigmatically titled *Alogon #1*, a work composed of seven angular wall units that followed a decreasing diagonal. 'The title, *Alogon*,' stated Smithson, 'comes from the Greek word referring to the unnameable, or to an irrational number.'[20] Two more series of works followed with the same title: *Alogon #2* and *Alogon #3*. Smithson makes reference to these on numerous occasions, evoking – at first without specifically naming – the Pythagorean origins of the term: the invention of the irrational number. '"*Alogon*" is something that suspends rationality, something you can find in some of the earlier pieces. There are three *Alogon* works, and they represent a kind of break with logic, the break with Gestalt.'[21]

In fact this work, which was created at the same time as he was reflecting on aerial art, is highly informative for an understanding of Smithson's thinking at that moment. He was concerned with the issue of scale, as it is brought into play by the aerial view, but as an indicator of our constitutive imaginary relationship to the world of perception. When we go up into the sky, the countryside resembles a map in three dimensions as 'the rational structures of buildings disappear into irrational disguises and are pitched into optical illusions', writes Smithson in his text on aerial art. 'The world seen from the air is abstract and illusive. From the window of an airplane one can see drastic changes of scale,

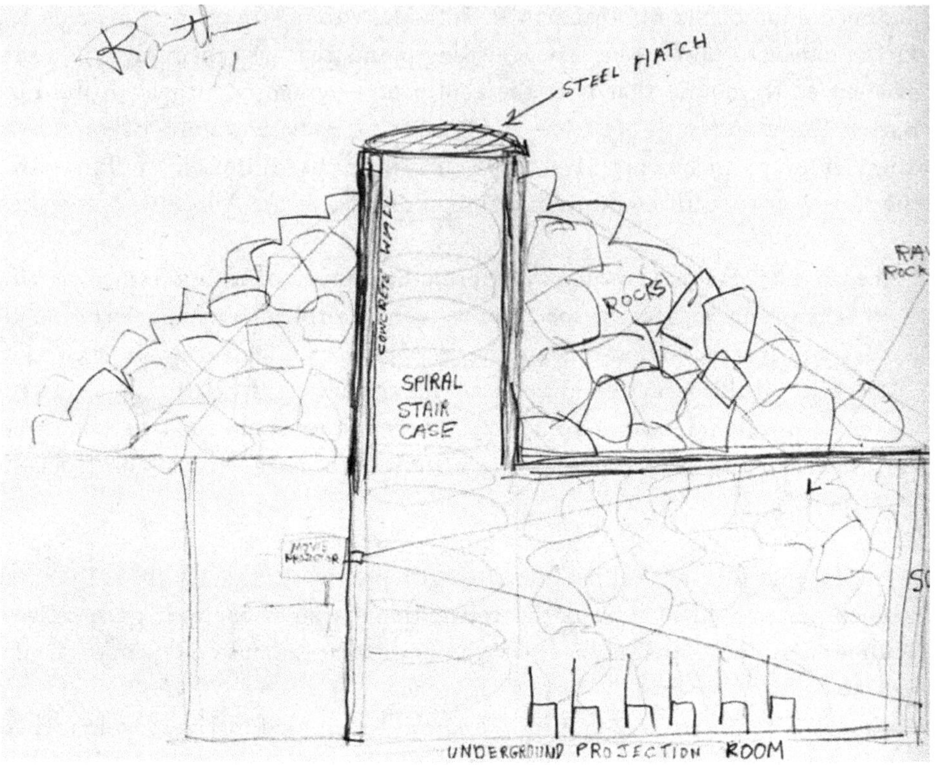

[15.5] R. Smithson, *Underground Projection Room* (Utah Museum Plan), 1971.

as one ascends and descends.'[22] For Smithson, then, scale has a quite specific significance that has to be considered alongside the mathematical notion of the incommensurable, of which we have just spoken. In fact, scale, as opposed to size, is something that cannot be put into relation with anything and it sends us back in a state of incommensurability: the 'surd situation'.[23]

This situation is that of our own subjectivity in the face of the world and the proposal Smithson put to the TAMS agency was related, according to him, to what he termed 'a certain kind of scale consciousness'.[24] Indeed, scale is to be understood here in relation to the site/non-site dialectic, because it is founded precisely in the passage of one (or a series of spaces) to another (or a series of other spaces), thus corresponding to the passage from one 'order' to another 'order' in the Pascalian sense. This could be the passage from the gallery to the site, or from cards, drawings, photos and films to what they represent, signify or designate – from, in the simplest terms, the imaginary to the real. 'Aerial art' merely emphasises this transformation of perception, or reversion of the visible into its other. Indeed, in speaking of the airport site, Smithson referred to the fact that the sub-soil contained sediments from the Cretaceous period. The site was bored with holes and trenches full of mud and rocks. 'If seen as a discrete step in the development of the whole site, the "boring" has an aesthetic value' Smithson writes. 'It is an "invisible hole" and could be defined by Carl Andre's motto: "A thing is a hole in a thing it is not."'[25] In one of the unpublished drafts of the air terminal article, Smithson moreover specified that in contrast to Morris or himself, 'Sol LeWitt and Carl Andre will provide works that will deal with the "sub-site" and exist as underground landmarks.'[26]

When Smithson began his research for the construction of *Spiral Jetty*, it was with all these thoughts and experiences in his mind. He had also devised a subterranean cinema, literally an 'underground projection room' which would be built next to the spiral according to the same plans as those drawn up for the TAMS project (Figure 15.5). This would have been an auditorium accessed by a spiral staircase, on whose walls one would view photographs of the work, while the film, *Spiral Jetty*, was being projected.[27] The work of the same name, whose images the film offers, is an impressive size; it is 1,500 feet long, 15 feet wide, and coils twice around itself. It scarcely rises above the water and its qualities, both graphic and picturesque, were not lost on Richard Serra.[28] The photographs we have indicate a very variable form, which accords with the particular point of view: it may be thin or fat, stretched-out or curled-up, or elevated in different ways on a mirror of water with multi-coloured reflections. Indeed, with respect to this changeability, Smithson commented that '[t]he scale of the Spiral Jetty tends to fluctuate depending on where the viewer happens to be'. He also said, picking up from his 1967 text on the development of the air terminal, that

> [s]cale depends on one's capacity to be conscious of the actualities of perception. When one refuses to release scale from size, one is left with an object or language that *appears* to be certain. For me scale operates by uncertainty. To be in the scale of the *Spiral Jetty* is to be out of it.[29]

All the film's beginning is devoted to the spiral project: the researching of the site, as well as the individual, historical and mythological accounts that accompanied the construction. Interwoven with these are reminiscences from the artist about his childhood and his fascination with dinosaurs. However, in the last part of the film, shot entirely from a helicopter, we are shown the spiral literally turned upside down, incandescent and irradiated by a blinding sun that seems to be burning from inside it, even while we are no longer certain whether it is rising straight into the sky or stretching out across the water. What the film really brings home is the mental and physical reality of the spiral, the extension of its real dimensions into its imaginary dimensions – in other words, its scale: 'After a certain point, measurable steps (scale [...]) descend from logic to the "surd state",'[30] writes Smithson with reference to *Spiral Jetty*. In his interview with Denis Wheeler he explains what he means by this: 'a surd area is beyond tautologic... not really beyond, there's no beyond. As a matter of fact, it's a region where logic is suspended [...] There's no commensurable relation, or it's incommensurable. So you're into a kind of irrational area.'[31] To fully understand this we must return to the term, 'surd', that Smithson used deliberately.

Originally *surd* came from *surdus,* which means deaf, a term introduced in Latin to translate the 'alogos' referred to by Euclid in his *Elements,* then used three centuries later to prove the theorem attributed to Pythagoras. The discovery of irrational magnitudes signified the impossibility of achieving a universal harmony: literally, the impossibility of *hearing* the music of the spheres. It is to this idea of irrationality that Smithson returns in the next part of his text, placing the word *surd* precisely in rapport with the *alogos* the artist used to describe some of his sculptures at the time of the project on the boundaries of Dallas regional airport: 'in the *Spiral Jetty* the surd takes over and leads one into a world that cannot be expressed by number or rationality. Ambiguities are admitted rather than rejected, contradictions are increased rather than decreased – the *alogos* undermines the *logos*.'[32]

The term used, surd,[33] as I have indicated, belongs to the vocabulary of mathematics and means 'that which cannot be expressed by a rational number'. As for immeasurable, it signifies that which is beyond all measure and is thus incapable of being measured. While a measurement is characterised by the relationship of one magnitude to another of the same nature, an irrational number, on the other hand, cannot be written in terms of a relationship between two other numbers, as with fractions for example. Now, we know that the 'geometric equivalent of a number's irrationality is the incommensurability of two segments of a straight line: that is to say that the length of one of the segments cannot be expressed in terms of fractions of the length of the other'.[34] It is here that the famous theorem attributed to Pythagoras intervenes to prove that the square root – once known as the 'surd root' – of two, is irrational to the extent that it cannot be written in comparative terms. And it is precisely this impossibility that characterises the Spiral Jetty. In this way, the artist Smithson has pushed the logic of scale to its very limits through rendering the work heterogeneous to its site: despite the fact that it is inscribed in its setting, it remains incommensurable.

Indeed, Smithson bestows on the notion of scale the Pascalian sense of 'order' – a sense that is in a certain way a transposition of the Euclidian theory of homogenous magnitude. 'Surd', or the incommensurable, points to the irreducibility of one order to another – of the order of the imaginary, for example, to that of the real. Thus one might say, to paraphrase Pascal, that the sum of the earth's magnitudes (*grandeurs*) will never equal the *grandeur* of *l'esprit* (mind). Smithson moreover stated that his concept of the universe was based on the Pascalian idea of 'a sphere whose circumference is everywhere and whose centre is nowhere', recognising in the French philosopher and scientist someone who 'was always troubled by these actual scale problems'.[35]

We can see thus the importance of Smithson's uncompleted aerial art project. If, as according to his own words, his accompanying reflections were seminal for the rest of his work, the inverse is also true. His thoughts are remarkably instructive for those who wonder about the view from an aircraft, in that they emphasise the mental and physical sense of displacement produced by the bird's-eye view. Smithson brings out the difficulties and *aporia* that our logical categories of thought encounter as we realise that what we see in this particular state of suspension probably has more to do with time than with space and with the metaphysical, rather than the physical. Smithson was fully conscious of this when he wrote in 'Aerial Art' that:

> [As of now,] aerial art can not only give limits to 'space' but also the hidden dimensions of 'time' apart from natural duration – an *artificial time* that can suggest galactic distance here on earth. Its focus on 'non-visual' space and time begins to shape an aesthetic based on the *airport as an idea*, and not simply as a mode of transportation. This airport is but a dot in the vast infinity of universes, an imperceptible point in a cosmic immensity, a speck in an impenetrable nowhere – aerial art reflects to a degree this vastness.[36]

NOTES

1 Kirk Varnadoe, *A Fine Disregard, What Makes Modern Art Modern* (New York: Harry N. Abrams, 1990).

2 This term was first used by Leo Steinberg, who uses it to describe 'the characteristic picture plane of the 1960s'. Steinberg says, 'I borrow the term from the flatbed printing press – 'a horizontal bed on which a horizontal printing press rests (Webster)', 'The flatbed picture plane makes its symbolic allusion to hard surfaces such as tabletops, studio floors, charts, bulletin boards – any receptor surface on which objects are scattered, on which data is entered, on which information may be received, printed, impressed – whether coherently or in confusion.' Leo Steinberg, 'Other Criteria', in *Other Criteria: Confrontations with Twentieth-Century Art* (London, Oxford, New York: Oxford University Press, 1972), pp.55–91; pp.82 and 84.

3 See Robert Morris, 'Aligned with Nazca', *Artforum*, 14(2), October (New York, 1975): 26–39. See also Gilles A. Tiberghien, *Land Art* (Paris: Éditions Carré, 1993, and New York: Princeton Architectural Press, 1995). Now in revised and expanded edition, Paris 2012.

4 Here we cannot agree with Varnadoe, who at the end of his text, curiously reinscribes Smithson in modernity with its rediscovery of ancient cultures such as the Nazca, seeing 'a common escape from the trivialities of individual style and urban existence in order to return the primordial anonymity of some vast, collective form', Varnadoe, op. cit., p.273. The connection certainly does not hide the originality of Smithson's approach, or the new interest that artists of the 1960s held for this kind of vision, in a direct rupture with modernity.

5 Brian O'Doherty, John Hightower and Paul Weiss also participated at this conference.

6 'Interview with Robert Smithson for the Archives of American Art/Smithsonian Institution (1972)', in Jack Flam, ed., *Robert Smithson, The Collected Writings* (Berkeley, Los Angeles, London: University of California Press, 1996), pp.270–96; p.291. Paul Cummings interviewed Smithson on 14 and 19 July 1972.

7 This unpublished plan has been reproduced in Ann Reynolds's well-documented book, *Robert Smithson: Learning from New Jersey and Elsewhere* (Cambridge, MA and London: MIT Press, 2003), p.136.

8 Paul Toner and Robert Smithson, 'Interview with Robert Smithson (1970)', in Flam, op. cit., pp.234–41; p.234. Smithson would also tell Paul Cummings that a good number of his reflections on crystalline structures came to him at the time when he spoke of 'the whole city in terms of crystalline network' (p.291). He spoke of the extent to which the TAMS project had 'got me to think about large land areas and the dialogue between the terminal and the fringes of the terminal – once again, between the centre and the edge of things'. He added, 'This has been a sort of ongoing preoccupation with me, part of the dialectic between the inner and the outer' (p.296). Paul Cummings, op. cit., pp.270–96; pp.291, 296.

9 Suzaan Boettger, *Earthworks, Art and the Landscape of the Sixties* (University of California Press, 2002), p.54.

10 See 'Four conversations between Dennis Wheeler and Robert Smithson (1969–1970)', in Flam, op. cit., p.210.

11 'The marked simplicity of the Dallas ring can only be observed from the sky' writes Valérie Mavridorakis. 'Whereas for Smithson, the aerial view corresponded to the stasis of a suddenly crystalised temporality, to Morris it appeared to be a return to the drawing board. From an aeroplane, the work indeed reveals itself to be flat and the viewer is thus taken back to painting. From then on, the model would be presented not on a table but fixed to a wall like a relief painting' Valérie Mavridorakis, 'Looping les projects pour l'aéroport de Dallas Fort-Worth', in *Robert Morris, estampes et multiples 1952–1998* (Geneva: Cabinet des Estampes and Chatou: Maison Levanneur-Centre national de l'estampe et de l'art imprimé, 1999), p.175.

12 Robert Smithson, 'Aerial Art', in Flam, op. cit., p.118. In 1968, Sol LeWitt would bury a metal box, 33 cm wide, beneath the house of Carel and Mia Visser, containing a work of art that was never publically identified and which belonged to the owner of the land. See, for example, Gilles A. Tiberghien, *La Nature dans l'art sous le regard de la photographie* (Paris: Delpire-Actes-Sud, 2005), reprinted 2010.

13 Robert Smithson, 'Gyrostasis' (1970), in Flam, op. cit., p.136.

14 'Given Smithson's grounding in the initial plans for the Dallas-Fort Worth Regional Airport, it is not surpising' wrote Robert Hobbs, 'that his first Nonsite (*sic*) involved a landing strip. What is fascinating is that he chose as his Site (*sic*) an airport that is almost the antithesis of the one in Texas: a small, sandy, rarely used government landing strip in the New Jersey Pine

Barrens.' Robert Hobbs, *Robert Smithson: Sculpture* (Ithaca and London: Cornell University Press, 1981), p.77.

15 'Discussion between Michael Heizer, Dennis Oppenheim, and Robert Smithson', *Avalanche*, Fall (1970), reprinted in Tiberghien, op. cit., p.277. Also in Flam, op. cit., pp.242–52.

16 Reynolds, op. cit., p.157.

17 Robert Smithson, 'A Sedimentation of the Mind: Earth Projects (1968)', in Flam, op. cit., p.111.

18 Reynolds, *Smithson: Learning*, p.159

19 On this anti-modernist strategy that one finds in the contemporary works of Richard Serra, Carl Andre and Robert Morris, see Anaël Lejeune's thesis, *Mise en théorie et mise en œuvre dans le travail de Carl Andre, Robert Morris, Richard Serra et Robert Smithson entre 1966 et 1973*, Louvain University, Faculté de Philosophie et Lettres. Département d'Archéologie, d'Histoire de l'Art et de Musicologie; academic year 2009–2010, under the supervision of Ralph Dekonnck and Alexander Streitberger.

20 Cummings, op. cit., p.292.

21 'Four conversations', op. cit., p.199.

22 Smithson, 'Aerial Art', op. cit.p.116.

23 'Four Conversations', op. cit., p.203.

24 Ibid., p.210.

25 Robert Smithson, 'Toward the development of an air terminal site (1967)', in Flam, op. cit., p.56.

26 Robert Smithson, 'Proposal for earthworks and landmark to be built on the fringes of the Fort Worth–Dallas Regional Air Terminal Site (1966–67)', in Flam, op. cit., p.354.

27 See Jean-Pierre Criqui, 'Un trou dans la vie. Robert Smithson va au cinéma', *Un trou dans la vie* (Paris: Desclée De Brouwer, 2002).

28 See, among others, 'Richard Serra. Interview with Peter Eisenman', *Zone 1/2* (New York: Urzone Press, 1986).

29 Robert Smithson, 'The Spiral Jetty (1972)', in Flam, op. cit., p.147.

30 Ibid.

31 'Four conversations', op. cit., p.199.

32 Smithson, 'The Spiral Jetty (1972)', op. cit., p.147.

33 According to Jack Flam, Smithson got his notion of the surd from, among others, Samuel Beckett's *The Unnamable*. Beckett was read by Smithson and by many other artists of his generation. See note 9, 'Four Conversations' (essay edited and annotated by Eva Schmidt), op. cit., p.231. The question also permeates Beckett's novel *Murphy*. Beckett had studied mathematics and was preoccupied by the idea of irrationality – see David H. Hesla, *The Shape of Chaos, an interpretation of the art of Samuel Beckett* (Minneapolis: The University of Minnesota Press, 1971). Beckett alludes to the Pythagorean fear of the irrational number *pi*. Thus in the book *Three Dialogues*, characterising the history of painting, Beckett speaks of 'a kind of tropism towards a light' [...] 'and with a kind of Pythagorean terror, as though the irrationality of pi were an offence against the deity, not to mention his creature.' Samuel Beckett, 'Bram Van Velde', in *Proust and Three Dialogues with Georges Duthuit* (London: John Calder, 1965), p.125.

34 See André Pichot, *La Naissance de la Science, T.2, Grèce présocratique* (Paris: Gallimard, Folio, 1991), p.150.

35 'Four Conversations', op. cit., pp.207 and 210.

36 Smithson, 'Aerial Art', op. cit., p.117.

16

On Google Earth

Mark Dorrian

An acquaintance that works in one of the ministries of the French government tells me of a strategy that he has developed to relieve the tedium of his job.[1] Upon the desk in his office there are two computers onto which, when he arrives each morning, he logs on. The first is reserved for ministerial business, but on the second he launches Google Earth, setting its virtual globe spinning far below him. Thus, while one machine presents him with the necessities of the day, glancing at the other offers something of an imaginative release from them, allowing him to fantasise that he is flying through the stratosphere, beyond the preoccupations, irritations and entanglements of close-to-the-ground life. If, to quote the authors of *Google: The Missing Manual,* with Google Earth one can 'swoop in like Superman from outer space', then my friend's solution is one that permits him to be simultaneously the superhero and his workaday alter ego Clark Kent (and this is something that even Superman himself could not achieve), flying over the planet while, rather more prosaically, continuing to fulfil his bureaucratic obligations below.[2]

One of the curiosities of researching Google Earth is that it can quickly come to seem as if everyone has – like my friend – a Google Earth story to tell. Thus, while it is usually the case that at the outset of a chapter like this one has to spend some time introducing the material to be discussed and expanding upon its less familiar aspects, it is symptomatic – and indeed is a key point of interest – that with Google one does not. There still may be some people on the planet with digital access who do not recognise the name, but they are getting fewer every day.[3] Google, with its extraordinarily dominant internet search engine, emblematises globalisation. Somewhat like those obscure singular yet infinitely complex institutions that lie below the surface of science fiction environments – institutions that are, like God, everywhere and nowhere at the same time and are consequently characterised by the absence of any differentiating noun so they become known as just 'The Corporation' or the like – Google can seem pretty much omnipresent, or at least well on the way to getting there. If totality was one of the dreams of early modernity – Faustian total knowledge, total control, total empowerment – postmodernity has reclaimed it with a vengeance, yet in a new way, the point now not being the reduction of difference through negation and the accumulation of knowledge within some Promethean individual, but conversely the ability to navigate (search) difference by managing the interface between things, as enabled by the prosthetic computational power of the processor. So, the pyramidal or perhaps helical structures of earlier imaginaries of escalating knowledge tend to give way to a more lateral, archipelago-like distribution in which slow historical ascent becomes superseded by the instantaneity of the network connection – a formation perhaps best indicated by the network pictures or internet maps with which we have become familiar[4] (Figure 16.1). Thus Google's stated objective to 'organise the world's information and make it universally accessible and useful';[5] and thus too a 2006 review essay on Google by John Lanchester for the *London Review of Books* entitled 'The Global Id', which thereby characterised it as a kind of collective planetary unconscious.[6]

Certainly, what strikes one about Google is the constant insistence on the colossal, the gargantuan and the exorbitant in its agenda, its technology and its statements. It displays that mixture of the absolute with the seeming negotiation of difference that we tend to describe as holism, which I take to be a benign encompassing of difference, as opposed to totalism, which is difference's negation. Famously the company was named after the googol, the massive number of 10 to the power of 100 (apparently the even more expansive name googolplex – 10 raised to the power of a googol – was first raised as a possibility).[7] The misspelling was by accident, at a stroke draining away some of the (Slavic?) strangeness of the original and endowing the word with a more verb-like quality and a suggestion of the visual; thus 'ogle' – www.ogleearth.com becoming the address of one of the major Google Earth blogs – and 'boggle'. And certainly, wide-eyed and slack-jawed astonishment seem the order of the day for this institution that has been ranked as the fastest growing company in the history of the world. Interestingly, when you make a search on Google, you are not in fact searching the internet itself: the technology is much more Borgesian. Instead, Google makes a copy that is constantly being updated of all the pages on the internet, which are downloaded onto a massive computer cluster that apparently comprises more than 1 million PCs, assembled, networked and optimised by the

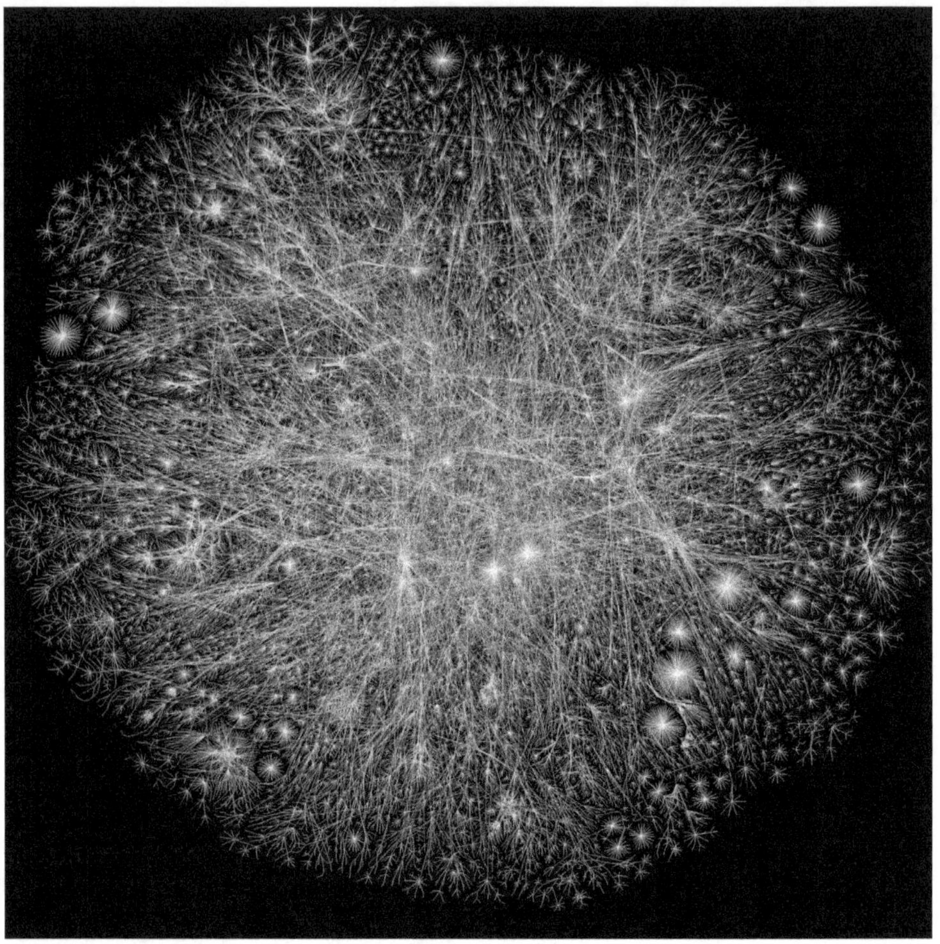

[16.1] Internet map, 23 November 2003.

company itself. The complex is described by the president of Stanford University, himself a Google board member, as 'the largest computer system in the world [...] I don't think there is even anything close'.[8] Already, by 2006, a report estimated that Google had more than 450,000 servers distributed across at least 25 global locations and interconnected by a high-capacity fibre optic network: as it concluded, it is the speed of light that ends up being the fundamental constraint.[9] As Google downloads what is in effect the entirety of the internet, it – to quote from John Lanchester's essay

> makes an index of every word on a web page, where it stands in relation to other words, whether or not a word is listed in a title, whether it is listed in a special

> typeface, how frequently it is listed on the page and so on [...] There are more than a hundred of these criteria, and Google gives a numeric weight to every one of them, for every searchable term on every one of eight billion web pages. When a query arrives – which it does at the rate of many times every second – Google searches the index for the relevant terms, measures the relevance of the results using all its various metrics [...] crunches out a single number for each page, and lists them, with the highest score at the top, usually within half a second or so. Even if you didn't know a thing about computers, you could tell that this involved a truly scary amount of computational power.[10]

The figures continue to expand and amaze. In his *Googled: The End of the World as We Know It,* Ken Auletta reports that Google's index contained 1 trillion web pages in 2008, and that in 4 hours it could index the equivalent of the complete holdings of the Library of Congress.[11]

If, as I have already hinted, Google almost uniquely seems capable of simultaneously encompassing the poles of the universal/singular opposition, then one way in which this seems to be manifested is in the extraordinarily intense subjective identification the company and its services inspire. In October 2006 the *New York Times* ran an article entitled 'Planet Google Wants You', which profiled Dan Firger, a law student at New York University and in many ways a typical inhabitant of Planet Google. Six to eight times a day, we are told, his mobile phone rings with text messages from Google reminding him of appointments logged into Google calendar. He searches the web with Google, talks via Google Talk, emails using Gmail, and so on. 'I find myself getting sucked down Google's wormhole,' he remarks. 'It's all part of Google's benign dictatorship of your life.'[12] The responses suggest, however, that this 'benign dictatorship' is experienced more as an extension, or even a *delivery,* of the self than it is as a transaction with another entity. If the latter is more the mode of experience of Microsoft, computing's so-called 'Evil Empire' and the butt of Google's 'Don't be evil' slogan (always 'forcing you to do things their way', as one complainant puts it), Google – to quote another commentator – 'literally augments your brain. I don't have to remember quite a few things now because Google can remember them for me. Google is an additional memory chip.'[13] Ultimately, however, the particular genius of Google is that it does not just facilitate the subject's command of information, but that it assembles and delivers it in such a way as to lead to a radical identification with what is given. Thus, to take one example, the *New York Times* article closes with a comment by Toni Carreiro, a web designer in California, who enthuses: 'That's what Google gives you – "me".'[14] And so we find that at the same time as Google gives you the world, it also gives you 'yourself', an effect not unconnected with the company's infamous user profiling techniques and storage of search histories, rationalised as being necessary for increased search efficiency but also of course sophistication in targeted advertising. When Google invested in the human genetics firm 23andMe in 2007, it was interpreted as a logical step in the quest to expand online user profiling.[15] As the British newspaper the *Guardian* has noted, Google knows more about the United Kingdom's citizens than does MI5, the state security agency.[16]

The dream of total knowledge, which is also a kind of total seeing, is an old theme, but here care has to be taken in distinguishing the particular kind of project that Google represents. In *From Counterculture to Cyberculture*, Fred Turner has examined how the anti-hierarchical and anti-corporate credos of radical 1960s thought fed into the digital discourses of the 1980s and 1990s. And certainly, the holistic ideology of Google's founding partners, Larry Page and Sergey Brin, owes more to the pan-earth ethic of California hippiedom of the 1960s and 1970s and the hippie-infused West Coast technoculture in which Page and Brin studied, at PhD level at least, than it does to any Enlightenment project.[17] I am thinking here of manifestations such as the *Whole Earth Catalog* (launched in 1968 in Menlo Park, California, where Google's founding partners would set up in a garage 30 years later), with its cover picture of the earth from space, which tried to make the 'wisdom' of others (other cultures, peoples, races, places, technologies, etc.) available. In this publication we can see a deeply liberal counterculture, whose watchwords were freedom and individual choice and which – if not exactly consumerist – sought an open access to and participation in the products, techniques and modalities of life of others that was at least a counterpart to that demanded by market capitalism. In the quest for personal development it seems there was almost nothing that one could not have, as long as it was not seen to compromise the equivalent pursuits of others. 'We are as gods and might as well get good at it', the 'Purpose' statement to *The Next Whole Earth Catalog* declared in 1980. In response to the institutional and bureaucratic conditions of formal power structures, the publication aimed, it said, to support the developing 'realm of intimate personal power' – 'the power of individuals to conduct their own education, find their own inspiration, shape their own environment, and share their adventure with whoever is interested'.[18]

So where is Google Earth in all this? We have taken this lengthy excursion before circling back to Google Earth because it allows us to discern the symbolic dimensions of the programme more clearly. Google Earth was released in 2005 and quickly became one of the most remarked upon and – in this era of generalised war and militarisation – contentious internet developments. But even in advance of the launch of the programme, the name Google Earth seemed highly loaded and symbolically invested. The planet, this earth, when qualified by Google appears to transform into an informational utopia – or even, in Kevin Kelly's eschatological phrase, a new 'Eden of everything' – that then exists as the final point on an expanding scale in whose lower reaches those earlier utopias of entertainment and science that were first branded as 'lands' and then 'worlds' find their place. The virtual globe that Google Earth presents is surely the symbolic counterpart of the corporation's mission to make everything available to you: Google gives you the world, and indeed, after the launch of Google Sky, the cosmos as well.[19]

If we are living, as has been claimed, in the age of the aerial image, then Google Earth is one of the principal phenomena that makes it so. Today the aerial view – the image *of* everywhere – seems to *be* everywhere, and it seems plausible to claim Google Earth as perhaps the most prominent manifestation and stimulant of this voracious contemporary appetite for views from above. Relations of all kinds on the ground are increasingly mediated in complex ways from the sky, a situation that Google Earth, through the massive availability of images that it facilitates, has played a key role in bringing about. Much valued for its spectacular and entrancing effects, the aerial view is firmly established as a recurrent feature of popular visual culture, media forms and touristic installations. When a representative for the London 2012 Olympic Games was interviewed on BBC Radio 4 on 6 November 2007, he was asked by the interviewer about the then still-to-be-unveiled design for the major stadium: his symptomatic response was that at least one thing was certain, 'it's a media event, so it will look great from the air'. Likewise, tourist concentration in the city is now focused upon the London Eye, a massive aerial viewing device marketed as 'the way the world sees London' that in 2005 was voted the ultimate world tourist destination (beating off such likely contenders as the Vatican and the Sydney Opera House).[20] At the same time, popular volumes of planetary images proliferate. Often tied to ecological rhetoric – such as Yann Arthus-Bertrand's *The Earth from the Air* – in these books scintillating images of the beauty and diversity of the earth's surface, of extraordinary definition and reproduced with highly saturated colours, achieve a kind of hyper-reality that appears simultaneously abstracted and highly palpable and that sublimates both pristine and devastated landscapes alike.[21]

Against this background, the principal question I want to ask of Google Earth is simply, what does it show us? What, and how, do we see when we engage the programme? Something that seems to me to be of great interest is its graphic interface, how we operate it, and what happens when we do. In particular I am concerned to think about the ways in which we are solicited by the images on the screen, and the kind of imaginative engagement with them – and by extension the earth itself – that they might be said to prompt. Google's mass elevation of the eye of the consumer into space carries with it consequences that demand a reconceptualisation of the view from above, one that effectively reverses some of the familiar historical understandings and connotations of aerial vision. Moreover, I am struck by the drift of various developments and trials, in which Google has experimented with ways of more effectively monetising the programme. In an article on the computer game *Spore*, Stephen Johnson has written of what he calls 'the long zoom', which he argues to be the characteristic visual paradigm of our time.[22] Exemplifying it by, among other things, Charles and Ray Eames' film *Powers of Ten* (1977) – a connection that is frequently drawn with respect to the Google Earth interface[23] – he stressed its epistemological aspects. The commercial possibilities and evident uses of the 'long zoom' in Google Earth, however, suggest another agency, one that is very precisely to do with the establishment of the commodity as the target of the zoom's spatial collapse. The promise here – at least from the point of view of revenue generation – is of a kind of virtuous circle of mutual targeting whereby Google Earth permits the commodity to target, via advertising, the cybertourist cum satellite-consumer, and then in turn to be geospatially targeted by her. A 2006 advertising campaign for Saturn cars, in which Google worked with a San Francisco-based advertising consultancy, can stand as an example of this. The campaign bundled together various Google products and services 'like clickable video clips, Google Earth and the geographic finding of computer users'. In an article for the *New York Times*, Stuart Elliott described how the advertisement worked:

> Visitors to a variety of Web sites in six cities around the country that are home to 22 Saturn dealerships will see what looks like typical banner ads for Aura, a new Saturn midsize sedan. Clicking on an ad will produce a view of the earth that zooms in on the dealership nearest to the computer user. The doors to the virtual dealership fly open, revealing the general manager who introduces a brief commercial about [the] Aura. After the spot ends, the general manager returns, standing next to an Aura and offering choices that include spinning the car 360 degrees, inspecting its engine, printing a map with directions to the dealership and visiting the Web sites of Saturn or the dealer.[24]

What happens, then, when we first launch Google Earth? When the programme opens and the screen image appears we find ourselves somewhere in space, not exactly deep space, but far enough away to see the entirety of the globe. In earlier versions of the programme the world appeared with the Americas facing us, not an insignificant fact and cognisant with the US-centric upload of information that some technical commentators remarked upon in early studies

(*Google Earth Study: Impacts and Uses for Defence and Security*, for example, produced in 2005 by the French Fleximage, a subsidiary of the European Aeronautic Defence and Space Company). In his 2007 *Google*.pedia: *The Ultimate Google Resource*, Michael Miller – in what is an instance of ideological misrecognition in its classic sense – makes a bizarre but unironic point regarding this: 'Anytime you start Google Earth, the view defaults to the extended zoom of planet Earth, focused on the continent of North America. This is a great place to start because you can get just about anyplace you want from here.'[25] The interface works through a principle of grasping, which intensifies the sense of the manipulability of the virtual object: through the hand icon that appears one can 'take hold' of the earth and spin it, or even invert it, which is a strangely disconcerting experience at first. Note that, at this elevation anyway, we are not moving around the earth, rather we appear to spin the globe in relation to a fixed position that we occupy. The hand cursor is a familiar one, recognisable from other graphics programmes (Acrobat, Photoshop, etc.), but here it gains an extra dimension. We are reminded of the cartographic tradition of miniature globes that we place our hands upon and revolve. The Google Earth interface seems to offer us a digital simulacrum of these, although with a now strikingly literalised planetary image.

So where exactly are we located when we open Google Earth? The implication is that we are in fact upon the moon, or at least on the way there. Certainly there is never the registration of any other body, except a generic star pattern, on the graphic interface. More specifically, I think that it might be argued that the Google Earth interface inherits and deploys, as a kind of 'underlay', one of the most famous, and popularly recognisable, images of the earth: the so-called 'Blue Marble' photograph taken by the Apollo 17 expedition en route to the moon in 1972[26] (Figure 16.2). In his brilliant commentary on images taken during the Apollo missions, Denis Cosgrove has pointed out the motivating and iconic role they played in emerging ecological discourses.[27] A key point here is the way in which the image of the planet from space produced a new kind of aerial view, one in which the terrestrial surface no longer filled the photographic frame. The world in the image gained a new sense of fragility when the contours of the planet became visible within its frame. The photographs of a bright earth engirdled by clouds suggested a pristine jewel-like planetary oasis isolated in the vast barrenness of space, a feeling provoked particularly by the famous 'Earthrise' image that was taken from Apollo 8 (1968), with its view of the distant earth rising above the foreground of the inert lunar desert.[28] As Stewart Brand would comment: 'Nowhere in the solar system is the contrast between a living and a dead planet so conspicuous as on the Moon at Earthrise.'[29] Moreover, in their liberation of the globe from all cultural signifiers – borderlines, grids,

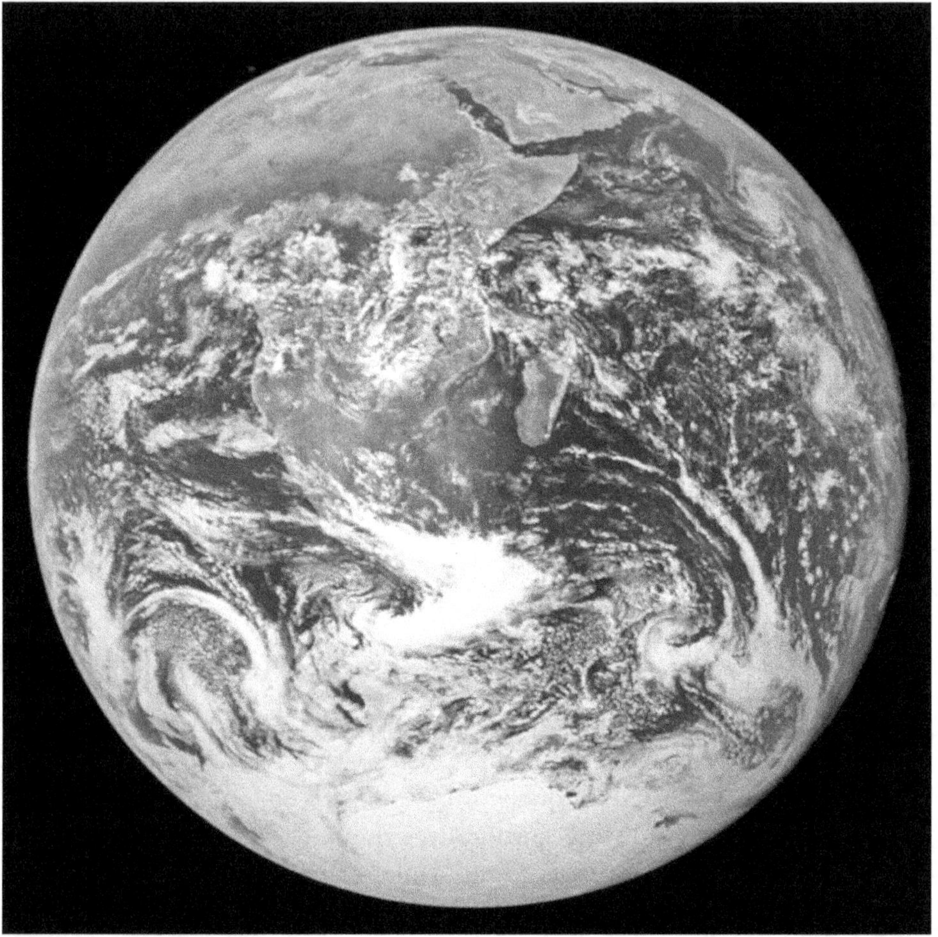

[16.2] The 'Blue Marble', 7 December 1972.

and cartographic codes – the Apollo photographs seemed to show a unified and perhaps even redeemed world purged of conflict, a planet that could be thought of as a single organism.[30]

If we accept that the Google Earth interface inherits and in some regard reperforms this image, then in what ways does it differ from it? The Apollo pictures are embedded in a very specific history, that of the Cold War space race and manned – and therefore heroic (as articulated through the iconography of the astronaut) – lunar exploration. The pristine singularity of the planet as conveyed by the images was predicated upon the singularity of the photographic image-capture event itself, the instantaneous and complete recording of the scene. Conversely Google Earth presents us with a non-auratic image in which

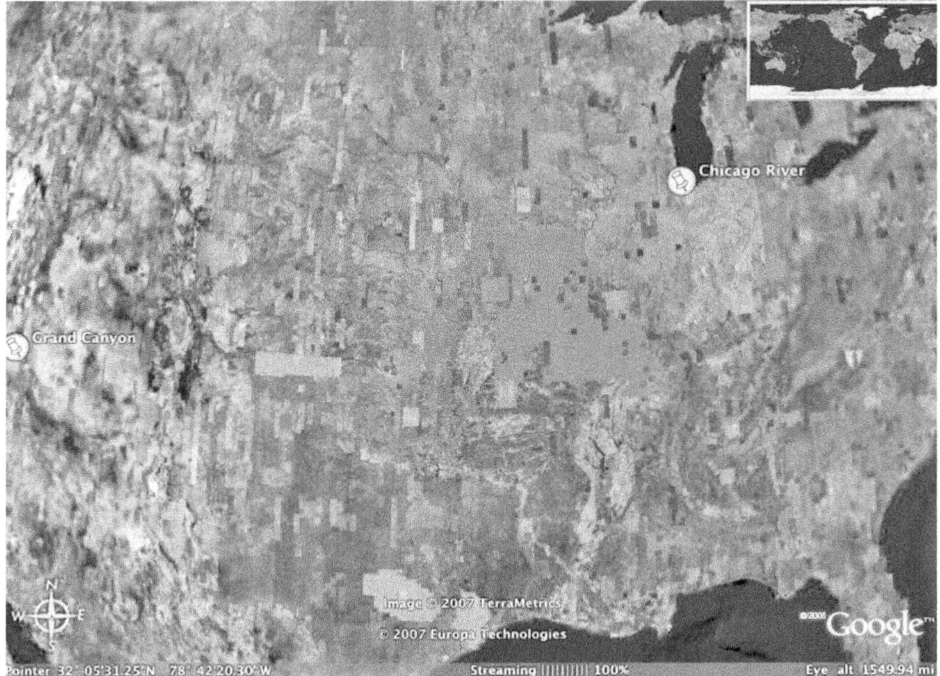

[16.3] Descending over North America in Google Earth, 2 February 2007.

the whole 'radiant jewel' of the Apollo images is fragmented – both spatially and temporally – into a panoply of geospatial data sets produced by orbiting satellites and lower-level image-capture devices, which are then digitally sutured together to form the global image. Even with the programme's informational layers switched off we can be under no illusion that this is any kind of 'natural' image (Figure 16.3). With its evidently constructed patchwork, the visual rhetoric of the globe no longer enunciates the 'wholeness of the object' but rather the 'wholeness of its searchability', for everything that retards vision tends to be drained away. Not only do clouds – 'magical' in the Apollo 17 image but obscurantist for Google Earth (although they do remain in the programme's screen icon, which is a kind of 'blue marble' logo), disperse – but also the world ceases to have a dark side and instead we have an entirely illuminated globe. On Google Earth the darkness of night never falls.[31] This is not a matter of stopping the sun in the sky, but rather of distributing and refracting its agency through the multiple orbiting devices that supply the image data from which the virtual globe is pieced together. This image of a mechanically encircled earth carries none of the sense of specular oscillation provoked by the Apollo images. For crucial to their cultural reception was the spectator's knowledge of what lay outside their frame – and indeed – behind the camera. The sense of the fragility of the planet was echoed and reinforced by the precariousness and exposure of the body of its representative, the astronaut who took the photograph. Knowledge of the provisional and contingent sustenance of this little piece of the earth, adrift from the biosphere and looking back at it, deeply intensified the spatial vertigo of these images and its implications.

One powerful effect of the Apollo images was to prompt reflection on the interrelationship between, and interconnectedness of, the planet's inhabitants. The pictorial registration of the earth isolated in the vastness of space suddenly made it seem small and relations on it necessarily close. A similar insistence on a new sense of proximity is evident on many commentaries on not just Google Earth, but on the Google phenomenon more generally. Randall Stross, for example, writes that 'Google has made the earth seem like a single cozy place' and titles the chapter of his book that discusses Google Earth, 'Small Planet, After All'.[32] Inasmuch as we accept this, then Google Earth – in its construction of a world of always-available proximity, a global totality that is always to hand – appears to be an intensification of the 'one-world effect' of the earlier images of the earth from space. It would be wrong to discount this, and I have heard aid-workers, earth-observation scientists and geographers speak optimistically, inevitably in connection with disaster situations, of the possibilities of the kind of global immediacy, the overcoming of distance between 'us' and 'them', that Google Earth seems to facilitate. Yet at the same time this raises all kinds of questions, not least those that issue from the gap that opens between the apparent omnipresence available to the Google Earth user and the specific limits of her vicarious experience as constructed by the programme: at the very least, it alerts us to the idea that the sense of 'global coziness' is likely to be less an effect of the programme *per se* than a relationship with it, one highly dependent on the user's social, political, economic and geographic situation outside the digital construction.

Equally, the presumption that Google Earth constructs closeness and coziness disregards its more uncanny aspects, the degree to which the sutured virtual globe transforms the world into a 'strange planet' rather than a 'small planet'. Certainly one has the impression that, post-Google Earth, the proper realm of the alien is no longer outer space but rather the digital surface of the planet or else its newly hollow interior, the entrance to which many internet images captured from Google Earth and posted online claim to have found. On the digital surfaces of Google's planet, strange and uncanny phenomena take shape that are eagerly reported and tracked in various blogs. Peculiar formations are seen to emerge, which beckon alien craft or physiognomically stare back into space and therefore also at the viewer. At the same time the apparatus of more earthly plots, plans and conspiracies show up in various ways, such as the notorious 'black helicopters' (for whose detection on Google Earth *The Register* ran a tongue-in-cheek competition)[33] or the so-called 'Area 51' military base in Nevada upon which so much speculation has alighted.[34] Even as it builds upon what the images show, conspiracy theory profits from the idea of the constitutive manipulability of the digital image, from the consequent uncertainty over its status, and from what might be described as the question of the 'politics of resolution' that Google Earth brings to the fore.

Since its release, much has been made of the national security issues that attend Google Earth, and the company's response has always been that its global image is constructed of data sets that are already available within the public domain. The responses have certainly been interesting: among others, complaints have – for example – been registered from South Korea, India, Taiwan (mis-named as a 'province' of China) and the city of Liverpool in England (because images of the city were not being updated quickly enough to show the results of its ongoing regeneration programme – too much still looked like a building site, or had still to begin).[35] In January 2007 the British newspaper the *Daily Telegraph* reported that Bahrain had blocked all access to Google Earth after opposition groups had used it to scrutinise royal palaces and their grounds and had consequently calculated that 'the ruling Al-Khalifa family owns about 80 per cent of the entire country'.[36] The United Kingdom also registered complaints and, according to the *Daily Telegraph* again, as a consequence British military bases in Iraq were 'blotted out'. So too, the article went on, were the Trident nuclear submarine pens in Faslane and intelligence centre GCHQ, in Cheltenham. The paper went on to say that, according to its own research, in addition to these, 'the entire aerial footage of Hereford, home to the SAS, has been fuzzed out'.[37]

This inevitably suggests that Google Earth might present us with a new kind of political map, one structured according to a different logic than those coloured political cartographies, organised by the vectors of national boundaries, with which we are all familiar. Instead with Google Earth the implication is that we have a politics of resolution, or definition, of the image, a new popular political map structured through image resolutions and the upload periodicity of data sets. US government legislation from the 1990s, for example, prohibits satellite imaging companies licensed in the US to release imagery of Israeli territory above a certain (low) resolution, unless it is already commercially available elsewhere. However, given the rapid international spread of imaging companies and technological developments, this is a restriction that has become increasingly ineffective.[38] The more general point to be made here is that censorship, concealment, camouflage – whatever one wants to call it – is not immediately or necessarily legible and so tends to be rather different from the large white spaces of earlier maps, which clearly signal that something is missing or has been excised. With the digital image, the effect is more of a stirring up or a fluctuation in the digital field, not a tear, or a rent within it, or a blot or crossing out on top of it.

Yet another, but related, way of understanding the resolution differentials on Google Earth is as a map of (predominantly Western) economic and political interests – which is to say, those of the customers of the commercial imaging companies from which Google derives its data sets. Areas that appear in great detail with a fast refresh rate are typically those with high real estate value. Disaster areas, conflict zones or places where state intelligence has been directed can also suddenly emerge with startling detail. Of an area on the Pakistan–Afghanistan border that 'suddenly became as detailed as the images of Manhattan' in March 2007, *Wired* magazine reported:

> Turns out, Google gets its images from many of the same satellite companies – DigitalGlobe, TerraMetrics, and others – that provide reconnaissance to US intelligence agencies. And when the CIA requests close-ups of the area around Peshawar in Pakistan's North-West Frontier Province, Google Earth reaps the benefits (although usually six to 18 months later). This is also why remote parts of Asia went hi-res after the Indian Ocean tsunami in 2004 and the Kashmir earthquake in 2005.[39]

At the same time, given that high image resolution has tended to intersect with the key locations of the 'digital first world', it comes as no surprise that a certain bravado can come to be attached to image definition in relation to national territories: more than once I have come across the phrase 'third world lo-res', which implies that being first world may come to mean not just having air-conditioned offices and a motorway network, but also having hyper clear territorial images on Google Earth.

And finally, one of the consequences of the popularisation, coherence and availability of geospatial data that Google Earth facilitates is that the surface of the earth begins to address the sky in a new, intentional, way: the terrestrial surface itself becomes manipulated as a media surface, not just virtually on the Google Earth interface, but literally. As the audience of geospatial data is no longer made up of only cartographers, scientists, military strategists and state operatives but rather – overwhelmingly – consumers, how commodities look from the sky, and how they address it, is a new concern. A newspaper reports that tourists, sceptical of the claims and photographs in holiday brochures, now use Google Earth to see the 'reality' of the situation (finding out that the hotel is next to a waste dump, or is still under construction, etc.).[40] Moreover, the earth's skin becomes a site for gargantuan advertising landworks addressed to satellites that take up the logic of the 'mashup' – the hybridisation of text, diagram and photograph that was pioneered for Google Maps – and transfer it to the terrestrial surface. If the standard narrations of the world-historical effects of digitisation tell of the wearing-away of the real by the virtual, these developments give a reverse instance in which – seemingly perversely – the virtual becomes subject to material realisation. Navigational technologies that display aerial images consequently register these landworks, not as an additional informational layer that can be switched off, but as part of the image layer itself. Thus a massive logo of Colonel Sanders appeared beside a Kentucky Fried Chicken outlet in Tenessee, a locator and brand-icon scaled for the era of 'satnav'.[41] In a similar vein, Anders Albrechtslund reports on a magazine that advertised its 100th issue by constructing a vast reproduction of its cover in the desert near Las Vegas, declaring that it 'can be seen from outer space using Google Earth' and calling it 'a UFO's-eye view'.[42] The aerial view in its contemporary form becomes less, as it has often been thought of in the past, a detached, dispassionate and privileged way of interpreting the world's surface, than a phenomenon which, by its very presence and new mass availability, produces specific, concrete effects upon it.

The most extreme examples of these tendencies though are undoubtedly the recent developments in Dubai, which are calculated to address the global real estate market through the sky. In the vast pictographic constructions of the so-called 'Palm trilogy' (the Palm Jumeirah, Palm Jebel Ali and Palm Deira developments), land-art precedents from the late 1960s and early 1970s such as Robert Smithson's *Spiral Jetty*, which always had a conceptual relationship with the aerial view, are unravelled and recalibrated for the conditions of the globalised postmodern economy. Clearly related to these are publications such as *The Middle East from Space* (2006), which then naturally takes the form of advertising, displaying the emirate's planetary-scale branding. The volume is published by Motivate Publishing, in which the UAE Minister of State for Finance is a partner and under whose imprint the book by the ruler of Dubai – Sheikh Mohammed Bin Rasheed Al Maktoum – titled *My Vision: Challenges in the Race for Excellence*, appeared the following year.[43]

Perhaps though, from the point of view of Google Earth, it is the development known as The World, which lies adjacent to the Palms, that appears the most suggestively articulated in relation to the new conditions and technologies of global aerial vision. The construction, as is well known, consists of an array of man-made islands fashioned, in Mike Davis' words, 'in the shape of an almost

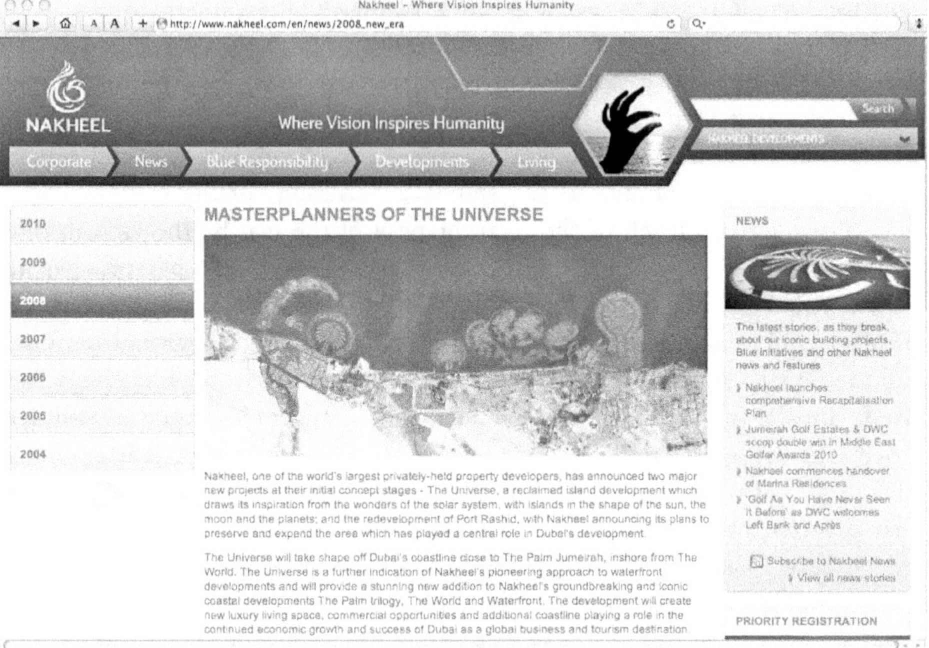

[16.4] Nakheel announces 'The Universe'.

finished puzzle of the world'.[44] The rhetorical gesture of its government-owned developer, Nakheel, is a little like that of Google itself: namely to give its – in this case – investors, the world. And perhaps not surprisingly the next step, as with Google's launch of Google Sky, turns out to be the cosmos. Or at least that is what was intended before the current financial crisis, when plans for a development around The World to be called The Universe were unveiled. In 2008 Nakheel announced the development under the banner 'Masterplanners of the Universe', but the following year it was placed on hold[45] (Figure 16.4). As it stands, the curiosity of navigating to The World via the Google Earth interface is of course the reiteration of the global image, the sense of the arrival at a picture of the world that looks back at itself and that is articulated both as a *mise en abîme* and, in its commercial strategy, as a *trompe l'oeil* for investors in the sky. Furthermore, the puzzle-like arrangement of The World to which Davis refers itself gains a reiterative character, given that it is initially encountered in the data set patchwork of the virtual globe that serves as the gateway to the other world toward which we zoom, and to which we will descend to find the patches reinstantiated at another scale, although this time resolved into real-estate parcels.

NOTES

1 This paper was originally presented at the workshop 'The Aerial View: Spatial Knowledges and Spatial Practices', held at the University of Edinburgh on 3 February 2007. An earlier version of the text has been published in *New Geographies 4: Scales of the Earth* (2011): 164–70.

2 Sarah Milstein, J. D. Biersdorfer and Matthew MacDonald, *Google: The Missing Manual*, 2nd edition (Beijing, Cambridge, etc.: Pogue Press, O'Reilly, 2006), p.108.

3 David Vise singles out South Korea as being particularly resistant to penetration by Google. David A. Vise, 'Google', *Foreign Policy*, 154 (2006): 20–4; 20.

4 See for example Martin Dodge and Rob Kitchin, *Mapping Cyberspace* (London and New York: Routledge, 2000).

5 http://www.google.com/corporate [accessed 22 March 2010]. Due to be completed in around 300 years according to Google CEO Eric Schmidt in a presentation to the Association of National Advertisers (USA) in 2005: see, 'We'll index the world by 2310, says Google', http://www.theregister.co.uk/2005/10/10/google_index [accessed 23 March 2010].

6 John Lanchester, 'The Global Id', *London Review of Books*, 28(2), 26 January (2006). http://www.lrb.co.uk/v28/n02/john-lanchester/the-global-id [accessed 23 March 2010].

7 David Vise, with Mark Malseed. *The Google Story* (Basingstoke and Oxford: Pan Macmillan, 2008), p.39.

8 Cited in David Vise, *The Google Story*, p.3.

9 John Markoff, 'Hiding in plain sight, Google seeks more power', *New York Times*, 14 June (2006). http://www.nytimes.com/2006/06/14/technology/14search.html?pagewanted=2&_r=1&ei=5070&en=5f47a9cc1f8a2faf&ex=1189396800 [accessed 23 March 2010].

10 John Lanchester, op. cit.

11 Ken Auletta, *Googled: The End of the World as We Know It* (London: Virgin Books, 2010).

12 Alex Williams, 'Planet Google wants you', *New York Times*, 15 October (2006). http://www.nytimes.com/2006/10/15/fashion/15google.html?ex=1189051200&en=1640e28bbf02e82e&ei=5070 [accessed 22 March 2010].

13 Ibid. At a September 2010 press conference, Sergey Brin announced that he wanted Google to become 'the third half of your brain'. http://bits.blogs.nytimes.com/2010/11/29/google-earth-pushes-boundaries-between-real-and-virtual/?scp=1&sq=%22google%20earth%20pushes%20boundaries%20between%20real%20and%20virtual%22&st=cse [accessed 1 December 2011].

14 Alex Williams, op. cit.

15 Robert Verkaik, 'Google is Watching You', *Independent*, 24 May (2007), pp.1–2; p.2.

16 Victor Keegan, 'That Ringing Sound is Google on the Phone', *Guardian* (Technology), 13 September (2007), p.4.

17 Fred Turner, *From Counterculture to Cyberculture: Stewart Brand, the Whole Earth Network, and the Rise of Digital Utopianism* (Chicago: University of Chicago Press, 2006).

18 Stewart Brand, ed., *The Next Whole Earth Catalog: Access to Tools* (POINT/Random House, 1981 [4th printing]), p.2.

19 Cf. Roberts' and Schein's discussion of images of the globe in advertisements by geographic information providers, in which they note: 'Views from above underscore the advertiser's totalizing claims of complete coverage, of being everywhere.' Susan M. Roberts and Richard H. Schein, 'Earth Shattering: Global Imagery and GIS' in John Pickles, ed., *Ground Truth: The*

Social Implications of Geographic Information Systems (New York and London: The Guilford Press, 1995), pp.171–95; p.174.

20 Arifa Akbar, 'London Eye on top of the world as it becomes best tourist attraction', *Independent*, 17 March (2005), pp.18–19. See Mark Dorrian, '"The Way the World Sees London": Thoughts on a Millennial Urban Spectacle' in A. Vidler, ed., *Architecture Between Spectacle and Use* (Williamstown: Sterling and Francine Clark Art Institute and New Haven, CT, and London: Yale University Press, 2008), pp.41–57.

21 For example, the 'picture of one of the worst things on the planet: the Athabasca oil sands in Alberta, Canada' selected by Bertrand as his best photograph. 'What you're looking at is essentially poison and pollution, yet the shot has great beauty.' 'Yann Arthus-Bertrand's Best Shot', *Guardian* (G2), 24 September (2009), p.23.

22 Steven Johnson, 'The long zoom', *New York Times Magazine*, 8 October (2006). http://www.nytimes.com/2006/10/08/magazine/08games.html?_r=2&oref=slogin&pagewanted=all [accessed 25 March 2010]. I am grateful to Amy Kulper for this reference.

23 For example, Vittoria Di Palma, 'Zoom: Google Earth and Global Intimacy', in Vittoria di Palma, Diana Periton and Marina Lathouri, eds, *Intimate Metropolis: Urban Subjects in the Modern City* (London and New York: Routledge, 2009), pp.239–70. For an interpretation of *Powers of Ten* in its Cold War context, see Mark Dorrian, 'Adventure on the vertical', *Cabinet* 44 (2012): 17–23.

24 Stuart Elliott, 'Marketing on Google: It's not just text anymore', *New York Times*, 22 September (2006). http://www.nytimes.com/2006/09/22/business/media/22adco.html?_r=1&ex=1188964800&en=0e8871e885436af5&ei=5070 [accessed 27 March 2010].

25 Michael Miller, *Google.pedia: The Ultimate Google Resource* (Indianapolis: Que Publishing, 2007), p.323.

26 Photograph reference: AS17-148-22727. Vittoria Di Palma also discerns a relation between Google Earth and this image in op. cit., p.264.

27 Denis Cosgrove, *Apollo's Eye: A Cartographic Genealogy of the Earth in the Western Imagination* (Baltimore and London: Johns Hopkins University Press, 2001), pp.257–67.

28 Studied by Robert Poole in *Earthrise: How Man First Saw the Earth* (New Haven and London: Yale University Press, 2008).

29 Stewart Brand, ed., *The Next Whole Earth Catalog*, p.1.

30 On the relation between the Apollo images and James Lovelock's Gaia hypothesis, see Robert Poole, *Earthrise*, pp.170–89.

31 In later releases there is an option to switch on a shading effect, which, however, disappears upon zooming in.

32 Randall Stross, *Planet Google: How One Company is Transforming Our Lives* (London: Atlantic Books, 2009), p.131.

33 Lester Haines, 'Google Earth: The black helicopters have landed', *The Register*, 14 October (2005). http://www.theregister.co.uk/2005/10/14/google_earth_competition_results [accessed 30 March 2010].

34 To sample a Google Earth UFO sighting in Area 51 see: http://www.youtube.com/watch?v=ucZKCrMvqu4 [accessed 30 March 2010].

35 Katie Hafner and Saritha Rai, 'Governments tremble at Google's bird's-eye view', *New York Times*, 20 December (2005). http://www.nytimes.com/2005/12/20/technology/20image.html?_r=1&ei=5070&en=4b89cb0ad323cec6&ex=1189051200&pagewanted=all [accessed 30 March 2005]; Lester Haines, 'Taiwan huffs and puffs at Google Earth', *The Register*, 4 October (2005). http://www.theregister.co.uk/2005/10/04/taiwan_google_earth [accessed 30 March

2010]; Lester Haines, 'Liverpool throws strop at Google Earth', *The Register*, 27 November (2006). http://www.theregister.co.uk/2006/11/27/liverpool_google_earth_outrage [accessed 30 March 2010].

36 'Picture is not always clear', *Daily Telegraph*, 13 January (2007). http://www.telegraph.co.uk/news/worldnews/1539400/Picture-is-not-always-clear.html [accessed 30 March 2010]. For more on this see: Ian Black, 'Bahrain protests will go nowhere while the US supports its government', *Guardian*, 16 April (2011). http://www.guardian.co.uk/world/2011/apr/16/bahrain-protests-us-supports-government?INTCMP=SRCH [accessed 2 December 2011].

37 Thomas Harding, 'Google blots out Iraq bases on internet', *Daily Telegraph*, 20 January (2007). http://www.telegraph.co.uk/news/worldnews/1540039/Google-blots-out-Iraq-bases-on-internet.html [accessed 30 March 2010].

38 For a report on the appearance of high-resolution images of Israel on Google Earth in 2007, see http://www.informationliberation.com/?id=23961 [accessed 30 March 2010].

39 On the website they helpfully provided a 'Search for bin Laden at Home!' link: http://www.wired.com/wired/archive/15.03/start.html?pg=10 [accessed 30 March 2010].

40 Charles Starmer-Smith, 'Zooming in: The world at your fingertip', *Daily Telegraph*, 5 November (2005). http://www.telegraph.co.uk/travel/733938/Zooming-in-the-world-at-your-fingertip.html [accessed 27 March 2010].

41 Lester Haines, 'Giant Colonel Sanders visible from space', *The Register*, 17 November (2006). http://www.theregister.co.uk/2006/11/17/colonel_sanders_mosaic [accessed 27 March 2010].

42 Anders Albrechtslund, 'Surveillance in Searching: A Study into Ethical Aspects of an Emergent Search Culture', unpublished paper, no pagination. I am grateful to the author for providing me with a copy of his essay.

43 http://www.motivatepublishing.com/library/default.asp?categorycode=About_mp&ID=About_mp [accessed 30 March 2010].

44 Mike Davis, 'Does the road to the future end at Dubai?', *Log: Observations on Architecture and the Contemporary City*, 6 (2005): 61–4; 61.

45 http://www.nakheel.com/en/news/2008_new_era [accessed 30 March 2010].

Index

www.ingramcontent.com/pod-product-compliance
Lightning Source LLC
LaVergne TN
LVHW010539100826
845148LV00001B/238

* 9 7 8 1 7 8 0 7 6 4 6 1 0 *